The Best AMERICAN SPORTS WRITING 1996

EDITED AND WITH
AN INTRODUCTION BY
John Feinstein

Glenn Stout, SERIES EDITOR

HOUGHTON MIFFLIN COMPANY
BOSTON · NEW YORK 1996

ISSN: 1056-8034
ISBN: 0-395-70072-8
ISBN: 0-395-70071-X (pbk.)

Printed in the United States of America

QUM 10 9 8 7 6 5 4 3 2 1

To my father, Harold Glenn Stout

Contents

Contents   ix

Foreword

AS I KEEP COMPANY with a room full of magazines and newspapers for much of the year, I have plenty of time to ponder all the things sports may or may not be. Believe me, if you read as much sports writing as I do, questions like that come up on a fairly regular basis.

The answers, however, usually come from unexpected places. Last year my father visited from Ohio and delivered the last remaining vestiges of my boyhood from the basement, most of which had something to do with sports. I received, among other items, an old pair of baseball spikes, the little league football helmet I wore while receiving two concussions, a deflated football, my T-shirts from Mosquito League baseball, a few trophies, every sports book ever published by the Scholastic Book Club (including the unforgettable first novel *Danger in Center Field* by one Willie Howard Mays Jr.) and an old National League baseball given to me by a neighbor. I immediately threw a grounder on our new asphalt driveway and scuffed off the National League stamp, but I still kept the ball.

The most interesting of these finds was a box of sports magazines dating from the late 1960s and early 1970s. Although my collection of the *Sporting News* did not survive the ensuing years of mildew and decay, a couple dozen copies of *Sport* did, as well as a smattering of other forgotten magazines like *Sport Scene, Pro Quarterback, All-Star Sports, Pro Sports* (my favorite at the time), and a variety of preseason annuals. There were even a few copies of *Sports Illustrated,* which cost too much for me to buy then. I unapologetically admit that the few copies I do have bear the stamp "Hilliard Ohio Junior High School Library."

When I tire of reading contemporary periodicals, this box is always worth a couple of hours of entertainment. The magazine covers are the best. At this moment, scattered upon my desk are the faces of Johnny Unitas, Bill Freehan, Lou Brock, and Bob Griese, and tabloid headlines heralding the stories contained inside, such as "Joe Namath — Is He Good or Lucky?" "Why Willie Mays Is Doing a Slow Burn" (probably because I've reminded him of his aforementioned novel), and "Pro Football's Cheap Shot Artists: They Won't Stop Until Somebody Gets Killed!" The covers of the venerable *Sports Illustrated* are of a different order. The issue of August 7, 1967, sports a garish painting of golfer Gay Brewer and promotes the scintillating story "Gay Brewer Tells How to Hit Golf's Best Shot — The Fade." Gay Brewer never excited my adolescent adoration, so why I liberated this particular issue absolutely escapes me.

But the real fun is inside. As amusing as the ads are for "Manny's Baseball Land," "Joe Weider's Killer Karate Krusher Course," and "An Important Message to Every Man and Woman in America Losing His or Her Hair," or *Sport*'s fashion photo feature "With Austin Carr and Don May(!)," or even the photo of the United States women's gymnastic team in *SI*, all of whom are distinguished from today's gymnasts by the fact that they have breasts, discernable paunches, and are at least sixteen years old, the stories themselves provide the greatest entertainment. Sorry to burst any nostalgic bubbles, but most of the writing isn't very good. This doesn't surprise me. My other writing projects often take me far back into microfilmed recesses of sports journalism. I am accustomed to reading what could never find a publisher today.

The issue of *Sports Illustrated* mentioned earlier demonstrated true wisdom by not even listing the writers on the Contents page, a practice that annoys me when I come across it now but may have been the right decision then.

I'm not saying that all the writing was poor, just as I am not saying that today's writers always adhere to a higher standard. There have always been good writers. But the Ed Linn's, Roger Kahn's, and other fine writers of earlier eras jumped off the page then. I'm not sure they would now. Not that today's writers are so much better and there is no more bad writing, but I think there is certainly less terrible writing today and many more good writers. There is also a larger, wider, much more varied marketplace for sports writing. The publications like those in the box that filled up issue after issue with newsprint and typewriting have, by and large, gone by the wayside. Oh, there are still some out there, including a few whose current incarnations disparage the title on the cover, but they don't dominate the genre like they once did.

It's a fact, but thirty years ago you'd never find memorable sports writing in a free weekly newspaper, a regional magazine, a Sunday supplement outside the *New York Times,* or in a newspaper from such an unlikely place as Wichita, Kansas. Once in a while, *Esquire* or *The New Yorker* printed something worthwhile, but most other general interest magazines eschewed sports as a topic.

These are precisely the places I now look to each year. I find the sports writing there as good, or better, than that found in most contemporary sports magazines. Every year I compile a list of Notable Sports Writing at the end of this book. Some are listed for reasons known only to me, but many of these stories, in any other year and with another guest editor, may well have made the book. To those readers for whom this volume is not enough, I urge you to flip to the back, look up these stories at the library or on-line, and create your own *Best American Sports Writing.*

Now what do all those magazines on my desk and the little commentary they spawned have to do with the common question of all the things sports may or may not be? Well, the more I thought about it the more I realized that the answer may be found, not just in those magazines my father brought to me, but also in the box they came in.

Remember when you were young and received a present and were sometimes far more interested in the imaginative properties of the box than in the confines of the gift itself? Well, it seems that, to each of us, sports is in some way a gift, something passed down from someone who had it before. I can trace my own love of baseball back to the age of 4 or 5, when I demanded the installation of outside lights in the back yard so my father could play whiffle ball with me when he got home after working fourteen hours and it was already dark.

Was it baseball I loved then? Not at first. It was the box, my father's coming home, me running out into the yard, and the fifteen minutes we'd spend together. Had this been a chore, or a demand, I may have grown up to detest the gift, the box, and the giver. As it was, I grew to love all three. Baseball, and sports in general, have been a palpable gift to me. In turn, I have been fascinated, intrigued, repulsed, and sometimes bored by all the permutations "sports" can take. But, in the end, sports has given me something far more valuable than my livelihood. It has provided another way for me to connect with a world beyond myself. Through sports, I learned to love reading, and through that, writing. Sports took me outside, allowed me to discover my own body, broke my heart and made me laugh, introduced me to friends and forced me to confront my enemies. It showed me what I could do, what I could not, and how to expand on each. Not that sports is the only way to accomplish this, or even the best way. But it is a way.

Of course, by itself, sports didn't really do any of this. I took the gift and box both, played with each, and followed where they led. Even now, I'm still trying to figure out precisely where this will take me, and it occurs to me that what distinguishes the writing in this or any edition of *The Best American Sports Writing* is that all the writers represented here are in the midst of a similar investigation. They are trying to determine the dimensions and limitations of sports, not only for themselves, but through the experiences of others. That is why this book can be done every year, and, I hope, is never quite the same. Each of us either accepts the gift or not, plays with the box or throws it away. How and why we do so is the only reason to keep turning the pages. I, for one, am glad enough to have received the gift at all. So, thanks, Pop, for bringing me the box.

Before I move on to other matters, I would be remiss if I didn't point out the demise of one of my favorite sources. Since its inception, the *Village Voice* sports section presented some of the most innovative, interesting, and imaginative sports writing published. The *Voice* sports section made a regular practice of covering events and people no one else did, and when they did cover the familiar, they usually did so in a way that was wholly unique. They also saw fit to comment, without caution, about sports writing and sports writers, subjects that are usually taboo in this nation's sporting press. Since the demise of the sports section a year ago, I find my task just a little less enjoyable. If sports writing is to be of continuing interest, it better not play it safe. The *Voice* did not. While the *Voice* itself was only rarely represented in these pages, I look forward to reading the *Voice* writers in other publications.

Each year, I read each and every issue of some three hundred sports and general interest magazines in search of stories that I believe might merit inclusion in *The Best American Sports Writing*. I also look at the Sunday magazines from about fifty daily newspapers and read as many newspapers as I can. I try not to miss anything, so each year I send requests to the editors of more than three hundred magazines and three hundred newspapers asking them to submit stories for my consideration, or better yet, provide me with a complimentary subscription to their publication.

Writers and readers are likewise encouraged to send me stories they've written or read that they would like to see in this series. Writers should feel particularly welcome to submit their own work. Many editors, particularly in the newspaper world, don't bother submitting anything, and those that do don't always submit the best stuff. In this volume alone there is at least one story that was turned down by a half-dozen publications before finding a home, another that wasn't included in a publication's own substantial set of submissions but was brought to my attention by a reader, and several that were submitted by the writers themselves.

Each year, I submit the best seventy-five stories or so to the guest editor, who makes the final selection. This year's guest editor, John Feinstein, supplemented my choices with a few of his own. To be considered for inclusion in next year's volume, each nonfiction story must have been published in 1996 in either the United States or Canada and must be column length or longer. Entries from on-line publications must be submitted in hard copy. Reprints or book excerpts are not eligible. I must receive all stories by February 1, 1997. This is a real deadline. Putting this book together is a labor-intensive process for both myself and the guest editor. Work received after my deadline usually sits around until the beginning of summer, so no amount of pleading in late submissions does any good.

All submissions must include authors' name, date of publication, publication name, and address. Photocopies, tearsheets, or clean copies are fine. Submissions cannot be returned, and it is not appropriate for me to comment on or critique individual submissions. Publications that want to make sure their contributions are considered should provide a complimentary subscription to the address listed below. Those that already do should extend the subscription another year.

Please send subscriptions or submissions to this exact address:

Glenn Stout
Series Editor
The Best American Sports Writing
P.O. Box 381
Uxbridge, MA 01569

I can also be contacted by e-mail at 104226.2445@compuserve. com. Please provide your snail mail address if you require a response. No stories may be submitted electronically. Copies of previous editions of this book can be ordered through most bookstores. Earlier volumes may be available from out-of-print book dealers. Collectors beware — please don't write me and ask for a copy because you just "know" I have extra copies around. I don't.

My thanks go out to the usual suspects, including my friends at the Boston Public Library and Thayer Memorial Library in Uxbridge, my editor Marnie Patterson, guest editor John Feinstein, Saorla and Siobhan. I'd also like to thank the dozens of readers who took the time to write me this past year and express their feelings about last year's edition. But, as in any other year, my greatest thanks extend to those who write about sports. This book is theirs.

GLENN STOUT

Introduction

THIRTEEN YEARS AGO, when I could still describe myself as a young reporter while keeping a straight face, I had a difficult decision to make. I had spent the previous two years covering politics for the *Washington Post,* a job I enjoyed greatly. Now, though, I had the chance to return to the sports department to cover the two sports I enjoyed most: college basketball and tennis.

What to do? If I stayed in politics, I would get to go to both political conventions in 1984, something I had always dreamed of doing. If I went to sports, I would get to cover the Summer Olympics, something I had been assigned to do in 1980 only to be pulled off the trip when the United States decided to boycott.

Back and forth I went, hoping somehow that someone would suggest I could do both. Political reporting, I was certain, was more *important.* Sports writing, I was equally certain, was more *fun.*

My friends who covered politics shook their heads when I spoke of my dilemma and said things like, "John, you're almost 28 years old. Isn't it time to stop covering games?" or, "Sure, go ahead and cover sports if all you want to be is a *sports* writer." They'd spit out the word "sports" as if it were some kind of affliction. It was a discomfiting notion, balanced only by the fact that Red Smith was a sports writer and Dave Kindred was a sports writer and Tony Kornheiser was a sports writer and so was Frank Deford. If men that bright and that talented were sports writers, I thought, it was likely that the disease wasn't terminal.

I was driving home one night, all of these various notions running through my head, when my perpetual fiddling with the radio dial led me to a broadcast coming out of New York. The New York Islanders, then the four-time Stanley Cup champions, were playing the Montreal Canadiens. It was late in the third period and the Islanders were clinging to a one-goal lead.

All thoughts of my future were put on hold as I listened to play-by-play man Barry Landers describe the Canadiens' peppering of goalie Billy Smith with shots in an attempt to tie the game. There was still a little more than a minute left as I wheeled onto my block and pulled up in front of my house. By now, the signal was fading, but by putting my head down near the car radio, I could hear Landers's call of the final minute. I sat like that, the engine running to keep me warm, until the Canadiens' final shot was steered away by Smith and the Islanders secured the victory.

I turned off the engine, jumped out of the car, and began walking up the steps to my front door. I was halfway there when I stopped.

"What were you just doing?" I said to myself.

"Sitting in my car in front of my house at ten o'clock at night with the engine running listening to the end of a hockey game," I answered. "Not a playoff hockey game even — a November hockey game."

I thought for another moment and realized there was a message here: anyone who will sit in a car listening to the end of a hockey game who has a chance to get paid to write about sports for a living should be doing just that. For better or worse, sports was always going to be my passion and my first love.

The next morning I went to see my boss, Larry Kramer, the metropolitan editor at the *Post*. I told him what had happened. He smiled.

"What you're telling me," he said, "is that, deep down, like it or not, you're a sports writer."

I nodded. "Exactly."

"Then," Kramer said, "I guess you should go be a sports writer."

If I said that I never once regretted that day or that decision, I would be lying. I still get a little bit cranky during the conventions or on election night. I would still like, someday, to find out first-hand what New Hampshire is like in February. But about 98 percent of the time, I am happily resigned to my fate. Thirteen years later I still listen to hockey games on the car radio — and baseball games and basketball games and football games.

Every year, I swear I'm going to make this my last Final Four because the event has grown so large, is so vastly overhyped by those of us in the media, and because the men who run the NCAA are such overstuffed, overblown hypocrites. And every year I'm back there on Monday night, looking around and wondering who will be good when October fifteenth rolls around.

I've even come to grips with this whole notion of what's important. The games themselves are, of course, unimportant. Unfortunately, there are always going to be people who make them sound like the Apocalypse times three. There is plenty wrong with sports and, in this book, you will read about much that is wrong and a number of people who have done wrong and gone bad.

But sports, I have found, *is* important. It is important because people care about it. If writing well about a hero like Cal Ripken Jr. or a fallen hero like Billy Cannon gives people pleasure and leaves them feeling as if they understand that person better than they did before, then the writer has accomplished something.

Presidential elections, it can be argued, are vastly more important than baseball games. There is no doubt that the decisions a president makes will have an impact on our lives. But didn't Cal Ripken impact our lives? Didn't watching him on that magic night in September of 1995 make us feel a little bit better, not just about baseball, but about ourselves? I got chills that night, just as I got chills watching Arthur Ashe winning Wimbledon in 1975 and the U.S. Olympic hockey team beating the Soviet Union in 1980, and Jackie Joyner-Kersee winning two gold medals at the Olympics in 1988, and Ben Crenshaw winning the Masters in 1995.

These are special moments that we remember and take heart from. Not so much because of the athlete's skill, but because of his or her will. Anything that reminds us of the extraordinary potential within us is important.

But sports are important for reasons that go beyond magic moments or mind-boggling achievements. They are important because they can provide us companionship at times when we need it most. In 1993, when my mother died very suddenly, I went to bed each night filled with dread. How would I push all the thoughts about my mother out of my head so I could sleep?

Thinking about my family wasn't a comfort, because I could think only about the pain they were all feeling — especially my father. For a while, I tried to focus on my next book project and what I had to do to begin organizing the work. But the book was about golf. My mother had been the one who introduced me to golf as a kid. Every time I thought about the book, I thought about my mom.

Finally, I hit on something: games. I would lie in bed every night and think about Tom Seaver's near-perfect game against the Cubs in 1969. Who was it who got the hit in the ninth? Jimmy Qualls. Where did he hit the ball? Left-centerfield. What was the final score? 4–0, Mets. I would bounce from there to the 1970 Knicks-Lakers final, my mind floating back to Madison Square Garden. Where did I sit for game seven? Section 406. How many points did Walt Frazier score that night? 36. From there I went to Mark Spitz at the '72 Olympics and on to Villanova at the '85 Final Four and Christian Laettner's shot against Kentucky in 1992.

Sometimes I would go through entire games in my mind. Other nights I would try to remember every college basketball game I had seen in — pick a year — 1988. Or the score of every Indiana game in 1985–86.

It worked. To this day, on the anniversary of my mother's death or on her birthday or wedding anniversary, I go to bed with a lineup of games and events in my head, knowing that eventually they will lead me to sleep.

I now know something I couldn't have known in 1983: sports *is* important. And, by extension, sports writing is important too.

Of course, that doesn't mean that all sports writing is good and all sports writers are good people. There is plenty of bad sports writing — just as there is plenty of bad political writing — and a lot of it is caused by that most common of human ailments: laziness.

Nowadays it is easy to be a sports writer and not work very hard. At almost any event you cover, the people in charge are more than willing to spoonfeed you an easy story. Play-by-play descriptions of everything that happens during a game are usually handed out within minutes of the final play as are quote sheets filled with wonderful and witty comments like "We won because we stayed focused and executed" or "We lost because we didn't stay focused and didn't execute."

Increasingly, contact with the athletes — and coaches — has become superficial. The creation of the dreaded "interview room," where players are brought postgame or postmatch, has made life easy for everyone. The athletes hand out empty, meaningless answers that sound as if they are being recited from a script (in some cases they are), and almost everyone feels compelled to just sit and write the answers down.

Often, trying to sneak up to the podium to ask a few extra questions is impossible because the athlete is being hustled out to do a "one-on-one" with ESPN, CNN, CNBC, or MTV. And if you try to follow along en route to that interview, you are likely to encounter some mean-spirited security people who think it is their job to make sure the athlete is protected from anyone wielding a vicious weapon like a pen or a notebook.

Of course, there is always the locker room. Then again, these days, there isn't always the locker room. Lately, the interview room is more often used as an excuse to keep reporters out of the locker room. Tennis has banned writers from locker rooms around the world, except at the U.S. Open. College basketball and football teams (often using the presence of female reporters as a sorry excuse) are closing their locker rooms to the media. Most pro football teams open their locker rooms only on game days or for limited times on practice days. The Washington Redskins' locker room is open each day from 12 to 1 P.M. Practice starts at 2 P.M. How many players do you think show up to chat with reporters between 12 and 1?

Which brings up another problem: most athletes not only believe they no longer need the print media; they despise and openly disdain the print media. In 1990, having become the number three–ranked tennis player in the world at the age of 20 and the first big American star since John McEnroe and Jimmy Connors, Andre Agassi decided he wasn't going to do any one-on-one interviews with members of the print media. He would attend mandatory postmatch sessions in the interview room — accompanied by his agent, his brother, his coach, his hitting partner, his clothing rep, and his fitness guru — and do selected TV interviews. That was it.

When I explained to his (since-fired) agent, Bill Shelton, that I thought Agassi owed the public that had made him into a millionaire a little more access than that, Shelton laughed at me. "We don't need you," he said. "We communicate with the public through our commercials." Scary, but not far from the truth.

The image of most athletes today — and it was Agassi who said "Image is everything" — is created in the public's mind to a frightening degree by the way they are marketed. Agassi, because he wears funny-looking clothes and lots of earrings, is considered "colorful." Deion Sanders is sort of cute and cuddly and sure can run fast. Michael Jordan is lovable and Dennis Rodman is hateable — in a lovable sort of way. But when Agassi's image was tarnished in 1990 because of a number of public relations missteps, his people began making calls to the media saying, "Andre will grant you an audience now."

It all can be quite discouraging. In fact, when people ask me about the difference between covering politics and covering sports, I often say that the major difference is that most politicians, even those running for president, still think they need the print media. When I covered politics in Maryland, it was much easier to secure time with the governor or the state's two senators than it was to get time with the basketball coach at Georgetown or the football coach at Nebraska or young Mr. Agassi.

What's more, with TV exploding and becoming more powerful every day, finding stories that haven't been told in some way, shape, or form by television has become more difficult. Game stories are practically outdated, partly because everyone can see the games live or at least see the key plays dozens of times later that night on highlights, and partly because starting times for major events have been pushed later because of the demands of TV. How many morning newspapers do you think carried definitive stories on the Massachusetts-Arkansas NCAA tournament game last March that tipped off at 10:50 P.M. Eastern Standard Time?

As ESPN develops into a media giant and more televison coverage is devoted to sports, even the good feature stories often end up there, if not first, then second — but with far greater exposure.

I remember reading a superb book several years ago, *Friday Night Lights*. It was about high school football in Texas and its grip on communities around the country. One chapter was on a high school team in Dallas, many of whose players had ended up in serious trouble after winning the state championship. About a year later, I saw a feature on ESPN about the same high school. No credit was given to the book. It became the TV network's story because they went out and reinterviewed everyone to make their reporting "original."

Even though sports writing has become more challenging, and, often, more frustrating through the years, those who aren't willing to make the easy trip to the interview room and feed their readers the canned quotes can still remind all of us why Red Smith and Dave Kindred and Tony Kornheiser and Frank Deford wanted to be sports writers once upon a time — and, in the case of the latter three — still do so today.

Good sports writing is not so very different than any other kind of writing: it is built first and foremost around good reporting. These days, good reporting stands out more than in the past because there just isn't that much of it out there. Faced with budget cutbacks, newspapers have shaved both their staffs and their travel budgets. Fewer reporters are given less time to do their best work.

Magazines also face this dilemma, although not to the same degree. They don't have to cover every game and every major event; they can pick and choose. That's why — unfortunately — most of the best sports writing these days is being printed by magazines. The good news is that the explosion of sports in this country has forced many magazines that once ignored sports to pay attention — and to hire people who can write well on the subject. *Vanity Fair* now has Frank Deford on its masthead, and *Esquire* has added Mike Lupica. Great magazine sports writing is no longer the eminent domain of *Sports Illustrated* writers and *The New Yorker*'s Roger Angell — although both are still at the top of their games and very much a part of this collection.

Angell and Deford are good examples of what I mean when I say that the best writing is the result of great reporting. Both men are known — and with good reason — for their style, wit, and ability to turn a phrase. But if you read them carefully, you quickly learn that neither is sitting in an armchair making dry observations on the nature of the games we play. Both are out there talking to the people they are writing about and to others about those people.

In 1992, when I was researching my book on baseball, I ran into Angell in Oakland during the first week in September. I knew that sometime in early November I would read his *New Yorker* piece on postseason baseball and grind my teeth knowing that he had probably said more in 10,000 words than I would say in 100,000 words when I sat down to write. Still, I was surprised to see him with the playoffs almost a month away.

"What are you doing out here so early?" I asked.

He looked at me as if I had asked him why he was breathing. "I'm preparing," he said. "I don't like to just show up on the first day of the playoffs not knowing anyone I'm going to write about."

Of course Angell could have shown up on the first day of the playoffs and known 90 percent of the people involved better than 90 percent of the people who would be writing about them. But 90 percent wasn't good enough for him. He wanted to come as close to 100 percent as possible. This approach is markedly different than that taken by many columnists today. They can't be bothered with the regular season or the nonmajors in golf or tennis. Then they show up at the Final Four or the U.S. Open or the World Series and start asking the beat guys questions like, "Who is this big German kid named Becker? Is he any good?"

If there is a common thread to the stories I have chosen for this book, it is that they all involve some very good reporting. Angell writes as lyrically as ever, but he doesn't attempt to do so until he's done his homework. Bill Gildea of the *Washington Post* is a beautiful writer, but what makes his stories on Indiana high school basketball come to life are the people he talked to and the places he went to. Michael Goodman's piece on the fall of Billy Cannon reeks of nose-to-the-grindstone reporting. The subject didn't give him very much, so he found people — and documents — who would.

In reading the stories, I tried very hard NOT to be balanced. I didn't want four basketball stories and four football stories and four baseball stories. I wanted the *best* stories, regardless of what they were about. Nor did I feel obligated to include — or not include — stories on subjects like fishing or butterflying or Scrabble, all of which were among the entries. I am not one of those who goes around saying that some games are sports and others are not. I go by what can best be described, I suppose, as the *Sports Illustrated* rule: if there is competition involved, it can be considered a sport. But I will admit that I know almost nothing about fishing and less about hunting, and even though I read everything Red Smith wrote about fishing (because I would read Red Smith on the subject of paint drying), it was often a struggle.

The only thing I can say about what follows is this: I would be proud to have had my name on every single story in here. Some may say that isn't a grand endorsement, but for better or worse, it's the best I've got.

One final story on being a sports writer. Shortly after the hockey epiphany that sent me back to the sports section at the *Post*, I went to lunch with two of my former metro colleagues, David Maraniss and Patrick Tyler. Maraniss would eventually win a Pulitzer Prize in 1993 and write the definitive biography of Bill Clinton. Tyler would go on to be a distinguished foreign correspondent for both the *Post* and the *New York Times*.

As we munched on moo goo gai pan, Tyler turned to me with an apologetic smile and said, "You know, John, I try to read your stuff in sports whenever I can. But I'm usually so busy in the morning that I don't have time to read anything other than the front section and the business section."

He looked at Maraniss. "Do you have that problem too, David?" he asked.

Maraniss smiled. "No, never," he said. "I always read sports first."

Fortunately for people like me, he is not alone. And, just as fortunately for all of us, there is still a lot that is worth reading.

JOHN FEINSTEIN

The Best
AMERICAN
SPORTS
WRITING
1996

DAVID DAVIS

The 13th Round

FROM LA WEEKLY

JERRY QUARRY fits the pool cue into his gnarled hands and bends
down to eye the angle of a long bank shot. It's just after noon on
a Friday, and the lunchtime regulars at the Sun Ray Inn have settled onto their barstools. Friday afternoons at the Sun Ray have a
rhythm all their own: hazy sunshine outside; ESPN, Budweiser, and
homemade clam chowder inside.

A steady stream of barflies approach the table to challenge
Quarry, who looks like a man out of time and place — say, late '60s
and early '70s Vegas. His neatly cropped brown hair is combed back
and held in place by a spritz of VO5 spray; he wears a tan golf shirt,
brown flared golf slacks, brown oxfords. His ruined face, with its
flattened nose, dimmed blue eyes, and mass of scar tissue, reflects
the ravages of a boxing career that began at age 7 and ended over
four decades later.

After each game of pool, Quarry and his companion, a reporter,
continue an ongoing conversation. The two have spent several days
together, watching hours of videos of Quarry in the ring and por-
ing over a scrapbook filled with hundreds of yellowed newspaper
and magazine clips. They've gone through nearly every chapter of
Quarry's life: his impoverished childhood, his victory as a teenager
in the national Golden Gloves championship, his quest for the
heavyweight championship of the world, how he made and squan-
dered a small fortune. Quarry has told of his drug and alcohol
abuse, his three failed marriages, his three failed comebacks.

Now, Quarry has a question. "What did you say you're out here
for?" he asks, genuinely puzzled.

Almost thirty years to the night since he made his professional boxing debut, Jerry Quarry is damaged goods. At 49, he suffers from pugilistica dementia, or chronic brain damage, caused by the accumulation of head blows he took in the ring. Neurologists estimate that up to 60 percent of all professional boxers eventually suffer from pugilistica dementia, but until now, only a handful of fighters have publicly acknowledged their disabilities.

In its early stages, the symptoms of pugilistica dementia resemble those of Alzheimer's disease. Quarry suffers acute short-term memory loss. He has difficulty with his equilibrium, he can't follow directions, and he can't perform even simple chores. Because he has problems with depth perception and gets lost easily, he can't drive a car or live alone. With no source of income other than a $614-a-month social security check and little chance of finding a decent job, he lives with his older brother, Jimmy, who pays for Jerry's medical treatment; Medi-Cal underwrites therapy to help Jerry learn to live with his injury. There is no other option. Despite his extremely successful thirteen-year career as a professional fighter, Jerry Quarry has no pension and receives no health-care benefits.

Jimmy Quarry, 50, a loan officer at World Savings & Loan, is a former amateur fighter who often sparred with Jerry when they were kids. Jimmy knows all about the inherent physical dangers of boxing. And he readily admits that Jerry is partly to blame for his present financial situation: with three divorces, a hearty appetite for the good life and a penchant for trusting the wrong people, Jerry went through the money he made during and after his boxing career.

But Jimmy, who speaks for his younger brother much of the time, is bitter that his brother literally boxed his brains out — and made a lot of people a lot of money — and has nothing to show for it. Through fundraisers and corporate donations, he hopes to raise enough money to fund the Jerry Quarry Foundation, a nonprofit organization that will pay pensions and provide health-care coverage to disabled fighters. The foundation would also retrain those ex-fighters who can still hold down a job.

Two plans to help injured fighters exist, one run by the International Boxing Federation (IBF), the other by the California Athletic Commission (CAC). But both are new and highly restrictive —

the IBF plan covers only those who fight in IBF-sanctioned fights;
the CAC plan, only those who fight in-state — and do not help the
majority of professional fighters, active or retired. If Jimmy Quarry
is successful, for the first time injured or disabled professional
fighters will have a place to which they can turn for comprehensive
financial help.

For Jimmy, the crusade is partly self-serving; with a pension, Jerry
would have an income. But he also genuinely loves his brother and
wants to help him. For Jerry, who, like many professional athletes,
sank deep into depression when his career ended, the foundation
is a lifeline. After years adrift, he has a purpose.

There's an irony to it all. In becoming the poster boy of a movement that asks the boxing world to take responsibility for those it
has harmed, Jerry Quarry exposes the essential contradiction of
the sport: its heroes are of necessity also its victims.

When you live mostly in the past, as Jerry Quarry does, the present
is uneventful, quiet. He and Jimmy share a small townhouse in San
Jacinto, some 95 miles southeast of downtown Los Angeles at the
foot of the San Jacinto Mountains. It's peaceful out there, and the
turf is familiar: Jerry often trained along these roads. He gets up
early and has breakfast, then takes a brisk walk — old training habits die hard. A couple of days a week, he heads over to the Sun Ray
(sometimes making the sixteen-mile round trip on foot) and visits
with his son from his first marriage, Jerry Lynn, who is a bar-
tender there. If Jimmy has arranged a Quarry Foundation fund-
raiser, Jerry will attend and sing a couple of songs or recite some
of the poetry he used to write. Though his speech is sometimes
slurred, he never forgets the words to any of his poems: "I look at
my past, great memories abound/For I fought, I bled and I cried/I
gave it my all round after round/And the world knows that I tried."

Those days are the exceptions. He spends most afternoons alone
but for a live-in nurse, watching TV or tapes of his old fights.

Several walls of the Quarry home have been turned into a shrine
to Jerry's career: photos of Jerry mugging with Jimmy and their
younger brother Mike, who fought for the light-heavyweight championship and is himself now brain-damaged; Jerry knocking down
Floyd Patterson; Jerry posing with Jack Dempsey and with Gene
Tunney. In many of the pictures, there is a man in the background,

a figure as significant in Jerry's life as any of his opponents — his father, Jack. For Jerry's story began, as many boxing stories do, with poverty and a father who hoped his sons could fight their way to a better life.

Some sixty years ago, 14-year-old Jack Quarry ran away from home to escape the Depression and the dust-bowl plains of Oklahoma and east Texas. He hopped freight trains west, learning to survive among the bums and hobos with his wits and fists — mostly the latter. Jack landed in California and followed the fruit; his legacy from those hardscrabble years was a wife, some rudimentary boxing skills and letters tattooed below his knuckles that when the two fists were held together read: H A R D L U C K.

The kids came fast and furious — four boys and four girls, starting with Jimmy and Jerry — and Jack moved the family up and down California at an even quicker pace. From Los Angeles to Fremont to Porterville to Compton to Bakersfield and back again: Jimmy estimates that he and Jerry attended twenty schools between first and sixth grade, and recalls living in government farm labor camps, picking cotton for twenty-one cents a day, and eating beans and potatoes for breakfast, lunch, and dinner.

Jack eventually escaped the fields, and the Quarrys settled in Bellflower, where Jack worked as a tire recapper for Goodyear. He had one passion — fighting — and he tried to pass it on to his sons, lacing up their boxing gloves and pushing them into the ring when each turned 5.

His training method was relentless, a combination of brutality and humiliation. One time, says Jimmy, he walked away from a fight during a softball game. Jack confronted his son, calling him a coward and a sissy. Then he made Jimmy get his baby sister's bottle and one of her diapers.

"He made me take off my clothes in front of the rest of the family, and pinned the diaper on me," relates Jimmy, his voice absolutely flat. "Then I was told to start sucking on the bottle."

Above all, Jack made sure his sons learned how to take a beating. Jimmy used Jerry as a punching bag in sparring sessions; in turn, Jerry pounded his younger brother Mike. Alternately disgusted and enraged by his father's domineering ways, Jimmy walked away from the ring at 20.

Jerry persevered. Despite a series of physical setbacks as a teen-

ager that included nephritis (acute inflammation of the kidneys),
a broken arm, and a broken back suffered in a diving accident,
he worked hard in the gym, sculpting his six-foot frame into 185
pounds of granite-hard muscle. A simple force drove him: Jerry
wanted nothing more than to please his father.

"Jerry never really bonded with our father, and he was always
insecure about that," says Mike Quarry. "When Jerry was sick with
nephritis, he went to school half days, and my father called him a
mama's boy. He became a boxer to try to prove himself."

By the time he was 16, Jerry had fought more than 100 amateur
fights. At 18, he'd been in more than 200, en route to compiling an
outstanding 170–13–54 record. More important, Jerry's success
won him the grudging respect of his father.

In 1965, Jerry captured the California Golden Gloves championships, then traveled to Kansas City for the nationals. Though he was
battling the flu, he knocked out all five of his opponents, a Golden
Gloves first. The decisive wins changed Jerry's life.

He had just graduated from Bellflower High, the first Quarry to
finish high school. Smart, well-spoken, and handsome (think of a
young Glen Campbell), he might have gone on to college and,
possibly, a white-collar career. Or, if he'd stayed amateur, he might
have won a spot on the 1968 Olympic team — and some time to
hone his talent and fill out physically.

But the power Jerry displayed in Kansas City gave Jack another
idea: Jerry should turn pro immediately. The reason? Jerry's devastating left hook could lead him to the heavyweight title and piles of
money. And when Jack said Jump, Jerry said How high?

In 1965, when Jerry turned pro, New York was the nation's premier
boxing town. But Los Angeles was a close second, in large part
because of the venerable Olympic Auditorium at 18th and Grand.
Promoter Aileen Eaton and matchmakers Mickey Davies and Don
"War-A-Week" Chargin mined Los Angeles's many boxing gyms for
talent, then presented the fighters at their Thursday-night shows.
And what talent the city produced: Joey Orbillo, Mando Ramos,
and Raul Rojas. Hedgemon Lewis and Danny "Little Red" Lopez.
Frankie Crawford and Carlos Palomino.

Jack Quarry instinctively knew that his son's marketability went
far beyond his punching power. Most of the nation's top boxers

were black and brown; after Rocky Marciano's retirement in 1955, only one white, Sweden's Ingemar Johansson, had held the heavyweight championship of the world (and Johansson's reign lasted just a year). As a "white hope," Jerry would automatically become a box-office draw and attract media attention.

Jack and Johnny Flores, a local trainer, signed "Irish Jerry" Quarry to a seven-year deal, and on May 7, 1965, the 19-year-old, crew-cut kid from Bellflower made his professional debut, whipping Gene Hamilton in front of 15,000 people at the Los Angeles Coliseum. Within a year, Jerry was established as a local favorite at the Olympic, racking up a 17–0–2 mark, with 10 knockouts.

Jack had predicted correctly: his boy was good enough for the pros, and the media did come running. They were measuring Jerry against the talents of other young heavyweight prospects — Thad Spencer, Clay Hodges, Tony Doyle, and Joey Orbillo — when Jerry fell to veteran Eddie Machem in the summer of '66, his first pro loss. But Jerry showed some of the tenacity that would mark his career by rebounding with two straight wins. That set up a showdown against Orbillo, the Wilmington-based "Harbor Hawk," in both fighters' biggest bout to date.

"I won the first three rounds, and in the fourth round, I came out throwing some jabs: boom, boom, boom," recalls Orbillo, who now works with the International Longshoreman's Warehouse Union in the Long Beach/San Pedro area. "And the next thing I know, I'm in a bowling alley at three o'clock in the morning. I'm, like, 'Who won the fight?' My friends picked me up, took me into the bathroom and said, 'Look at yourself. Think who won the fight.' That Jerry Quarry. Man, he was a hard hitter."

To understand Jerry Quarry today, you have to know his past fights. As Jerry's caretaker and number-one fan, Jimmy has collected every major bout on videotape. To sit with Jimmy and Jerry and watch all of them in a single afternoon is to see a life rise and fall in a fast-forward blur.

Here's Jerry in '68, unmarked and handsome, talking with Howard Cosell before he strides into the ring and painstakingly dissects Thad Spencer, using a vicious left hook to set up his powerful right.

Next, it's Jerry and Jimmy Ellis battling for the heavyweight championship after Muhammad Ali was stripped of the title for refusing induction into the Army. Jerry looks tentative and stiff, his excellent counterpunching skills nullified as Ellis routinely beats him to the punch. The fifteen-round fight isn't even close. Quarry loses the decision and Ellis becomes champion.

After the fight, X-rays would reveal that Quarry, who says he had complained of back pain to his father, had fought the entire fight with a broken back. "My father and Johnny Flores shot Jerry up with Cortisone because they didn't want to miss out on the big payday — $125,000," says Jimmy bitterly.

Jack Quarry denies that he knew Jerry had back problems during training camp. "Jerry told Johnny Flores that his back was hurting," he says. "Jerry never told me he had a problem with his back."

Jerry considers the loss to Ellis the most heartbreaking of his career; he's convinced that had he not been injured or had his father not made him fight that night, he would have beaten Ellis for the title. When the fight comes on, he rises from his chair and hurries from the room.

Rewind, eject. Jerry returns to the room, and the show continues. Insert, play. He defeats the highly regarded Buster Mathis. "I left-hooked him to death," chortles Jerry. Then, in 1969, he takes on Joe Frazier, perhaps the hardest hitter and hardest worker in the heavyweight division. The two men rush to meet in the center of the ring and begin to pound each other. Every so often they step back, as if to admire the damage they've wrought, then rush forward again. The brutal pace can't last, and Jerry takes the brunt of the punishment, his right eye bloody and swollen shut for the last four rounds of the fight. In the seventh, it's stopped.

Still, Jerry refuses to fold. The next video shows him a year later knocking out number one–ranked contender Mac Foster in Madison Square Garden. The upset win propels him into a 1970 showdown with Muhammad Ali, back in the ring after his three-and-a-half-year exile. The fight is an event — white hope vs. militant black Muslim — but it's over quickly. Ali, looking ring-rusty, prevails after a nasty gash opens up over Jerry's left eye late in the third round, forcing the stoppage of the fight. Quarry claims the cut came from an Ali head butt; repeated viewings of the sequence when the blood starts flowing are inconclusive.

Two years later, Quarry meets Ali again for the NABF heavyweight championship belt. Jerry sports a paunch and is sluggish; Ali thrashes him, keeping him at a distance with a stinging jab. But Jerry bounces back again, whipping Randy Neumann, then Ron Lyle, yet another number one–ranked contender, then Earnie Shavers. The string of victories leads him into a second showdown with Smokin' Joe Frazier, who's older and slower but just as powerful. By the time the fight is stopped in the fifth round, Jerry is bleeding profusely from the nose and mouth and from cuts over both eyes.

The last tape, 1975. Nine days after his thirtieth birthday, Jerry meets young strongman Ken Norton, who comes onscreen looking like a conqueror, his V-shaped torso smooth and hard as brown metal. Quarry no longer resembles his trim, neatly groomed 1968 self. He looks sloppy, with bushy sideburns and unruly hair; his face is red and puffy, and a small gut hangs over his waistband. He wades in toward Norton, who plays matador with Jerry, catching him with a random assortment of rights and lefts. By the fifth round, Quarry has become a veritable punching bag, his chest and face splattered with his own blood. Finally, as Norton pounds him against the ropes, the referee mercifully stops the bout. After the fight, Jerry announced his retirement.

Stop, rewind, eject. One sits, contemplating the tape's message: Jerry Quarry epitomized what a professional boxer should be — dogged, impervious to pain, powerful. And that Jerry Quarry was a fighter who never, ever gave up.

"There's no quit in a Quarry," Jack used to tell his sons, and Jerry took it to heart. Every time the sports writers thought he was through, he came back. But because he never won the heavyweight title, and thus never fulfilled his father's ambition for him, Jerry thought — and still thinks — of himself as a failure.

Many boxers think that way, for they look at their sport in black and white: you win or you lose. The only other colors that matter are red, for blood, and green, for money.

Of these, green is the most important. The Mob used to run boxing; nowadays, several boxing organizations, TV networks and promoters dominate. Along with the managers, they control where, when and whom the fighter fights — and for how much. A fighter's trainer determines how far he will run each day and where he'll work out. Each gets a cut of the fighter's purse.

In making their decisions, the powers that be (and those that have been) have rarely considered the fighter's own welfare. After 1892, for example, bareknuckle fighting was banned and padded gloves were adopted, not to protect the fighters' heads, as many mistakenly believe, but to protect their hands. In fact, because padded gloves allow fighters to swing and hit with greater force, their use has increased the severity of brain damage. Because some states have rules that suspend fighters who have been knocked out, greedy managers habitually have taken their fighters to another state, where they fight under assumed names and thus avoid the post-knockout suspension period. In addition, few states have required licensing and medical tests for trainers, who, ultimately, are responsible for the condition of the fighter's body. It is the trainers, after all, who decide whether a fighter is too badly injured to continue during a fight.

The fighters, with very few exceptions, have had little or no control over their own careers. They're disposable, and the smart ones recognize this: they call themselves pieces of meat or whores.

If boxers are whores, that would make the governing bodies and promoters pimps. Then, the spectators, the witnesses to the violence in the ring, would be the johns. Boxing wouldn't be what it is without them. The spectators' presence gives meaning to a fight, validating it as "a sport" or "a game." Or as "the sweet science" or "the manly art of self-defense." The spectators support the sport with their wallets; in return, they demand it provide action. They applaud a fighter for leaving his blood on the canvas; it is the ultimate sacrifice. When they don't get what they want, they boo. Or they do what fans used to do up in the balcony of the old Olympic Auditorium: when a pair of fighters danced around and didn't fight, they passed a cup, filled it with piss and then threw it into the ring.

Who damaged Jerry Quarry? His father did and he did and boxing did. But so did we.

Fighters know that they'll have to live with some physical damage after they retire. That's part of their code, and most wear their bashed-in noses and scar tissue and cauliflower ears with pride. But what many don't plan for is how to manage their postfight lives. What does a man do when his whole identity is fighting and he physically can't do it anymore?

Jerry did what most every retired fighter does. Two years after his loss to Norton, he went back into training, pushing himself for a comeback fight in the newly created cruiserweight division. He beat Lorenzo Zanon, but the feeling that he was on a mission to become champion was gone.

Meanwhile, his personal life began to unravel. When he wasn't fighting and required to stay in shape, he drank heavily and gained weight. His first marriage, which had ended in the early '70s, was followed in quick succession by two other failures; the last ended with Jerry assuming the paternity of a child he still swears isn't his.

His son Jerry Lynn, then a teenager, lived with his father for long stretches during the '80s. "Those were the hard years," he says. "He'd come home drunk, then go into his room and cry. He didn't know what he was going to do with his life."

Depressed, floundering, Quarry attempted two more comeback fights in 1983. He won both, but his 38-year-old body absorbed tremendous physical damage. "I didn't even know about them until he came home all cut up," says Jerry Lynn. "The most damage was when he fought James Williams in '83. He took sixty-some stitches in his face and scared the shit out of me. It was so bad, Red Cross set up camp outside his dressing room."

Jerry retired for a third time after the Williams fight. He had earned about $2 million in the ring, but with three divorce settlements, alimony and child-support payments, nonstop partying, and the loss of his principal source of income, he had to cash in the investments that were meant to support his retirement years. Houses and property in Orange County and Hawaii slipped away; so did his small retirement nest egg.

Quarry struggled to hold down a number of jobs: fight commentator for CBS, Miller Lite pitchman, bodyguard/road manager for Three Dog Night, actor, PR man, lounge singer. Nothing stuck; either he hated the work or he couldn't make the grade. And he found he missed being in the spotlight.

In 1992, nine years after his last official appearance in the ring, he made one last comeback. According to Jimmy, Jerry allowed some "business partners" to talk him into the fight. "They were telling Jerry that he had to get in shape to do a movie about his life, but all they cared about was making money by getting him back in the ring," he says. "He was no longer a fighter. He was trying to please his so-called friends."

Because Jerry declined to appear before the California Athletic Commission, it refused to issue him a license to fight. Nevada also turned him down. But Colorado doesn't have a boxing commission, and Jerry went there to fight Ron Crammer. Jerry lost a six-round decision, then came home with his front teeth knocked out, his right eye cut and a glaze in his eyes. He was 47, and had earned about $1,000 for the night's work.

After the Crammer fight, Jimmy says, Jerry's disabilities really started coming out. "He'd get up from the couch and say, 'I guess I'm going home.' And I'd say, 'What do you mean you're going home; where do you live?' He'd say, 'Woodland Hills.' I'd say, 'You're here.' And he'd say, 'Oh, I was just checking you guys out.'"

Jerry's sister Dianna took him to Dr. Peter Russell, a San Luis Obispo–based neuropsychologist. Russell's examinations revealed that Jerry had "suffered significant cerebral atrophy and neurological impairment." Further testing showed a severely impaired short-term memory. The cause, according to Russell, was repeated trauma to the head.

The connection between Jerry's condition and boxing echoed findings that had begun to appear in the 1980s in the *Journal of the American Medical Association* (*JAMA*). Advances in technology and testing — including magnetic resonance imaging (MRI), computerized axial tomography (CAT) scans, and neuropsychiatric testing — were allowing researchers to confirm medically what had for years been anecdotal material about "punch-drunk" fighters. According to one study done in the New York area, over 60 percent of professional boxers who'd fought a large number of bouts would end up with chronic brain damage. Unlike the harm caused by a knockout, when a boxer renders another unconscious almost instantly, chronic brain damage — more subtle and hard to measure — is the result of an accumulation of blows. Other factors that contribute to the severity of the condition include the number of fights, and at what age the boxer began and ended his career. The more fights, the more likely he will end up with cerebral atrophy; aging exacerbates the condition.

The findings fueled a debate between the medical and the boxing communities. Those in the boxing world argued that it was difficult to substantiate that fighting caused brain damage, since no "baseline measurements" — i.e., the original condition and subsequent changes to the brain — existed to prove causality. Neurologists countered with multiple studies of select fighters that showed only boxing could have caused the damage.

Ironically, just before his '83 comeback, Jerry took part in a *Sports Illustrated* study about brain damage among boxers. Neurologists hired by *SI* administered a CAT scan and a neuropsych exam. They concluded then that Quarry, though still functional, had "problems with certain cognitive functions — short-term memory and perceptual motor ability."

Today, Jerry says he doesn't remember taking the tests. But the results of those tests, when compared to those done by Russell, could provide researchers further insight into the rate at which a fighter's brain atrophies.

As the debate continued, *JAMA* editors began a campaign to outlaw boxing. In 1984, under the headline "Boxing Should Be Banned in Civilized Countries — Round 2," Dr. George Lundberg urged, "Either boxing should be abolished, which we favor, or blows to the head should be made illegal." To emphasize his point, he described what happens inside the skull upon impact: "The fist hits the head, and the skull moves immediately. The brain lags a bit, then it glides and swirls and bumps around. Brain fibers are torn, brain cells die, small blood vessels are torn, and little hemorrhages occur. This repeats itself hundreds and thousands of times."

Working under the assumption that boxing wouldn't be banned any time soon, Lundberg and other doctors drew up a list of recommendations to minimize damage to boxers. They included the establishment of a "'National Registry of Boxers' for all amateurs and professional boxers, including sparring mates . . . to record the results of all licensed bouts"; authorizing ring physicians "to stop any bout in progress, at any time, to examine a contestant and, when indicated, to terminate a bout that might . . . result in serious injury for either contestant"; and standardizing and upgrading state and local boxing commissions' medical evaluations.

Since the publication of its recommendations, *JAMA* has periodically repeated its arguments, but none of its suggestions has been adopted nationwide. Boxers — and their managers and promoters — agree that a national registry is vitally important: it would prevent boxers who've been knocked out in one state from fighting in another under assumed names, and it would require the licensing of all trainers, thus stopping inexperienced cornermen from handling fighters.

But most in the boxing community continue to deny that a widespread problem with chronic brain damage exists. When a fighter grows mentally disabled, they prefer to blame alcohol, drugs, and aging.

The California Athletic Commission, which oversees the state's boxing operations, has become one of the most progressive in the world, in part because California hosts so many professional and amateur fights. In 1994, some ninety pro boxing cards, and twenty kickboxing or martial-arts cards, took place in California, the most in the United States. California's boxing shows grossed $3 million in gate receipts and $3.6 million in broadcast fees.

Dr. Robert Karns, the chair of the physicians' advisory committee to the state's athletic commission, says that California already follows many of *JAMA*'s recommendations regarding boxer safety and physician responsibility. For instance, says Karns, when a fighter gets knocked out in a California bout, he is barred from sparring for thirty days and from competing for forty-five days.

"We're one of the only states where a physician at ringside may stop a fight," adds Karns. "Also, each fighter who fights in California must be examined and undergo a separate, state-approved neurological exam before being licensed."

Karns does not believe boxing should be banned. "Boxing's the only sport where it's you against me, matched in equal weight and skill," he says. "It's not like football, where you have 300-pound linemen smashing 180-pound quarterbacks." He adds that some changes have been made over the last two decades to protect fighters: championship bouts have been shortened from fifteen rounds to twelve, and there has been widespread installation of padding on ring posts to decrease accidental injuries to the head.

"Jerry Quarry is a product of boxing in the sixties and seventies," says Karns, who emphasizes that California denied Quarry a boxing license before his '92 comeback. "I honestly believe that if everyone follows strict rules, boxing can be a sport where people can have a career and walk away healthy."

That's only partly true, because the basic purpose of boxing remains to separate one's opponent from his consciousness. That means delivering blows to the head, and that means damage. Nor do neurologists distinguish between blows to the head that occur during sparring and those that occur during fights. And while boxers spar with padded headgear, the protection that headgear gives the brain is minimal. "It keeps a fighter from getting cut accidentally, in case two guys bump heads," says trainer Bill Slayton, who helped supervise Jerry's budding amateur career at the Teamsters Gym in downtown Los Angeles. "That's the main purpose for it, because you can still get knocked down. As for the gloves, well, the padding there protects the hands, not the skull."

Slayton vividly recalls the sparring battles Jerry and his younger brother Mike would wage in the gym. "Mike and Jerry used to go through some terrible wars," he says. "There was no animosity between them; it's just they would work."

The sparring Jerry and Mike did with each other may have done each as much harm as their fights. Mike, now 44, has taken classes for his short-term memory problem, but he admits that the disability will probably grow worse. "Jerry was subject to hitting me too hard during sparring," says Mike. "He never tried to knock me out or nothing, which he obviously could have, but he did go hard on me. A couple of years ago he apologized to me for beating up on me."

"Their whole lives, my brothers were conditioned by my father to take a punch," says Jimmy, sadly. "That's why they could take punishment."

Jimmy and Jerry didn't watch last month's super-middleweight championship fight between Gerald McClellan and Nigel Benn the first time it was televised by Showtime. They didn't see McClellan getting knocked out, collapsing unconscious in his corner, then being rushed to the hospital for the removal of a blood clot in his brain. They didn't hear the prognosis that McClellan will never fight again and may never live a "normal" life.

Assuming he lives, McClellan will join the many fighters incapacitated by boxing. For Jimmy, the list is already too long. "If they don't come up with some sort of plan to protect the fighters better, I'm all for banning boxing," he says. "I still love the sport. I still watch it every chance I get. But every day I see my brother, and every day I hurt.

"We won't let chickens fight. We won't let dogs fight. We won't even let them trip horses, because it's cruel to those animals. Yet we will let two men get in a ring and beat their brains out for our entertainment, because we don't care what happens to them."

That boxing still doesn't take care of its own remains one of the most shameful chapters in sports. Most observers, in and out of the boxing community, agree that because only a small handful of fighters wield any semblance of power, control of the sport rests with the powerful governing bodies like the IBF, the World Boxing Council and the World Boxing Association, and several promoters. And, because no one national organization exists to oversee what they do, boxing's chaotic and destructive ways persist.

This could change, of course. The governing bodies and promoters could allow boxers a voice in the sport. But that would mean yielding control. They could better regulate boxing's ancillary professions (including trainers, managers, and promoters). But that would involve committing time and energy to developing and monitoring supervisory programs. They could allow one governing body to regulate the entire industry. But that would mean losing power. They could require all boxers to take biannual CAT scans and other neurological tests and help set up a comprehensive pension and health-care plan. But that would mean giving up profits.

Jimmy believes that the Jerry Quarry Foundation will succeed precisely because he plans to bypass boxing's powers that be. "If you look at the history of boxing, it's always been a paternalistic atmosphere," says Jimmy. "The plans that have come from boxing have never succeeded because someone has always dropped the ball."

In one way, Jerry's an unlikely choice for the role as boxing's conscience. Never particularly eloquent, now he repeats himself constantly, trotting out a homily for every occasion. "Boxing is a one-on-one confrontation with your life," he'll say over and over, "and payback's a bitch." About his marriages, he'll tell you, "Three times up, three times down, this li'l dummy doesn't go another round."

But, in another way, the part fits him perfectly. Jerry Quarry's face and words and deteriorating mind reveal him as a man whose dedication to boxing cost him everything: the sport that made Jerry Quarry also destroyed him.

"Boxing is a very cruel sport, and getting in the ring is not an easy thing to do," he says. "But the situation after you retire from boxing is hellacious."

Did he ever think he'd find himself in this position?

"No," he answers.

Is he bitter?

No, he says. "It's a part of life. Life's just a steady climb to the bottom."

TOM JUNOD

The Savior

FROM GQ

GRANT HILL is happy among the hoodlums. He doesn't like the
word "hoodlums," because it's unkind, and so he tries to think of
some other term that might describe those he met at the party . . .
but no, let's be honest, they were hoodlums, all right. Terry Mills,
Grant's teammate on the Pistons, was throwing a charity party in
downtown Detroit, at some big old theater, with his name all up
in lights — "TERRY MILLS" — and for some reason the hoodlums
just decided to come. The party was the place to be, if you were a
hoodlum. There were guys in these long mink coats, wearing these
big mink hats, and you just know they had guns stuffed in their
pockets. There were these crazy women running around, who were
with the hoodlums but who were all drunk and lubricious, and
ready to go. And in the middle of this chaos was none other than
Grant Hill, along with two of his teammates, Johnny Dawkins and
Rafael Addison.

Now, anybody who knows anything about Grant Hill knows that
he's not supposed to be at a hoodlum party — that he's supposed
to be visiting an orphanage or something, because, after all, this is
the guy who's so good, so clean, so freaking nice, that he's going to
help us love sports again. Hell, even the hoodlums had to know that
Grant Hill was something of an anomaly in their midst, and so you
might think that they would try to corrupt him, or just mess with
him in some way. But you'd be wrong. The hoodlums loved Grant
Hill. They welcomed Grant Hill. They shouted, whenever he came
near them, *"Grant Hill! Grant Hill! Grant Hill!"* as though he were
the King of the Hoodlums or, as Grant has said, "Dr. Detroit." *Grant*

Hill! Grant Hill! Grant Hill! And you know what Grant Hill did? He didn't hold himself above them, if that's what you're thinking, because he wasn't raised that way. He was raised to acknowledge everyone, to treat everybody the same, and that's exactly what he did: he acknowledged all the hoodlums. No, he did more than that — he went around relating to each one, to the extent that Addison and Dawkins just kind of walked behind him, looking at each other, shaking their heads, allowing him, Grant Hill, to make introductions and to be their shield. The women were all over Grant, of course — so drunk and lubricious that it looked like they were going to fight over him — but Grant just talked to them, all of them, fat or skinny, drunk or sober, and you better believe that at the Hoodlums' Ball there were plenty of each. And then, whenever a hoodlum in a mink coat came over, Grant would say to Addison and Dawkins, "Man, we got to get ourselves one of these coats," and the hoodlum wouldn't take offense or give any indication that he sensed someone was mocking him. No, he would just look at Grant and then look back at his coat and say "Yeah, well, heh-heh, it is *fine*, isn't it?"

Grant Hill's just a kid, and he's managed to turn a whole nation of fans, coaches, reporters and professional hucksters into a hoodlum chorus. He's just 22 years old, a rookie in the NBA, and yet he goes out on the road with the Pistons and the crowds at hostile stadiums — at the Garden, for crying out loud — don't just cheer him, they greet him, they stand and beckon, they call his name in welcome. *Grant Hill! Grant Hill! Grant Hill!* He spends ten minutes with reporters and columnists, and because he acknowledges them, because he offers them politesse and deference instead of the usual helping of surliness and suspicion, the grateful wretches pronounce him perfect, as though his every utterance were an echo of some higher order, and he didn't have as little, or as much, to say as the next idealistic young millionaire schooled in the resolute banality of the postgame interview. He averages eighteen points a game for the last-place Pistons, and he is at once the first rookie ever to lead the NBA in All-Star voting and, arguably, the first player ever to lead the voting by virtue of his own virtue. He sells sneakers for Fila, pitches soda pop for Sprite, and touts trucks for GMC, and he has been named the most marketable young player in the NBA, although — as Grant is the first to admit — he really hasn't done anything yet.

Why, then, has he been anointed? Well, you could say that the mere fact that he is not a hoodlum in a world replete with hoodlums — that he is not an asshole in a sports universe replete with assholes — has qualified him to wear a crown. You could say, as Grant does, that "with the baseball and hockey strikes, and the years of greed, here comes someone who just wants to play, so maybe it is perfect timing for everyone." You could say that the NBA needs Grant to fill the void left by the departure of Michael, Magic, and Bird. You could say . . . oh, hell, you could say a lot of things: that Grant is, in the words of the poet Charles P. Pierce, "our first post-Gingrich superstar"; that he's a harbinger of the day when the value police will finally break down the doors of the locker room and make all those muscled miscreants toe the line in the name of God and country; that because he is said to "act white" and "play black," he makes a black man's game palatable to the white folk who have started imputing a connection between "in your face" and "in your house.". . .

Or you could just say what Grant says, and what the hoodlums at the Hoodlums' Ball all instinctively knew the minute he walked into the room: "I don't think I was groomed to be an athlete. I was groomed to be a prince or someone going into politics — a public figure or a king."

For the first three days of his life, in October 1972, Grant was known simply as the Boy Hill. Calvin Hill had so desperately wanted a son that he had permitted himself to think only of having a daughter and to entertain only a list of girls' names. When Janet Hill, in fact, gave birth to a boy, the infant went nameless until Roger Staubach visited the hospital, listened to the names the Hills were considering, heard the one he liked and, in an act of wisdom and impatience, issued an edict: "It's time to name him, and we're going to name him Grant."

He was royalty from the start, then. How can you be anything less when your parents are Calvin and Janet Hill? Calvin Hill graduated from Yale University and became a star running back for the Cowboys, and then the Washington Redskins and the Cleveland Browns. Janet Hill shared a suite with Hillary Rodham at Wellesley and went on to own a Capitol Hill consulting firm with her partner, Clifford Alexander, a former secretary of the army. Oh, sure, the Hills will tell you that they raised their son to be neither an athlete nor a king — that their only specific purpose was to raise him as a man of character — and there is no reason to doubt them. All the same, if God ever wanted to start a production line for the creation of athletes and kings — or for the creation of athletes who stir nostalgia for the days when we believed that athletes *were* our kings — he would locate it in Calvin and Janet's home. It was there, you see, that Grant grew up listening not only to his father and his mother but also to Roger Staubach and Paul Warfield and Ozzie Newsome and Michael Washington and Kenny Houston and Brig Owens, who were athletes, sure, but also noble men convinced of the nobility of their calling.

"I think that just listening to my friends talk, Grant picked up a lot of things — the dos and don'ts of being in public," Calvin says. "There was a sense that you have to do something with fame and fortune — that there was a certain power to being an athlete."

Indeed, because Grant was the only child of only children, his parents made sure that their house bustled with esteemed men and women who could — by counsel and by example — show him what kind of behavior the world would expect from him and what kind of behavior he could expect from the world. "My parents stressed the importance of education, athletics, and the right people," Grant says. "I didn't have to go outside my house for any of that. Everything I needed, everything I had to hear, was right at home."

They called themselves the Boring Family. Grant's friends called them the Huxtables, and called Janet the General. Stories of her stringent command are a matter of record and, increasingly, of legend: how Grant was forbidden to use the telephone six days a week, and indeed was permitted just one hour of telephone time on Saturdays; how, when Grant once broke curfew, she threw his watch against a wall, saying "You don't use it, anyway!"; how she had the watch fixed and presented it to him, gift-wrapped, on his birthday. What is cited less frequently is Janet Hill's insistence on the value of talk: how she would, each afternoon at four o'clock, excuse herself from whatever she was doing — even meetings with her most crucial clients — to call Grant, to tell him what her day had been like, so that even when he was home alone he had a sense of connection, not only with his mother but with what she had to do each day, which was to go to work.

The Hills did not quite realize what they had managed to accomplish — the kind of son they had managed to raise — until one evening during Grant's senior year at Duke University, when they were asked to be on a radio talk show with him. Grant was on the phone from Durham; Janet and Calvin were on the phone from their home in Great Falls, Virginia; and the host, because of constraints of Grant's time, asked Grant to speak first. "We just listened," Calvin says. "We didn't say anything, and we were mesmerized. He was so witty and articulate, it was like reading Henry James. Then the host says, 'Now, we're going to ask questions of his parents,' and we're like, 'Ah, uh, duh' — we're stumbling through because we still can't get over Grant."

And it was then that they had an inkling of what their son's life, and their lives, might be like; that he had something, and that he might, one day, be able to show the world what the Hills have of course always known: that athletes should be the best of us and not the worst.

It is a risky strategy for a corporation to bank on the marketability of virtue, because it is one of the sad truths of human experience that virtue, over time, tends to become less virtuous. A few years ago, Howe Burch, the marketing director of Fila USA, had the idea of marketing Riddick Bowe as a friendly athlete, and not only as a friendly athlete but as a friendly boxer. Burch was so taken with his idea that he used Fila's considerable clout in Italy to arrange for Bowe to have an audience with the pope. Well, why not? After all, Burch was trying to define his company against freaking Nike, and Nike had already signed up every badass who went to work in short pants. Why not try virtue? Why not try the pope? Why not go for contrast? How could Burch have foreseen that one day Bowe would ask if he had to take off his shirt for a commercial — "Yeah, Riddick, you're a boxer. You're in the ring. You gotta take off your shirt" — and that when he finally did, fat would drip down his body like fudge on a sundae? How could Burch have known that Louis Farrakhan would show up at ringside to cheer Bowe, that Bowe's manager would start sporting "FREE MIKE TYSON" T-shirts, and that Bowe, dressed in Fila from head to toe, would punch out some poor stiff at a press conference?

And how could Burch have possibly predicted that the player he signed out of the 1993 basketball draft, Jamal Mashburn of the Dallas Mavericks, was going to feud with his coach and play for such a surpassingly shitty team that the smell seemed to stick to the skin of his signature-edition sneakers?

It may be assumed, then, that Howe Burch approached the 1994 basketball draft with some trepidation, especially since he was already committed to the slogan "Change the game," which he translates into the vernacular as "You can be a champion without being an asshole." He did not consider Glenn "Big Dog" Robinson, the projected number one pick, especially marketable, so he focused his attention on the presumed number two, Jason Kidd, and the presumed number three, Grant Hill. Burch wasn't sure about Kidd. Sure, he had some renegade pizzazz, and you could call his line of sneakers and clothing Kidd Stuff, but he seemed a little low-key and introverted, and then one morning Burch picked up the newspaper and read that Kidd had been involved in a hit-and-run in California. . . . Well, Burch didn't need that, no, and so thereafter he and Fila concentrated exclusively on Grant Hill.

Got him, too — snatched him away from freaking Nike by offering him something Nike couldn't: the future. Grant would have his own shoe, the Hill. He would have his own cross-trainer, and his own hiking boot, and his own line of casual clothes. Nike had, well, everybody, from Sir Charles to Mister Robinson to, what's his name, Dan Majerle, but Fila would have Grant, and Grant would have exactly what he wanted: the chance to swing the course of Fila's destiny the way Michael Jordan once had swung the course of Nike's.

Now Howe Burch can wake up in the morning and open the sports section and drink his coffee with a smile. He is immune. "Did you hear that story about Thurman Thomas?" he asks. "You know, the one where he tells the kid that he fumbled because 'I was up all night fucking your mama'? Nice, huh? Well, I love it when they do stuff like that, because it just distances Grant from the rest of the market." So go ahead — jam the rosters with motherfuckers and trash-talkers and crotch-pumpers; let assholes overrun the league, or the entire body of holy endeavor and unholy enterprise known as sport: Howe Burch won't care. He will be delighted, in fact, because he has Grant Hill, and Grant Hill, who is not an asshole, is changing the game.

Grant stands in front of a camera and talks. A microphone, suspended on a boom, captures the deep voice that issues from underneath his scrubby mustache and puts his words on tape. He is not saying anything special. He is not doing anything special. He is being himself, and what he is, after all, is a kid, thin, angled, slouchy, watchful, with soft, bright eyes and elfin ears and a shaved scalp that gives him the appearance of an outsize child drawn in unfilled outlines — a sweet, smart, comic-strip character with a head shaped like a light bulb and a body six feet eight inches tall. He is being filmed for a commercial; he is supposed to be selling sneakers, and yet he can do anything he wants, or nothing at all, and the camera will keep rolling, and from time to time the art director will nod and say "Boom, that's a spot."

Grant has freed them. Because of who Grant is, what Grant is, Sam Gulisano, the art director, and Robbie Austin, Sam's copywriting partner at the advertising firm of FCB, are free to simply let Grant be Grant. He has freed them, because if he were not who he is, what he is, they would have to make up something. They would have to turn Grant into a fictional character. They would launch him over a backboard or make him wear a dress.

But Sam and Robbie know exactly who Grant is. He is the son of the esteemed Calvin and the esteemed Janet. He is a graduate of Duke University, where he won two national championships and, in his senior year, very nearly won a third with a team he had to carry. He is a kid who, when he signed with Fila, stipulated that $120,000 of his contract would be set aside for a summer basketball league in inner-city Detroit. He is class, he is quality, and so after a few stabs at making things up — a commercial in which Grant, as a little boy, jump-shoots peas into the lake of gravy in his mother's mashed potatoes; a commercial in which Grant, as an English gentleman, upbraids some trash-talker for his improper use of language and then dunks in his face — Sam and Robbie hired the team that made the documentary *Hoop Dreams* to shoot a campaign entitled "A Rookie's Journal."

"Reality — that's what we're after," says Robbie.

"Totally unscripted," says Sam.

"Totally. This has to be Grant's."

"This has to come from him."

"It's absolutely real," says Robbie. "I can honestly say there's never been a commercial as reality-based."

In "A Rookie's Journal," Grant never deigns to be a shill; he never sullies himself with the job of selling sneakers. He just talks into the camera, about himself, his life in the NBA, his feelings, and then, at the end of the commercial, the Fila logo flashes on the screen, with the slogan "Change the game," and that's it — no artifice, no punch lines, no advertising, and yet . . . "Because it's Grant," says Sam, "you can get like, fifty spots in a day."

For instance, on the first day of shooting, Sam and Robbie are watching Grant play with a soccer ball. He's spinning it on his fingertips, he's dribbling it like a basketball, he pretends he's a quarterback, fading back to pass — and Sam and Robbie run to the cameraman and say "Did you get that?" because they know that the exuberance they have just seen is a spot. Then Grant sits down with the makeup artist, and, as she does his eyes, he says, "I've never played basketball in eyeliner before," and, well, as Sam says, "Boom, that's a spot." Then Grant starts talking about one of his idols, Julius Erving, and how Erving recently gave him his home phone number and Grant called the number just to hear Dr. J's voice on the answering machine — boom, that's a spot. Indeed, once we accept the premise of the campaign, which is that even if everybody else is an asshole, Grant Hill, certainly, is not, then anything Grant says, or does, is not only charming and delightful, it is curative, it is — boom, a spot — good for us.

"*Boooo!* You suck! You suck, Big Dog!"

It is a doleful evening in December, on the stricken plain between Detroit and Flint, in a crater of concrete and klieg lights known as the Palace of Auburn Hills, where the mediocre Milwaukee Bucks have come to challenge the dismal Detroit Pistons. The Palace is loud and crowded, but let's face it: the evening would be utterly without enchantment — just another excuse for hot dogs and Dutch milk — did it not promise an encounter between Grant Hill and Glenn "Big Dog" Robinson, the two rookies whose incipient rivalry the NBA has worked assiduously to promote.

"Right now, there has been a perception of a lack in the very elite top-superstar category," says the league's deputy commissioner, Russ Granik. A lack. Well, yes. That's one way of putting it.

Right now, though, the rivalry between Grant Hill and Glenn Robinson does not exist. It's not even close. Grant has been chosen; Big Dog has not. Grant is on the cover of the NBA's own *Hoop* magazine; Grant plays piano on *Letterman* and pulls it off so easily that it becomes his defining moment thus far. Big Dog — well, as Rex K. Nelson, who oversees community affairs for the Pistons and serves on the NBA's marketing advisory committee, says, "Robinson has some work to do as far as image and articulation. I mean 'Big Dog' — that's not really marketable, unless you work for a pet store."

They are friendly, Grant and Big Dog. They like each other. Indeed, Grant has been meaning to talk to Big Dog, to ask him whether what's been happening to Grant on the road — the odd approbation of enemy crowds — has been happening to him as well. He does not have to ask. The answer is no, because Big Dog — well, you know about Big Dog, don't you? He is the one who wanted too much. He was the NBA's number one draft pick, a thick jump shooter out of Purdue whose agent asked the Bucks for $100 million over ten years and then, after a holdout, settled for the less epochal figure of $68 million. He has become a symbol of heedless greed, just as Grant Hill has become a symbol of effortless grace, and now, as he is introduced, in his standard-issue black sneakers (he has not yet settled on a shoe contract) and in tube socks tugged all the way up his skinny calves, a woman waves a sign that, next to a crude image of Grant, asks "HEY BIG DOG — WHO IS #1 NOW?" and some asshole behind the Milwaukee bench is yelling "*Boooo!* You suck! You suck, Big Dog!". . .

. . . until the lights go down, and the arena fills with the theme song for some generic apocalypse, and the crowd stares up at a huge video cube blazing with the image of a four-point buck being blown to bits by a flaming basketball shot from the portals of the Palace. "Yeah! Yeah! Yeah!" cries the guy behind the bench, and then the Pistons come out, spotlit, and a roar goes up for Number 33, the humble hero.

Grant is a hero, of course, as much for what he didn't do as for what he did. He didn't hold out, for one thing — didn't insult all the hardworking folks now rising to cheer him. His agent, Lon Babby, was too smart for that — too astute a reader of the Zeitgeist, too aware of the opportunities that would come Grant's way if he just worked things out with the Pistons, signed his $45 million, eight-year contract and got into camp on time. Hell, Babby wasn't even taking a cut. He was positioning himself in regard to other agents in the same way Grant was positioning himself in regard to other basketball players. He was different. He was a lawyer, getting paid by the hour, and so he did not have to be professionally intransigent. He could afford to be reasonable, just as Grant could afford to be reasonable, just as Big Dog . . .

Well, who knows what Big Dog could afford? While Grant drove a Mercedes in high school and has participated since college in limited partnerships that give him part-ownership of eight urban-contemporary radio stations, Big Dog grew up poor in Gary, Indiana. Big Dog has never been in the position to be selective, to refuse things. On the evening of the collegiate draft, both he and Grant were invited to appear on one of the home-shopping networks to hawk their rookie trading cards. Grant declined, and this is cited by Lon Babby as evidence of his restraint. Big Dog accepted, and this was cited by newspaper columnists as evidence of his rapacity. Who cares that Big Dog has never turned his back on Gary, Indiana? Who cares that he still goes home to spend time with the kids for whom he is a blazon of hope, or that he puts his money into Gary's youth programs, just as Grant Hill puts his money into youth programs in Detroit? Big Dog asked for $100 million, didn't he? Well, then, Big Dog must be greedy, and now, as the game begins, Big Dog hits his jumper ("Yeah, *that's* worth $100 million!"), then misses a foul shot ("Sixty-eight, Glenn! Sixty-eight!").

Christ, they know everything, these fans, and are fixated on facts and figures. When Grant misses, though, they don't yell "Forty-five, Grant! Forty-five!" No, even when Grant looks like a rookie, clanking a jumper or losing the ball on a streak to the basket, the crowd is behind him: "Let's go, Grant!" "You're doing fine, Grant!" "Keep taking the shot, Grant!" And when Hill blocks Big Dog's shot and takes the ball downcourt himself, gliding between defenders on a parabolic path to the hoop with Big Dog in futile pursuit — well, there is in the audience this little coiled, quickening hush, until Grant, cutting to the basket, shifts in the air and dishes across his body to an onrushing Piston, who goes in for the slam . . . and the hush dissolves into a jolly uproar.

They each score fifteen tonight, in a game the Bucks lead from the opening tip to the final buzzer. By the end of the evening, however, the score, and the game, hardly matter; the apparatus by which the NBA at once promotes and devalues its product has taken over, and Sir Slamalot, the Pistons' plumed mascot, is delivering pizza, and the crowd is dancing to "YMCA," and when Big Dog leaves the court, there are no more boos, and no cheers, either: There is nothing.

That *nothing* — that big, clanging, soulless void at the heart of sports? Grant Hill wants to fill it. That's what you have to love about him, and that's certainly what guys like Howe Burch and Sam Gulisano and Lon Babby love about him: how much he wants it, how willing and eager he is to get out there and be the guy who changes the game. He's 22 years old and already he's talking about being *remembered;* about some kid's thinking about him, Grant Hill, the way Grant Hill used to think about his idols, Arthur Ashe and Julius Erving. He doesn't even care that in the process of being remembered he will be pinioned by the encumbrances of fame; indeed, when he goes to a restaurant one evening and is set upon by autograph-seekers and is told that one day he's going to wind up like Joe Montana or Michael Jordan, unable even to go out to enjoy a simple meal, he says, "The problems that Montana and those guys have, I want to have those problems, because that means I went to a certain level."

He is driven by . . . youth? pride? competitiveness? noblesse oblige? Yeah, sure, all of that, but also a sense of singularity, a sense of being apart. Because Grant is a *Hill,* the only child of Janet and Calvin, he is not quite anything else, and yet he has been taught by his parents that he must live his life among everyone else. He is who he is and he is who he is not. His talent, other than for basketball, is for crossover; he exists between poles, and so he is electric with possibility — the Elvis of the hard court. Grant is not white, though he was raised to be comfortable among whites and he makes whites comfortable; he is not of the inner city, though he is comfortable in the inner city and regards its inhabitants as his people; he is not a hoodlum, though he is happy among the hoodlums. He is, by simple virtue of being alone, a natural politician; his world is one of constituencies, and he goes out and *wins them over,* with his own identity as his ideology.

He is animated by a sense of mission, and in his mission he is his parents by proxy. His father did not spike the ball after a touchdown; Grant does not talk trash after a slam. He says, "Don't get me wrong; I talk on the court. When a guy makes a nice move, I tell him 'Nice move.'" He operates in some place between innocence and intention. He does not trash-talk because it is not in him to trash-talk, and also because he considers the custom of trash-talking "demeaning" and wishes to curb it, to live up to the old-fashioned imperative of "raising the race."

"The perception of trash-talking is mainly of black athletes," he says. "People don't think whites do it, and when a black player comes along who doesn't do it, all of a sudden it's like a big deal — all of a sudden, it's like 'This is something rare.' It bothers me that there's so much negative written about black athletes. I want something positive written."

He does not care that some people in his own marketing team have located his appeal in the fact that he is considered "a good Negro" and "the great black white hope." "I'm not going to change who I am to please anybody," he says. "If I walk into a room full of white people, I'm going to act the same as if I walk into a room full of black people. I acknowledge everybody. I know I'm black. I've been black all my life. I don't have to walk a certain way, dress a certain way. I don't have to do anything to prove my blackness."

Is he being used? Is he being used not to elevate but rather to diminish the image of other black athletes, to give columnists an excuse for writing "Yeah, all these guys are assholes save for Grant Hill . . ."? "Everybody gets used," he says. Then, later: "It makes me uncomfortable when I'm put *against* people, like [Washington's] Chris Webber. People saying 'Chris doesn't act like Grant Hill' — it makes me uncomfortable, all these comparisons. Every time something happens negative to a black athlete, why am I always compared to that person? You know — '*Grant* doesn't do this, *Grant* doesn't do that, *Grant's* not greedy.' It's uncalled for. It's like all of a sudden I'm a measuring stick."

And yet . . . Grant *is* the measuring stick, and he chooses to live as the measuring stick. Although he is lonely, he spends most of his

time alone. He goes to movies alone. He goes to bookstores alone.
He goes to restaurants alone, when he is not driving alone to the
fast-food window. He is at once incorruptible and fearful of corrup-
tion. He not only abstains from alcohol, he has never *tried* alcohol,
never so much as had a sip, because he knows that alcohol ruins
lives, and the prospect of ruin frightens him. He is afraid of gambling, because "gambling is a disease," and he is afraid of tattoos,
because he can't imagine allowing anyone or anything to contami-
nate his flesh, and afraid of earrings, because "I don't know, with
AIDS going around — that piercing stuff just scares me."

Grant went out once with a teammate to a casino and a strip
joint. He gambled, modestly, and then, at the strip joint, when his
teammate started "acting crazy" and "acting rude," cursing out the
dancers and calling them "bitches and hos," Grant slipped them
each $50, to leave the impression of goodwill. He never went out
with that teammate again. No, instead, he bought five video arcade
games for his basement, so that he could entertain himself without
cost to his character and insulate himself against some irrevocable
instant in which he finds his name — and his parents' name —
besmirched. He has invested everything he is in what he is not. He
is not a hoodlum, no, and he will never be one. He is not an
asshole, and for this simple reason we are desperate to love him, as
a way of loving what we used to love — as a way of loving sports.

KAREN KARBO

Polite, Feminine, Can Bench Press Dennis Conner

FROM OUTSIDE

THEIR OWN public relations people invited me here — to the San Diego compound where the women's Team, the all-female crew of the yacht *America³*, is training for the 1995 America's Cup competition — but no one seems to know I'm coming. It's 6:15 A.M. For ten minutes I've been standing at the gate in the chain-link fence, which is topped with three strands of penitentiary-style razor wire. The morning is overcast and humid, the sky the color of an old bruise: odd weather for the city with the most temperate climate in the country. Blond crew members trail past in baggy T-shirts and ancient gym shorts, sweat socks, and Birkenstocks.

"I wish we could let you in," says one apologetically, slipping her key card into the electronic lock. "Someone'll be here soon." I'm here to see how an all-female crew, the first in the 143-year history of the world's most prestigious yacht race, might do things differently in this very male sport, so I make a note: polite.

Eventually, someone does come. Tony, from security. He's a non-blond with bulging arms that advertise his occupation. He checks my name off on a clipboard and points the way toward the weight room, where from 6:30 to 8:30 the girls, as they call themselves, work out six days a week, and have since last June and will at least until the Defender Selection Series, which begins this month, determines whether they'll go on to the finals in May.

Tony is SoCal friendly now — "You goin' out on the boat? Cool! Have a good one!" — but later, after the day's training session is over and *America³* and her stablemate, *Kanza*, have been hauled out of the water, their glossy white hulls swathed in blue skirts to protect their secret keels from prying eyes, he'll circle me from a distance, slapping his fist against his hand, anxious to have me gone. Anyone who has not signed the *America³* lifetime confidentiality statement is considered a "potential competitor." Even one girl's aged grandparents, visiting for a day from Indiana, were treated as if they might be sniffing around for secrets.

The weight room is basic, far less glam than your local Gold's Gym. Here and there a few posters have been taped up, mostly dazzling shots of *America³* winning the Cup in 1992 with oddball billionaire Bill Koch, its owner and the progenitor of the Women's Team, at the helm.

Some of the girls head out for a run, others hop onto stationary bikes, and still others are sent by Dick Dent, former trainer for the San Diego Padres, to the Versa Climbers. They hook themselves up to heart-rate monitors and crank out a mile to John Mellencamp's "Hurts So Good."

It's a weird, inspiring sight: a roomful of healthy, athletic women, ranging in age from 21 to 36, almost all sun-bleached blonds with caramel tans and broad, strong shoulders. Superficially, they appear to be a huge family of sisters. There are two Merrits, two Sarahs, two Stephanies. There are graduates from Yale, Wesleyan, Cornell. There are three Olympic medalists, three former Yachtswomen of the Year, one aerospace engineer who works in NASA's Microgravity Division, two world-class weight lifters, one former cast member of the weekly TV show *American Gladiators*. They are, variously, five-foot-three, 135 pounds; five-foot-seven, 150 pounds; five-foot-eleven, 170 pounds. They were chosen from a field of 650 applicants by the coaches, James (Kimo) Worthington and Stu Argo, both men, both members of the winning 1992 crew.

After the aerobic portion of their workout, the girls move on to the weight machines.

"Who're you?" asks Stephanie Armitage-Johnson, curly blond bangs, bright green eyes, her T-shirt limp with perspiration. I make another note: friendly. Armitage-Johnson, one of the world-class weight lifters, is assistant strength and conditioning coach for the University of Washington Huskies football team. I peek at the training log on her clipboard and see that she lifts in the triple digits.

I get an aloof, businesslike nod from Dawn Riley, sleek in red sports bra and royal blue bicycle shorts, gold necklace and earrings. To forestall the creation of a hierarchy, no positions have yet been assigned, but Riley is a likely candidate for helmsman. She is the best-known sailor among the girls and was the only woman on the *America³* crew in 1992.

"Hurts So Good" plays over and over. It's an anthem, a key part of the workout. This is revealed by Sandra Bateman, the organization's associate director of communications and public relations, who joins herself to my hip at 7:30. Dressed in deck shoes, navy blue shorts, and a white *America³* polo shirt, she's rail thin and . . . blond. Her impossible job is to make sure that when I leave the compound, I take with me the same impression I have at this moment: that here is a group of wholesome, hardworking women who embody the image on the official Women's Team T-shirt, the famous figure of Rosie the Riveter, her hair neatly covered by a red polka-dot kerchief, her biceps flexed, under the legend WE CAN DO IT!

Sandra Bateman is a wealth of charming anecdotes. She tells me how, once, when a TV crew came to film the girls, they were forced to turn the music off because the station didn't have air rights to the song. Instead, the station provided some easy-listening stuff that drove the girls crazy. "They need the beat," she says. "It keeps them pumped."

We are standing near the plate glass window that separates the weight room from the trainer's room. I've taken an interest in the Team Roach Collection. Earlier, Jane Oetking — who bears the double distinction of being one of the crew's two New Zealanders (married to an American, she has dual citizenship) and a brunette — strode in with a big bug to add to the display. Two inch-long specimens had already been taped to the window with white first-aid tape and labeled "Joan" and "Jen." Jane's beetle — not a roach at all — was squirming when she fastened it to the window and, hooting with laughter, scribbled "Jane" on the tape. Now Sandra Bateman watches mutely as I stare at the bugs. "Three of the twenty-four women in the crew are mothers," she says finally. "Half of them are married."

I know this already from the reams of press releases generated by her office. In addition to rehearsing all their medals and awards and achievements, the material lists each girl's marital status — not for the information of potential suitors, clearly, but to establish, somehow, that these are *nice* girls, *good* girls. Some of whom, it is also coyly noted, can bench-press their husbands.

The Defender Selection Series, which begins on the twelfth of this month, will pit the Women's Team in round-robin fashion against two other American crews, Team Dennis Conner and PACT '95, a Maine-based syndicate of young racers. The winner will defend the Cup against the foreign boat that wins the Challenger Selection Series, held simultaneously, also off San Diego.

The other teams, so far, anyway, are exclusively male. And that, of course, has prompted everyone — from two-time Cup winner Dennis Conner to the crew members of PACT '95 to the counter help at Bay Mart Liquor, down the block from the *America³* compound; from national sports commentators to Vegas oddsmakers to every journalist assigned to this and every other America's Cup story from now until May — to ask the big, dumb, inescapable question: All things being equal, can the girls beat the boys?

They can. People who know sailing know this, because they know that in sailing, particularly match cup racing, nothing is equal, ever. The 1995 America's Cup competition will not be a nautical version of Bobby Riggs versus Billy Jean King. Minute by minute, things change — the sea, the wind, the weight of the air; the boat, the sails, the tactics used by the opposition. A sailor must be agile, confident, able to recognize in a heartbeat a stroke of luck and play it out until, again, things change. In accounts of past America's Cup races, halyards are always snapping, sails are always ripping, water is always being taken on for mysterious reasons. Sailing on this level is a test of skills that are by and large immeasurable: the ability to adapt, cooperate, improvise. Can women do these things as well as men? Sexists would say that they can do these things a whole lot better than men.

But when people ask, Can the girls beat the boys? what they really mean is, Are the girls *strong enough* to beat the boys, and if they aren't, can they win the Cup anyway? One fear is that the women will lose precious seconds every time they tack; on Koch's winning 1992 crew, the grinders, who operate the winches that raise and lower the 150-pound sails, were football players, and there's no question that a linebacker can get a sail up faster than even the brawniest husband-heaving Olympic rower. But seconds are also lost when crew members disagree, when ego clouds a skipper's judgment, when tactics are bold but ultimately ineffective. Somewhere in there, some say, the women might find an edge.

In any case, the girls-versus-boys question is as quaint as playground gossip. The real question — unfortunately, from the viewpoint of purists — is this: Can *America³*, and then the boat that is now being built for the Women's Team based on the designs that Koch bequeathed along with his Cup-winning yacht, beat the boats that the guys put on the water?

What we're talking about is not sailors, but technology. And when we talk about technology, we're talking about money. Lots of money. One edge the women do have — and this almost everyone is agreed on — is their ability to attract funding. The *America³* organization, of course, won't reveal the size of the war chest, but it already counts among its corporate sponsors Citizen Watches, Dry Idea deodorant, *Glamour,* Lifetime, and Hewlett-Packard.

In a time long ago and far away, America's Cup funding was discreetly drawn from private sources, fished from the pockets of Vanderbilts and Liptons and, more recently, Ted Turner. The $68 million that upstart Koch spent in 1992 was viewed as Simply Too Much. (Conner spent $20 million on his winning 1987 campaign, A Lot But Not Vulgar.) Some say Koch "bought" the race, but what he really did was transform it even more thoroughly from a sport into a business and a science.

Himself a graduate of M.I.T., Koch to an unprecedented extent brought together not only renowned yacht designers and naval architects, but also computer scientists and physicists, experts in software and hydrodynamics, to work on *America³*. He introduced elaborate wind- and water-tunnel testing, created a Velocity Prediction Program, invented a new kind of lightweight sailcloth. He allegedly amped-up the already rich tradition of spying on the competition, engaging in the kind of over-the-top espionage found in a Tom Clancy novel with an undercover boat, *Guzzini,* that was dedicated to monitoring the competition's boat and training runs. (The Koch organization insists that *Guzzini* was merely decorated with the trappings of a spy boat in an elaborate gag.) All this — coupled with the fact that Koch, a Kansas native who had been sailing only eight years and certainly had no previous America's

Cup experience, chose to skipper *America³* himself — sealed his reputation as the Jethro Bodine of yacht racing. Jethro nonetheless beat Conner 7–4 in the Defender Selection Series and then creamed the Italians in the finals, 4–1.

Last March, in another stunt that flummoxed the yachting world, Koch bought three hours of satellite TV time to broadcast to the world, in a snazzy to-do at the Plaza in New York, that he would be turning over *America³*, *Kanza*, and several million in seed money to an all-women crew. The publicity photo showed a handful of outdoorsy beauties — some of whom, incidentally, were not chosen for the final team — arranged around a fatherly-looking Koch. Each wore cream-colored slacks, a navy blue blazer, a classy strand of real pearls. It was time, the party line went, for women to have an opportunity to prove themselves in this traditionally all-male sport.

This detonated an avalanche of speculation, mostly in the media, that still shows no signs of slowing. Why on earth would Koch do this? What were his motives? Was this a publicity gimmick? A whim? The end result of market research telling him that an all-women crew would have an easier time finding corporate sponsors than a recycled '92 crew? A cynical and egotistical impulse based on Koch's belief that the America's Cup is, as he has been quoted as saying, "a battle of management and organization first, then technology, and finally a boat race"? I won on my boat, the fastest boat in the world, Koch seemed to be saying; I bet I can put a bunch of girls on it and still win. Or is the Women's Team, from a more charitable view, simply a projection of Koch himself, a group of outsiders brought together by the ultimate outsider, a man who claimed the Cup against 100-to-1 odds? At press time, bookmakers hadn't yet placed odds on the women's chances, but some say they'll be even higher.

In any case, the girls don't seem to care. On a concrete level, Koch's motivation is irrelevant; the 1995 America's Cup competition really is a chance for the world's top female sailors to show what they can do with one of the world's best boats. Dawn Riley, who was courted by both Team Dennis Conner and PACT '95, is emphatic: "Being part of a crew that's all female is not a reason to sign on. No serious sailor would."

"Well," I say, "I have to ask. Why *is* Bill Koch doing this?"

She looks only moderately impatient. "There's a first for every-

thing. After this I imagine there will be co-ed teams, and I'd like
to see that. What people seem to lose sight of is that Bill mounted
this campaign with an all-female team because he thought he could
win. The point, always, is to win, and he thought an all-female crew
could do it off San Diego." (Indeed, as this issue of *Outside* went
to press, the Women's Team, sailing *America³* in the first race of
the 1994 International America's Cup Class World Championship,
beat both Conner and PACT '95, placing second after John Ber-
trand's *One Australia* off San Diego.)

It's an important point. The sea off San Diego is much different than it is off the western coast of Australia, where Conner re-
claimed the cup in 1987. San Diego has lighter air and more swell
than you might think. It's shifty. It requires reflexes, tactics. "We can
win in these conditions," says Riley, "and Bill knows it."

Breakfast is a carbo-rich meal of granola, French toast, and linguini
with clam sauce at Tarantino's, the Italian restaurant next door to
the *America³* compound. I sit across from Christy Evans, who tells
me how she has a life on hold back in Boston, a boyfriend she
hasn't seen in two and a half months, and a job selling office
furniture. I imagine it's the saleswoman in her that makes her so
voluble. "I was so jazzed to be picked!" she says. "There were other,
more experienced racers, girls with bigger races under their belts,
but they chose me. I was so honored."

Like all the women on the team, she's spent almost all of her
sailing life being the only girl on a boat full of guys. "Men are
more aggressive," she says. "They like to yell. I'd like to say they're
gruffer, but you look at some of our helmsmen, and they're pretty
gruff. There is this difference: a man'll criticize a woman in front of
the rest of the crew, whereas he won't criticize another guy. Once I
made a mistake and was pulled off the bow; if I'd been a guy, that
never would have happened."

After breakfast there's an all-crew meeting in the sail loft, the
second floor of a warehouse reached from an outside stairway. At
one end is a table surrounded by a snarl of folding chairs. A good
three-quarters of the space is occupied by sails spilling across the
floor. Mark Irwin is on his hands and knees, carefully mending a
ripped sail. "These girls tear as many sails as the guys do," he
observes. "I like to see that. It's a sign of aggressive sailing." He
grins up at me. "Also, sometimes, just plain old bad luck."

"O.K.," says head coach Kimo Worthington, starting the meeting. "Did everyone get my memo? If you haven't gotten one, get one. If you got one, read it. This is serious business."

Assistant coach Stu Argo, like Worthington a soft-spoken man, paces around the sail loft during the meeting, hands in his pockets. He's smaller than many of the girls, his eyes hidden beneath the brim of a baseball cap. Argo and Worthington are the interface between Koch's shadowy ambitions and the tangible particulars of the girls' grueling day-to-day training schedule. No one in the history of the Cup has had a job like theirs, and it's hard not to picture them as bewildered male teachers at a girls' school.

"The topic here is sexual harassment," says Worthington.

"Cool!" says Merrit Palm.

Worthington clears his throat. He's trying to be professional about this, but these women seemingly don't care about his discomfort any more than they care about the politically correct way observers tiptoe around almost all the issues they evoke. "It's about . . . if you're being asked to do something and you don't want to do . . ."

"Oh, great," says Diana Klybert. "This means my social life is screwed."

Everyone cracks up. Susie Leech Nairn, the aerospace engineer, pipes up, "Oh, no, don't say that in front of the journalist."

Sandra Bateman promptly pulls me over to a long table littered with *America³* posters, showing the boat and individual pictures of each team member. "Did you see these?" she asks. "All the girls need to sign them. Then they're auctioned at fundraisers. We have a lot of fundraisers. You should see these girls when they're all dressed up. They're beautiful girls, so *feminine*."

For the year or so that the Women's Team members will spend training and competing, they will get paid for this shore work — tending the boats, prepping them each day, and putting them to bed each night — but in order to retain their amateur status, they aren't compensated for their actual sailing. I ask Sandra Bateman what they are paid. "I can't tell you that," she answers, "but it is comparable to what the men get paid for the same work."

"Not sixty-nine cents for every dollar?"

"No, no, no. We're obviously very sensitive to that."

Every morning it takes nearly an hour and a half to prep *America³* and *Kanza* before setting out. While Crosby, Stills, and Nash bleats from a tinny sound system on *Chubasco,* the tender docked nearby, everyone falls to their assigned tasks, inspecting the winches, going over the hull. There are nine sails on each boat and eight sails stored on the tender, and they all have to be brought down from the storage racks, built by the women themselves, to the dock; it takes four women, two on either side of the load. Lisa Charles, one of the smaller girls, dons a harness and shimmies up the mast to inspect the rigging. The Two Stephanies, as they are called, a weight lifter and a rower, haul aboard ice chests filled with lunches.

On *America³* Sarah Cavanagh is "lifting the skirts," the security tarps that shield the keel from spies. A rawboned and quiet New Englander, she's been sailing since the age of 3 and has a degree in yacht design from the Landing School in Kennebunkport, Maine. She goes about her work with a calm efficiency that borders on the phlegmatic. "Guess you shouldn't be down here yet," she says to me. "We don't take the skirts off until the boat's in the water. There's nothing to see, really, but still . . ."

Behind me, I hear Sandra Bateman's voice: "Here! I got you some lunch!" She hands me an unripe banana and a mashed brownie.

"I'm just down here checking out the keel," I quip, but Sandra Bateman doesn't laugh. It's as if I've made a hijacking joke at the airport.

In recent years the America's Cup has become infused with a dizzy paranoia focused on keels, the clunky, hidden appendages that are the philosopher's stone of match cup sailing. The way the syndicates pursue the perfect keel design, you'd think there didn't need to be anyone on the boat at all: create the perfect keel and come collect the silver cup.

It started in 1983, when *Australia II* wrested the Cup from Dennis Conner's *Liberty* — and became the first foreign winner in the history of the race — with the aid of a bizarre winged keel that no one had paid much attention to until the boat started pulverizing the competition in early matches. The next time the Cup was held, in 1987, competitors began actively spying, flying over each other's boats in helicopters and hiring divers to poke around in the dead of night. This year, spying is supposed to be prohibited, but the skirts are there, and the red, white, and blue eagle insignia painted on each side of *America³* is situated so that the keel can't be seen in clear water because of the reflection.

At 10:30 *Chubasco* tows *America³* and *Kanza* out into open water. Simple, elegant vessels with pearl-white hulls, they lack engines, railings, heads. Nothing to keep you from falling overboard and nowhere to relieve yourself. The three girls who have gone overboard so far have been dubbed the *America³* Swim Team.

The tow-out takes an hour. *America³* will race with a crew of sixteen, but for training purposes each boat operates with twelve: five on the foredeck to hoist and handle the head sails, four grinders on middeck, and the helmsman, tactician, and navigator in the afterguard.

Dawn Riley sits on deck, a blue canvas book bag full of dog-eared papers cradled in her lap. "My floating office," she calls it. "Every Saturday I weed it out, and by the end of the week it looks like this." She's writing an article for *Glamour* on "barrier-breaking" events in her life.

"One of our girls wrote about living with dyslexia," offers Sandra Bateman.

"Barrier-breaking?" I say. "Isn't it kind of obvious?" Dawn Riley was pitman on *America³* during the 1992 Defender Selection Series. "You'd think," says Riley, and then tells me about a day when John Caponera, from Comedy Central, came sailing. They were doing spoof and staged a silly scene in which a bunch of the crew members were supposed to be pushing him overboard. "This is the kind of stuff we have to put up with," she says, and I blurt out that I don't imagine Comedy Central thinks there are any potential sight gags over at Team Dennis Conner.

Sandra Bateman interrupts. "Maybe now is a good time to talk to Annie." Annie Nelson is a PR person's dream. She is married, a mother of two young children, a sort of sporty Vanessa Redgrave. At 36, she's one of the older crew members and counts among her accomplishments windsurfing across Lake Titicaca. Her husband, Bruce Nelson, is a naval architect who works fourteen hours a day for Team Dennis Conner.

"It's fine," she says of crewing while managing the nonstop duties of motherhood. "Just harder than I thought." She tells me a story about losing her au pair of one week. "The other girls don't get it — what it is when a child's up all night with an earache." Not only don't the other girls get it, but her husband's teammates don't get it. Of course, they don't need to get it.

"But the kids?" I ask. "They're doing O.K.?"

The question makes her teary-eyed. "They're fine," she says. "Oh, look at me. I'm just tired."

We begin to sail. For an hour or so, *America³* and *Kanza* race against each other, running tests. What they're testing, I'm not allowed to know. Stu Argo murmurs commands in a tone so conversational that he could almost be talking to himself. He's the only man aboard, of course, and during downtime the girls tease him with private running jokes that I have no way of deciphering. He seems to enjoy being treated like the family pet.

Cavanagh, the navigator, sits at the stern, measuring the relative speed and distance of *Kanza* with a radar gun. Nelson, today's tactician, talks to *Kanza*'s crew via walkie-talkie. Her voice is soft, and she tells me that she and the other crew members are being coached on projecting their voices. They're casual about the secrecy until Nelson asks *Kanza* what they're using for a target and then quickly and firmly corrects herself: "Don't answer that." This is the course they'll be using for the Cup; anyone could be listening.

The tests go on. Six-minute tests, three-minute tests. I keep waiting for the tests to end and the real sailing to begin, for the sun to come out, the wind to pick up. The girls are so relaxed, it's almost like they're passengers. Then Argo or Nelson will announce that it's time to make a change, and everyone will slide into action. Every time we come about there's the loud, spook-house groan of the sheets sliding through the winches, the lightning-like crackle of the sails shifting. Then, nothing. We putter. I'm offered a windbreaker.

It's not unusual for America's Cup races to be run in 28-knot winds, 35-knot winds, winds that tear sails from the rigging, that force the boat to heel so that the entire crew has to hike outboard to keep from capsizing. Gales that humble and challenge the greatest sailors in the world. Today, the air is sultry and almost completely still; it's like no southern California day anyone can remember.

"We've got a very ugly chop here," says Nelson, sighing. "Is it . . . spitting?" *Chubasco* radios that, yes, rain is expected. The digital gauge measuring true wind speed shows four knots. It falls to 3.5. We stop for lunch.

The girls are not happy with their lunches. It's become a favorite thing to complain about. Today, the peanut butter and jelly sandwiches could serve as ballast, and every day there is some kind of sci-fi salad drenched in a vinegary dressing and enough fruit roll-ups to stock a nursery school for a year.

"Food for 2-year-olds!" crows Jane Oetking. Her New Zealander's twang makes everything she says more hilarious than it might be otherwise. She unrolls an apricot fruit roll-up and, biting out two eyes and a nose, lays it on her face. "A new facial treatment," she says. Someone takes a picture. "*Glamour* wants us to be glamorous," she says. I suggest that if *Glamour* wanted to do a true service to its readership, it would print the crew members' heights and weights. "That'll be the day," she laughs. The wind sinks to three knots. Incredibly, it begins to rain. "During the entire 1992 Cup season, it only rained five times," says Argo. "Can you believe this?"

They haul down the mainsail and fasten its blue cover in a way that makes a tent, and then everyone in the afterguard sits beneath it. An engineless boat on the open sea is quiet. We bob around and around. Every so often, we're caught in the trough of a wave and everyone goes, "Whoa-oh-ugh."

"Testing for seasickness," Nelson announces to *Kanza* on her walkie-talkie.

"We've never had a journalist on board who's gotten sick," says Riley. "This could be a first."

Oetking says, "Imagine some fatty, lukewarm sausage mixed with a wad of drain hair."

Argo says, "Or you know when you're really hung over and you go in the morning to take a swig out of the carton and the milk is sour?"

"There's always projectile baby vomit," reflects Nelson.

"Girls," says Sandra Bateman. She's lying on the stern with her eyes closed, one thin hand on her forehead. I can't tell whether she's feeling sick, too, or whether she's suddenly overwhelmed by the strain of being the house mom. I don't envy her job, making sure the world sees the Women's Team as spunky and adorable instead of human.

For if Koch's take on the America's Cup is true, it is excellence of organization and technology that wins races, and it takes piles of money to buy excellence of organization and technology, and the

way you get piles of money in the modern age of big boat racing is
to sign on corporate sponsors, and the way you get corporate sponsors is to put forth a team of nice girls who don't make jokes about
sexual harassment, who don't complain about their lunches, who
don't try to make a visiting journalist throw up. It's the old, old
story: They must be tough enough to compete, brutal enough to
win, without giving offense. They must wear their pearls.

I have never been seasick, but just to be safe, I took a Dramamine
when I got on the boat. It doesn't seem to be working. My jaws
tighten up, my tongue swims in saliva. I fish the card of pills out of
my pack and read that you're supposed to take the stuff an hour
before getting on board. Nelson leans over and whispers, "Stare at
the horizon. It'll help."

What helps is the announcement that at 2 P.M. the day is
scrapped. Even the stern Riley is embarrassed. "You've had such a
bad time!" she says. "You didn't see what we could do!"

Chubasco returns, throws us a line, and begins the long tow back
to the harbor. On *Kanza*, three girls sack out on big, pillowy sail
bags. Half of the crew on *America³* disappears below deck for a nap.
Riley returns to her *Glamour* article. Some of the girls play solitaire
on a laptop; others take pictures of one another. Pelicans glide
by, giving us the occasional imperious sideways glance. This is the
worst sailing day the Women's Team has had since training began
last June.

"This," sighs Riley, "is sailing."

After hours, the place to go is the Brigantine, a restaurant on
Shelter Island that flies the *America³* standard over the bar and
makes a killer house margarita with Cointreau, served in a cocktail
shaker. The women are local celebrities here; they get half off meals
and drinks. Racer chasers and autograph hounds can spot them by
their large $300 *America³* watches, their universal sun-bleached hair.

The Brig is crowded on a Friday night. We have put in our names
for a party first of six, then eight, now ten. Crew members and staff
keep showing up. Several of us take our Brigantine margaritas out
onto the deck. The girls are in high spirits. The running joke of the
day resurfaces — the main event of the next week will be "trying
out new lunches." At the sound of the words "trying out," as if on
cue, the head of a man drinking on the tier below us snaps around.

One of the women grabs my elbow and drags me inside as she whispers to another, "That's Paul. I think he's trying to sign on with Dennis."

It's no secret that all the good spying happens at bars. Beans are spilled, secrets inadvertently revealed. These girls like to eat and drink. They order beef, extra sour cream for their baked potatoes. They drink a lot and know a number of raunchy jokes. Around midnight they'll head off to a party with some Navy SEALs. (I'll politely decline their invitation.) They're *sailors*.

At dinner, someone brings up the sexual harassment issue, and a story is told on Stu Argo. A reporter once said to him, "Here you are, spending twelve hours a day, six days a week, with these twenty-four women. Surely you must have a favorite." Argo pondered this. A normally quiet man, he grew even quieter. "Rather than answer that," he said, "I'll draw you a picture of the keel."

RICK REILLY

The Ultimate Price

FROM SPORTS ILLUSTRATED

WHEN THEY came to tell Geri Stephenson that her marine was dead, she didn't have to ask which one.

She knew. She had known ever since General Norman Schwarzkopf got on television that morning and said, "The marines lost two light armored vehicles." One of the LAVs was blown up near Khafji, Saudi Arabia, where Geri's first son, Dion, was stationed. The news didn't give names, but it said the seven marines killed in the explosion were the first U.S. casualties of Operation Desert Storm.

She knew. Typical Dion. Had to be the first in everything.

Death had its choice of Stephensons that night. Dion's younger brother Shaun had followed him to Desert Storm. Typical Shaun. Anything Dion did, Shaun did right behind him. Anything Dion did, Shaun wanted to do better. And the only thing Shaun wanted more than to be *better* than Dion was to be *exactly like* Dion. That's the funny thing. Shaun, who was 19, had wanted to be in that LAV that night, wanted to fight the Iraqis alongside his 22-year-old brother, but the brass hadn't gone for it. Instead, Shaun was on a tank-landing ship two hundred miles from Khafji.

Geri knew. Schwarzkopf hadn't mentioned tank ships.

All that longest day she had stared through the window, expecting them, dreading them, hating them. She needed to be alone with her terror that night, so she and her husband, Jim, went to sleep in separate beds, she in their room, he in Dion's, the one with the walls almost entirely covered by swimming medals and soccer ribbons and prom king pictures.

When they finally came, at 2 A.M., she peeked through the venetian blinds and saw an Army chaplain and two Marine corpsmen waiting on the stoop. Two officers from the Bountiful, Utah, police department waited in a black-and-white on the steep street out front. Five people, as though the message they bore was so heavy that it took that many to carry it.

"May we come in, Mrs. Stephenson?" the chaplain asked.

She was sheet-white, wide-eyed, and numb.

"No," she said.

Dion was a marine right out of the birth canal, like *the* leatherneck himself: his father. Jim Stephenson was the gung-holiest marine ever to get inside a pair of camouflage utilities. "I think of myself as a warrior," he says, and he was. He went behind enemy lines in Vietnam. After his tour he joined the Army reserves and became a Green Beret. You want a hard-ass, squared-away bastard, get a marine-slash-Green Beret. Whatever his boys turned out to be, Jim knew one thing: he would have them ready to do their duty. "They don't have to be marines," Jim would tell friends. "But they have to do their duty." The only confusing part was whether their duty was to their country or their father.

When the boys were three, for instance, Jim began giving them "p.t.'s" — timed physical training tests. At six, the kids were eating C rations. When they were eight, Jim hung a knotted rope from the top branch of a thirty-foot tree in their back yard in West Covina, California, and timed the boys going from the bottom to the top. By the time they were 10, Jim was bicycling alongside them, hollering out encouragement, as they ran cross-country. By 16, the boys had been to Devil Pups, a two-week marine-style camp for kids, complete with all the discomforts of real boot camp: no TV, no music and no visits from parents. "Tell you what," says the Warrior. "They come back from that, and they're answering, 'Sir, yes, sir!'" It is never too soon to be a soldier.

Jim's adoptive father, Edward, was a decorated Navy gunner in World War II whose fixed machine gun was set ablaze by Japanese fire. Without calling for help, he single-handedly put out the flames and resumed firing. Jim's adoptive mother, Alice, was a Wave. When Jim was 14, his father, brother, and sister died in an airplane crash. Jim stood sentry beside the coffins for eight hours, tearless.

And yet when Geri bore their first son, Jim could not get over the fact that he finally had somebody connected to him by flesh, and he wept like a schoolgirl. "This is *me*," he said. "My child. This is my blood." After Shaun's arrival, Geri would gently complain sometimes that she and Jim never had a night alone, that maybe the boys didn't need to come with them to the movies again, but Jim couldn't leave them. "See, I never had the kind of guidance you need to really excel," Jim would explain. So he would take the boys even to the weight room, where he often lifted with an Austrian bodybuilder named Arnold Schwarzenegger. And at each task, each challenge, each morning, Jim told his boys the same thing: "Let's go kick some butt!"

By high school these two boys were like a Doublemint gum ad come to life. There was nothing they couldn't do, nobody's heart they couldn't win, no honor they couldn't earn. One time Shaun arrived at a date's house, and the girl's mother saw those *An Officer and a Gentleman* looks that could stop a secretarial pool — those chocolate eyes, that perfectly square chin, and that letter jacket festooned with pins and medals — and asked him, "Are you for real?"

In 1983 Jim got a job as a Delta Airlines mechanic, and the family moved to Bountiful, where in high school Dion made the state tournament in swimming three years. Shaun came along two years later and made state in swimming three years, beating many of Dion's records. Dion was a star left wing in soccer. Shaun starred at wide receiver in football. Dion was voted Best Kisser and captain of the drama club. Shaun was Wally Cleaver polite and the starting shortstop besides.

"Shaun worshiped the ground Dion walked on," says their closest friend, David Hearn. "Maybe that was why Shaun was always trying to outdo him, just to make it even." The truth was, Shaun ached to do something completely different. Dion was going to be a marine, but Shaun wanted only to play football and to fly. His jones for flying began when he was 12 and he saw the Blue Angels perform. His addiction to football came the same year from watching the game on Saturdays with the Warrior. Shaun's two dreams fused magically the day he saw the Army-Navy game on television. The United States Naval Academy: here was the most wonderful place in the world, a place where you could be a soldier, play football, and prepare to fly all at once. Making it to the Naval Academy became Shaun's one true aim.

"Go after it," Dion would tell him. "You are capable of more than me. You've got more upstairs." If Shaun made it, he would be the first in the family to go to college.

"An officer in the family," the Warrior said. "Wouldn't that be something?"

But Shaun failed. He turned down football scholarships from Weber State and Southern Utah State, but he kept barely missing the minimum test score to get into the Academy. He took the ACT three times, the SAT four. By then Dion had graduated number one in his boot camp, graduated number one from infantry school, jumped from airplanes at 30,000 feet and scuba dived at 100 feet, and he had made Force Reconnaissance, the marine equivalent of the Navy SEALs or the Army Special Forces: the marines who were trained to go behind enemy lines, to gather information, to draw enemy fire just to learn enemy positions. Basically, the hell-raisingest marines there are.

"Dad, I want to do what D's doing," Shaun finally said, and it did not take long for the Warrior to get over losing a naval officer and relish gaining another marine. "Well, bud," he said, "let's go kick some butt."

So Shaun went charging after Dion, graduating number one from the same boot camp, number one from the same infantry school, soaring through the same jump school, earning his scuba bubble and making Force Reconnaissance, only more quickly than Dion had. Shaun even broke all the obstacle-course and physical-training records Dion had set at Camp Pendleton. You grow up a Stephenson, boot camp is basically Gymboree. And yet Shaun wouldn't throw out that old dream. "I wanted to start right off being number one in everything," he says. "I had to be if I wanted to get into the Naval Academy."

His hope was that he and his brother could fight side by side, but Dion went off to the Persian Gulf in August 1990 — raised his hand to be on the first plane headed there. Before he left, he and Shaun smoked a cigar behind the barracks at Camp Pendleton. Six months later Shaun was right behind him.

What's stupid is that Dion didn't have to die. He was assigned to security duty at a Saudi camp where soldiers rested up from their long desert patrols. But the sonofabitch only wanted to be on the front line. He kept insisting that he be sent back with his guys, the seven others on the LAV, to fight "So-damn Insane," as he referred to the Iraqi president in his letters home. *What are we waiting for?* he would write. *Let's go get him!*

And so they let Dion go back. He spent uncountable hours with his mates, patrolling the vast nothingness of the desert in the LAV, which Dion had dubbed and painted *The Blaze of Glory*, after a Bon Jovi song from the movie *Young Guns*. The guys would be out there for mind-numbing weeks at a time, seeing nobody else, showering once a week out of five-gallon water bottles and staging dung-beetle races to battle the monotony.

Sometimes the sun and the sand and the isolation began to drive them stark raving bonkers. At one point the vehicle commander screamed, "What does it matter! We're all going to die out here anyway!" It was at times like those that Dion would take over. He would suddenly announce, "Time to scorch a binger!" Everybody would sit in a circle in the sand in the middle of the night, bite the filter off his cigarette and smoke it as fast as he could. They would all get dizzy and then laugh and then fight and cry and laugh some more. It was a trick Dion had learned from his father. When Dion and Shaun were little, Jim would resolve fights by making the boys put on boxing gloves and fight until they were bloody and exhausted and sobbing, and then Jim would make them hug and say they loved each other. Bonding, gung ho–style. "Dion was the one who held that whole vehicle together," says Ron Tull, the LAV's driver.

Maybe Dion felt something coming, because one night he wrote each member of his family a letter. To his mother, he wrote, *God has to bring me home to you. . . . I love you so much.* A few nights later, on January 29, the guys dug in the LAV at a barren outpost known as Umm Juhal. While Dion slept, Tull got word that recon had found a column of more than one hundred Iraqi tanks heading their way.

"D! They're coming, man! We gotta get up! We gotta go!"

Dion awoke with a grin and said, "This is it, Tully. Time to kick some butt!"

But the Nintendo war that is waged today does not care all that much for soldiers and glory and kicking butt, not with thermal-imaging ground missiles that can kill tanks at 4,500 meters. *The Blaze of Glory* never engaged in combat. The boys never got closer to the

Iraqis than 1,000 meters. They just sat and watched as the pilots lit up the distant sky.

But then, suddenly, horribly, it was they who were lit up. A U.S. A-10 Warthog dropped a phosphorus flare next to the LAV that made it as visible in the night as a drive-in movie. "Those freakin' A-10s skylined us!" somebody screamed. Two guys in a missile carrier next to the LAV jumped out and tried to bury the flare, but it was like trying to bury an airport searchlight. In the LAV there was a sickening hush. Surely the Warthog pilot knew he'd made a mistake. Surely the boys had not just been marked as enemy by their own air force.

Seconds later another Warthog fired a U.S.-made Maverick missile — the tank killer, the missile designed to break the skin of a vehicle and then wreak hell inside, exploding like a grenade and releasing a hurricane of shrapnel, a thousand knives flung in all directions. Dion was sitting in the back of the LAV when the Maverick came flying through the back hatch. It hit and fragmented, churning, burning, severing limbs and heads and releasing a force so powerful that it blew off the closed and locked driver's hatch and sent Tull flying after it. Days later a military spokesman would have an explanation: "Friendly fire."

When Tull awoke, the LAV's tires were still on fire, and what was left of the 15-ton vehicle was still crackling and snapping. Tully couldn't feel his broken back or the second- and third-degree burns on his body or the sand under his hands. All he wanted to do was crawl back to the LAV. But every time he'd move, he'd pass out. Not that it mattered. The seven young guns inside *The Blaze of Glory* were dead.

God didn't bring Dion home, but Shaun did. Shaun spent February 4, 1991, the day before his twentieth birthday, flying his brother's remains home on the last leg of the trip from Saudi Arabia. He boarded a Delta jet, one his father had often worked on, in Dover, Delaware. Shaun's hands were still bruised from beating holy hell out of the C.O.'s locker onboard the USS *Frederick*. That was just after the C.O. had said, "Shaun, I've got some real bad news for you. Your brother was killed tonight." Shaun just threw tearless punches until his hands bled. This time, though, there would be no hugs afterward.

They pulled into the very ramp their father worked on at Salt

Lake City International Airport. The Warrior did not come to greet them. "I could've never worked on that ramp again," Jim says. "Every time I stepped out there, I would've thought about D."

Shaun was driven up his own street, which was lined with scores of people holding candles and singing *God Bless America*. He walked up the stairs into his parents' room, where his mother refused to hug him. If you do not let army chaplains into your house, they can't tell you your son is gone. And if you do not hug your grief-stricken other son, the grief can't exist. Shaun turned and bear-hugged the Warrior.

A week later the whole state threw Dion the biggest, slowest parade Salt Lake City had ever seen. Folks say that back at the Cathedral of the Madeleine, where the biggest bunch of flowers was from Schwarzenegger, cars were still pulling out of the parking lot and into the procession when the hearse arrived at the Bountiful Cemetery, fifteen minutes up the freeway. The governor cried that day, and flags across the state could only make it halfway up their poles, and elementary school crossing guards saluted as the funeral procession passed.

Even General Alfred Gray, the commander of the U.S. Marine Corps, was there. He had flown back from the Persian Gulf to see one of his men buried. Afterward Shaun told him, "I want to go back. I want to go back and avenge my brother's death."

Geri just lowered her head. Gray said, "I'll see what I can do."

But the military usually doesn't send a man to a theater of war where a family member has been killed, so Shaun was assigned to recruit marines out of the office in Salt Lake City. "Kind of hard, you know?" Shaun says. "Trying to get a kid to sign up for a war where your brother just got killed."

Looked like flying and football were also gone. If Shaun could not go back and fight and make them notice him, how would he ever play football for Navy? But then the phone rang.

President Bush was calling to say how sorry he was that Dion had died in friendly fire, and how proud he was of Dion and what he'd done for the country. "He was the best," Bush said in a trembling voice. "A good marine."

The Warrior had one thing to say. There was already talk about this friendly fire business. The parents of the victims were beginning a lawsuit against the maker of the Maverick, and the Warrior would have none of it. "Sir, you did the right thing by getting into this," he told Bush.

Through that week the Warrior told the papers, "Friendly fire is a part of combat," and, "If that pilot came to our door right now, we'd invite him in. . . . My son's gone, but this pilot has to get up every day and say, 'My missile killed these men.' That's a heckuva thing to have to live with." And when the mini-cams were gone and the lights were finally off and his family asleep, the Warrior would bury his face in his pillow and cry.

A few days later General Gray called and asked Shaun what his plans were. Shaun gulped a little and said, "Well, I've always wanted to attend the Naval Academy."

Gray said he would look into that, too.

Within two weeks there came a letter from the U.S. Naval Academy announcing that Shaun Stephenson had won an appointment by order of Senator Orrin Hatch (R., Utah), Representative Jim Hansen (R., Utah), and the president of the United States.

It's all you can do to keep from throwing a punch when you are a 22-year-old Force Recon marine with five citations for meritorious service and one lost brother, and some 19-year-old midshipman in a bad haircut screams at you about discipline.

It was all Shaun could do to keep from laughing when those officious upper-class detailers came bursting in for that first inspection, ready to start barking and pencil-ticking and pulling down shirts that weren't hung right (top button buttoned, facing the same direction, colors together), and they found . . . nothing. The room was flawless, every shoe was a mirror, every corner perfect. You grow up a Stephenson, plebe year is basically Moose Lodge initiation night.

Inspections weren't Shaun's problem at the Naval Academy. Grades were the problem. He needed a year at the Naval Academy Prep School just to make it to plebe year. Didn't matter if the president or the pope got you your appointment; if you didn't have the grades, you were gone. "People think my road was all laid down by the president," Shaun says. "If I get my diploma — when I get it — I'll have had to work twice as hard as everybody else."

He came close to flunking out that year. He had been King Jock at Bountiful, and he had never had to worry about the books: a lot of his high school teachers were his coaches. "I had never taken calculus, chemistry, physics, computer science," Shaun says of his year at the prep school. "I'd never even used a computer before." Like his grandfather, like his father, he was not good at asking for help. Hadn't had to.

And that's when he found someone who could get him through: an old friend — Dion. "I started to think about how he would handle things," Shaun remembers. "Dion could talk to anyone. And every time I started feeling sorry for myself, I thought of what he went through, and everything I was worried about just seemed so petty." Besides, in a macabre way, it was Dion who had gotten Shaun inside the Navy yard. "He paid the ultimate price," says Shaun. "I wasn't going to let him down."

He let the air out of his pride. He got tutors. He would help some 4.0 nerd with weapons class in exchange for help in trig. The grades started rising. Unfortunately, it was the football that went nowhere.

His plebe year Shaun walked on but never suited up. Every day he would look at the depth chart for wide receivers, and every day he would see no change. At the bottom, dead last, it read *Stephenson*. He would practice all week. He was no bigger than your local grocery sacker, and in practice 230-pound linebackers would turn him into a smudge mark. Then the game would come, and Shaun would be sitting up in the stands with his friends, aching on the inside. "He was a great guy," says George Chaump, then the Navy coach. "But he hadn't played in a long time, and he was small, and his feet weren't the quickest."

Shaun's sophomore year Chaump asked him to leave the program. "I liked him," says Chaump, "but we only had 140 lockers. We had to keep the size of the sqad down." When you have a hard time cracking that top 140, things do not look good.

And yet Shaun wouldn't let the dream shrivel and blow away. He went out for lightweight football, a brand peculiar to the East Coast, which is like varsity football in all ways except that no player can exceed 159 pounds. "I think Shaun made that with room to spare," says his lightweight coach, Bill Beckett.

At lightweight Shaun was a vision. Navy shared the league title his sophomore year and finished second his junior year. Shaun made all-league. His teammates learned his story. The one everybody called Recon caught passes and returned punts and was the inspiration of a team that drew 3,000 midshipmen to the Army game. And still Chaump had no interest.

Friends would go up to him and say, "This kid can really play. You ought to give him a chance." But the coach never did. Shaun was Rudy in a different blue and gold. With only a year left, he was two rungs below hopeless.

But then Chaump was fired after his third straight loss to Army. Charlie Weatherbie, a former Air Force assistant, came in. And then this hit Shaun's E-mail: anybody who wanted to try out for the football team during spring drills was welcome. *Anybody.*

What Shaun had before him was a heaven-sent, platinum-plated break. He worked out madly with his friends on the varsity, worked on his speed, worked on his jumping. Unfortunately, the offense that Weatherbie planned to run was the spread, which would reduce the number of wide receivers on the field from three to two and have twice as many running plays as passing plays. Still, Shaun swam on against the current.

On the first day of spring practice, he looked at the depth chart and saw that his name was still right there near the bottom. Then, just to take the odds clear off the tote board, he broke his thumb. Fine. Put it in a cast. He was not missing this.

Then an odd thing happened. Every night Weatherbie and his staff would sit down, exhausted, and look at film of 150 kids practicing, and every night they would find themselves saying the same thing: "Wait. Run that back. Who's the kid making the great block?" And, "Was that 18 again?" And, "You know, this kid, Stephenson? He's getting the job done."

In the spring game Shaun caught three passes for 54 yards — making one reception as he dived into the end zone for a touchdown (with a cast on the broken thumb, no less) — and madly blocked anybody he could find, including the chain holders. Finally, when Shaun was given the Vice Admiral William P. Mack Award as the most improved player in spring practice, there was nothing Weatherbie could do. The new depth charts were posted the next day. At the top of the list of receivers, above the recruited players and the ones who stood a helmet taller than Shaun, above the 4.5 sprinters, was the little walk-on from Bountiful who was somehow missing the quit gene.

He called home and told his mother, "You're going to be going to a lot of football games next year, Mom."

And still, the happy ending wouldn't come. At the last scrimmage this fall, before Navy's opener at SMU on September 9, when more than twenty of Shaun's friends would fly to Dallas to be part of this joy that grew from so much grief, Shaun tore a ligament in his left knee. He might be out for three weeks, six weeks, the year — nobody was sure. As he stood on crutches the night of the scrimmage, he was completely out of stiff upper lips. All the marine drained out of him. Player after player came up, all of them towering over him, gently rubbing his head and leaning over to whisper in his ear, and yet he could not be strong. He had come so far.

"I'm sorry," he said through tears. "You just don't know how much this team means to me."

The Warrior is even prouder of his son in death than in life. "Because of what he stood for," Jim says. "Dion was willing to stand up for people in a country he knew nothing about." But honor and duty and glory are best left to marines and fathers and warriors. For mothers, war is just another way to get your son sent home under a colorful cloak. Jim wears his son's death with pride, but Geri wears Dion's Mickey Mouse watch instead. There are days she misses him so much that the hands seem to stop completely.

Michael, the Stephensons' third son, is 14 and the triplicate. He is handsome, a soccer star, and unfailingly polite. He has already signed up for Devil Pups. Pictures of Dion and Shaun in their dress blues hang over his bed. The other day Michael said, "Dad, I might want to do what Shaun's doing."

Geri tries not to hang her head. "I worry," she says. "But I'll just let him do what he wants and say my prayers every night."

She may need to double them. Shaun spent last summer aboard an aircraft carrier, the USS *Carl Vinson,* his first step toward becoming a fighter pilot. The rule is that brothers cannot die in the same theater of war, but Bosnia is a long way from Khafji. Geri thinks about it. Shaun followed Dion everywhere else; will he follow him someday in another long, slow parade?

That is a worry for some other day. Right now Geri has this wonderfully happy middle to believe in. Turns out the doctors had no idea how fiercely Shaun would rehab the knee. Instead of six weeks, he should be back in four. He should start his first college football game, against Duke, this Saturday, and Geri and Jim will be there to witness it, just as they will be in Philadelphia on December 2, when Shaun will be part of that magical Army-Navy game that started it all for him. And so, three exits past the place where dreams usually give out, it will finally be real. After four and a half years of sorrow and disappointment and setbacks, the fighter-pilot-to-be will be wearing Navy blue and gold, ready to kick some serious butt. And that leaves only one question.

Hey, Recon, are you for real?

TOM VERDUCCI

The High Price of
Hard Living

FROM SPORTS ILLUSTRATED

THE HOOD OF the silver-blue Mercedes resting in the circular driveway of the new $1.2 million house in Rancho Mirage, California, is
still warm. On this Wednesday afternoon in mid-January, Darryl
Strawberry has just returned from providing a urine sample at a
local hospital as part of his drug-testing agreement with Major
League Baseball.

"There's a lot of sobriety out here," Strawberry says of the
Coachella Valley as he offers up bottled water and stretches out on
a leather sofa. The valley also has perfect desert weather, streets
named after movie stars, and more than 80 golf courses, 600 tennis
courts, and 10,000 swimming pools, one of which is just over Strawberry's left shoulder on the other side of the patio doors.

Strawberry chose this resort community as his home last May
after seeking treatment for cocaine abuse. "And I don't even play
golf," he says. He is living in self-imposed exile, talking about his
former home cities, New York and Los Angeles, as his versions of
Sodom and Gomorrah.

"It became a lifestyle for me," Strawberry says. "Drink, do coke,
get women, do something freaky . . . all that stuff. I did it for so
long. I played games when I was drunk, or just getting off a drunk
or all-night partying or coming down off amphetamines.

"With alcohol and drugs it was the excitement. That's how I got
addicted. It was an exciting way to escape from everything else.

Coming to the major leagues at such a young age and coming to
New York . . . maybe someplace else it would be a little different, but
New York is a party place, an upbeat place.

"Man, I put up some good numbers. But I look back and wish
I could've done it like I'm doing it now: clean. I just got tired of
[the lifestyle] after eight, nine, ten years. They would have never
caught me because I'd done it [drugs] for so long. I grew up in a
fast place, L.A."

Strawberry had provided a urine sample the previous day as well.
The day before that, on Monday, Strawberry had spoken at a Martin Luther King Day rally at the El Cerrito Community Center, a few
miles north of Oakland. He had talked about the importance of
keeping children off drugs and alcohol, referring to them several
times as "the young youth today."

"I've been through drugs and alcohol myself," he had said into
the microphone. "I overcame that through the grace of God."

The cocaine he had scored less than forty-eight hours earlier, on
Saturday night, lingered in his system as he spoke at the rally. More
fatefully, it was in the urine samples he provided on Tuesday and
Wednesday. He didn't realize, as he sprawled across his couch,
telling a reporter he was clean, that he'd been caught.

It begins with one beer, the way an inferno starts with a spark or the
way a massive freeway pileup begins with one car. Dwight Gooden's
pattern of self-destruction continues when he orders another beer
and then another. On this night, in June 1994, the lights and the
music and mostly the alcohol at the Manhattan nightclub are sooth-
ing him.

He has been a hard drinker since 1986, when he was 21 and in
his third year in the majors — abstaining from alcohol only on the
two nights before a starting assignment and, flushed with youth,
money and stardom, indulging on all the others. At 22 he landed in
a drug rehab center after testing positive for cocaine. Now, nearing
his thirtieth birthday and into his third straight losing season, he is
drinking out of self-pity. The alcohol hits him like Novocain; it
numbs the pain of his depression but cannot remove it.

The beers are not enough, so, as he often has, he switches to
something harder. Vodka has always been a favorite. It makes him
forget about his combined 22–28 record in 1992 and '93, about

how terrible his team, the New York Mets, has become and about
the injured toe on his right foot, which has kept him on the disabled list for the past five weeks. The drinks keep coming.

Man, I'm hammered, he thinks. He presses on deep into the
night, so deep that he still is drinking when he notices the place is
closed, the doors are locked and everybody else except the people
who work in the club have gone home. That's when one of the
employees pulls out the bag of cocaine. *You want some?*

I know I shouldn't, he thinks. But that notion passes quicker than
one of his old fastballs, dissolving completely into the fuzziness of
his alcohol-polluted mind. What the hell, he thinks. I'm on minor
league rehab for my toe. They won't test me.

Within forty-eight hours a representative of the testing agency
used by Major League Baseball arrives in Binghamton, New York,
home of the Mets' Double A affiliate, to collect a urine sample from
Gooden.

The career paths of Darryl Strawberry and Dwight Gooden began
as parallel lines — twin, unbending inclines headed straight to
Cooperstown. How could it be that instead we are left with this ugly
tangle of trouble? They both were National League Rookies of the
Year, the 21-year-old Strawberry in 1983 and Gooden, at 19, the following season. When Gooden started his first major league game,
in '84, Strawberry ripped a home run to center field for the game-
winning RBI. Before either one of them had turned 25, they were
stars, millionaires and, in '86, world champions as members of one
of only four National League teams in this century to win as many
as 108 regular-season games. How did those parallel lines wind up
as twisted as those on a New York City subway map, the two of them
intersecting over and over again?

Intersections: In the off-season following the Mets' World Series
victory, Gooden was arrested for brawling with Tampa police and
Strawberry was ordered by a Los Angeles superior court to stay away
from his wife, Lisa, whose nose he had broken with a punch to the
face. So when Strawberry reported to spring training in 1987 and
discovered he had been assigned a locker next to Gooden's, he
cracked in his typical dark humor, "Look, it's Assault and Battery
together."

Six weeks later Gooden spent Opening Day in Smithers Alcohol-

ism and Treatment Center in New York City, being treated for
cocaine use, while Strawberry, wearing Gooden's uniform pants,
drove in the winning runs with a three-run home run. Three years
after Gooden checked into Smithers seeking treatment for drug
abuse, Strawberry checked into Smithers for alcohol abuse. Both of
them now admit they sought treatment half-heartedly. Little wonder then that last year Strawberry and Gooden both had occasion
to check into the Betty Ford Center in Rancho Mirage for cocaine
abuse. One going and the other coming, they missed each other by
only 79 days.

Last August 14, Strawberry picked up Gooden upon his release
from the Betty Ford Center and drove him the one mile down
Bob Hope Drive to Strawberry's new home. He escorted Gooden
through the grand marbled foyer and into the living room.

"Doc, you've got to get out of Florida," Strawberry said. "You've
got to change your environment to keep from using. The most
important thing they told me at Betty Ford was to change the whole
atmosphere and get away from the people who use."

Gooden has maintained his home in St. Petersburg since moving
there in 1987 from his birthplace, Tampa. Within a week after
leaving the Betty Ford Center last summer — and three days after
attending a counseling session in New York with Robert Millman, a
psychiatrist who represents Major League Baseball, and Joel Solomon, a psychiatrist who represents the players' union — Gooden
was drinking and using cocaine again with friends in Tampa. And
five months after that, Strawberry tested positive for cocaine.

"It just goes to show you," Gooden says now, "it doesn't matter
where you are. Drugs, alcohol . . . it's everywhere. What's more
important is that you can never let your guard down."

Another intersection: Today neither Strawberry nor Gooden has
a team to call his own. They are suspended from baseball. They are
the eighty-sixed Mets.

And yet they are so different. Strawberry is a complex puzzle.
None of the Mets was better around children when making charitable appearances. Even now he is pouring a healthy portion of
what's left of his money — he's estimated to have earned about $25
million as a baseball player — into the Strawberry Patch Youth
Project, a San Francisco Bay Area drug and alcohol prevention
program that he founded with Ron Jones, one of his closest friends

and a former drug dealer. Strawberry is, even as he approaches his
thirty-third birthday, as naively eager for love and acceptance as a
puppy in a pet-shop window. He has a natural capacity to charm
people. He can turn any room into a happy place merely by strolling
in with that cool, smooth, long-legged glide, and he can energize
any ballpark, hit or miss, with that beautiful, looping swing.

Sadly, he can just as easily transform himself into something
rotten. His transgressions contradict — even obliterate, for many
people — that core of goodness. Alcoholic, drug abuser, batterer,
and now convicted tax cheat. His career has been a long screech of
tires during which all you could do was wait for the crash. The
chronic tardiness, the enormous mood swings, the erratic behavior
offered a cacophonous prelude to disaster for all to hear. "A walking
stick of TNT," says Strawberry's former Met teammate Ron
Darling, who's now a pitcher for the Oakland A's.

Contrasted against Strawberry's dark streak was the apparent
benevolent light of Gooden: accommodating, consistent, industrious,
quiet. Indeed, after 1985 the tight friendship between the two
ballplayers loosened to a comfortable acquaintance. They were not
as close as the public thought. Or, as Strawberry says, "I never partied
with Doc."

"The few times Dwight was late for anything," Darling says, "everyone
would ask, 'Is the cab stuck in traffic? Was he in an accident?'
When Darryl was late, you thought right away, Darryl screwed up
again. Doc was Teflon and could do no wrong. Darryl was a ticking
time bomb."

The way Strawberry remembers it, his first experience with cocaine
occurred in 1983, soon after he was promoted to the major
leagues. He liked to drink beer and he had smoked pot sometimes,
but now two of his veteran teammates were asking him to try something
new. "There's a couple of lines in the bathroom for you, kid,"
he remembers them saying. "This is the big leagues. This is what
you do in the big leagues. Go ahead. It's good for you."

Strawberry tried the cocaine. Damn, he thought, that's good.

So began a career whose trademark has been its volatility. He
did not create a new controversy every day; it only seemed that way.
In a seven-day span in June 1987, Strawberry overslept twice, each
time needing a teammate to roust him from his hotel bed with a

phone call from the ballpark; was fined $250 and benched for two games for those latenesses; charged the mound after almost being hit by a pitch; and blasted a 450-foot home run. So often did he drop bombs that when asked about his weird week, he replied in all earnestness, "Weird? Why? Just because I was late twice, got benched, was fined and had a fight? It's part of the game."

Still, what happened within a four-day span earlier this month was shocking even by his standards. Between February 6 and 9 Strawberry received a 60-day suspension from baseball because of the positive drug tests, was released by the San Francisco Giants, and pleaded guilty to the charge of failing to report and pay tax on more than $350,000 earned from appearing at card shows from 1986 to '90. Sentencing is scheduled for March 15. As part of the plea arrangement Strawberry is expected to be sent to prison for three months and held under house arrest for another three months.

Last week, according to Jones, Strawberry entered his third rehabilitation center in the past five years.

"Every time I think he's coming out of it, something else happens," said Richie Bry, Strawberry's agent from 1980 to '88, even before learning about this month's positive drug tests. "You don't know what to believe from him anymore. I think Darryl is basically a good person but very immature and subject to being influenced heavily by other people, some good and some not. He's easily misled and easily succumbs."

The recent bout with cocaine cost Strawberry what appeared to be a perfect fit for him. During his twenty-nine games with the Giants, who signed him after his release from the Los Angeles Dodgers last May, Strawberry enjoyed the benefits of playing for an understanding manager, Dusty Baker; having Barry Bonds and Matt Williams in the lineup, which allowed him to play a supporting role for the first time in his career; and having his older brother, Michael, on the team payroll as his personal chaperon. Strawberry lost all of that on January 14, when he hooked up with some friends for a Saturday night out in San Diego.

"He had all of that riding and still went back to cocaine," says Jones, who says he is reformed after going to prison twice, once on a drug charge and once on a weapons charge. "That's how powerful that —— is. Darryl told me [he used again because] he felt a lot of pressure was on him, like going to jail and his ex-wife bothering him. Darryl has never been one to be honest with himself."

Until the recent relapse Strawberry said he had been clean since last April 2. That night began with a private lecture in the office of Dodger manager Tommy Lasorda, before an exhibition game in Anaheim against the California Angels. "Get yourself going," Lasorda barked. "We need you to carry us."

How many times have I heard that? Strawberry thought. Only my whole career. Why is it always on me? I'm tired of it. I don't want to hear it anymore.

He hit a home run in his last at-bat that night and then disappeared into his own black hole of despair, drinking and drugs. He got so high he never went home. His new wife, Charisse, called his mother, Ruby, late the next morning, which was a Sunday. Darryl had weekend custody of his two children from his first marriage, Darryl Jr. and Diamond, but after staying at his house they were to return that day to his ex-wife, Lisa. Did Ruby know where Darryl was? Ruby was rushing off to church, so she let her daughter Regina talk to Charisse and left without being clear as to what the call was about.

When Ruby arrived at the Blood Covenant Christian Faith Center in Pomona, California, where she also works as a secretary, the parishioners comforted her. They had heard news reports that Darryl was missing. "It's going to be O.K.," they said. Ruby had no idea what they were talking about.

Strawberry remembered that the Dodgers had an exhibition game in Anaheim that afternoon — the last before the regular season began on April 5 — but he could not muster the energy to go. I'm tired, he thought, too tired. I am not going through another season like this. The partying, the drinking. . . . I'm just so tired.

Late in the day he phoned his lawyer, Robert Shapiro, and agreed to meet with him the next morning. Shapiro, who two months later would be on national TV representing a fugitive named O.J. Simpson, brought Darryl into his office while Ruby, Charisse, and Michael waited outside. Shapiro told Strawberry it was time he admitted he was an alcoholic and a drug user. For years Strawberry had been afraid to make that admission because he was worried, for one thing, about how it would be received by his family, his team, and the media.

Shapiro told him he would take care of everything, including how it played out in the press. When the door opened, Shapiro gestured toward the family and asked Strawberry, "Is it O.K. to share it with them?" Strawberry nodded and told them.

"Tears welled up in my eyes, and I had a big lump in my throat," Ruby says. "It made me realize some of the things that were going on. I couldn't understand some of the things that were happening with him. He didn't care what was going on with the family. He was not in touch with us.

"Now that I look back I can understand a lot of his behavior. I used to wonder why he never made eye contact with me when he talked. I kind of brushed it off. You know, he was always on the go, never had much time. He was always kind of looking over my head, looking for someplace else to go or something.

"I remember one of the first things he did after he left the Betty Ford Center. We were sitting in my home, on opposite sides of the room. I told him, 'You know, that's something you never used to do.' And he said, 'What's that? What are you talking about?' And I said, 'You can look me in the eyes when you're talking to me. You never used to do that.'

"From what I understand now, a lot of things were going on before he came back to L.A. That was something we weren't aware of."

Marking the beginning of a life gone wrong is an inexact science. When did the downward spiral begin for Darryl? With that night after his rookie season when he met Lisa Andrews at a Los Angeles Laker game at the Forum? With that first powerful hit of coke? With his sophomore year at Crenshaw High in South Central Los Angeles, when he was disciplined by his baseball coach for having a bad attitude and quit the team? Or with those childhood nights when he remembers his father, Henry, would come home loud and angry after drinking and gambling? Darryl, the middle of five children, remembers being hit by his father "for little things" before Henry left Ruby in 1974, when Darryl was 12.

"It starts with abuse: verbal and physical abuse," Darryl says. "It leaves scars you carry to adulthood." Ruby doesn't remember Henry's striking Darryl so much, saying, "I'm not that kind of mother. I would not have allowed it with my kids." But she does concede it's important if "that's the way he remembers it." Teammates and friends always have noticed how Darryl has sought love, often desperately.

"Yes," Ruby says, "because Darryl didn't have the father he wanted, or one who acted the way he thought a father was supposed to. It caused him to act out in different ways. Some children need that father figure, especially boys. Darryl needed it, but he didn't have it and looked for it in other places."

The Mets selected Strawberry with the first overall pick of the 1980 draft, their decision clinched when Strawberry, then fresh out of Crenshaw High, posted an impressive score on a test that measures aggressiveness, mental toughness, and self-confidence. After giving Strawberry a $200,000 signing bonus, New York had scout Roger Jongewaard accompany him to its Kingsport, Tennessee, rookie league team. "I went with him as a buffer because of all the attention he was getting," Jongewaard says. "Darryl did such a great job handling it, he really didn't need me."

Less than three years later, in 1983, Strawberry was in the big leagues. He had 26 home runs that season, beginning an unprecedented run of hitting more than 25 home runs in his first nine seasons, all but one of them with the Mets. Only two other players in history had hit that many homers in more than their first *four* seasons: Frank Robinson (7) and Joe DiMaggio (6). During that span Strawberry never hit 40 home runs in a season, and he averaged 92 RBIs — a relatively low total for someone with his power. He also missed an average of 21 games a season in those years. And he played just 75 games over the 1992 and '93 seasons because of a herniated disk that required surgery.

"He should have averaged 100 RBIs and 40 home runs," Jongewaard says. "He has underachieved. And that's a hard thing to say because he put up some very good numbers, but that's how much talent he had."

Those sort of expectations alternately inflated Strawberry with pride and wore him down. In typical Straw-speak, one day he would promise "a monster season" and the next he would complain about having to carry too big a load. His quotes were often outrageous and typically hollow. He continually drifted, as if pulled by the current, and if he ever sought moorage during his years with the Mets, he did not find it at home or in the clubhouse.

"I was at their wedding," a friend says of Darryl and Lisa's marriage, "and they were at each other's throats from Day One. It was like they hated each other from the start. And his mother didn't like her at all. That put a drain on Darryl. And it was no secret how they went through money. It was almost like a contest they had to see which one could outspend the other."

Darryl married Lisa in January 1985, two months before signing a six-year contract worth $7.2 million. Much of that money was scheduled to be deferred. It wasn't long before he dipped into that account.

The Strawberrys would separate and reconcile routinely over the next seven years. Once, at dinner with another couple, Darryl and Lisa shouted obscenities at each other so loudly in a restaurant that "we were embarrassed," says one of the other diners. "I said to Lisa, 'Why don't you try being nice to him?' And she said, 'If you only knew what he puts me through.'"

One of Lisa's attempts at reconciliation occurred in Houston during the 1986 National League Championship Series. Darryl says he spent one night drinking with friends at the hotel bar, and when he returned to their room he found Lisa had chained the door shut. He banged furiously on the door as they screamed at each other. When she finally opened the door, Darryl uncorked a punch to her nose that sent her to a hospital.

"It was scary," he says. "I did some of the same things in my marriage that I felt my father did to me and our family. It's unfortunate it had to happen like that, but I was turning into him. That's what I found out later from the people at Betty Ford."

Lisa filed for legal separation and an order of protection on January 29, 1987. She and Darryl reconciled eight months later. On June 2, 1989, Lisa began divorce proceedings. The Strawberrys reconciled again later that year. At 3:45 in the morning of January 26, 1990, during a fierce argument in which Lisa whacked Darryl in the ribs with an iron rod, he pulled out a .25 caliber pistol and pointed it at her. He was arrested and jailed briefly on suspicion of assault with a deadly weapon, but no charges were filed.

Recalling that night in his 1992 autobiography, *Darryl*, he wrote, "Just be glad, I remember saying to myself as I tried to find something positive in this whole mess, that you aren't involved with drugs." That, of course, was a lie. Eight days after the fight, at the Mets' recommendation, Strawberry checked into Smithers for alcohol abuse. As it turned out, this was a convenient move to help avoid prosecution. That was another one of Darryl's lies. "Going to

Smithers was my cover-up," he admits now. "I never even bothered telling them about the drugs."

Strawberry continued to drift. On November 8, 1990, he signed as a free agent with the Dodgers. "My first choice was to be back home," he said at the ensuing press conference, only to turn around moments later and say, "The Mets were the only organization I wanted to play for."

He tried religion, claiming in January 1991 that he was born again. He was free of drugs and alcohol, he said, while rationalizing, "I can have a glass of wine or beer if I choose. I choose not to." An L.A. teammate said that was a lie and that Strawberry still was sucking down beers. Born-again teammates on the Dodgers, Brett Butler and Gary Carter, would invite him to breakfast, but Strawberry wouldn't show.

"It wasn't a farce," his mother says. "I think he was genuinely trying to get his life together. But at the same time he did not want to admit to anyone how much trouble he was in."

Darryl and Lisa split again in January 1991, and she resumed divorce proceedings on May 28, 1992. The divorce was finalized on October 15, 1993. Lisa was granted the couple's house in Encino, a 1991 BMW 750i, a 1989 Porsche 928, a 1991 Mercedes SL, $300,000 in cash, $40,000 in attorney's fees (in addition to the $55,000 Darryl had already paid for her attorneys and accountants), and $50,000 a month in spousal support. Darryl was ordered to pay another $30,000 a month in child support.

"His marriage was a bad one from the beginning," Ruby said in 1991. "Darryl wasn't that kind of person until he got involved with Lisa."

Lisa Strawberry did not respond to *SI*'s attempts to reach her through her attorney.

On December 3, 1993, less than two months after his divorce was finalized, Strawberry married Charisse Simon. The wedding occurred three months after Strawberry was arrested on a battery charge for allegedly striking her. Simon did not file charges. The couple has an 11-month-old son, Jordan, and is expecting another child in June, the fifth for Strawberry by three women. (In 1990 Strawberry was found by means of a blood test to be the father of a child by Lisa Clayton, of Clayton, Missouri, who had filed a paternity suit against him.)

Strawberry's domestic problems affected him on the field. He admitted during spring training in 1987 that there were periods of "several days, even weeks where I didn't concentrate at all." Then his deportment grew worse. That year he reported late to work at least four times (once remarking, "It's tough getting up for day games"), walked out of training camp once and begged out of a critical game against the first-place St. Louis Cardinals with a virus after spending the afternoon recording a rap song. After that, Met teammate Wally Backman remarked, "Nobody I know gets sick twenty-five times a year." To which Strawberry responded, "I'll bust that little redneck in the face." And all that happened in a year when he had career highs in batting average (.284) and home runs (39).

"When a guy gets to the ballpark at five-thirty, six o'clock at night and he's sending somebody out for a burger or chicken and it's his first meal of the day, that's a sign of trouble," says Steve Garland, a former Met trainer. "And that happened a lot."

"You could always tell the days Darryl didn't want to play," says former Met Dave Magadan. "I mean, you *knew*. He'd show up looking as if he was knocking on death's door. You knew he wasn't going to play or you'd get nothing out of him."

On those days Garland or one of the New York coaches would mention to manager Davey Johnson that Strawberry appeared as if he wanted to sit the game out. " —— him," Johnson would snap back.

"That's right," Johnson says now. "I'd get the farthest away from him that I could so that he had no chance of getting the day off. My attitude was, he was going to play — screw him. Maybe he'll understand he has to keep himself ready to play and get his damn rest. Usually he'd be so mad at me, he'd go out and hit two home runs. It happened more than once."

"I don't know about that," Magadan says. "Most of those times Darryl was a nonfactor."

Johnson knew Strawberry was cheating himself on the field and called him into his office on numerous occasions. The speech, Johnson says, was always the same: "You've got to take care of yourself. You've got to get your rest. You can't keep this up." Strawberry would nod and say, "Thanks, skip. I hear you. I'm going to turn things around." And the minute Strawberry walked out the door he would forget what he had heard.

Says Bry, Strawberry's former agent: "Management is so afraid to say anything to players, especially the high-paid ones. They see them on a daily basis. They're scared to death of the players, afraid to confront them if they know something's wrong. That's what happened with Darryl."

On September 18, 1989, in anticipation of a New York loss, Strawberry and Kevin McReynolds began undressing in the clubhouse in the ninth inning of a game at Wrigley Field. The Mets staged a rally, however, forcing the two players to scurry back into their uniforms as their turns in the batting order approached. Johnson fined them $500 each and called a meeting the next day.

"Mac knew he was wrong, but what he really didn't like was being linked with Strawberry," Johnson says. "What really upset me was that during the meeting Darryl was saying, 'What's the big deal?'" Johnson and Strawberry nearly came to blows. Several players, including Darling, prevented a fistfight only by stepping between them. "What most people don't know," Darling says, "is that that kind of confrontation happened on planes and buses and in the clubhouse between Darryl and Davey maybe twenty times. That happened all the time."

Strawberry could be mean and antagonistic, especially from his usual spot in the back of the team bus. He would shout loud enough so that Johnson, sitting in the first row, could hear him. He once ridiculed Johnson so viciously for not giving enough playing time to outfielder Mookie Wilson that Johnson had to fight back an urge to run to the rear of the bus and pummel Strawberry. On another day Mackey Sasser, a Met catcher troubled by an embarrassing hitch in his throwing motion, was not as restrained. He charged Strawberry and came away from the assault with blood gushing from his nose.

"Darryl always thought [ragging on people] was funny," Magadan says. "But a lot of times it was vicious. And he wasn't always drunk. A lot of times it was on the bus right after a game."

Nobody caught more heat from Strawberry than Carter, the veteran catcher who struggled with injuries from 1987 through '89, his last two years with the Mets. "It got to the point of being very malicious," says Carter. "But a lot of it had to do with his drinking. You just let it go. I knew what it was all about. It was about money. He hated it that I was making more money than he was, even though I'd tell him, 'Darryl, you're going to make ten times as much money in this game as I ever did.' It was the same thing with Keith Hernandez. That's why they had the fight."

In spring training of 1989, while lining up for a team picture, Strawberry suddenly took a punch at Hernandez, the Met first baseman, shouting, "I've been tired of you for years!"

"That was where it really started to unravel for Darryl," Darling says. "He lost a lot of respect, and I think he was embarrassed. Keith and Gary were at the ends of their careers, and the team was passing to Darryl and Dwight. And they were never able to lead the team in the same way. They were never able to take the team from Keith and Gary and take it another step."

As the pressure grew and as the Mets failed again and again to make it back to the World Series, Strawberry began to see himself more and more as a victim. "Other guys would have a bad year and people would make excuses for them," he says, "but if we didn't win it was my fault. My own teammates would say things about me. I could never figure that out.

"Listen, I hold myself accountable for all that's happened. I take full responsibility for what I did. But me and Doc were two young stars, black players, who came to New York, and the expectations were extremely high. I don't think any other two players in any sport came to New York at that age with expectations so high. The pressure, it was so great. That's why I want to help kids now. I didn't have anyone say, 'Let me help you.' If I had had someone like that around, maybe I'd have had a different way of dealing with it."

When Strawberry, at 21, and Gooden, at 19, joined the Mets, they became a part of a team that played hard and lived harder. That group evolved into a ball club fueled by an intense desire to be the best but very often driven also by alcohol, amphetamines, gambling, and drugs. Young, impressionable, and unsophisticated, Strawberry and Gooden were driftwood in the current.

"When Doc came out of Smithers in 1987," Garland says, "he talked to me about how prevalent the drug use was on the team. He started calling off names. He rattled off more than ten — more than half the team. Probably around fourteen or fifteen. And I thought the '84, '85, and '86 teams were wilder."

Gooden recalls the time on a team charter in 1986 when the door to one of the bathrooms popped open, revealing a teammate inside using cocaine. "A lot of us saw it," Gooden says. "We just looked at each other and said, 'Nobody saw nothing.'"

Between 1986 and '91, of the twenty-two Met players who appeared in the 1986 World Series, eight were arrested following incidents that were alcohol- and/or battery-related (Strawberry, Gooden, Darling, Rick Aguilera, Lenny Dykstra, Kevin Mitchell, Bob Ojeda, and Tim Teufel) and a ninth was disciplined by baseball for cocaine use (Hernandez). The charges against Aguilera, Mitchell, and Ojeda were eventually dropped.

Johnson, the New York manager from 1984 through part of the '90 season, has admitted he drank too much in those years. He kept a refrigerator stocked with beer in his Shea Stadium office. A former Met player even remembers one of the coaches smoking pot on a beach in Florida during one spring training.

Moreover, Johnson says he knew "a couple of the New York veterans, not including Strawberry, were using amphetamines." Says Garland, "The guys who used amphetamines, maybe the numbers weren't great, but those who did use them used them almost every day. They depended on them so much they felt like they couldn't play without them."

After the 1986 season the Mets traded Mitchell, who had grown up around gangs in San Diego, because he scared the suits in the front office. They worried he was corrupting Strawberry and Gooden. "It was a mistake," Johnson says. "Mitch would have one or two drinks, but that's it. He was a good influence on them. He played hard. He had the street smarts they lacked. He could spot trouble and tell people to get lost. They needed that."

Says Gooden, "Davey's right. They should have never traded him."

The most influential player on those Met teams of the mid- to late-1980s was Hernandez, the smarmy first baseman who, during 1985 drug trials in Pittsburgh involving twenty-three baseball players, admitted using cocaine while he was with St. Louis in the early '80s. Hernandez advised Strawberry on how to break out of a batting slump: Go out and get totally smashed. Strawberry remembers the time Hernandez told him he'd found the perfect drink, of which he needed only five or six in a night: "dry martini," Strawberry says, laughing.

The other veteran pillar of the team, Carter, was ignored or, worse, ridiculed. His crime? He was a conservative family man. "There was a lack of respect for Gary Carter," Garland says. "He was clearly in an overwhelming minority — or should I say an underwhelming minority."

The game was changing in those years, what with salaries and the memorabilia business beginning to boom; with the social status of players shifting, as revered icons became disposable celebrities; and with cocaine, as it was in the rest of American society, readily available.

Says Darling, "Darryl and, to a lesser extent, Dwight were the first athletes I'd ever seen who surrounded themselves with an inner circle of about eight to ten associates. I felt like I never really knew either one of them. These people will tell the big star whatever he wants to hear. Their whole existence is contingent on one thing: making the man happy. It was not a real world."

The vortex of these changes — the money, the empty adulation, the cocaine — spun more quickly for a team from New York. The Mets became such a sexy, star-studded team that they were chased by fans carrying video cameras, the newest high-tech assault weapon of an increasingly aggressive audience. Just getting out of a hotel became an exercise in subterfuge.

The Mets were a portable party. Who among them would dare to be the grinch who turned down the music? What stick-in-the-mud would confront a teammate about drinking too much? The dynamics of the baseball clubhouse, especially the New York clubhouse, would not allow that. "All ballplayers like their beer," says a Met insider. "The difference with this team was they liked all the stuff harder than beer."

And so any talk about overindulging was done with a winking eye and a chuckle. Strawberry would see Gooden with liquor and say, "Man, you drinking again?" And Gooden would catch Strawberry doing likewise and remark, "Man, you're an alcoholic." Just something else to laugh about, that's all it was.

When Gooden got out of Smithers in 1987, his counselor there, Allan Lans, was given added responsibility as the Mets' psychiatrist. But Lans was distrusted by many players, who figured he was a spy for management. Gooden would joke to Strawberry, "Doctor Lans says you're a time bomb waiting to go off," and later Doc would simply say, "Tick, tick, tick. . . ." as he walked by Darryl.

Strawberry often left the clubhouse after games with cans of beer in a paper bag. On travel days, he and Gooden would pack large bottles of Stolichnaya vodka in their carry bags to take aboard the team charter planes.

"If we wouldn't have partied so much, we would have won more," Strawberry says. "We had a team full of drunks. We'd go into a town and couldn't wait to go out drinking and partying, always asking each other, 'Hey, where you going tonight?' If we had twenty-four guys on the team in those days, at least half of them were hard drinkers or drug users. That was a hard-living team."

"What I remember," Gooden says, "is we'd be on the road and we'd come back into the clubhouse after batting practice and we'd be saying, 'Yeah, let's kick some ass and then go out and show everyone we own this town.' Whether it was Montreal or St. Louis or whatever, we wanted people to know it, like we were taking over the place."

Several players were so heavily involved with poker playing that Johnson or one of his coaches occasionally sat in for a few hands in the clubhouse. "My fear," Johnson says, "was that the stakes were getting out of control, and one player would be into another player for a dangerous amount of money. That bothered me more than anything. I didn't want to see guys get hurt financially. Then there'd be animosity."

Johnson was fired during the 1990 season, in great part because Met management saw the players getting away from him. He disputes Strawberry's assessment that the team drank itself out of more titles. "I enjoyed those teams, and we were in contention every year," he says.

But Magadan, sometimes one of Strawberry's harsher critics, says, "I would agree with Darryl on that. We just lost perspective. I think a lot of guys lost sight of what our goals were. We'd go on a six-game road trip, say to Chicago and St. Louis. And instead of thinking, Let's win five out of six or six out of six, guys would be thinking, In Chicago I can go out to this restaurant and this bar, and in St. Louis I can go here and there. It was almost as if the games were getting in the way for some guys. They'd rather skip them and just go out."

Last August, on one of his first nights back home in St. Petersburg after his stay at the Betty Ford Center and his counseling sessions in

New York, Gooden grabbed a cold beer from his refrigerator and jumped into his black Mercedes. One for the road. He headed north on I-275 to Tampa for a night out with friends. Already under a sixty-day suspension from Major League Baseball, he was risking an even harsher sentence. So what? He was feeling worthless and alone. Everyone seemed to be giving up on him.

The beer started his familiar chain reaction: a few more beers that led to hard liquor that led to cocaine. "If I don't drink, I have no desire to use coke," Gooden says. "You could put a bag of coke in front of me right now and I'd have no desire for it at all. Once I drink, especially when I get drunk, the desire is there. The hard stuff leads to coke. It was the same thing over and over.

"My problems have never been here in St. Pete. I was always getting into trouble in Tampa. It's strange. I have a son in Tampa, and I go there all the time to see him. If I go to Tampa during the day, I'm fine. But in Tampa after the sun goes down, it's like I'm a vampire. I change. Get a beer for the ride, meet my friends, go to a club, and I'm in trouble.

"Why did it happen? That's one of the things I'm trying to work out with my counselor. It's tough trying to pinpoint it. It's not any one thing. It's not that simple. Why go out and get ——faced to the max? I still can't pinpoint it."

Gooden was the greatest pitching prodigy ever. He struck out more batters (276) in 1984 than any rookie in history. At 20 he was the youngest Opening Day pitcher this century and the youngest Cy Young Award winner ever. He is the only pitcher this century to have 200 strikeouts in each of his first three seasons. Of the first 100 games he started in the big leagues, he lost only 19.

"He was by far the greatest pitcher I'd ever seen," Darling says. "I pitched behind him in the rotation, so I always charted his pitches. Those first two years, I swear, it seemed like he was 0 and 2 on 75 percent of the hitters. It was like Little League, where the other team has no chance except to bunt. If you told me Dwight was going to win 300 games and strike out 400 people one year, I'd have believed it. That's how good he was."

In the months after he was voted Rookie of the Year in 1984, Gooden, then living in Tampa, began using cocaine occasionally behind the closed bedroom doors of house parties. Life was so easy. It had to be celebrated.

"My nearest sister is thirteen years older than me," says Gooden, who has five older siblings. "I don't want to say I was spoiled, but I had what I wanted growing up. Once I got to the big leagues, it happened so quickly for me. I got caught up in it."

Says Strawberry, "Doc came into the big leagues at 19. By 20 he was a big drunk hanging out in strip clubs."

"Not true," Gooden says. "It was my third year when I started to drink heavily."

By then, 1986, rumors about his drug use began to swirl. People called the Met front office claiming to have knowledge of it. Gooden missed an exhibition game because of a friend's car accident, he claimed. He missed the team's ticker-tape parade following the World Series victory because, he says now, he was hung over from the night before and overslept. He called off his engagement to Carlene Pearson and fathered a son, Dwight Jr., by another woman, Debra Hamilton of Tampa. Then he had that brawl with the Tampa police after they stopped his car.

So on March 24, 1987, at Gooden's urging, his agent, Jim Neader, met with Met vice president Al Harazin to work out a voluntary drug-testing plan. Gooden was supposed to attend the meeting but did not show. "Test for everything," Neader said. The next day, Neader told Harazin, "Go ahead, test away." So the following day, the Mets took a urine sample and sent it to St. Petersburg General Hospital.

"I feel like I have to do it," Gooden said at the time. "I want to convince the Mets more than I do anyone else."

On March 30 a test came up positive for cocaine. On April Fools' Day the Mets confronted Gooden with the test result. His first reaction was to deny it. Then he broke down and cried.

"It was an absolute bombshell," Johnson says. "I thought it wasn't true. He was on time, worked hard and set a good example for the other pitchers. He had one of the best work ethics I've seen."

Gooden's life was a lie, and the Mets unwittingly helped perpetuate it. Under the overzealous mothering of the front office and its publicity staff, Gooden was told when to speak, whom to speak to and, sometimes, what to say. Such was management's paranoia that during Gooden's first workout at Shea Stadium after his first drug rehabilitation, reporters were sequestered in an auxiliary locker room with a guard posted at the door. The press was even refused access to the press box. The Mets weren't about to let Gooden become a loose cannon like Strawberry. Problem was, they failed to let Gooden be himself.

"I became this person I really wasn't," he says. "People said I was this quiet, nice, shy kid. Sometimes I just wanted to yell, '——' or '——' or just blow somebody out. But I'd always stop myself and say, 'I'm not supposed to be like this.' Jay [Horwitz, the team's public relations director] would ask me to do an interview, and even if I didn't want to do it, I'd say, 'O.K., I'll do it.'"

"The problem with Dwight," Johnson says, "is he couldn't say no. He was too nice. Evidently, he knew people in Tampa who could get you in trouble. It was like he was the lucky one, and it would be wrong for him not to be their friend, like he wanted to prove to them he wasn't acting like a big shot and turning his back on them."

Says Gooden, "That's 100 percent true. I have to be more vocal — in any situation." Gooden, despite Horwitz's concern, decided on his own to be interviewed for this story.

"I'm not going to sit back and just take things in anymore," he says. "I have to be me. I'm going to be a little more selfish."

Gooden checked into Smithers in April 1987 immediately after testing positive for cocaine. He felt awkward being there and re-fused to open up to Lans. I can handle this myself, he thought. You're not much of a man if you have to go to someone else with your problems.

The counselors tried to teach him how alcohol acted as his gate-way to cocaine, but the lesson didn't stick. Three weeks after he checked out of Smithers he was drinking again. "If I won, I went out drinking to celebrate," he says. "And if I lost, I went out drinking to forget about it."

After Gooden's four weeks in Smithers, Major League Baseball began testing him for drugs as often as three times per week. As he continued to test clean over the years, baseball officials relaxed their vigilance. First they stopped taking samples on the days that he pitched. Eventually the frequency of the testing shrank to four random tests over each half of the baseball season. And, Gooden says, Lans began cutting back on Gooden's aftercare, excusing him from Alcoholics Anonymous meetings in New York because Gooden was such a celebrity that his appearances there were a distraction.

Meanwhile, Gooden's drinking problem deepened. With Strawberry gone to Los Angeles, the Mets plummeted to fifth place in 1991 with a 77–84 record. It was the first time Gooden had played on a losing big league team. New York's deterioration continued, with 90 losses in '92 and 103 losses and a last-place finish in '93. Gooden suffered the first two losing seasons of his big league career in those years. He tried finding solace inside a bottle of beer or vodka. It was a never-ending search. It was in those years too that his arm started feeling unresponsive.

"I didn't think it happened before, but in '92 and '93 all the drinking started to affect my performance," he says. "It was cumulative. After a while, abusing your body catches up to you. I'd be the first to admit it."

In December 1993, after one of his nocturnal sojourns into Tampa, another drug test turned up positive. Inexplicably, according to a high-ranking major league official, baseball's medical people chose to let it slide without informing the executive council or the players' union. "They didn't do him any favors by doing that," former trainer Garland says. "It does make you wonder if there were any other times they did the same thing."

But the dirty test last June was not ignored. The Mets told Gooden he was facing probable suspension for violating his aftercare program. Gooden, in deep denial, told friends that it was no big deal, that he simply had missed a test because of oversleeping. He learned of his sixty-day ban on June 24, a day he was scheduled to start against the Pittsburgh Pirates. The Mets, paranoid as ever, coaxed him into going ahead with his start anyway. After all, baseball wasn't ready to announce the suspension, so what would people think if Gooden was scratched from his start? It turned out to be the worst performance of his career. "If I had to do it again," he says, "there's no way I'd go out there."

At first, Gooden says, Millman and Solomon, his counselors in New York, did not recommend that he undergo another inpatient rehabilitation. His aftercare program, including the testing regimen, needed to be stepped up. Gooden, after meeting with the doctors on July 1, went home to St. Petersburg. At an outing over that Fourth of July weekend, he decided, "Well, I'll just have a couple of beers."

He continued to slide. "I always knew one or two guys who had the coke," he says. "It wasn't like I had to go driving through some

bad neighborhood and roll the window down." Once, on the morning of scheduled drug tests, he called up Lans and said, "I was using
last night. Should I still go ahead with the test?" Lans advised him,
yes, he should let himself be tested.

Finally, on July 22, he checked into the Betty Ford Center. When
he broke the news to his wife, Monica, that he was heading to the
clinic, she looked puzzled and asked, "Why?"

"She didn't know how bad it was," he says. "She'd always be asleep
in bed when I'd be coming home late."

But three weeks after Gooden left the clinic, his depression returned and his cocaine use continued. "Looking back on it," he
says, "I should have called Jim [Neader] and told him what I was
feeling. It's almost like you want to isolate yourself from the world. I
didn't want to see anybody, even my family."

Then on September 15 the Mets confirmed that Gooden had
again violated his aftercare program. Baseball withheld any further
action, essentially allowing him more time to pull himself together.
But more samples came back dirty. On November 4 he was suspended for the 1995 season.

"People ask, 'How can you use when you know you're getting
tested?'" Gooden says. "It's not that easy not to. I remember when
Otis Nixon tested positive again [in 1991, while with the Atlanta
Braves]. I was like, Oh, man, how could a guy do something like
that with so much on the line? Now I understand."

Gooden claims he has remained clean since then and has the test
results to prove it. "I want the tests," he says. "It's one thing to say it
and another to have the proof to show it."

He has devoted himself to his three-times-a-week Alcoholics
Anonymous meetings and his two-times a-week sessions with a personal counselor in New Port Richey, Florida. One of the members
of his AA group is a 70-year-old man who has been attending such
meetings for the past thirty years. Gooden was shocked to hear him
talk about episodes of still wanting to go back to alcohol. Another
AA group member explained he has had nine relapses and is working hard to stave off a tenth.

"I see why," Gooden says. "You can never have this thing beat. I
have to accept that. I still have my days where I get down. The
difference is it doesn't stay with me as long as it did in August and
September."

On January 27 Gooden flew to New York to meet with Millman

and Solomon. As the plane descended to LaGuardia Airport, the side on which Gooden sat banked toward Shea Stadium, as if genuflecting. Gooden caught plain sight of the giant horseshoe with the great expanse of green laid out so invitingly inside. Overwhelmed, not with sadness but with joy, he nearly cried. At that moment he wanted to be standing on the mound, a fresh baseball in his hand, the possibilities all new again.

"C'mon, let's get inside and talk," Gooden says, gesturing toward his Mercedes as the rain begins to fall. The wheels are equipped with brilliant rims that gleam even in the late-morning gloom. Gooden selected the rims and ordered another set for Monica's Mercedes convertible. To keep himself occupied, he has turned his love for customizing cars into a serious hobby. At the moment he is tinkering with a 1974 Porsche and a 1969 Chevy. Renovation. It is what he's doing with his life.

Slipping behind the steering wheel, Gooden is still perspiring slightly from one of his typically grueling workouts with Larry Mayol, his personal trainer. He appears to be in terrific shape, and when he throws the baseball, he says, it feels like it is flying out of his hand again. "Not having alcohol in your system," he says, "it seems like it makes you meaner, quicker."

Wearing blue Met shorts and a blue nylon Met training jacket, he looks and talks as if he still were the Met ace. In fact, he has no employer, which would seem to be a daunting proposition for someone who supports an extended family. Beginning in 1987, with a $320,000 house for his parents and a $530,000 house for himself and Monica, Gooden has purchased five of the seven homes on his block, a waterfront cul-de-sac. One of the houses is the home of his nephew, Florida Marlin outfielder Gary Sheffield. Gooden wants to buy the remaining two houses from their current owners and then erect a security gate at the entrance to the street, though he says, "It's Gary's turn to buy."

Gooden, who last year finished a three-year contract originally worth $15.45 million and has earned about $25 million during his major league career, says he is financially secure. What he wants is simply to pitch in the major leagues again — even before his suspension is scheduled to end in November. He says he has been told by baseball officials that he could be reinstated by mid-summer if he shows he has put his life in order, a claim Major League Baseball does not confirm. He has a standing offer from the Mets to start talking about a new contract as soon as he is reinstated to the game. He wants nothing other than that.

"It just feels like New York is my home," he says. "I belong to New York. It seems like I did all my growing up in New York.

"Obviously, I'd like to apologize to the fans for my actions, but I can honestly say I'm on the right track. I'm getting myself in the best possible shape physically so when that chance comes I'll be ready. It may be time to quit feeling like it can be 1985 again. But I'd be lying if I said I don't want to win twenty games again.

"I keep having these daydreams about coming back. If they let me come back in June or July, I can picture winning Comeback Player of the Year and going to a dinner to get the award and giving a speech. I go over that speech all the time."

The rain has let up and the faintest bit of sunshine appears. He has to be on his way now. He has an appointment with his counselor this afternoon and an AA meeting in the evening.

Before he goes, he is asked about being paired in infamy with Strawberry. The two of them started out as stars and were going to be the dominant players of their era, sure as sunrise. Now here they are, on the outside looking in, with messy lives to clean up and careers as uncertain as they were once assured. Doc and Straw. Teammates once again.

"It's sad," he says. "The stories are kind of similar. Except Darryl was more vocal and I wasn't. Maybe if I was more vocal and if he wasn't, maybe it would have turned out better for both of us. Maybe."

MICHAEL GOODMAN

An Utter Disaster

FROM THE SPORTING NEWS

DR. BILLY ABB CANNON — Louisiana football legend, confessed counterfeiter — waves me into the tiny, cluttered cubicle he calls his orthodontist office. Outside, his waiting room is empty of both staff and clients. As usual.

Cheap green and yellow vinyl chairs hooked together line the walls. One hundred or so magazines are piled on white formica coffee tables. *Esquire, People, Family Journal.* The magazines on top are dated April and May of 1994. Many are addressed to someone other than Cannon. The toilet and sink in the bathroom are splotched with rust.

"It's a very depressing place," says Paul Manasseh, a retired LSU sports information director who lunches and visits with Cannon weekly at Cannon's office in Baton Rouge. "Billy sits in that office all day long, all by himself. He had to get an answering machine because of bill collectors. He never picks up the phone until he knows who it is."

Cannon's two X-ray machines — one is broken — have not been used since 1986 when he was released from federal prison in Texarkana, Texas. He served two and a half years as head of a ring that counterfeited $6 million in $100 bills.

Now, Cannon contracts out X-rays because he has been "financially unable" to pay the $55-a-year safety inspection fee for X-ray machines, according to a letter filed September 9, 1993, with the state attorney general. The letter from his attorney was in response to two lawsuits by the attorney general totaling nearly $1,000 in fines and court fees for nonpayment of $110 for safety inspections.

Financial desperation, Cannon says, forced him to *invite* a reporter to sit down with him, probably the first time in more than a decade.

At first, Cannon wanted $1,000 to talk. Through an intermediary, Cannon was told the *Sporting News* does not pay for interviews. The possibility of a book deal resulting from the article was discussed. No argument. Successful books have been written about far less controversial sports figures.

"Billy wants to talk. He's at his office," relayed the intermediary, a close friend.

Cannon offers me a seat. He raises a cola bottle to his lips. It is full. But not with soda. He squirts a stream of tobacco juice dead center through the bottle's small opening.

"Chaw?" he asks, offering a pouch of Red Man tobacco. I don't chew. But chew I do. Cannon tosses over an empty spittin' bottle and the pouch labeled "The Flavor of America . . . America's best chew." We talk and spit with tobacco plugs wedged between cheek and gum.

"I'm broke," Cannon says. His voice is matter of fact, almost nonchalant. "I'm busted. I'm going down. I'll probably file bankruptcy." He concedes even his 1959 Heisman Trophy has been bartered to a restaurant owner for display in return for free lunches and to protect the Heisman from creditors.

The people of Baton Rouge still haven't fully recovered from the shame of Cannon's 1983 counterfeiting scandal.

Now this.

Again, it seems, Cannon will embarrass, disappoint and betray the football-obsessed fans of this state capital strung along the Mississippi River. Many, if not most, still cling to the glory Cannon gave them and LSU: the 1958 national championship. The 89-yard punt return for a touchdown to beat hated Ole Miss in 1959.

Physically, Cannon still oozes power. Big, burly, with a meaty face, square jaw, cropped jock haircut. His hatred of the media is clear during the thirty minutes he endures my presence. His eyes glitter with suspicion. His voice is edged with contempt. His smile through pressed, colorless lips is more of a smirk and sneer.

The phone rings. His message machine announces: "This is Dr. Billy Cannon. I am presently with a patient. If you will leave your name . . ."

Cannon listens to the message. "Another bill collector," he mutters.

He brightens. "I can tell you stories that would fill a book. I can tell you things you wouldn't believe."

"So," I pose, "tell me. Give me a taste, a sample."

I pull out my notebook. Cannon freezes. His eyes narrow. "How much of a cash advance can I get right now? What's in it for me?" he asks repeatedly.

Cannon is reminded that cash advances for books are unpredictable. Perhaps something. Perhaps nothing. First, the article.

Cannon's face mottles with anger and frustration.

"I need money *now*," he snaps. "No cash advance for a book, no article! What's in it for me, *now?*" Cannon is told an article is forthcoming, regardless.

"I'm gonna punch you out and throw you out," Cannon snarls.

I stand, take out two false teeth, hoping Cannon has no stomach for beating up a reporter he invited into his office.

Cannon sighs. "Just leave," he grumbles. I pause at the door and ask for the third time: "Why, Billy, did you print the phony one hundreds?"

He responds with the same answer. "I took a shot." Then adds, "It didn't work."

Why Cannon turned counterfeiter is, in the words of Smiley Anders, local newspaper columnist and Cannon's high school classmate, "one of the great unsolved mysteries in Louisiana."

For twelve years, the people who know, or think they know Cannon best, have tried, in their disappointment and bewilderment, to solve the mystery. Simplistic, pat answers for human behavior — Cannon's behavior — have been as hotly disputed among psychiatrists as they are in Baton Rouge.

The best answer may be in Cannon's arrogant, remorseless retort: "I took a shot. It didn't work."

A look at Cannon's life reveals a youthful wildness, a greediness, an insolence toward society nurtured and ingrained through decades of hero worship and special treatment.

"Billy's gone through life figuring he could do anything and get away with it . . . that he was above the law," says Manasseh, the retired LSU sports information director who was the only person from LSU to stand with Cannon when he was sentenced to prison.

"Friendship. Loyalty. Those are some of the good things about Billy," Manasseh says. "In 1975 my daughter needed oral surgery. Billy recommended a dentist. She died from complications from anesthesia. The dentist was not to blame. Billy was at the funeral standing in the back with tears in his eyes. To this day Billy blames himself. Another time, before he went to prison, Billy put braces on my son. Months went by, and I didn't get a bill. I asked, 'Billy, where's the bill?' He'd reply, 'Oh, don't worry about it.' But because I insisted, he charged me $200."

Manasseh shrugs. "Billy's basically a good guy. He's a devoted family man to his five children and the wife he married in college. But he does some dumb-ass things. He's got a streak in him . . . a quirk. He's a very complex person. I'm no shrink. Go figure it."

Today, Cannon leads a quiet life, according to friends — Thomas J. Moran, Manasseh, and others.

"Billy'll have a beer, but that's about it," Manasseh says.

Moran adds, "You never see Billy out at night. He goes home."

Home is a faded yellow-brick, one-level house he bought in 1961 in what is now an upscale manicured suburb fringing the Sherwood Forest Country Club. He drives a late-model Ford pickup. He lives with his wife of thirty-nine years, Dorothy, his high school sweetheart. Three of his four daughters have married and moved. His youngest daughter, Bunnie, 25, is assistant director for the LSU Recreation Center. His son, Billy Jr., is in construction in Baton Rouge.

Occasionally, Cannon eats lunch at the Golden Pelican Bar and Grill a few doors from his office.

Renee, a tavern regular in her forties with burgundy-rimmed glasses, says Cannon is a "very charismatic guy with a confident sense of humor" who readily autographs the stream of bar napkins thrust at him.

Once, Renee recounted, Cannon bumped into a former patient and asked what he was doing.

"I'm in the printing business," the patient responded.

Cannon shrugged. "I was in the printing business myself."

Cannon grew up in a tough neighborhood on the north side of the tracks.

"North of the tracks back then was white trash and blue collar," says J.R. Ball, editor of the *Tiger Rag*, a weekly off-campus magazine that covers LSU sports. "Cannon was known as a thug, a punk."

Paul Dietzel, Cannon's LSU football coach, knows as much as anybody about Cannon's early years.

"When Billy was just a boy, his father's arm was caught in machinery at a plant and ripped off," Dietzel says. "His father became bitter and hateful toward the company — fell apart — because he felt they never treated him right, never took care of him. Billy's dad never recovered from that mentally or physically. Billy's mother had to take in washing, laundry . . . clean houses. She held the family together. I think they were on relief, on welfare, for a while. I know people . . . neighbors, friends . . . had to give Billy clothes so he could go to school. LSU eventually gave Billy's father a job as a janitor. All this created an attitude really early in Billy's life and became, maybe, his downfall."

Cannon entered Istrouma High School in 1952. "In his freshman year, he was tall, skinny and bow-legged . . . a cocky kid . . . devil-may-care," says Anders, the columnist. Cannon's natural speed and strength were obvious. "Billy spent summers working with Alvin Roy [who became a trainer in professional football, now deceased]. When Billy came back each year, he was bigger and bigger, faster and stronger. None of us [students] could believe it," Anders says.

All of a sudden Billy blossomed into a fabulous athlete and football player in high school. He became Billy Cannon Superstar and was in the spotlight from that time on. Then fifteen kids went on a rampage against, well, what were called "queers." When the write-ups came out in the press, the only name used was Billy Cannon. He was the news.

Cannon's notoriety also blossomed. He and two buddies smiled sweetly, but slyly gave the finger in a 1955 basketball yearbook photo.

On a dull night, Cannon and pals would go downtown and "put the roll on a queer . . . slap the queers around," according to Cannon's attorney, Robert L. Kleinpeter, and past interviews given by Cannon's former principal.

"Billy got away with a lot," Al Harrison, a probation officer in the 1950s, told the *Sporting News* recently. "The coach and principal would come down and keep him out of trouble. He was a rough kid who had some compulsion to do nefarious things."

Finally, one of Cannon's beating victims filed charges just before Cannon's senior year in high school. Cannon received a ninety-day suspended sentence and probation. Baton Rouge couldn't have cared less. Cannon could do no wrong. LSU in general and football in particular are the heart and soul of this town.

Cannon was a 195-pound running back who scored 39 touchdowns his senior year, was named All-State and All-America, and led his high school to a state championship. He would later run the 100 in 9.4 seconds and throw a 16-pound shot 54 feet.

As Cannon neared graduation in 1955, he became the most recruited high school player in America.

But Cannon was a hometown boy. He was LSU-bound.

Rusty Jabour was 4 when his parents moved into the student housing built underneath the end-zone seating of LSU's Tiger Stadium. It was 1958.

"I'll never forget the thunder of the fans jumping and screaming above me," says Jabour, now an information officer for the attorney general of Louisiana, "As I look back, that deafening roar above me was for Billy Cannon taking the [undefeated] Tigers to a national championship. I can still hear it."

Cannon clinched the Heisman Trophy on Halloween night, 1959. With Ole Miss leading, 3–0, in the fourth quarter, Cannon snagged Jake Gibbs's punt on the 11-yard line. Six or seven tacklers bounced off Cannon during his 89-yard touchdown run. To this day, local radio and television stations replay The Run on Halloween night.

"I watched the ball bounce down by the 10, and I kept saying, 'No, Billy, no!' Then it became 'Go, Billy, go!'" Dietzel says.

"You have to understand it was a hot, muggy night and late in the game. The players on both teams were exhausted. But not Billy. He was so strong, so fast, he basically ran through the whole team. He was 210 pounds and ran the 100 in 9.4 seconds and could throw the shot put 55, 56 feet. It was one of the greatest runs in college football. I have a film clip of it. I still watch it more than I'd like to admit."

Despite his ability, Billy was still trouble. "Billy would get into a tiff, a mood, and just not practice," Dietzel says. "I'd haul him into the office and say: 'Billy, you're getting all the headlines. You're the star and these guys are working their butts off and you throw tiffs.

How does it feel to be the most disliked guy on the team? If I were them I wouldn't block for you.' Billy would look at me in amazement. 'They say that about me?' Then he'd hustle and roar around in practice for a few weeks and then throw another tiff. But he was a good team player when it was necessary. At halftime, he'd go to each player and shake them and tell them to get off their nests. Billy Cannon was hard to understand."

(Dietzel says that, by comparison, Johnny Robinson, another running back at LSU with Cannon, was far wilder than Billy as a teenager in Baton Rouge. In a twist of fates, Robinson now runs a halfway house in Louisiana.)

Billy Cannon began his professional career wheeling and dealing. He signed with teams from the National Football League and the newly formed American Football League. A journalist from Los Angeles called Cannon "the most repugnant young profiteer ever to sell his talents to anyone who'd bid."

First, Cannon signed a contract in November 1959 for $50,000 over three years with the Los Angeles Rams of the NFL. He held a press conference with then-Rams general manager Pete Rozelle. Then on New Year's Day 1960, between the goal posts of the Sugar Bowl, Cannon, before 83,000 fans, signed another contract with the Houston Oilers of the AFL. That contract offered him $100,000 over three years, a $10,000 gift for his wife, a slightly used Cadillac, and a promised chain of Cannon gas stations selling Cannonball Regular and Super Cannonball.

A Rams-Oilers legal battle followed. The Oilers won.

Cannon got the Cadillac but not the gas stations. He led the league in rushing in 1961 but hurt his back in 1962. He was traded to the Oakland Raiders in 1964 and ended his career in 1970 as a tight end. Sports writer Rich Koster described Cannon ending his career as a "loner . . . who snarled at sports writers." During the off-seasons, though, Cannon had gone to dentistry school. With five children, Cannon knew he had to prepare for the future. Because of his popularity, Cannon's practice flourished to an estimated $300,000 a year.

But Cannon was not satisfied. "Billy thought he could make $50 million," Moran says. "Billy never could stay away from living on the edge . . . a risk-taker. He was always working an angle to make a buck any way he could. Look at what happened with Billy Jr."

In 1980, Cannon's son, at 18, was a probable first-round draft pick as a major league shortstop/outfielder. Publicly, Billy Sr. sent telegrams to the twenty-six major league teams advising not to waste a first-round pick on his son because he was going to college. Privately, the Cannons were meeting with George Steinbrenner, owner of the Yankees. Billy Jr. was drafted by the Yankees and signed for a reported $350,000 bonus. Then–baseball commissioner Bowie Kuhn vetoed the signing. Kuhn said the other owners had been misled by Billy Sr.'s telegrams.

Billy Jr. went to Texas A&M and was the Dallas Cowboys' first-round draft pick in 1984 as a promising linebacker. He signed for a reported $1.9 million over six years. Despite advice to pay a $36,000 insurance premium in case of injury, Billy Jr. didn't. Eight games into his first year he suffered a spinal injury. Doctors warned of paralysis if he were hurt again. Billy Jr. claimed negligence by the Cowboys and filed a multimillion-dollar lawsuit. It was settled in 1992.

But Billy Sr. had his own woes. What follows is the story of folk hero turned desperado. What happened is based upon public records and interviews with Cannon, his friends, his attorney, and the federal prosecutors who sent him to prison:

Cannon invested in real estate, a shopping center, an office building, and other ventures. He also gambled heavily on sports and bought racehorses. Luck, Cannon discovered, favors nobody — even football heroes.

By 1983, Cannon was involved in nearly forty financial lawsuits with lending institutions, real-estate agents, utilities and private citizens. A sampling of these lawsuits:

• Cannon borrowed more than $246,000 "in 23 various promissory notes" in 1981–82 from First Progressive Bank of Louisiana and "failed and refused" to pay until May 1983, when he reached an undisclosed settlement.

• Cannon bought a condominium for $122,000 in 1982 and never made a payment. The condo was sold at auction for $60,000 in March 1983.

• Cannon borrowed $55,000 in December 1981 and made no payments. A judgment was entered against him in February 1983.

• Cannon bought a Mack truck in July 1982 for $87,880. His first payment of $1,464 was due in September. He never made a payment. The matter was settled out of court in 1985, while Cannon was in prison.

(Cannon's financial misadventures continued after his release from prison. Since then, he has been involved in at least a dozen more lawsuits.)

One Cannon venture in 1980 was printing souvenir T-shirts, according to Randall Miller, the assistant United States attorney who prosecuted him. The shirts were printed by John Stiglets, a convicted counterfeiter.

"Cannon complained to a friend he needed to borrow more money," Miller says. "The friend told Cannon, 'Why borrow money? The guy printing those T-shirts makes the best money around.'" Miller adds: "At the time, Billy Cannon needed money like a dead man needs a coffin. He bankrolled Stiglets with $15,000 and got in deeper and deeper."

Stiglets set up shop in Texas. During the next two years, he printed $6 million in $100 bills. The plan was to pass the money far from Baton Rouge, but the counterfeiting ring had grown to a half-dozen or so. Not everybody was paying attention. The Secret Service was tipped in late 1982 that a man had bought a Bible, vitamins, and jeans in three different stores with three $100 bills. Hmmm.

He was arrested. More $100 bills were taped under his car hood and found at his house. They were phony.

"Under questioning the guy said Billy Cannon was behind it all," says Stan Bardwell, then United States attorney. "The Secret Service agents were almost reluctant, embarrassed to tell me because it sounded so far-fetched."

Bardwell, it turned out, grew up with Cannon, though on the right side of the tracks. "I wasn't surprised. I knew his reputation as a punk . . . a bully . . . doing anything he damn well pleased."

Fifty-five federal agents descended upon Baton Rouge. Six wiretaps were placed on the phones of Cannon and other suspects.

Months passed without a break. Finally, on July 8, 1983, Cannon left his office about noon with a suspected accomplice. Agents followed, but Cannon's car "disappeared" on an unmarked dead-end street. The car reappeared at Cannon's office.

That afternoon, two men in a pickup — suspects — headed for

the same dead-end street, making U-turns, stopping, pulling over, and constantly "looking around to see if anyone was following them," documents reveal.

Agents watched the pickup drive to the dead end and vanish into grass four to six feet high. The pickup emerged. The men drove to a warehouse and unloaded two large plastic garbage bags. The bags held about $1 million in counterfeit $100 bills. Agents returned to the tall grass and dug up two empty Igloo coolers. The property belonged to Cannon. He spotted the agents the next morning and was told they had a search warrant. He shrugged and drove to Jefferson Downs racetrack near New Orleans. He was arrested upon his return.

The seventh-largest counterfeiting ring in American history was no more.

"I expected Cannon to be a smart ass who was going to fight it all the way," says Miller, the federal prosecutor. "Instead, he was the opposite. He seemed relieved. His attitude was: 'You got me. I'm gonna take my medicine like a man.'"

Miller says Cannon's eyes widened when he learned agents spent the night tromping over his property. "You're kidding!" Cannon had gasped. "We took two dozen poisonous snakes outta there a few days ago."

Miller laughs over the anecdote. He turns serious. "Cannon did something else that struck me. We hit a break in debriefing him. Then, out of the blue, like he was talking to himself, Cannon said, 'Maybe now, some people won't be as mad at me as they are.' Cannon looked at me and realized I overheard him. He felt compelled to explain: 'Everybody wanted me to take part in the Special Olympics. I couldn't do it 'cause I knew you all were investigating me, and I didn't want to embarrass anybody. Now maybe they'll understand.'"

Cannon led agents to other buried coolers packed with counterfeit bills. He pleaded guilty to conspiracy to possess and deal in counterfeit money. He cooperated with prosecutors and testified against his five cohorts in hope of avoiding prison.

At the sentencing, Cannon told Judge Frank J. Polozola: "What I did was wrong, terribly wrong. I have done everything within my power to correct my mistakes . . ."

Polozola replied: "If the name of the person I was about to

sentence was not Dr. Billy Cannon, what sentence would I impose? The court refuses to allow those who have fame and fortune or status in life to commit a crime and then have a slap on the hand while imposing jail sentences on others who are less fortunate."

Polozola gave Cannon the maximum: five years in prison and a $10,000 fine. He sold his practice to another orthodontist and surrendered his dentistry license.

Cannon entered federal prison in Texarkana, Texas, on September 12, 1983. His lawyer and others beseeched Polozola to reduce or modify the sentence. Their arguments included:

• Cannon's sentence was harsher than the other defendants', given his cooperation.

• Cannon's immediate family would be "virtually unable" to visit him because Texarkana is so far from Baton Rouge (307 miles). His "infirm mother and elderly mother-in-law are unlikely to visit him at all."

• Cannon's December 1983 induction into the National Football Foundation Hall of Fame was revoked.

• Cannon "was unable to witness his son's final year of collegiate football."

• Cannon had to "remain in the same clothes" for one week because prison officials lost his other clothes.

• Cannon is bored. He has nothing to do in prison.

The judge replied he was "confident that one or more jobs can be found at the prison for Cannon to perform . . ."

As for Cannon's claim that five years was unfair, the judge said that if Cannon had not agreed to testify against his fellow counterfeiters, "Cannon's maximum exposure in this case would have been one hundred years or more." The judge ruled that a sentence reduction "only would encourage a belief that persons with fame and fortune receive preferential treatment . . ."

Cannon was a loner in prison. He discouraged visitors.

"I was planning to go see him," Manasseh says. "But I was told he didn't want to see anybody. He just wasn't particularly interested in seeing anybody." Even Billy Jr. once told a reporter that he visited his father only two or three times.

"There was nothing good about [prison]," Cannon later told a writer from the New Orleans *Times-Picayune*. "I was away from my family, and that is the worst punishment of all." Cannon added that he did receive many letters from supporters, including a "wonderful, uplifting letter" from the person who presented him the Heisman Trophy — Richard M. Nixon.

Cannon served two and a half years, then went to a Salvation Army halfway house in Baton Rouge, He was released November 28, 1986.

Not everybody cheered. "Jailbird! Jailbird! Jailbird!" a woman screeched. Recalling the incident, Cannon once remarked, "I wonder if she thinks I don't know I was in jail."

"There's still a lot of ill feeling in this town," grumbles Manasseh, Cannon's close friend. "Some people will not forgive. Deep down, they think Billy betrayed them. He's got that onus on him the rest of his life. He's paying the price."

After prison, Cannon's license was reinstated, following a forty-hour refresher course with Dr. John Sheridan at the LSU School of Dentistry.

"Billy Cannon was like a god to me growing up in Baton Rouge," Sheridan says. "And now Billy Cannon himself walks into my office. Despite the counterfeiting, it's hard to forget what he did for Baton Rouge and LSU."

As the years passed, Sheridan says, it was clear that Cannon could not rebuild his practice. "He's still revered as a football hero, but that counterfeiting deal, prison, the craziness of it all . . . I guess it makes people wonder, and wonder enough to see another orthodontist."

Sheridan adds, "The sad, pathetic thing, the pity of it is that Dr. Cannon is a good orthodontist." Sheridan thought for a moment. "But I'll have to admit, Dr. Cannon is the only dentist I've ever heard of that chews tobacco."

Thomas J. Moran proudly guides me through the packed lunch crowd of one of his six restaurants, T.J. Ribs — Baton Rouge's most popular rib joint and a hangout of the sporting crowd. The walls are lined with signed basketballs, footballs, helmets, trophies, pictures, uniforms, baseball cards.

With a flourish, Moran says, "There it is!" He points to a five-foot-high, six-foot-by-six-foot, glass-enclosed trophy case protected by brass railings and anchored to brick pillars near the entrance. Inside, on a pedestal looking down upon the autographed gun boats

of Kareem Abdul-Jabbar and Shaquille O'Neal is Billy Cannon's
Heisman Trophy.

Moran beams. "Billy says it's real silver — not bronze like the
others — 'cause his trophy marked the silver anniversary of the
Heisman." We study the 36-pound striking sculpture of a running
back.

"How come it doesn't look silver?" I ask.

Moran frowns. "That's what Billy tells everybody." He pauses. "I
never really had it tested."

Well, actually, the trophy is kind of, sort of, but not really silver.
It's not even silver-plated. "It's what they call 'silverized,' or oxi-
dized," says Jamie Crimmins, athletic director of the New York
Downtown Athletic Club, which handles the Heisman Trophy
Award. "It cost $54 to have that silverizing done. But the last time I
saw Cannon's Heisman in the restaurant, the silverizing was gone
. . . worn off . . . maybe tarnished. It looked just like any other
Heisman Trophy."

Crimmins says it costs about $2,500 to make a Heisman. There is
no argument, however, that a memorabilia collector, particularly in
Louisiana, might pay far more for Cannon's Heisman.

Cannon's trophy first appeared in T.J. Ribs in 1986 — the year
the restaurant opened and Cannon was released from prison. It became common knowledge among Moran's friends that he bought
the Heisman from Cannon for an undisclosed amount.

Cannon bristles when asked if he sold his Heisman. He stares
sullenly, then angrily squirts an extra long stream of tobacco juice
into his bottle. His voice is edgy. "Let's just say it's being protected
[against creditors]."

I call Crimmins, the Heisman official. He groans. "Billy and I are
personal friends. I know he's got financial problems. But to put all
this in about the Heisman Trophy . . . this will open a can of worms.
I think, maybe, this was the kind of thing where he gets to eat a free
lunch."

Moran says, "I bought [the Heisman], but that's not for publication." Moran was told it's the worst-kept secret in Baton Rouge, and
Cannon won't deny it.

Moran grimaces. His voice drops. "Billy always lived in a world of
adulation. . . . The star. He won everything he ever tried. He felt he
could do anything he wants to do. He began doing things of his

own imagination. A lot of people 'took' him, and when it came to the nut-cutting, many bailed out."

Moran rethinks his comment. "Hey, Billy gave so much to this state and I think he deserved . . . he's a good family man, goes straight home at night . . . no drinking, no playing around."

Moran looks away. His voice turns hoarse. "Billy's so broke. He's going down. I promised him he's always got a place to stay . . . always will have three hots and a cot."

KENNY MOORE

The End of the World

FROM SPORTS ILLUSTRATED

WE BEGAN BY the Ethiopian central prison. We drove a dented 1967 VW Beetle slowly down a muddy, unmarked Addis Ababa street, passed the Libyan Embassy, turned right and tried not to stare at a haphazard compound of cement and corrugated sheet-metal buildings. Across the road, in the rain, goats and trucks bleated and brayed at each other. Men urinated against a wall. An arch marked the main gate. In the lee of a crumbling yellow plaster watchtower, a half-dozen guards wearing thin blue overcoats watched us go by, eyes instantly locked on the *faranjoch,* the foreigners. A thought came: the things you do for Olympic brotherhood.

Or maybe simply the idea of Olympic brotherhood. Captive inside the prison was a man I had not seen in twenty-three years. I had never had more than fragmentary conversations with him. We had simply raced each other in two Olympic marathons. Was it conceit to think because of that, I knew him? Knew him well enough to believe he couldn't possibly deserve to be there? Knew him well enough to try to outwit the Ethiopian prison system to get that simple message to him?

The man was Mamo Wolde, the 1968 Olympic marathon gold medal winner. Last May, Amnesty International revealed that in '92 Mamo had been rounded up with thousands of other Ethiopians suspected of involvement in the horrid human-rights abuses of the Communist regime that had been deposed the year before. He had been imprisoned, without having been formally charged with a crime, for the past three years.

Learning that, from a tiny item in the *Los Angeles Times,* had jerked me to my feet. *Mamo Wolde?* He and countryman Abebe Bikila were the greatest one-two punch in Olympic marathon history. Abebe won in Rome in 1960 (barefoot, finished in torchlight under the Arch of Constantine), and in Tokyo in '64 (shod, did calisthenics on the stadium infield after destroying the world best time), thereby beginning the great African distance running avalanche.

In Mexico City in 1968 a leg injury forced Abebe to drop out after ten miles. Mamo, who had already taken the silver in the 10,000 meters, won that marathon, making it three in a row for Ethiopia. I placed fourteenth in Mexico City, but I remember Mamo only as a black-and-green wraith, vanishing ahead after fifteen miles, his pace remorseless. He won by three minutes.

So the whole of our relationship was based on something that happened in the last eleven miles of the 1972 Olympic marathon in Munich. Mamo was so soundless of foot and breath that often I only knew he was running beside me by the sight of his distinguished widow's peak. With six miles to go, Frank Shorter was a minute ahead of us and increasing his lead. But when Mamo and I looked back, we seemed to have left the rest of the field behind.

We both run with our toes pointing out slightly, so at times our shoes brushed. "I'm sorry, I'm sorry," Mamo would say.

On a rough path in Munich's English Garden, with five miles to go, a dehydration cramp shot up my right hamstring. Mamo watched me slow and hop, grabbing my leg, and then he turned and ran on. He looked back one last time. This is what I cannot forget. *His face was filled with regret.* He seemed to be saying it wasn't supposed to happen this way. We were supposed to race on together, and the stronger would take the silver and the other the bronze. In fact, Belgium's Karel Lismont caught us both and finished second. Mamo got the bronze. I followed in fourth, on my twinging thigh, some thirty seconds behind, a gap that gave me a clear view of Mamo over the last couple of miles but no hope of catching him.

The postrace scene has long since taken on a strobe-light selectivity. I can clearly see how stunned Shorter was at winning. But I don't see Mamo. We must have shaken hands, congratulating, consoling, but if we did, the memory is gone.

*

I never saw Mamo again. He went home to Addis Ababa, where he had been promoted to captain in the Palace Guard of the aging Emperor Haile Selassie and was promised a nice house, like the one that had reportedly been given to Abebe before he died in 1973. Mamo never got it. In '74 Haile Selassie was overthrown by Ethiopian military leaders who, under Mengistu Haile Mariam, created a ruthless, hugely paranoid Communist government known as the Dergue, the Amharic word for committee.

Mengistu outlawed private land ownership and put collective urban planning under the authority of local councils called *kebeles*. This fueled resistance in northern Ethiopia's rural areas, and Mengistu met the opposition with terror. For seventeen years all human assembly was assumed to be subversive. Ethiopians needed written permission for a wedding party. Chatting on a street corner could lead to interrogation by council tribunals or Revolutionary Guards — armed citizen enforcers.

Ethiopians deemed disloyal were killed by the thousands. The Dergue reportedly made its morgues run at a profit. A family claiming the body of a loved one was charged ten Ethiopian birr ($1.60) for each bullet used in the execution. Since more holes meant more revenue, death squads reportedly were asked to observe a two-bullet minimum.

All this seemed to mean that Mamo, who had been identified with the deposed emperor, could be in great danger. Being an Olympic champion and a national hero does not ensure safety in a nation that is ruled by fear of counterrevolutions and whose leaders are always on the lookout for a rallying point for insurgency.

Yet Mamo was hardly that. He had never seemed a martial sort of man or even ambitious beyond his sport. He seemed to owe his captain's rank more to his Olympic success than to personal or political connections to Haile Selassie. He was not of a rebellious tribe. The only Ethiopians he seemed to want to inspire to action were his country's young runners, several of whom he coached. But so effectively did the Dergue embargo information that for years if I thought of Mamo at all, it was only to wonder what had become of him and benighted Ethiopia's incessant war, famine, and purge.

In May 1991 the Dergue, having lost military aid from the collapsing Soviet Union and East Germany, was overthrown by the Ethiopian People's Revolutionary Democratic Front. Mengistu, who was responsible — through his Red Terror and by blocking aid to famine victims — for hundreds of thousands of deaths, escaped to Zimbabwe.

In late 1991 the new Ethiopian government rounded up more than two thousand alleged officials of and collaborators with the Dergue, many of whom surely do deserve punishment for the regime's homicides. In this sweep, Mamo Wolde was caught up and imprisoned. In '92 Ethiopia created a Special Prosecutor's Office to investigate, charge, and bring to court the suspects. But in May of this year [1995] Amnesty International said that no charges had ever been filed against Mamo and that it had seen no evidence to suggest that he was implicated in human-rights abuses. Amnesty appealed to Ethiopia to either charge or release those in his situation. Ethiopia did neither. In August, Mamo was still confined in the Ethiopian central prison, in a section known as the End of the World. There he would sit, prosecutors had told Amnesty, until more important cases were dealt with. But Amnesty did not learn what crime, if any, Mamo was suspected of. Ethiopia was still being gallingly tightfisted with information. I started calling African contacts, trying to learn more.

I wasn't alone. After word of Mamo's plight got out, the International Olympic Committee and the International Amateur Athletic Federation (IAAF), the world governing body of track and field, demanded explanations from Ethiopian sports officials. But since those officials were also members of the Ethiopian government, they got back only hand-wringing. "We have been advised to await the verdict of the court," said Sibehat Belya, vice president of Ethiopia's National Olympic Committee. At the World Track and Field Championships in Göteborg, Sweden, in August, IAAF officials admitted that all they could do was inquire and exhort.

Whether they knew him or not, all the Olympians I spoke to were astounded to learn of an Olympic champion's imprisonment. Not that they felt a gold medal guaranteed moral perfection, but what is more at the heart of the Games than the forsaking of violence? So sacred did they hold the Olympic truce that the ancient Greeks put down their arms on the battlefield in the days of the Games. Who can look on an Olympic 100-meter final or heavyweight wrestling final and not see combatants subsuming the most powerful human ambitions into peaceful competition?

Such was the feeling of another 1972 Olympian, 800-meter bronze medalist Mike Boit of Kenya, who is now his country's commissioner for sports and represents Africa on the IAAF Athletes' Commission. I was in Göteborg covering the championships when I ran into Boit, who urged me to go to Ethiopia, try to see Mamo or at least discover all I could about his case and condition, then lay the information before the Athletes' Commission. "The combined voices of Olympians," he said, "must be heard."

So I flew to Addis Ababa, which is set 7,500 feet above sea level, on dark, hilly earth that was then being turned to black mud by cold rain. The essential fact of Ethiopia is that it is high, up to 10,000 feet above sea level. Its central mountains claw from the sky virtually every drop of moisture blown northwest from the Indian Ocean and so become the source of the Blue Nile. Their long rain shadow is the Sahara Desert.

Ethiopia is a country most known for its suffering and poverty, yet few people have a richer history than the Ethiopians do. They, perhaps fancifully, claim that the highlands were first settled by a great-grandson of Noah, named Ethiopic. Some ninety-seven generations later, his descendants were ruled by the queen of Sheba, who traveled to Jerusalem, bedded King Solomon, converted to Judaism, and bore him a son, Menelik. Menelik brought back to Ethiopia not only a thousand people from each of the twelve tribes of Israel, but also the Ark of the Covenant (What is said to be the Ark can be found this day in the St. Mary of Zion Church in Axum). Menelik was first in the Solomonic dynasty of emperors that ended some 237 monarchs later, with Haile Selassie.

Christianity, which arrived in Ethiopia in the fourth century, came under assault in the seventh century when the great plateau region was encircled but never conquered by Islam. For nearly a thousand years even the trade routes to the highlands were cut off by the stalemate between the forces representing the two religions. This long isolation produced, to many Western minds, one of the world's most feudal, xenophobic, argumentative cultures. British novelist Evelyn Waugh, who covered Haile Selassie's coronation in 1930, wrote of "the prevarications, the evasions . . . the lethargy and cunning. . . . Tricking the Europeans was a national craft."

These were the people I would persuade to let me visit their rejected national hero? *These* were the people who would tell me why he was locked up? Fortunately I was not alone. Antonin Kratochvil had flown in from Prague. A former Czech freedom fighter whose natural photographer's combativeness had been sharpened by life and work in repressive regimes, he was very clearly the right man for the job. Yet photographing the slaughter in Rwanda had made him sensitive to the ever-present possibility of violence. I said I trusted him to not take too many chances.

"Give me your little plastic camera," he said. "I can hide it in my scarf when we go to the prison."

Maybe trust is too strong a word.

Even before we left for Ethiopia, we were faced with a choice. Ethiopian Olympic officials wouldn't talk to us unless the Ministry of Information certified us as journalists. But once the government knew we were journalists, we assumed, there would be no way we were going to be allowed near a prison, let alone Mamo.

So we bagged the officials and came in on tourist visas. Kratochvil planned to say he was a designer and trainer. My pitch would be personal: as an old friend and competitor of Mamo's, I would say I was stopping over in Addis simply to see him and cheer him up.

I tried this out first in a phone call to the Special Prosecutor's Office. I was transferred to a prosecutor named Abraham Tsegaye. His English was precise, his tone unnervingly bland. He said that some trials of the architects of the Red Terror had begun but that the courts were in a "period of hiatus" to allow defense attorneys more time to prepare. At present, he said, there were 1,300 detainees. "No charges have been filed against Mamo Wolde," he said, "but we are preparing to make charges when the courts resume, perhaps in two or three months."

I took a breath and asked the crucial question: "What are you charging him with?"

"With taking part in a criminal act."

"What criminal act?"

"A killing. . . ."

I went queasy. I had come all this way on the strength of a backward glance. Suddenly it didn't seem such an ironclad guarantee of innocence. "What killing?"

"Mamo Wolde is suspected of being involved in killing one person while he served as a Dergue Revolutionary Guard."

"Revolutionary Guard? How could he have been a Dergue Revolutionary Guard? He was in Haile Selassie's Imperial Guard."

"The Imperial Guard was disbanded by the Dergue," said Abraham. "The Revolutionary Guard was then organized in 1975 along Communist lines to incite the public to 'defend' the revolution against its enemies. Mamo could have joined."

I grabbed at a straw. "What do you mean, 'could have'?" I said. "Did he or didn't he?"

"I don't know," said Abraham. "I'm basically a spokesman."

"Who accused Mamo of this crime?"

"The victim's family. Of the possibility of his collaboration with others."

"Was there a hearing before a judge?"

"Yes. . . . Well, perhaps not a hearing in the way you mean, with testimony. Our investigator gathered statements. Then the court sat with the investigator and Mamo Wolde and looked at the file and decided there were sufficient signs of his implication. So the court ordered him taken into custody."

"Did Mamo Wolde have access to a lawyer?"

"Not now. Not until he is charged."

"If I was detained for three years without charge, I'd sure have a lawyer."

"Well, in your country every time you shake hands with someone, you need a lawyer. In Ethiopia it is not such a way."

"Can you give me permission to visit Mamo?"

"I'm sorry. I don't have that authority."

He hung up. I must have looked ashen. Kratochvil brought me a glass of water and said prosecutors always put the worst face on things. Then he brightened. "Does Mamo have a wife?" he asked.

Mamo did indeed, and when we called her, she invited us to visit. So, on the last day of August, on a rocky lane not far off a main road, some children directed us to a door in a long, corrugated metal wall. As we pounded on it, the reverberations seemed to carry around the block.

A young man admitted us to a yard where corn and squash grew. He led us around a small house made of mud over a framework of sticks and held together with a coat of paint. In the back doorway, dressed in their Sunday best, were Mamo's wife, Aberash Wolde-Semhate, 24, and their 5-year-old daughter, Addiss Alem Mamo, and 3-year-old son, Tabor Mamo. Tabor's brave little handshake was cold and trembling. The young man who had let us in was Samuel, Mamo's 19-year-old son by his first wife, Aymalem Beru, who is now dead.

Inside we were shown to a dim sitting room. The wood floors were smooth and clean. Incense was in the air. Aberash poured us glasses of *talla,* a home-brewed beer. "If a guest does not accept the food and drink offered in an Ethiopian home," our interpreter had warned us, "the host feels so bad, it's like a natural disaster."

Aberash lifted her glass and solemnly apologized for Mamo's not being able to welcome me into his house. As we drank, I lifted my eyes and saw, hanging on the wall, Mamo's Olympic gold medal for the Mexico City marathon and his silver from the 10,000. The Munich marathon bronze was nowhere in sight.

"I am so thankful for this," Aberash said. "For your remembering that your runner friend still lives."

I admitted to her that I didn't really know Mamo that well. So Aberash opened a photo album and gave us a thumbnail sketch of her husband. He was born sixty-four years ago in Ada, about a marathon's distance southeast of Addis Ababa. He is a member of the Oromo tribe. "He is a *strict* [Ethiopian] Orthodox Christian," she says. "During the Dergue, party committee meetings were on Sunday mornings to keep members from going to church. Mamo solved that by going to church before dawn."

Aberash was introduced to Mamo seven years ago, shortly after his first wife died. "Before, when I was in school, I ran a little, not seriously," she said. "But I read about and I loved them, both of our heroes, Abebe Bikila and Mamo."

She dropped her eyes, a little embarrassed. I don't know what I expected to find in Mamo's home, but the simple, rustic room and Aberash's tender loyalty hardly seemed consistent with a totalitarian absentee master. I took heart, and I asked the questions that I feared the most.

"Had Mamo indeed been a Revolutionary Guard?"

"He told me he was nothing," said Aberash. "He was on a *kebele* committee — a committee for development — and also coached."

"The prosecutor's office said he will be charged in a killing," I told her. "Was he involved?"

"No," Aberash said. "No. Here is what happened. This was in 1975, at the height of the terror. Mamo said one night he was phoned by [a top *kebele* official] and ordered to put on his dress uniform, with his pistol, and go to a certain nightclub. Mamo thought this was protocol, that he was to meet an important visitor. When he got there, he saw that the official and some others had a boy with his hands tied. He was about 15. He might have been in some youth group fighting against the Dergue. The official ordered Mamo not to talk. Then the official and another man took the boy out and shot him. Then they told Mamo to go there, to the body of the boy. At first he refused, but at that time to refuse an official was to be dead yourself, so finally he went. The boy was dead. The official told Mamo to shoot the body again because there had to be two holes. The policy. Mamo said he went to three meters [ten feet] away and shot and purposely missed. Lots of people saw him miss. In 1992 many witnesses said Mamo didn't kill anybody. Only one accused him. The official who shot the boy wants to blame Mamo to save himself. But the prosecutors said they had to keep Mamo in detention until they bring charges. But they never do. He just waits."

As I listened, I looked again at Mamo's medals. The Mamo in Aberash's story had acted as I imagined I might act if plunged into a world of such choices. I began to revive a little.

Mamo had been receiving a small pension from his government service. When he was imprisoned, the money stopped. "I couldn't feed my children," said Aberash. "I applied to the athletics people, and now the IOC gives a little every month." Also, Samuel has dropped out of school and gotten a job as a welder's assistant.

Mamo was briefly allowed out of prison twice, once when he was ill and once when he told Aberash he thought he was being freed. Each time he stayed in Addis Ababa with his family. Each time he was re-arrested. In a way, this was the most galling thing I learned, since it seemed to prove that Mamo is no risk to flee his country. "He wants to go to trial," said Aberash. "He wants to clear his name."

If he has to wait, I wondered, why couldn't he wait at home?

Mamo's latest detention had lasted two years and six months by the time I arrived in Addis Ababa. His health had not been good. "He was very sick in prison, with bronchitis, liver and stomach problems," said Aberash. "He's lost a lot of hearing in one ear. He was in the prison hospital for a month and a half, in the winter."

Prison food is terrible, but families are allowed to bring supplemental rations four days a week. "On Tuesdays and Thursdays the guards take the food and tell me to leave," said Aberash. "But on Saturdays and Sundays family members can go in and see the prisoners for a few minutes. You are lined up in a field, six feet apart, with a fence in between. I think Saturday you should try to come along."

So Saturday at noon, loaded with chocolate, cookies and cigarettes for Mamo to use in barter, Kratochvil and I drove Aberash to the prison. She had warm chicken stew in a plastic carrier. She did not believe the prosecutor was being truthful when he told us that Mamo would soon be charged.

Outside the prison gate perhaps two hundred people — women and children and old men — were shuffling into one end of an open shed that had four long rows of benches. At the other end guards took names and allowed twenty people at a time to enter the prison. Through the open gate we could see them being searched. Kratochvil had my tiny panoramic camera hidden in his voluminous white scarf and was blazing away at the prison and the people.

Many of the visitors were obviously middle class. The children stared at the *faranjoch* out of wonder rather than want. Down the rows went urchins selling peanuts, bad fruit, and Olympic lottery tickets that had Abebe Bikila's picture on them. I bought five tickets for ten birr. The seller shook my hand and wished me luck. I began to feel a wild hope. We just might waltz in here.

But when we stood up with Aberash and the people near her and moved toward the gate, we were cut out as if we were hyenas among goats. A comely female guard explained to us that foreigners were simply never allowed to visit a prison. It was a matter of national security.

While Aberash was inside, the guard went on to say that the only one who could conceivably authorize our entry was the police commissioner. As we were asking his whereabouts, Aberash came out. There were tears in her eyes. "Mamo said to tell you that your remembering, your coming has restored his morale and his faith," she said evenly. "He feels both great happiness and sadness. Happy at your coming. Sad that he can't greet you properly."

I had the same emotions. It suddenly hit me what a long shot I must have seemed to him. Hell, what a long shot I really was. It was good to have let him know he wasn't forgotten, but I was damned if I was going to go home without seeing him now.

Working our way up the chain of command, we went to four

police stations in search of the commissioner. Our story became better with each telling, until Mamo and I were long-separated brothers. The higher their rank, the further out of the uniform the Ethiopian police officers were. The shift commander's candy-striped shirt was no match for his paunch. He had a Texas long-horn on his huge belt buckle. He told us that the commish wasn't available until Monday morning. We made an appointment.

The next day we gave Aberash and Samuel a lift back to the prison. Kratochvil had brought a larger camera this time, and he took a picture of Aberash in the waiting shed. His action was seen, and suddenly we were encircled by police. One of them kept re-peating that they'd had problems with people saying terrible things about their country. "Everybody in *every* country," guard after guard repeated, "*had* to know taking pictures of prisons and police stations was *forbidden*."

Kratochvil said he had not taken any pictures of the prison, just of Aberash, and offered them the film. They took it, but this did no good. One guard, a skinny, wasted man with a warped hand, kept yelling that we were incredibly cunning foreigners, and it was their duty to consider everything we said a lie and simply arrest us. Finding himself in the minority, he held out for summoning higher authority.

Aberash stood up for us so forcefully that she was instantly made to sit down in the waiting shed and was ordered to shut up. Calls were made, and we were told to wait. After half an hour Kratochvil, our interpreter and I were ordered in through the gate and put on a butt-polished wooden bench against a wall facing a sandy court-yard. "Now *we* are detained," said Kratochvil.

We waited. The prisoner's visiting family members were being searched in front of us. The female guards who were going over the female visitors were anatomically thorough, to the point of running a hand up under skirts and deep into crotches.

We waited. I told the members of my team that no one is as patient as a marathoner, and they should hang in. All nodded. I took myself literally and strove for that frame of mind you want in the first twenty miles: alert but with aggressiveness in check, anxi-eties suppressed. And as has been known to happen in a marathon, a familiar question arose: What the hell was I doing here?

The answer came more easily than it does on the road. I wasn't just hoping that Olympic commonality might mean something to some sadistic prison guards. I was trying to do a little good. I remembered what Irish miler Eamonn Coghlan had said to me a few years back, when I told him that I was envious of his sub-four-minute miles after he turned 40: "Runners don't exactly win men out of bondage. But journalists can."

Well, this was the first time I'd had a chance, so it didn't seem hard to discipline myself to be calm. Besides, how brutal could a night in an Ethiopian prison be when Mamo had done a thousand of them?

As if in answer, a guard loudly slammed a magazine into his AK-47 and watched our reaction. "So arrogant," whispered the interpreter.

I looked at the ground. If one of these guards had an accident with his gun, this tiny peak of black basalt protruding through red pumice could be the last thing I'd see. I am not an adrenaline junkie. It didn't take getting into this fix to teach me that risks have to be well justified. But once you are in a fix, it doesn't really matter whether your aim is noble or base; you have no choice but to see it through.

In my mind, I started listing recent events of suffering — the Serbs shelling the Sarajevo marketplace, Zaire's president trying to force a million refugees back into Rwanda, Kashmiri separatists decapitating a Norwegian tourist — as if to imply that Mamo's was but a drop in the bucket, that his suffering was not worthy of real sacrifice to alleviate.

This was a sign that my nerve was eroding exactly the way it does in a long, hard marathon. Your thoughts turn fatalistic. There is no hope of winning now, you think. It's as good as over. Why keep hurting?

This you learn to fight. It's never over. If you can't win, you can pass someone. If you can't finish, you can shoot for the next aid station, and then the next. So I tore my thoughts from hopeless mass misery and fixed them on Mamo Wolde, the specific, fragile, 64-year-old man locked in a cage a hundred yards away, and I was back running with him in Munich. This time, when my cramp hit, when he turned and winced, I imagined him finding words. "Hold on," he said to me. "Hold on."

Suddenly a four-door pickup roared in, and a young man with a leather jacket and blue suede shoes got out and inspected us. This was someone who identified himself simply as Major Neguesse, and all around deferred to him. The whites of his eyes were the color of strawberry jam. We explained everything all over again to him, after which he went inside and called his superior.

We waited. It seemed a good sign when a uniformed guard moved us into the shade on the other side of the courtyard. But from there the interpreter could hear the insatiable hunger for our heads expressed by the man with the crippled hand.

We'd been held for four hours. It clouded over. We were moved back across the courtyard. They kept asking for our passports. We kept saying we'd left them at our hotel.

Over the wall wafted the melodic voices of a women's choir from the nearby Ethiopian Orthodox church. Amid their angelic music, our salvation arrived, in the person of a man introduced to us as Captain Shanbel, maybe 35, with a pointed, freckled nose. He was holding a hissing walkie-talkie. In English he told us that we had to prove who we were. We asked him to let us go get our passports at the hotel. He said we could, with an escort.

Outside the gate Aberash and Samuel were still waiting. They were told to go home, so they watched us set off across Addis Ababa with a policeman in the back seat of our car and a huge armored vehicle with half a dozen officers in it right behind. You should have seen the face of the Hilton doorman when we pulled in.

As Kratochvil and I ran inside, Kratochvil dashed ahead and was safely up in an elevator before officers Neguesse and Shanbel caught up with me in the lobby. By the time they'd accompanied me to my room, appropriated my passport and told me that I had nothing to worry about as long as my papers were in order, Kratochvil had already flushed the undeveloped film of the previous day's photos of the prison. The officers took his camera for good measure. We said we would see them on the morrow, and then spent an hour calling everyone we knew. We tried to sound calm. We've, uh, been in the prison and, uh, they held us all day, and now they have our passports. If you don't hear from us, say, by tomorrow night, you probably should contact the United States Embassy. . . .

We got up early the next day and drove through mists to the office of the police commissioner, who took one look at us and said he wouldn't be responsible for *faranjoch*. Be serious. We had to go to the Ministry of Internal Affairs. The interpreter swallowed hard.

The downstairs courtyard at the ministry looked like a crowd scene from *Gandhi*. Hundreds of rain soaked people were mobbing the office that issued exit visas. By contrast, the tiny office for foreigners had cobwebs on the desk. We were sent upstairs to a room where the sign on the door read only THE CHIEF. It had bustling secretaries. The power went out. The secretaries opened the curtains. The power returned. After an hour we were ushered in.

The chief was Internal Affairs Minister Mahete. She wore a red dress. Her angular face was forceful, and she looked a little sour, perhaps because on her desk was a volume titled *Immigration Laws of the United States*.

As the interpreter made our pitch, I tried to seem nonthreatening. I must have looked like one of the kids begging at the stoplights. She stopped the interpreter, made some calls, shook her head, called in a secretary and dictated a three-sentence letter to the prison authorities. She had given me permission to see Mamo.

At the prison we held her letter before us like a cross toward a vampire. The gate rolled open. The guards who had hassled us the day before looked at the document and fell back against the walls. We were given an escort down a stony path. The buildings — one with no roof — were spread apart, with weedy land between.

Major Neguesse bowed us into his office. He gave us back our passports and camera. His eyes were still red, but now he looked almost friendly. He said he hoped we understood that they had only been doing their duty. We understood.

"Well, then, let us see your friend."

A cluster of guards led us down a sloping path toward a two-story building that could have been an old theater. Wooden rails on posts ran out under an awning from its double doors, as if to keep a great many men in line. No prisoners could be seen, only guards. I peered in through the doors. A staircase led up. Guards were coming down it, and among them was a slender man in a green and white sweater and a distinguished widow's peak.

I threw aside my guards. He fought through his. He and I embraced on the steps. He was bony through the sweater, but warm and strong. And excited. "It all comes back," he said. "I remember you had a goatee."

"I thought you would be gray."

"Thank you, thank you from my family for this. Remember me to the brothers, the Olympic brothers."

"You *are* remembered," I said. I told him I was carrying the best wishes of the IOC, the IAAF and at least a dozen friends from the Olympic movement, as well as a standing invitation to be grand marshal of the Honolulu Marathon, back in the islands where I now live. As the list went on, he lifted his eyes and arms. "These are words from God," he said.

I hugged him again. He didn't seem bruised. He had on flip-flops and blue socks. I said, "We just have to get you out of here."

"This is a good government now," he said, an eye going to the listening guards. "It will release me soon, I'm sure. It will see that the charge was false. It will realize it was a bad man trying to save himself."

"Is there anything that you need?"

"I never got my house from the emperor. I had to live all these years in the mud house you saw. All I need in the world is to get out, remake it in stone, and live with my children in safety."

We had maybe eight minutes together. A guard must have given Mamo a sign, but I didn't catch it. He took my forearms in his hands. "It restores my soul," he said. "It is something I can feel in my body, that people outside the country remember." Then they led him back upstairs.

Later I would call prosecutor Abraham once more. He now felt Mamo might be charged "before the end of the year." Every time I asked, it seemed, the date receded further.

Granting that Mamo had to stand trial, I said, could he not be bailed out in the interim? The prosecutor replied that Mamo's was not a "bailable offense."

"It's been three years," I said. "Doesn't the Ethiopian constitution guarantee a speedy trial?"

"It does," he said. "But it doesn't say *how* speedy. Remember, we are investigating a government that conducted systematic, state-supported human-rights abuses for seventeen years. So guarantees of rights may not apply in these extraordinary circumstances. But I assure you, the delay is not intentional. It's simply budgetary. We have so few resources."

I was inclined to believe him. But I was also emboldened, by my sharpened sense of the man Mamo Wolde is, to include in this account the prosecutor's telephone number and address (011-251-1-120-828, or P.O. Box 6842, Addis Ababa), so that the world's Olympians and human-rights activists might respectfully remind Ethiopia that justice delayed is justice denied.

There was a feast that night at Mamo's house. Aberash, who had been astounded at our success, prepared traditional *injera*, a wheel of spongy, sour, fermented bread made from a grain called *teff*. This we used to sop up several kinds of *wat* (stew). The *talla* flowed, and at the end Aberash performed an elaborate coffee ritual, roasting the beans on the charcoal brazier, grinding them in a mortar. and then putting them in a pot on the same coals.

While she waited for the coffee to strengthen, she warmed frankincense in a little clay pot. The children crept quietly into the fragrant room. The rain rang on the roof. Even Kratochvil seemed to be at peace, although he had revealed that he had taken my little disposable camera in his pocket into the prison, and that it had practically killed him not to be able to photograph my reunion with Mamo.

It seemed absurd then that I had thought that coming here had been some sort of moral risk. We were Olympians, Mamo and I. In the rage of competition we had obeyed the rules. We had each denied the voice of our inner killer and settled things the honorable way. I had always known that much about him, and it was always ample reason to press his captors for fairness.

The traditional Ethiopian coffee service has three rounds. We drank two and left the third, to symbolically ensure our return.

I closed my eyes, savoring, and in that moment I saw Mamo again, in his threadbare sweater, going up those prison stairs. But this time I was the one to turn around and give the long look back. This time, I was the one to cry out that this is wrong, to tell him that this isn't the way things should be happening.

JOEL REESE

Down and Out

FROM TEXAS MONTHLY

GOLDEN RICHARDS HAD been my hero for eighteen years. When I was a tow-headed kid growing up in the suburbs of Chicago, the blond wide receiver for the Dallas Cowboys was my idol. With his blazing speed, quick hands, and yellow hair, in the words of one fawning article, "splaying from beneath his helmet like dried palm fronds," John Golden Richards was proof to me that perfection existed. He was the fair-haired boy on America's Team. He made acrobatic, one-handed catches and cuts and fakes that left corner-backs grasping at air. He caught the 32-yard touchdown on the second play of the Cowboys' 1977 conference championship against the Minnesota Vikings. He caught the game-clinching touchdown pass against the Denver Broncos in Super Bowl XII. Tossed not by quarterback Roger Staubach but by fullback Robert Newhouse, it was the first running-back-option pass completed for a touchdown in Super Bowl history. God had smiled on Golden Richards. And I loved him. I owned every one of his football cards and had memorized his stats and birthday (December 31, 1950). When I was a kid, my bedroom walls were plastered with newspaper articles, his name underlined in shaky red marker. And the adulation didn't stop at adolescence. Even after he retired — a couple of seasons after the Cowboys traded him to the Chicago Bears — I bought a Bears jersey that bore the number 83. Sometimes, when I was feeling low, I looked at the Golden Richards football card I always carried in my wallet. For years I fantasized about meeting Golden.

Now I was writing an article about him and his career and what had happened to him since retiring. He had been arrested on

December 14, 1992, for forging checks he had stolen from his
father to buy prescription narcotics. I read incredulously of his
arrest on a cold December morning during my first year of graduate school in journalism at the University of Montana. In the sports
section of the *Missoulian* was a one-paragraph story that said Gold-
en had no money, no job, and no place to live and had lost everything because of his addiction to pills. About a year later, my thesis
adviser approved a story about how Golden had gone from catching a Super Bowl touchdown to being arrested for forgery. After
many phone calls, I found him and persuaded him to talk to me,
and here I was, with Golden on a sunny winter afternoon in 1994 in
his hometown of Salt Lake City. We were in his car; the plan was to
drive around Salt Lake City, and he, the second eldest of six boys
and one girl from a good Mormon family, would show me the high
school where he had established his reputation as one of the best
athletes Utah has ever produced. He had played for the Granite
Farmers, competing in football, basketball, track, and he almost
single-handedly won the state track meet for Granite in 1969. He
had also excelled at football, playing half-back and returning punts,
running toward the end zone, which was painted with a golden G
for Granite. He scored five touchdowns in his first game. In high
school he dated his eventual wife, the beautiful Barbara Johnson.

But that was long ago. Golden had since been through rough
times. He had been addicted to painkillers for years. His life had
been a series of turns for the worse — rehabilitation efforts (including Alcoholics Anonymous) followed by relapses, near-over-
doses, and drinking binges. Golden spent a week in jail for the
forgery after being arraigned on his forty-second birthday. Apart
from the forgery arrest, I had a vague idea, at the time of our
meeting, of the extent of Golden's troubles. I forgot about my
disappointment in him because I was riding with him in his wife's
car — his third wife. He was driving, and I was asking questions.

"Goddam, my radiator light is on," he said. "We need to go get
some water."

He pulled into a gas station and parked by the water hose, in
front of the pay phone. We went inside and he bought a monster Pepsi. We went out to the car and he opened the hood. He
unscrewed the radiator cap. Green antifreeze dribbled onto the
ground. "No problem there," he said. He slammed the hood shut

and turned toward me. "Say, listen, my teeth are killing me," he said, looking away, his sunglasses reflecting the passing cars. "My dentist said it's from being knocked around so much on Sundays. I've had three root canals. I can't go in to see him until tomorrow. I took some Tylenol this morning, but it's not working. Do you have any painkillers, Tylenol 3, or anything like that?"

Warning lights went off in my head. Last night at his apartment, Golden had told me about his addiction to painkillers but said he was clean and everything was O.K. Now he was asking me for pills.

"I don't have anything like that," I said.

"Do you think your friend does?" he asked, referring to Sean, the guy with whom I was staying but did not know very well.

"I don't know. I don't know if he's around," I said.

"Can you give him a call and see if he's home?" he said, pulling a quarter out of his pocket. The moment hung there. Golden held out the quarter. I knew I should say no, forget it, this makes me really uncomfortable. But I wanted to cooperate with him so he would cooperate with me. I wanted him to like me. I took the coin and dialed. I wanted Golden to step away so I could fake the call, but he stayed, leaning over my shoulder. I could smell the leather of his bomber jacket. His face was yellowish, and the hands that had cradled so many touchdowns clasped the metal edges of the phone booth.

"Hello, Sean? Listen, I'm with Golden and his teeth are really hurting. Do you have any prescription stuff? Tylenol 3?"

"I don't know. Let me look," Sean said. He put the phone down.

"What's he doing? Is he checking?" Golden asked. "Let me talk to him," and he took the phone from my hand. "What's this guy's name?" he asked. I told him.

"Hey, Sean, Golden Richards here. How you doin'? Listen, my teeth are really bad and I need something for 'em . . . Mepergan? What's that? . . . O.K. . . . Well, listen, buddy, I'd be glad to reimburse you for them . . . You sure? . . . O.K., buddy, well, listen, what do you do? . . . Photography? Hell, buddy, I can set you up, get you all sorts of jobs taking pictures of sports teams and stuff like that . . . I'd be glad to help you out."

We drove to Sean's apartment. He wasn't home, so I used the key he had given me. Golden went to the dining room table, where Sean had left the pills. He looked at the label. "You think he has

anything else?" he asked, his eyes flitting around the apartment. He
still wouldn't look at me.

"I don't know," I said.

"He said there might be more in the bathroom. Where's the
bathroom?" he asked.

"Down the hall and to the left."

Golden went down the hall. I heard him rummaging through the
medicine cabinet.

When I first met with Golden the night before, everything had
been perfect. It was our get-acquainted night, his chance to check
out this guy who had driven nine hours from Missoula, Montana, to
probe into his life. I had traveled down Interstate 15 through Dil-
lon, Montana, spending an unexpected night in a motel because
the temperature on the Monida Pass was 40 below and the wind
had reached 70 miles per hour. The next day was clear and crisp,
the sky gleaming blue as I drove into Murray — five miles south of
Salt Lake City — where Golden lived.

I was speechless when Golden Richards opened the door with a
handshake and a "glad to meet you, Joel." Here was the man I had
idolized like a father since the age of ten. He looked a little hag-
gard; his eyes were not as sharp as I had thought they would be, and
he moved slowly. He was still trim and immediately friendly, but his
skin had the leathery look of someone who smokes too much and
sleeps too little, perhaps an effect of having been addicted to painkillers, off and on, for more than twenty years. He looked smaller
than his six-foot height and wore new-looking Wrangler blue jeans
and a button-down white cotton shirt. He invited me into the tidy
apartment. We sat across from each other in the living room, whose
windows looked out onto the Wasatch Mountains, the room glow-
ing orange in the sunset. On a shelf next to a small plaster Jesus
were pictures of him and his new 25-year-old wife sitting by a tree.
We went out to his porch and he smoked a cigarette — something
he said maybe I shouldn't mention because he didn't want to be a
bad influence on kids.

We talked about current events, a recently signed Middle East
peace accord, and his career in sports. Coming out of college, he
had assumed that he would have to make it into the NFL as a free
agent, which he was prepared to do. He had been surprised when

the Cowboys traded for an earlier pick in the 1973 NFL draft so they could choose him in the second round, ahead of eventual teammate and Super Bowl Most Valuable Player Harvey Martin, as well as Dan Fouts, Tom Jackson, and Joe Ferguson. He would join the Cowboys to replace Bob Hayes, the player everyone knew as "the world's fastest man." In college Golden had idolized Hayes and had worn number 22 because it was Hayes's number. He talked about his greatest moments in the NFL. "Everyone assumes my most memorable moment was the Super Bowl, but it wasn't," he said. "It was every time it was 3rd and 6 and I caught an 8-yard out to keep the drive going. The camaraderie in the huddle. Those plays are the most memorable."

Golden was pretty calm, but he drank several Pepsis while we talked. He accidentally kicked his cup and spilled brown cola on the rug. "Shiite Muslims," he said as he dodged into the kitchen to get some paper towels. He was articulate and thoughtful and was open about his past drug use. He occasionally clucked his tongue and shook his head. "The crazy days of the NFL," he said with a slight smile. He sat back and looked at me as I talked, listening and thinking before answering. He asked about my life, how I ended up here, why I chose him as my favorite player.

"I guess it was the hair," I said after a moment. "And everyone told me I looked like you."

"Yeah, I can see that," he said.

I took out the yellowed *Chicago Tribune Magazine* I had kept since the age of 10 — dated November 5, 1978 — which featured a cover story on Golden after he was traded from the Cowboys to the Bears. We realized that I was nearly the same age, 27, as he was in the picture on the cover, looking evenly into the camera, football tucked under his right arm. He had been traded to the Bears after the Super Bowl season; he told me he was traded for first- and second-round draft picks and the Cowboys had to shut down the switchboard after the trade because the team was inundated with angry calls. He talked about how he got hooked on drugs, said the Cowboys had started him on painkillers to keep him playing. "I went to my doctor in Salt Lake because I felt so damn terrible," he said. "I thought I had the world's worst flu. The doctor asked me if I was on any medication. I told him, 'Not anymore.' He asked what I had been taking, and I told him I didn't know. He asked what it looked

like. I told him it was yellow and said 135 and 'endo.' He sat back
and said, 'You're going through withdrawal.'"

That's where the struggle began, but it was over now, he said. He
brought out his four-month-old son, Jay Golden, and talked lov-
ingly to him. "You're going to do anything you want, little man,
aren't you," he cooed. "I'm not going to make you do anything. I'm
not going to be one of those Little League dads who lives through
his son. Look at these hands," he said, gently holding his son's tiny
palms. "Look at the size of these mitts. He's going to be slam-dunk-
ing soon."

By the time I left, Golden and I were buddies. "We'll see you
tomorrow, young man," he said, clapping me on the back. He
waved before he closed the door. He was all right. He had been to
the bottom — one would be hard-pressed to think of something
lower than stealing checks from one's own father to buy pills — but
he was back. He told me that he was going to be starting a job that
week analyzing data for a California-based health-products company. He was back on track, and I was happy for him.

As I drove through Salt Lake City, the sun set and the evening
breeze blew through my hair. I tuned the radio to the local college
station. "Heroes" by David Bowie came on. "We can be heroes, just
for one day," the Thin White Duke sang. "We can be us, just for
one day."

But that was last night. Now Golden came out of Sean's bathroom, holding the bottle of pills. "They don't have anything else,"
he said. He went to the phone and called a pharmacy — a number he apparently had memorized — to find out about Mepergan
(a brand of meperidine also marketed under the familiar name
Demerol), which is a narcotic painkiller combined with an antihis-
tamine. He asked a couple of questions, then hung up, and we left
Sean's apartment to tour Salt Lake City. He drove. I tried to put the
incident behind me.

We drove around the city and he showed me the large pink house
where his parents live, the fields where he and his brothers had
played football, where he had learned the moves that made him a
star in high school. He suggested that I write his memoirs. "Tarnished Thoughts About Golden Times," he said he wanted to call it.
"We'll get you some real money, get some shoes to replace those

Converse," he said with a smile, referring to my ratty white canvas hightops. I laughed and blushed, but the morning's events hung in the air between us. We drove up to a quiet, exclusive cul-de-sac and he pointed out a large brown house where he and Barbara, his first wife, lived back in the good days. I asked him about his second wife and what had happened with her. He began a rambling tale about how she had attacked him one night and then called the police. "It was the craziest damn thing," he said. His voice slowly got softer and raspy, and I could barely hear him. He wasn't making much sense. He talked for several minutes, then asked me, "What was the question again?" He kept licking his lips.

"You were talking about your second wife," I said.

"Oh, right. Yeah, that was a messy situation. Boy, I tell you . . ." Then he was mumbling again. He appeared to be lost and kept turning into dead-end streets and stalling the car. He pulled into a strip mall to go into a video store and I followed him.

"Say, how much money do you have?" he asked. "I'm just wondering because, you know . . ." he said, trailing off.

In the store he seemed to grab boxes at random and stare at them, his mind not processing the cover of *Weekend at Bernie's*. Something was definitely off, but I hadn't seen him take any of the pills, and I had been with him the whole time.

Golden grabbed *For the Boys*, with Bette Midler, and a Nintendo hockey game and walked unsteadily to the counter. "Do you want the instructions for that?" the teenage cashier asked him.

"What?"

"The instructions. For the game," the kid said, his gum clicking in his mouth.

"What?"

"This here. This is a Nintendo game, a cartridge."

"Oh," Golden said, holding the cartridge up in front of his face. "No, I don't want this." He tossed two crumpled bills onto the counter and we walked out. I carried the movie.

I went out to the car and turned, and he was still standing on the curb. He looked pale in his jeans and bomber jacket, mouth open, knees slightly bent, legs bowed like an old cowboy's. He tried to put his sunglasses in his shirt pocket, swiping repeatedly and missing the pocket each time. He wobbled to the car and got behind the wheel. His skin was chalky.

"Why don't you let me drive?" I said.

"No, I'll be fine," he said. He couldn't get the key into the ignition, again and again stabbing the steering column.

He did get the car started but stalled it there in the parking lot, then finally got out onto a road. He was weaving, crossing the center line. Suddenly he pulled into the parking lot of an office complex. He parked and we sat there, silent. Finally, I mustered the courage to ask, "Are you feeling O.K.?"

He was leaning back in his seat, eyes closed, mouth agape. "I'm just kind of like, I don't know," he said. "The rest of my head."

I asked, "Golden, how many of those pills . . ."

"Say, do you want a cold drink?" he asked, motioning toward a restaurant at the end of the lot.

That was a coherent sentence, I thought. Maybe he's O.K. "No, thanks."

The car started rolling toward the restaurant. I looked over at him. Golden's eyes were shut, his head lolling backward. He was blacking out.

"Golden, better hit the brakes. You're about to hit that wall."

"Oh, shit," he said, slamming on the brake pedal.

"Say, how many of those pills . . . How many did you take, a bunch of 'em?" I asked.

"I just, I don't know," he said. "I felt crazy, like jumping right through that window . . ." His head tilted back again.

"Why don't I drive?" I said. "It looks like you're getting sleepy there."

". . . blinding in my eye, can't function," he said. "O.K."

I got out and walked around to the driver's door and helped him out. He was no longer a man; he was a drowsy, disoriented child. He held onto the car as he walked around the back. He stopped and bent over the license plate. "Is this the kind you punch?" he asked.

"Um, no," I said.

The engine sputtered as I drove. "How many of those pills did you take?" I asked. "The ones we got at the apartment."

"When you're an addict, you have to take all of them," he said, suddenly semi-lucid.

"Do you think of yourself as an addict?"

"No, not really," he said, head back against the headrest. His eyes drifted shut.

I drove in silence, looking over at him occasionally to see how he was doing. "They could come in, o-and-25, and beat the Cowboys," he mumbled.

"Who's that?" I asked.

"The Rangers," he said.

I got to his apartment complex, helped him up the stairs to his apartment, and sat down on his couch. I checked his jacket and found the pill bottle in the front left pocket. It was empty. Golden was crawling on all fours in front of the couch. I ran into the bedroom, called an emergency hotline, and told the attendant what had happened. "Where is he now?" the attendant asked.

"He's on the floor of his living room."

"Go see if he's still breathing."

My God. "O.K." I ran back to the living room and Golden was passed out in the classic drunk position: face down on the carpet, arms at his sides, knees bent. I leaned over and heard breath rasping out of his mouth. His hair hung around his purplish face and his eyes were shut. I ran back to the phone.

"Yes, he's still breathing."

"O.K. Call 911 immediately."

The paramedics arrived a few minutes later. One went over to Golden and started taking his vitals. I leaned against the wall, unable to watch. His blood pressure was 170 over 110. "His pupils are unreactive and constricted," a paramedic said. They put oxygen tubes up his nose. They sat him up and asked him if he had taken any pills.

"No, sir," he said, squat on the floor, legs flat in front of him.

"What day is it — Monday, Tuesday — what day is it?" one asked him.

"Tuesday," he said. His eyes rolled back. It was Saturday.

"Be straight with us here, Golden," one said. "What's going on?"

"In regards to what?" Golden asked.

"In regards to why we're here. They said you were unconscious on the floor."

"Probably a woman said that," Golden said, his head falling backward, then snapping back to attention.

"You weren't unconscious on the floor?" the paramedic asked.

"That'd be one two three one one five," Golden said.

"His eyes keep going back," another paramedic said. "Bring the stretcher up. He's going to go."

One of the paramedics looked at the picture of Golden catching a touchdown for the Cowboys and said, "This Golden Richards?"

"Yeah," the other responded.

"This is sad," the first one said.

"This is really sad," the other said.

I felt hot, fat tears roll down my cheeks. Golden lay there on the stretcher as they wheeled him out, eyes wild and uncomprehending, blue tubes up his nose. I followed as they took him to the ambulance, the neighbors looking at us from their porches. A round-faced policeman started grilling me, asking me how he got the pills.

"I got them for him," I said.

"You got them for him?" he asked. "Why? Did he pay you? Who are you?"

He's going to arrest me, I thought. He thinks I'm Golden's pusher.

"Look, I got them for him because he said his teeth hurt," I said. "I didn't know. I wanted to help him. I'm his biggest fan."

I drove to the hospital and joined his wife, Amy, her son, and her dad in the emergency room. We sat there against the wall, under the stifling fluorescent lights, playing with Jay Golden's hands. "This is it," she said to her dad. "He's going to Arizona," referring to a rehab center there. I didn't much feel like it, but I asked her a couple of questions about Golden, how long he had been straight, how many times this had happened before. I thought I should act like a reporter.

"I don't know," she answered to each one. "I guess it's safe to say I don't know my husband very well," she said with a nervous laugh.

I left the hospital and drove back to Sean's apartment, my face slick and sticky and my hands shaking. I remember trying to pinpoint when Golden took the pills and thinking he must have taken them in Sean's bathroom. That night, Golden called me. "Say, sorry about today," he said. "Thanks for your help."

"That's all right," I said.

"Yeah, the doctors don't know what the hell happened. They said it was either a grand mal seizure or an allergic reaction."

"Golden, I found the empty bottle in your coat."

He paused for a moment. "Well, I don't know what the hell's going on," he said. "But it wasn't the pills."

*

In the life of Golden Richards, there are two realities: his and everyone else's. His story must be told by others because by the end of my interviews with him, I found much of what he said to be untrue. It begins, as one might expect, with an idyllic youth. When I talked to his high school coaches or his Scout master, they became hyperbolic. "He was a great kid, a really great kid," said Hal Erickson, his track and basketball coach. "I thought the world of him. We were all his fans." Golden's Scout master, Rita Reese (no relation to me), said the young Golden sticks out in her memory. She remembered Golden's grandfather standing up at Golden's twelfth birthday — when Mormon males receive the priesthood — and saying: "If ever there was an appropriately named young man, Golden is it." She added, "He was a totally golden person. And I could have stood up and said, 'Hear, hear.'"

After dazzling his elders with his athletic feats at Granite High, Golden went on to Brigham Young University in Provo in 1969. On a sunny afternoon on BYU's beautiful campus at the foot of the Wasatch Range, it is easy to see why Golden was so revered. Young men with their hair neatly parted stroll around with backpacks casually flung over their shoulders, looking like they just stepped out of an Eddie Bauer catalog. Women in white shorts and gray BYU sweatshirts smile warmly. It seems a natural environment for a charismatic, handsome guy like Golden Richards. He ran the 40-yard dash in 4.2 seconds and, with his fleetness, set records that stand today. He racked up 219 punt-return yards against North Texas State in 1971. That season he compiled a nation-leading 624 return yards and returned 4 punts for touchdowns. He caught 36 passes in 1970 and 14 in 1971, leading the team in receptions both years.

But Golden said he got tired of the run-oriented offense of the team and transferred to the University of Hawaii in 1972, where he caught 23 passes for 414 yards and 5 touchdowns before injuring his knee. Every article I've ever read about him says he transferred because he wanted more passes. But BYU coach LaVell Edwards said it wasn't the offense that compelled Golden to move from Provo to Honolulu. "It was grades," Edwards said. "He had difficulty keeping his eligibility because he didn't attend classes conscientiously. He flunked out of school."

A 1972 BYU press guide backs Edwards's claim: "It's the unexpected losses that are painful, and the Cougars experienced a major setback with the departure of Golden Richards, an academic casualty."

I talked to Golden on the phone twice after his apparent overdose, visiting him again a couple of months later. He was still friendly, but edgy and hurried. I was no longer just a worshiping fan; I was someone who had seen him zonked on pills. Predictably, the interview wasn't easy. I asked him about the grades. "I've heard that — it's a bunch of bullshit," he said. "I had a B average and twenty-three more credits than I needed as a junior. That's a verifiable fact."

I told him that the BYU press guide does verify a fact, but not his way.

"Look, why would I be eligible at Hawaii and not BYU? They're in the NCAA. It doesn't make any sense."

But there was a provision at the University of Hawaii stating that athletes who transferred there didn't have to sit out a year before playing, as they do at most other schools. Golden spent most of his year at Hawaii recovering from a knee injury. He thought the injury would keep him from being drafted, but Tex Schramm, the Cowboys' general manager and president from 1960 to 1989, says he was at Golden's big game against North Texas and was awed by Golden's speed. "We were always looking for speed in receivers, and Golden had that speed," Schramm said. "He was so fast. And he could use it on the football field. That's an important difference between a track man and a football player. Some can't use their speed on the field, but he could."

It was a natural match. The golden boy packed his bags and went to Dallas to play football in front of the world-famous shimmying Dallas Cowboys cheerleaders and 65,000 rabid fans. The Cowboys had lost the 1971 Super Bowl to the Baltimore Colts on a last-second field goal, then rolled over Miami in 1972, and the city was hungry for another win. "He had the name and the long, flowing hair," said Frank Luksa, a columnist for the *Dallas Morning News* who covered the Cowboys for fifteen years. "He was very highly regarded and people liked him. They liked his playing style — he was undersized but fast and an underdog figure in a game where everyone was bigger than he was."

The veterans on the team were skeptical of this new guy with the

122 Down and Out

hair and the quick feet. And then the name. Sure he was fast, but Golden Richards? "I always wondered, was that his real name or his stage name?" asked Thomas Henderson, who was known as Hollywood in the glory days and was famous for dunking the ball over the goal post. "They loved him in Dallas. You know, he was *Golden Richards*. He had a choice of women he could see. The golden boy, from Paul Hornung to him, has always been a kind of wonderment for white athletes. With a name like 'Golden,' being the golden wide receiver on America's Team — he fit perfectly."

Golden captivated the city, and indeed the nation. Barbara says that at one point he was receiving a thousand pieces of fan mail a week from all over the country. He was doing commercials. He told me about trysts with cheerleaders and pop singers (never during his marriage, though). He hung out with Kris Kristofferson and Willie Nelson. Charity work. Celebrity golf outings. Speaking engagements. He and Roger Staubach were the most-requested Cowboys to speak at banquets.

He could play too. Mike Ditka, who was then the wide-receiver coach for Dallas, said Golden was a real talent his first few years. "He made some great catches," Ditka said. "He was a great player. He practiced very hard. And he hit people too. One game he knocked . . . what was that guy's name, number 46 on the Bears?"

"Doug Plank?"

"Yeah, Plank. He knocked Plank right on his ass. And Plank was a big guy."

"There was certainly greatness in Golden Richards," said Danny White, the quarterback who succeeded Roger Staubach in Dallas. "He was with the Cowboys when I got there in 1976. I was like a little kid around his heroes — Staubach, Lee Roy Jordan, Tony Dorsett. Golden Richards was one of those guys."

There is one particular catch that comes to mind. It's a Monday night game, the Cowboys are playing the Kansas City Chiefs in Dallas, and Staubach tosses a bullet from about the Chiefs' 26-yard line toward the end zone. Golden is running across the back line, and it looks as if Staubach has thrown it over Golden's head, but Golden leaps, extending fully, and tips the ball with his left hand. He and the football move parallel toward the back of the end zone, the ball end over end and Golden in an extended tumble, arms outstretched. Half-falling, half-diving, Golden gathers the ball in his left hand just before he hits the ground. He pulls it to his chest and slides along the AstroTurf, coming to a stop with his silver pants on the blue end-zone carpet, white jersey on the white out-of-bounds paint. Two officials shoot their arms skyward. The crowd roars. In 1989 the catch is chosen by fans as the second best in Monday night history — second to a catch made by a man who played in the NFL for one week.

But two words made themselves a part of Golden's life, two words that come into the life of every pro football player: "pain" and "fear." Golden had messed his knee up good at Hawaii — he said the doctors told him he would never walk without a limp, let alone play football again. He overcame that, but the knee never was quite the same. And he may as well have gone onto the field with a bull's-eye painted on his chest. He was just the kind of guy defenders hated. Cliff Harris, the Cowboys' free safety for ten years, says he was good friends with Golden, but he would have gone after him if they had been on opposing teams. "Wide receivers love to think of themselves as having more refined skills, of being more proper," said Harris, who now works with an insurance company in Dallas. "They hated it when you hit them because it would mess them up, mess up their socks, which were pulled up just right. And Golden fit that profile. You've got a tough guy's sport, and you've got a guy with flowing blond hair who is fast and fragile playing a tough guy's sport. And the fans loved it. But the players wanted to crunch a guy like that."

All that crunching took a toll. There were stinging blows to the ribs, back, legs, and face. The Golden face. Bad teeth run in the Richards family, but Golden's were worse. He had a series of root canals and countless trips to the dentist. The pain, for a man who admittedly has a low threshold for it, became unbearable. So the doctor prescribed Percodan, a tremendously powerful and addictive drug. It wasn't long before Golden was hooked.

"He never blacked out, ever," Barbara told me. "There were times when he got very, very drowsy, and it was apparent there was something strange. But he masked his drug habit very well."

Even his closest friends on the team — Harris; Charlie Waters, a strong safety; and roommate John Fitzgerald, who played center — didn't know there was a problem at first. "I knew he was taking them, but I never knew how bad it was," said Fitzgerald, who is now vice president of an insurance agency in Dallas. Fitzgerald found out about Golden's abuses from a mutual friend after Golden had been retired for a couple of years. But Fitzgerald was quick to add, as was every other player I talked to, that drug use in the NFL was much worse than anyone knew. Golden popped painkillers, but everyone did.

"Let me tell you something," said Henderson, who had battled a cocaine addiction for years. "When you play the game of football, it looks graceful — these guys look like gazelles running around out there. But when you're running twenty-four miles an hour and some guy hits you, and you strain, and you fall and hit the ground, it hurts. Sometimes it hurts forever. First you start on aspirin, then Tylenol 3, then codeine, then Percodan, then you know some doctor and he gives you a hundred."

Golden says that is what happened with him: he was banged up, his teeth hurt, and he was in pain. Then he had to decide. "Here you are, you're in the show," he said. "Somebody hands you something and says, 'You can play or you can not play. If you don't want to, that's your decision. But if you want to, these pills will help you play better.' So I took them and took them and took them."

Once Golden was addicted, he didn't know where to go. How could he, the blond kid everyone loved, admit to a drug problem? If the team found out, they would cut him or trade him. He would end up in Green Bay or Philadelphia — then the NFL's equivalent of Siberia. He was afraid, and it affected his demeanor. He became secretive. Ditka remembered that Golden's behavior changed after his first season. "I confronted him somewhere along the way," he told me. "I said, 'Golden, I don't know what you're doing, but you're doing something wrong. You're a bundle of nerves.' He was walking on pins and needles. Before, he had been a relaxed, happy-go-lucky guy. Something was different."

But the games were scheduled and the seasons went on. By 1977 the Cowboys were knocking on the door of the Super Bowl. They played Minnesota in the NFC championship in Dallas, with the winner going on to Super Bowl XII. On the Cowboys' second offensive play, at the Minnesota 32-yard line, Staubach faked a screen and tossed a rainbow toward the end zone, and Golden pulled it in with a breadbasket catch. Dallas 6, Minnesota 0. The Cowboys won 23–6. There was much rejoicing in Dallas, but not for Golden.

He left the locker room to drive home, to face another night battling his addiction. Something happened to him, he told me, as he drove on I-35 away from the arena. "I remember this so clearly. I pulled over and looked back in my rearview mirror and saw the light pouring up from the inside of the stadium," he had said that first night at his apartment, telling me the same story he had told a reporter for the *Dallas Morning News* the previous year. "And I started to cry because I knew I had two more weeks there. Here I was supposed to be in one of the most exciting times of a football player's career, and all I am is in despair because I had to propagate this addiction for another two weeks. I had to take the pills to play, and I was sick and tired of it. I just wanted the season to be over with so I could feel better and start taking care of myself."

But this was no time for emotional collapses. The Cowboys were in the Super Bowl against Denver's vaunted Orange Crush defense, and they'd better win. Dallas expected nothing less. But Golden was barely hanging on. "I don't know how he played," Barbara said. "He was in such bad shape."

Super Sunday arrived, and the big game was held in the mammoth New Orleans Superdome. From the beginning, it didn't look like much of a game. The Broncos were pathetic. Their quarterback, Craig Morton, a former Cowboy, had tossed four interceptions by halftime, tying the Super Bowl record for an entire game. The Broncos fumbled another four times. But the Cowboys couldn't put them away. Efren Herrera had missed three field goals, and the Cowboys' offense hadn't clicked. America's Team was up 20–10, but backup quarterback Norris Weese had come in to give the Broncos some life with his scrambling ability. The game wasn't over yet. Then, in the fourth quarter, lineman Harvey Martin sacked Weese and forced a fumble, which Dallas recovered at the Denver 29. On the Cowboys' first play, Coach Tom Landry whispered, "Brown right formation, X opposite shift, toss 38, halfback lead, fullback pass to Y." A trick play. Staubach pitched back to fullback Robert Newhouse, who ran left on a sweep. Suddenly, he stopped and heaved the ball toward the end zone. Golden had sprinted past the Broncos' secondary, who had bit on the run, but safety Steve Foley recovered and was closing in. Too late. The ball arrived over Golden's right shoulder and he hauled it in. Touchdown. Cowboys win, 27–10. The season was over, the good guys had won, and Golden's catch had sealed the game. He and Barbara left for Utah to get him away from the pressures of Dallas, to try to save him. But on April 2, 1978, that effort failed. Golden overdosed, and it nearly killed him.

He had returned to Texas for a speaking engagement, but going back to Dallas, the city that loved him so, brought back the pressure, and Golden went to his standby. "It was the old Gee-I-have-a-toothache-is-there-a-doctor-who-can-give-me-a-prescription line," Barbara said. "And they did, and it was a pretty serious drug. I can't remember what it was, but it was something you wouldn't want to mess around with. And he took a lot. By nine o'clock he was pretty out of it, and by ten you could tell he wasn't all there. Then he started seizing and turning blue."

Barbara called the paramedics and Cowboys doctor Pat Evans, who met the ambulance at Baylor University Medical Center. Evans, who wouldn't be interviewed for this story, has said Golden's overdose wasn't such a big deal. But Barbara angrily disagrees. "That's crap," she told me. "I was there. It was a big deal. Later it was dismissed, classified as routine flu symptoms. Who knows how they covered it up."

Later that year, Golden was traded to the Chicago Bears for a third-round draft choice — not for the first- and second-round picks, as he had told me. The people I spoke with who knew of the overdose said it was the reason for the trade. But Schramm denies any knowledge of an overdose. "I know nothing about that," he said. "In fact, this is the first time I've ever heard anything about it. I don't agree that he had a drug problem when he was playing. I think he had a clear head all the time he was playing for us."

Golden went to the mediocre Bears and produced — well, produced as much as anyone could with Bob Avellini throwing the ball. He caught a career-high 28 passes in 1978, but the nagging injuries got worse. He caught 5 passes in the 1979 season, then went on the injured-reserve list for a tear in his right knee. He later learned that he had played that season with a broken arm. In April 1980, disappointed with the man who was supposed to revive their offense, the Bears released Golden. He went to Denver to try to catch on with the Broncos but hurt his hand and was cut. He retired in 1980 at the age of 29.

Since 1980 Golden has had a sporadic, shaky history. He hosted a cable hunting-and-fishing show called *ESPN Outdoors,* which ran in the 1981 season. The show's producer, Lee Martin, said Golden was an ideal host and that he never knew of any drug problem. "We never had any situations where he was late for a shoot or didn't show up — he was a great asset because he got involved with everything. He was such a charmer. People really took to him."

The show ended, and Golden went to work in public relations for an energy company in Salt Lake. The addiction kept going, though. It wouldn't end. But the marriage finally did in March 1984. "I couldn't put up with it anymore," Barbara said. "And I became the bad person, the cause of Golden's troubles."

Barbara says Golden was so charismatic and charming that he was able to finagle pills out of just about anybody. But he finally exhausted his options, which at one point led him to the door of Rita Reese, his former Scout master. Reese said that one day Golden came to her door and told her that he had a terrible headache and he needed some pills. "I've had two sons go through chemical addiction," she told me. "One is dead and one made it. So I was aware, and I knew enough not to give him any kind of narcotic. So he left. He crossed the street and told the neighbors his wife had a toothache."

There are other questions about Golden's life since retiring that may never be answered. Where did he stay when he was broke? Who supported him, and with how much? Reese said the local bishop arranged for the church to help Golden for a while. When we spoke, Golden was vague about his activities, referring to various jobs he had held and occasionally acknowledging his numerous stays in rehab clinics. But he became unclear and edgy when pressed for details. "It's not like I dropped off the face of the earth," he said.

As I talked to his friends and former teammates, many asked if Golden still had his football memorabilia. The Super Bowl ring is perhaps the most treasured of all football mementos, but he had been broke, and it could have brought a lot of money. Several ex-teammates asked if he still had the ring. During my first visit with him, Golden said all his souvenirs were still at his parents' house. And the ring? He said he had left it at the house of a former girlfriend who was now demanding money for it. He said she was asking for $2,500 to $3,000. When I visited with him several weeks later, he told me a variation on the same story, apparently forgetting that I had heard it before. I asked how much she was asking. "I don't even remember . . . something like six, seven, eight hundred," he said. I asked for this woman's name, but he said he didn't want to tell me so the lawsuit he was about to file would surprise her.

Ken Sowby, the former manager of Salt Lake's Baseball Cards Etc., said Golden's jerseys, shoes, and helmets had all come in for sale. They weren't that popular until Golden was arrested. Within minutes of that announcement, Sowby said, everything was sold. And he said a friend of Golden's offered to sell him Golden's Super Bowl ring. "He was asking eleven hundred dollars for it, and I offered about half of that to see how serious he was," Sowby said. He then recalled how he had met Golden years before and Golden had let him see the ring. "I held it in my hand. He said he'd call me back, but he never did. He was such a supernice guy; he made me feel like I was the greatest thing in the world because he was letting me try his ring on," Sowby said, then paused. "I have no thoughts at all that he still has it. I'd bet anything he doesn't."

Golden worked for a while as a machinist for his father-in-law's plastic fabricating plant in 1993, but he went to work one day and slowly lapsed into incoherence. "He got almost nonfunctional," recalled Amy's father, Stan Mendenhall. "He got disoriented. My son took him home. He never did collapse. It wasn't as though he was really drunk. And he said, at that point in time, he wasn't aware that he had taken anything. He said he thought somebody had put something in his soda as a joke, but I don't believe that."

There were several common occurrences in the interviews I had. Everyone had theories as to why Golden was hooked for so long, and so heavily. Another common element was sadness for a man who cannot gain control of his life. Ditka said that although Golden might have initially gotten pills from the team doctors, he needed to take responsibility for his own situation. "I don't think it's so much a sickness as a weakness," he said. "I never think you can blame the doctor. I think the option is always there for the player. We've all done it. But you don't become hooked on it. Because when you do get hooked on it, it's a one-way road to nowhere."

So the lesson is, Play the game, perform on Sunday, don't drop the ball. Do what you have to do. Take whatever you have to take. But don't get hooked. That may not be so easy when you start taking codeine and Percodan. These are physically addictive drugs, and stopping them may be, as many find, impossible. Golden said he wasn't ready for the silence, the day-to-day life where no cheerleaders await a correct decision at work. "That was pretty tough for me," he said. "I think the drugs filled a void, an emotional void. The natural high was replaced with a chemical high."

Then there is the addictive personality, a physiological condition that leads some people to get addicted to substances such as caffeine, sugar, alcohol, or in Golden's case, opiates. I remember Golden's smoking — which he says he has since quit — the Pepsis, the enrollment in AA.

"When I read about Golden's arrest in the papers, I called and got a message to him," Thomas Henderson said. "I said, 'If you need help, give me a call.' He never called. I've been sober since 1983. I was addicted to crack cocaine. He might think his addiction to pills is tough, but wait until you get your mouth around that little crack pipe. I wouldn't give him any money, any pills. But I can tell him that I've been through the hell of addiction, and I know what that's like. But I also know the beauty of recovery. And I know how to live. But does Golden Richards want to live? I had to get over the myth of Hollywood. Can Golden get over the myth of Golden? Can he be John Richards?"

Maybe he can. Danny White thinks so. "There is a lot of greatness there, a lot of character," White said. "It may have been covered over a couple years, it may have been tainted, but it's there. I know his family, his background, and I know he has the potential to overcome anything he needs to overcome." Maybe he tried every day. But when I knocked on his door, an adoring fan, telling him how he was always my hero, asking if he remembers this catch or that play, maybe it all comes flooding back and overwhelms him. Maybe the memories come back of when he was famous, a man who happened to fit America's definition of perfection. The speed. The hair. The grace. A Mormon boy from a big family in Salt Lake City who captured the national imagination, and who thought no one would want him if they knew of the habit he had developed.

I haven't talked to Golden in more than a year. The last I know of him is what I saw on a video sent to me by channel KTVX in Salt

Lake City, which did a story on him this past summer. In it, reporter Carl Arky interviews Golden and shows clips of his playing days. The segment begins with photos of him at Granite, BYU, and as a Cowboy, then cuts to a shirtless, tanned Golden at his new job — driving a bulldozer. There are several shots of Golden and his son, Jay, strolling next to a small lake, Golden encouraging Jay as he throws rocks into the water.

Later, Golden, whose long hair is even blonder from being bleached by the sun, tells Arky the same things he told me: that his drug habit began when the Cowboys gave him a choice of pills or sitting out, that "the champion never becomes a champion unless he has tasted canvas." But, he emphasizes, he is getting his life in order: "I'm doing Golden a favor this time," he says. "I'm doing it for me."

At one point in the interview Arky asks Golden what it was like to spend a week in jail. "That was a real low spot," Golden says, biting his lip. "I never thought I'd be in jail." And he starts to cry.

I anticipate that Golden will never speak to me again after reading about what happened when I visited him, which is difficult for me. He might hate me, think that I came into his life to sabotage him, when it was actually the opposite. I wanted to spend some time with him — with the hope that perhaps we could be friends. Watching your hero collapse from an overdose is not exactly the stuff lifelong dreams are made of.

A couple of weeks after I first visited him, I called and we chatted for a while, and then I asked him about what had happened on that day in Salt Lake City. He told me that he thought the pills were a nonnarcotic muscle relaxant and that he took the whole bottle because they were old and he thought their potency might have expired. I told him that some people might not believe that. He became annoyed. "I don't care what some people might think," he said. "I don't have to explain myself to anybody, but since it's you, I'll tell you. The other day I went to the dentist. And the dentist was going to give me some pain pills. I asked what was in them, and he said they were fine. I said O.K., then I said, 'Do these have any codeine?' and he said, 'Yes.' I said, 'Whoa! No, thank you kindly!' And I didn't, I got a nonnarcotic pain pill. That was the reality of my situation, not what happened with you. That wasn't the reality."

He says that he has been told that the whole incident was a result

of a reaction to sulfa drugs that he had taken for an upper respira-
tory tract infection. I think back to when the hotline operator told
me to listen for his breath, to see if he was still breathing. And I
can't help but think that I nearly killed him, and I wonder what I
would have done if I had bent over and heard no breath coming
from his mouth. Friends tell me I shouldn't think about that, that I
saved his life. But he wouldn't have overdosed in the first place if I
hadn't gotten the pills for him. More than likely it will happen
again, and maybe the next time he won't wake up. Maybe there will
be a couple pills too many, and when the next person puts his ear to
Golden's mouth he won't hear anything.

    Now that I have met my hero, I don't know that I am any better
off than I was before, when he was a face on a football card. My
images of Golden will forever be of him opening the door that first
night, standing over my shoulder at the phone booth, lying pros-
trate on the floor of his living room. And there is one more that will
always remain with me. In the Golden Richards file at the BYU
sports information office, there are a few pieces of memorabilia,
including some black and white pictures of Golden as a student. In
one of them a heartbreakingly youthful Golden sits on the bench
during a night game, looking out at the field. Bundled in a large
BYU jacket, his hair tousled, his arm clutched around him, he looks
vulnerable — you don't want to see him anywhere near the football
field. You want him tossing the Sunday paper onto your porch,
singing in the BYU choir, dating your daughter. Not the target of a
strong safety with anger seething in his eyes. Golden looks lost amid
the roars and the rage.

TOM FARREY

Hard-Core Hoops

FROM PACIFIC

THE ROAD TO prison is a two-way street, in that an outsider can always turn back at any moment.

It starts near the entrance to the Fort Lewis Army base, with the weapons of war on the right, before descending down through a dark gauntlet of tall, thick trees that blocks all light except an angelic ribbon of pink-orange dusk that runs along the very top. With nothing to look at, the visitor is left alone with his thoughts and fears.

The road empties into a Norman Rockwell landscape of wood-frame homes, stand-alone mail boxes and a small, quaint neighborhood grocery. The car stops at the waterfront, next to railroad tracks where an engine rumbles by, shaking his insides. Waiting for the train to pass, he stands next to a mother holding the tiny hand of a girl in navy sailor hat and matching dress. *That could just as well be my little girl,* he thinks, as she retrieves a crushed penny from between the rails.

He's also thinking about bailing, walking onto the part of the pier that splits right for a ferry to Anderson Island. How easy it would be to hop that boat, take a ride for a couple of hours, tell his teammates later that he was confused. His wife would not object.

But he proceeds, over the two thick yellow lines urging caution, past the red signs saying authorized persons only, into a government-style hut where he is greeted by a sign that warns:

No FIREARMS,
Dangerous Drugs,
Explosives,
OR DANGEROUS WEAPONS ALLOWED!

His senses are alive, taking in everything, as a large, uniformed man in the window, perhaps a former pro wrestler, says, "Basketball game tonight, huh?" *What did he mean by that — "huh?" Why is he smiling so cryptically? What's he know that he's not sharing?*

He is too scared to ask, now that his teammates have arrived. As a basic American male, he would rather enter a fight with Godzilla than concede, in front of his buddies, that fire-breathing oversize reptiles frighten him. Besides, he's propelled by an urge equally as irrational as fear: the urge to play basketball in the best possible setting, against the best possible players.

This is his Final Four.

So, he takes his temporary prison ID card. He walks through the metal detector and under the row of black-and-white pictures, dating back to 1893, of tough-looking, cigar-chomping prison wardens, men whose job it was to watch over criminals like Mickey Cohen, Charles Manson, the Birdman of Alcatraz. He steps onto a passenger boat driven by a prison official who was once attacked by inmates on this ride, who had to fight them off to save his life.

There is no turning back now.

He is going to prison.

Voluntarily.

That very thought occurs many times on a recent Wednesday to the members of Evergreen Excavation, one of the several recreation-league men's teams scheduled to play this season against the McNeil Island Correctional Center team. As a unit, Evergreen isn't having much of a season, at 1–4, and now they are going to try to play McNeil with only four players — a construction worker, timber-mill worker and two salesmen. The others skipped out late for various, suspicious reasons.

Their best player, who formerly played college basketball, said an appointment came up that night — his first, hallelujah, in two weeks!

Another, a truck driver, called ahead to say he couldn't make the 6:20 P.M. boat.

A third said his other team, in the Air Force league, had its game rescheduled for that same night and that, of course, he has an obligation to that team first.

The competition alone is enough to scare off rivals. Teams formed under the Pierce County Parks and Recreation Department have been coming to the McNeil Island prison for decades, almost always leaving in defeat. McNeil is regularly the Meridian League champion, having lost only three games in the past seven years against competition made up usually of former prep players. There may not be a more dominating basketball team in the state of Washington during that time, on the pro, college, high school, or recreation level.

Of course, the Islanders have certain advantages. All of their games are home games. They are the only team with a coach. Their talent pool is deep, with more than 80 of the 1,100 prisoners annually trying out for 12 spots on "the varsity." Prison life leaves them plenty of time to hone their game. They have their own gym.

And talk about hostile crowds. Everyone courtside is a felon. Some are robbers, others rapists, drug dealers or murderers at McNeil, a medium-security facility. With nothing better to do on Wednesday nights, they cram into the small facility, whooping, fist-pumping, betting. Gambling is common on prison basketball games, with players sometimes paid as much as $40 to make sure their team covers the spread (effectively making the players professionals).

For the strong of heart, a trip to McNeil is the closest a rec-leaguer will ever get to playing a game at Boston Garden. In this old, sweltering gym, in fact, former Celtic player Emmette Bryant, a member of the NBA championship team of 1969, coached the McNeil team for several years in the 1980s as the prison's recreation director. The benches and certain areas of the court are painted in Celtic green, although, as Bryant notes, "that's also known as institutional green."

The Los Angeles Lakers once played an intrasquad scrimmage at McNeil when one of their star players, Elgin Baylor, was in the Army and based at Fort Lewis. His officers wouldn't release him for practice in Los Angeles prior to the playoffs, so the Lakers flew to Seattle. They rented the nearest gym outside Fort Lewis and had inmates officiate the game (prompting Laker player Jim Krebs to bark at one point, "After that call, I know why you're here!").

To entice teams to make the trip, McNeil is the only gym in the Meridian League that allows dunking. That is, if a player can get up in the air — and over the water. A man once wanted to play so badly at McNeil Island that he submitted the mandatory personal information, hoping that when the state did a security check it wouldn't notice he had an outstanding warrant. He was arrested at the ferry dock.

Not everyone is so eager to go to McNeil, however. Pierce County has to pay referees an extra $10 to officiate games at the prison, and even then many of them chicken out. Teams of policemen and lawyers won't play there, fearing retribution, and a third of the teams that do sign up back out at the last moment.

Fortunately for Evergreen Excavation, they have Steve Miner, their burly center/timber-mill worker, who is reassuring his teammates on the boat ride over that there's nothing to worry about. He's telling them that he played over there several years ago and that it's no more intimidating than an ordinary rec-league game. When he starts to describe the gym atmosphere, though, he is interrupted.

"Uh," says Charlie Washburn, a prison official sitting nearby, "I think you're talking about the McNeil Island annex." He is speaking of the minimum-security annex. Where the prisoners are older and the gym newer than at the main facility, which plans to open a new gym this spring because the old one is falling apart.

Miner pauses, looking around. Then he yells, "TURN THE BOAT AROUND!!!"

He is half-joking, which also means he is half-serious. As always in the Meridian League, the visitors have signed up for more than a game. They'll get an experience, and if they're lucky, an education.

Game time. If the prisoners are going to find any freedom in this facility, it's going to be right here within the dimensions of a smaller-than-regulation-size basketball court that's been home over the years to some of the best players produced by the state, former high school stars from Garfield on down.

Old heads who have been incarcerated before at maximum-security facilities like Walla Walla, where prisoners are locked in their cell twenty hours a day, consider life at McNeil a form of adult daycare, with its dormlike rooms and lesser restrictions on movement. But to first-timers like Shedrick Dyson, a loquacious 26-year-old from Seattle, it feels like misery.

Room checks every morning, body counts six times a day, including twice in the middle of the night. The same low-grade food each week. The spirals of razor wire circling the prison grounds, a reminder that you are a threat to society and cannot be trusted. No, McNeil is not Fantasy Island.

"Without basketball, I don't know what I'd be doing in here," Dyson said. "From the time I walked into this prison, I started playing. The very first night. I just walked in and said, 'Anyone want to play?' First night I probably scored 35.

"Once I get on the court, it's like I'm outside the institution. I could be at Green Lake or Seattle U., because those are the places we played on the streets. Every time the sun comes out, Green Lake's the spot, no doubt about it. I've played against Gary Payton, Shawn Kemp, all the guys, Detlef Schrempf, just out on the playground. Michael Cage, Cortez Kennedy, Rick Mirer.

"I got Nate McMillan once at Green Lake. He just kind of finger-rolled it. I came from the other side and swept it off the glass, you know. He's like, 'Good block.' That's one of the highlights of me ever playing basketball."

Teammates on the McNeil varsity consider Dyson a cartoon figure. They tease him about his grand appearance: the pencil-thin mustache, the impeccable haircut, the exaggerated sense of self, and particularly, the $115 shoes he wears only when playing basketball. They say he scores only because he never passes the ball.

Dyson bristles at the criticism but concedes, in the stuttering manner of an alcoholic coming to terms with his illness, "I-I-I am a selfish person." Basketball, as always, is a mere reflection of the person. Dyson had a job as a car detailer in Seattle but wanted a swanky ride himself, couldn't afford it, so he sold crack cocaine on the side.

Now he's locked up, with a 2-year-old son on the outside and a family wondering what in the world went wrong. None of his five brothers and two sisters has ever been incarcerated, he says.

His mother, a live-in nurse, wrote him a letter in October, as he was being assigned to McNeil.

Hi Shedrick,
I know you are feeling like no one cares about you, but that's not the issue here. Things are just tight right now for everyone but it will get better. Trust me. I'm working very hard at getting this in order, but I'm doing it . . .

Well, here's some of the things I'd like you to do for me. Pray a lot and try to get through this. Don't let the system use you. Use the system by escaping it and doing a lot of the things you enjoy doing. Try to get you a job that can help you when you get out. There are a lot of different people there, of all nationalities, races and colors. Try to break down that line and make friends and try to always give, rather than receive. Before you think of raising your fists at someone, think of me and your family and take the time to sit down and write us.

> Love you always and forever,
> Mom

Dyson plays each varsity game with the letter tucked into his left shoe, for strength.

All that Evergreen Excavation sees, though, are the tops of those leather Converses, which is exactly what Dyson wants. In competition, he wants his opponent to take notice of these eye-grabbing shoes with the bold stripes and masking tape over the front, like spats. He said he tapes them to protect the toe area from ripping, but it also serves as a distraction.

"They'll look down at 'em and I'm gone," said Dyson, who cleans his shoes regularly with suede spray to maintain their luster. "By the time he looks up, I'm all the way to the rim already. They can laugh and joke about it but I use every little tool I can use. Everything. Everything."

The first quarter ends with McNeil leading Evergreen Excavation, 25–14. Dyson comes off the bench to hit a three-pointer from the corner, one of three baskets he scores during the game.

As the second quarter begins, most of Evergreen Excavation's points have been scored by prisoners the team picked up to fill the player shortage. Steve Miner, with six points, is the only regular member of Evergreen Excavation who has scored.

He is also the only one who appears comfortable in the gym, at least initially.

With the rest of his team, Miner made the chilling walk from the boat dock to the gym. He was escorted through three electronic prison gates, pausing in the sally port long enough to glimpse the rows of handcuffs behind the protected glass, then shown into the prisoners' area. He was unnerved by the sound of that final gate closing behind him, a sound that prison officials joke is worth five points at least for the home team.

Miner walked up three stories and into the cramped gym, where the 156 inmates there for the game studied the visitors from a single row of seats along the wall. Others looked on from behind the metal fence of an adjacent weight room. To Miner, it seemed there were more like 500 in attendance because of the noise of weights clanking and inmates talking, all of which reverberated off the gym's peeling, concrete walls.

But once the game started, all cares disappeared for Miner — not just about his immediate surroundings but from everyday life, the day-to-day stress of paying bills and meeting obligations. That is why he plays basketball, and in a roundabout way why he came to an elevated dungeon like McNeil.

"My life's changed a lot in the last three years," said Miner, who's gotten married and had a child, with another on the way. "I was single, a bouncer at a club, dating a lot of people. I was going fifty miles an hour all the time. Now I've got to slow down, and for me that's hard."

Literally. "It seems like I'm always getting speeding tickets. I feel like every time I'm out in the car I get pulled over. I've also gotten into my fair share of bar fights . . . Basketball helps me relax."

Prisoners aren't the only ones seeking freedom. People on the outside exist in a world of increasing restrictions. They spend unwanted hours each day in their cars, or offices. They get caught in traffic jams, long lines, bureaucratic red tape, and political dogma that assigns titles to everyone, whether it be "Gen Xer" or "feminist" or "white male." The boxes people live in are getting smaller, even as their options are growing.

As it happens, the game of basketball is all about people trying to make the most of their limited space without coming to blows. It is about perfecting the art of going around opponents, not through them. It is about achieving happiness within strict geographical confines, even as the neighbors get more ornery.

It is a model game for the twenty-first century, if the population charts suggest anything.

All Miner wants to do, though, is get Evergreen's inside game going. Throwing his six-foot-four-inch, 240-pound body around the paint, Miner got his hands on the ball early. But to cut into the lead, teammates started hoisting three-point shots that missed the mark, often leading to fast-break baskets for the Islanders.

When Miner finally does get the ball and drives inside, his shot is blocked affirmatively, prompting a guttural howl of "WUUUUU-UUUUU" from the crowd.

Miner comes to the bench, a river of sweat looking for replenishment. Sorry. Prison rules don't allow visitors to bring special fluids like Gatorade, to prevent the sneaking of alcohol to inmates.

Score at halftime: 59–29, McNeil. Everyone knows where this game's headed. The McNeil coach, Grey Benjamin, comes over to the Evergreen bench to recommend that the clock run continuously through the second half, even during free throws, so that Evergreen can make the 8 P.M. boat back to Steilacoom. No one objects.

From beyond the three-point line, Don Womack lets loose a shot that splashes down twenty-five feet away in a cushion of nylon net. He loves watching the shot, the way it feels leaving his fingers, its high, beautiful arc, the anticipation as the ball falls back toward earth, then finally the sense of total accomplishment as it filters through the net.

Little else in Womack's life is so perfect. He was a confused boy from Tacoma when he first got into crime, at age 13, taking cars on joy rides. Later when his drug habit got expensive, he started selling the cars he stole. Now 25, he's pretty much been locked up since he was 14, in various juvenile and adult institutions.

He was introduced to basketball at one of those juvenile facilities, Mission Ridge near Bremerton, where a counselor showed him a little fadeaway jumper. As the tall, skinny kid grew, he started taking the shot from farther out on the perimeter. Before long, he was a certifiable gym rat.

And breaking all the rules.

In the yard one day at McNeil, Womack said, he was cornered by several white inmates — "the ones with tattoos" — who informed him in racist terms that in prison, basketball is a black sport and that he shouldn't mix with black inmates. Out of fear, he stopped playing in the gym, instead sneaking outside to shoot on the hard courts by himself every day for hours.

But eventually he made his way back inside, where perils of a new variety existed. Some of the black players accepted him but a few of them did so, he said, "for the wrong reasons." In some prisons, he said, there's a perception that young white men who hang around black men are interested in homosexual sex.

One day when he was 18, he was hit over the head with a lead pipe by one of those prisoners, "just as a warning that I was 'posed to do what he wanted me to do," he said.

Womack says the tension at McNeil has relaxed in recent years with the construction of new living facilities, and that he gets along with everybody. But crossing the racial divide still has its consequences, even on the basketball court, one of the few places where inmates from the various racial groups interact voluntarily.

"The black guys still talk crazy every once in a while, you know, trying to get you all frustrated," he said. "And it does get to me when they're saying 'white boy, white boy,' even though they don't mean it in a disrespectful way. That's just how they talk when they're talking. But it irritates the hell out of me. I'm like, 'My name is Womack, I'm a white *man* or something.'"

He is one of two whites on the twelve-man varsity roster and one of a mere handful of whites and Hispanics who even tried out for the team.

But he is a basketball player, above all.

Third quarter ends with McNeil leading, 88–46.

As a contest, the game has completely degenerated. The waves of McNeil substitutions, five at a time every four minutes, have sapped their opponent of any last chance at a comeback. Just about every other trip upcourt for Evergreen Excavation, a McNeil player steals the ball and tosses it quickly the other way for an easy basket.

It's gotten so ugly the crowd is cheering for Evergreen. Womack flips off one of the inmates, and gets benched.

But most of the players are still getting what each of them needs, personally, out of the game.

Anthony "Little Barkley" Hickenbottom, 25, a muscular inmate new to McNeil, is roaring to the hoop, just like his younger brother, Roberto Bergersen, does for the University of Washington as a scholarship basketball player. Hickenbottom likes playing against outside teams because it allows him to feel "human" again, not criminal.

Running the team ably from the point guard position is Eric "Prime Time" Langston, 30, who uses basketball as a way to keep in shape until he is released into the outside world, where he wants to put to use his training as a computer technician. He is captain of the team, which pays for its balls, uniforms and league fees with funds raised by the prisoners.

Down low in the key is Emanuel "Veteran" Milton, 46, the oldest player on the court. A self-described Vietnam vet who is missing most of his teeth, who had his dentures stolen with his coat while playing hoops in Salt Lake City, Milton is waving for the ball on his gimpy knees, looking for that sweet, "un-*stop*-pable" fadeaway that's been with him all these years.

"If I had my choice on dying, it'd be on a basketball court making my turnaround jumper," Milton said, flashing a gummy grin. "I'd have a heart attack, the ball would hit the bottom of the net and, boom, I'd be gone.

"Hopefully if I get to heaven, God will put me on his varsity team."

Final score: 117–59. McNeil moves a step closer to another Meridian League title. But judging by the players' eagerness to slap hands with the losers, the Islanders aren't so much drunk with victory as they are intent on leaving the right impression. They thank Evergreen Excavation for making the trip and encourage them to return, anytime.

Evergreen Excavation likes the idea. It occurs to the players that the game was virtually devoid of trash-talking and rough play, contrary to what they had expected. Maybe they just didn't give the Islanders enough of a run; the inmates got testy in a close loss a couple weeks later to a team called Da Boyz. But they say they have to go back to youth-league ball to remember a game so cleanly played.

Best of all, they came face-to-face with their fears. Maybe they didn't get the life stories or even the names of their opponents, but they got physical and emotional images, and in the wonderfully expressive language that is basketball, came to know the prisoners on some level.

"I probably talked about the game more in the two weeks prior than the two weeks after," Miner would say later. "You anticipate it more than anything. You talk about it with your friends, about what Guido the Killer Pimp might do to you, all the scenarios. But when you come back there's not much to talk about, because not much happens."

It's worked that way for years at McNeil, where prison officials say no one from a visiting team has ever been attacked. The outsider goes inside the McNeil Island prison, deep down scared for his safety, and he comes out with 16 points, 10 rebounds, 3 assists, and a clearer understanding of the people who call the place their temporary home.

Next time, maybe he walks downtown past the drug pushers and street life with a little more comfort, because he's traded sweat with them under the boards. Maybe the news stories about crime don't seem as menacing, because he's looked into the eyes of society's worst, been guests in their house, and on some basic level, they're not as alien as he assumed.

Doesn't mean he has them over to dinner at his house. Doesn't even mean that they're ready to go back into society. Some people don't know what to do with their freedom; they mistake freedom for license. But the point is, the visitor has found his measure of freedom — inside some of the meanest walls erected.

"I'd go back there to play," says Peter James, an Evergreen player. "I'd go back there in a minute."

It's only a game, they say. But teams in the Meridian League, including the McNeil Islanders, know better.

MICHAEL BAMBERGER

Living with a Lie

FROM SPORTS ILLUSTRATED

IN THE COMMUNITY of golf, Ben Wright, the CBS golf broad-caster and longtime golf writer, is invited to the best parties. He's an amiable, well-spoken man bursting with opinions and stories, delivered in a lovely British accent that isn't quite Oxbridge, but close. He describes his mother as a "minor Scottish aristocrat," and he prepared for London University at an all-boys English public school, Felsted. He has spent four decades in golf's elite circles. Everything about him contributes to a veneer of refinement. His boss's boss, David Kenin, the president of CBS Sports, calls Wright "a complex, sophisticated guy." John Bentley Wright, corpulent and jolly, highly compensated and often smelling very good, calls himself "a ham."

Every so often he slips up, and a coarser element of his personality, a Fleet Street side, emerges. In a recent interview with *SI* he described a former editor of his at the *Financial Times* as "a raging fag." (And he followed that with "I have nothing against homosexuals.") In 1992, writing in *Southern Links,* an American golf magazine now known as *Links,* Wright alleged that Muirfield's club secretary demanded "girlie pictures" in exchange for press credentials for the 1959 Walker Cup, which Wright was to cover for the London *Daily Mirror.* "I pleaded that I had no access to the newspaper's pin-up photographs, which were in any case nothing like as daring as the bare-breasted lovelies daily exposed nowadays in the British tabloids," he wrote. Later, to settle a libel suit, Wright dispatched a letter of apology and a $1,000 check to the secretary, the late Paddy

Hanmer. "Seldom right but never in doubt" — that's what they say about Wright, good-naturedly, in the CBS trailers.

It was in a CBS trailer — on the second Thursday of May, shortly before noon, on the grounds of the DuPont Country Club, in Wilmington, Delaware, site of the 1995 McDonald's LPGA Championship — that Wright met Valerie Helmbreck, a reporter on the *News Journal,* a Delaware newspaper. They spent a half hour together, and neither his life nor hers has been the same since.

Helmbreck began her story, which ran on the front page of the *News Journal* on Friday, May 12, with a quote from Wright: "Let's face facts here. Lesbians in the sport hurt women's golf."

He was also quoted as saying, "They're going to a butch game and that furthers the bad image of the game." He was quoted as saying that homosexuality on the women's tour "is not reticent. It's paraded. There's a defiance in them in the last decade." And, "Women are handicapped by having boobs. It's not easy for them to keep their left arm straight, and that's one of the tenets of the game. Their boobs get in the way."

Wright, the story said, believes that the LPGA's homosexual image hinders corporate support; that the tour's leading players, including Michelle McGann and Laura Davies, lack charisma; and that modern women pros are wrong to emphasize power over finesse.

And with that, all hell broke loose.

Before the story was published, word of the interview reached Wright's boss, Frank Chirkinian, the executive producer of golf for CBS, who was in Wilmington. Early that afternoon, Chirkinian called Helmbreck at the *News Journal* and told her that they needed to meet. Helmbreck, who did not know Chirkinian, asked him to spell his name and reveal his title. He ignored her request, and the terse conversation ended when Helmbreck hung up on him. The story had been out only a few hours on Friday morning when Wright, who is 63, was urged to leave Wilmington and go to CBS headquarters, in New York. There, for six hours, Wright and Kenin discussed the interview and the story it produced. Each man was accompanied by a lawyer. At the *News Journal* on Friday, Helmbreck and her editors received scores of calls, some from readers voicing opinions but many more from newspapers, magazines, radio stations and television programs, seeking comment. Helmbreck wouldn't talk, and the newspaper's editor said the paper stood by the accuracy of its story.

Late on Friday, Kenin released his findings: "I am convinced that the offensive statements attributed to Mr. Wright were not made." He also said that both Wright and CBS Sports had "been done a grave injustice in this matter." Wright offered two releases of his own. In a statement for reporters, Wright said he never used the words "boobs" or "butch" with Helmbreck. He maintained he never said lesbianism on the women's tour is "paraded" or that lesbians were bad for the image of the game. He wrote that he would "not discuss lesbianism with a stranger, just as I would not discuss my three divorces with a stranger." In a statement for the players, posted in the DuPont Country Club locker room Friday morning, Wright wrote, "I am disgusted at the pack of lies and distortion that was attributed to me." He said the same thing on CBS's Saturday coverage of the tournament. Looking directly into the camera and perspiring, Wright called Helmbreck's story "not only totally inaccurate but extremely distasteful."

Helmbreck's piece, a 1,100-word story in a cautious, responsible small-state daily, had all the elements needed to ignite a modern press brushfire: gay sex, male chauvinism, political incorrectness, sports, network television, and a faintly famous figure — a TV personality — to wrap the whole thing around. The *New York Post* captured the moment in a five-word headline for its Saturday paper: THE BOOB ON THE TUBE.

The story had a short shelf life. It was a national story for a day or two, then interest sagged. Ultimately, the Wright-Helmbreck escapade proved to be an unsatisfying little saga, lacking a clear resolution. The interview wasn't tape-recorded. CBS put its word up against Helmbreck's and created reasonable doubt. "They could easily stomp on her," says Richard Sandomir, who covered the story for the *New York Times,* "so they did. Had it been a reporter they knew, Ben would have been gone."

In 1988 CBS fired Jimmy (the Greek) Snyder when he said on TV that blacks were physically better suited for sports than whites. In 1990 CBS suspended Andy Rooney of *60 Minutes* for three months for making remarks that some gays and blacks found offensive. CBS was pressured into pulling Gary McCord from this year's Masters because the Augusta czars didn't like McCord's idea of humor. But

Ben Wright stayed onboard. He didn't have to defend the opinions and quotations, which many people viewed as defensible, because, he said, they weren't his. LPGA officials gave him the benefit of the doubt. When gay-rights groups called for Wright's head, or at least an apology, he ignored them; in his view there was nothing to apologize for. He said the story was a "pack of lies"; his network supported him; and the duo of Bentley and McCord, a team valued by CBS, was saved. Later, Wright received a four-year contract extension. The only victim was Helmbreck and her reputation as a reporter, and no one at the network seemed to care about that. "The woman has disappeared, as far as I know," Wright said recently.

Then Ben did a silly thing. The great raconteur didn't stick to his story. On June 13, a month after the incident, at the summer home of Nancy and Jack Whitaker in Bridgehampton, New York, during the week of the U.S. Open at Shinnecock Hills, Wright attended an elegant dinner party. Barbara and Jack Nicklaus were there. So was Dan Jenkins, the sports writer and novelist who helped Wright get his start with CBS in 1973. "I asked him, 'Did you say it?'" Jenkins, a former *Sports Illustrated* writer, recounted recently. "And he said, 'Of course I said it. But I was granted complete anonymity.' What I don't know is if he was joking. He'd had about two bottles of wine."

Details of the interview emerged in other places. Ken Doig, a veteran tour caddie and a part-time CBS employee, said he eavesdropped on the interview because he couldn't believe what Wright was saying to Helmbreck. Doig, the oldest son of a well-regarded Canadian golfing family, said he likes Wright but that Wright's response to Helmbreck's story was disingenuous. "Her story was accurate," said Doig, who works occasionally for *SI* as a photographer's assistant. "I heard Ben say boobs. I heard him say lesbianism hurts in getting sponsorships." Doig has worked odd jobs for CBS at the Masters, and at other tournaments, since 1977. Asked why he wanted to come forward in the matter of Wright versus Helmbreck and jeopardize his employment with CBS, Doig said, "I'm a golfer, and golf is a game of integrity. I believe in telling the truth."

When contacted by *SI* last month, Wright, an incorrigible talker, said that he could not discuss the Helmbreck story without permission from Kenin, and permission was not granted. ("I'm not going to give him the opportunity to talk and get himself in trouble again," Kenin said.) In a brief telephone interview on the subject, Wright characterized Helmbreck as divorced, involved in a custody battle, possibly a lesbian. It was, Wright said, his bad luck to run into her around Mother's Day, when Helmbreck was upset because she wouldn't be able to see her children. Wright described Helmbreck as having a feminist, gay-rights agenda. "I was totally misquoted. She put into my mouth words she told me," Wright said. "She granted me anonymity. She chose to nail me. It's hurt me terribly. It's aged me ten years. She's a very unhappy woman."

But none of Wright's statements check out. Helmbreck is married — "happily married for fifteen years," she says — to an assistant city editor at the *News Journal.* They have three children. She has been a reporter on the *News Journal* for more than a decade and has lived in Delaware most of her forty-three years. She is currently a features writer and was formerly a TV critic, which is why she was assigned to write about the television coverage of the LPGA Championship. Helmbreck writes often about food and in October wrote a light piece comparing herself with her mock heroine, Martha Stewart, to whom she bears a resemblance. In her twelve years on the *News Journal,* she has been charged with misquoting someone on only one other occasion. That was in 1990, when actress Kathleen Turner was staying in Wilmington at the Hotel duPont. Helmbreck quoted the hotel manager as saying that Turner was not as attractive in person as she appears on the screen. The manager said he was misquoted; the *News Journal* backed Helmbreck. For her foray into golf, Helmbreck said her original plan was to write about the differences between women's and men's golf telecasts. Helmbreck says she took notes throughout the interview with Wright and that the entire session was on the record, except when Wright told her it was not. She declined to reveal what was not on the record. *SI* secured an internal memo from the *News Journal* that describes the part of the interview that was not on the record. According to the document, Wright said that Helmbreck could use, but not attribute to him, the "fingernail test." According to the memo, Wright said that players with short fingernails are gay, and players with long fingernails are not. Helmbreck made no reference to the fingernail test in her story.

Wright has many supporters, JoAnne Carner among them. The LPGA Hall of Famer said Wright's line about women golfers and their breasts was originally her own, a joking way to explain the differences between men's and women's golf. Dottie Mochrie, an LPGA player, said she couldn't imagine Wright intending to say the things he was quoted as saying. Still, she was surprised by what Wright said at the October 2 opening of a golf course, Cliffs Valley in Travelers Rest, South Carolina, designed by Wright. The ceremony, attended by 1,500 people, featured an exhibition by Mochrie and Jay Haas, among others. During the introductions Wright mocked Haas for his performance in the Ryder Cup. When he was through, Wright, according to people present, said to the crowd, "This is payback because at dinner last night Jay asked me about lesbians." There was nervous laughter. "I was a little disappointed that it was brought up again," Mochrie says. "I thought he could've been more sensitive."

At this point, more than six months after the interview, Chirkinian recognizes that Helmbreck's story must be at least *partially* true. "Something must have been said, for it to get into print," he says. Kenin's view appears to have evolved over the past half year. "CBS never said it was a pack of lies," he said recently. "There's a community element to it. She's outside the community. Ben didn't know that at the time. This was a case of one not understanding the other."

Chirkinian said Helmbreck did not understand Wright's sense of humor. "[But] whether Ben Wright was serious or joking, if he admits to [the quotes], he's fired," Chirkinian said. "With our corporate lawyers? Ben would have walked the plank. And to walk the plank for that? I don't think so."

Helmbreck is still in Wilmington, a working reporter. Sometimes when she calls people for a story, they recognize her name. They know she was involved in some messy thing with a golf announcer for CBS. It's frustrating for her. Wright, she says, is a man of his generation, that's all. She has had to live with the consequences. "In this business," she says, "you can be a nut, you can be a drunk, but the one thing you can't be is dishonest." Helmbreck stands by her story. Given the chance, she would write it the same way again.

ROGER ANGELL

Called Strike

FROM THE NEW YORKER

WITH SOME BASEBALL games, the best of them, you can take a look back afterward, in memory or on your scorecard, and find the unexpected play or late at-bat that turned the thing around. This doesn't happen with anything like the same regularity in other team sports, and it's one of the reasons that baseball offers hope as one of its steady ingredients: balm for your pain; restoration for your foundering, down-on-its-luck team; and that little three-run rally by the good guys in the bottom of the eighth which starts when your number-seven batter lifts a feeble Roman-candle pop that just falls in behind first base and sends a runner scurrying along into scoring position. For many disconsolate fans, I think, this is exactly what happened on the last day of March, when United States District Court Judge Sonia Sotomayor issued an injunction against the baseball owners after ruling that their actions during collective bargaining with the Players Association had been in violation of federal law. The ruling ended (or at least suspended for a while) the longest and most bitter labor dispute in professional sports — the 234-day players' strike that shut down play last August, snatched away the late pennant races, and, for the first time in ninety years, wiped out the World Series. The ugliness extended itself through an off-season of icy silences between the embattled parties, interspersed with pious stonewallings, heavily lawyered but fruitless negotiating sessions, newsless news conferences, and self-serving positionings and urgings by senators and congresspeople, and even by the president. The infuriating standoff came within two days of becoming something far worse: the onset of a major league season

contested by eager but talentless "replacement players," hired by
the owners with no other purpose than to bust the union representing their own regulars and stars.

It didn't happen, thanks to Judge Sotomayor's first-ever baseball
ruling: a hell of an at-bat. The players ended their walkout, and the
owners, after considering and discarding the option of a retali-
atory lockout, saw their appeal for a stay of the injunction denied
(the three judges on that panel said scalding things about the
owners' lawyers' conduct of the negotiations), and only then threw
in the towel. Spring training — a shortened, catch-up session for
the real players this time — began again; a flurry of trades and
late contract signings (many of them at vastly reduced rates) allowed the clubs to begin shaping their rosters; and fresh opening
days, for a shortened, 144-game schedule, were proclaimed. If, in
retrospect, the owners again looked like the losers in this, the
eighth outbreak of hostilities in the baseball labor wars over the
past twenty-three years, there were other smoking ruins to contem-
plate this time around, including the loss of more than $700 mil-
lion in revenue, and the disaffection of large sectors of the audience for what used to be called the national pastime.

Disaffected (well, almost) and doubtful, I waited a whole week
before heading off to Arizona for some sun and fly balls, and
perhaps a margarita at the Pink Pony with some of my back-from-
Elba fellow-exiles. Spring training, as always, disarmed me with its
moments and its stories. I was there when Lou Piniella, who now
manages the Seattle Mariners, got himself thrown out of a game
in Peoria while arguing over a foul ball with a replacement umpire (the umps, too, were out on strike this spring) — which is, all
in all, hard to do. The ruckus allowed some of us to recall a comment by Piniella's wife, Anita, a few years ago, after a similar eye-
bulging, neck-swelling, hat-stomping outburst by her combustible
hubby. "I'm forty-three years old," she said, "and I'm married to a
four-year-old." Then someone told me how Lou, in a more relaxed
moment, had been supervising batting practice on a recent morning when he offered to buy a steak dinner for his celebrated young
star Ken Griffey, Jr., if he could make contact with the next pitch.
The kid took him on, but failed, amid general hilarity. Lou kept
hectoring him about the bet until one morning when the manager
walked into the clubhouse and found a twelve-hundred-pound
Hereford steer standing in his office.

In Scottsdale on another day, Ron Fimrite, the *Sports Illustrated* sage, consulted his program while we waited for the first Giants batter of the game to step in against the scary six-foot-ten southpaw Mariner ace Randy Johnson. "'Dax Jones, center field,'" Ron read out. "Well, *there's* a name I've never heard of —" He was interrupted by a short, sharp noise as Jones knocked Johnson's first pitch over the left-field fence. "Until now," he finished smoothly.

Later in that game, I jotted down some reminder notes about Barry Bonds, the Giants' superstar, as he came up to bat, thirty feet away: zebra-striped Nikes, dangling crucifix earring, supercilious ease. With a slight, blurred movement, he dispatched the ball over the right-centerfield wall. What you want to remember about Barry is *wrists*.

And then, late one morning in Phoenix, I stopped on my way up the aisle in the nearly deserted Oakland Athletics park — the workout was ending, and the team was about to board a bus to their afternoon game — to see who it was who was taking such a loud b.p. in the cage. I didn't recognize him at first, but he was meeting each pitch with the same smooth, balanced, right-handed picture swing, and the balls were flying on a line into every sector of the empty outfield: left, right, center, and now a crisp drive that bounced on the right-field foul line — all base hits. Here and there around the field, the last remaining players and coaches stopped whatever they were doing and stood and watched. Then I realized that the batter was Brian Harper, the veteran catcher-outfielder-designated hitter, who had joined the club only that morning as a late free-agent sign-on. Harper, I knew, had always *killed* the A's at the plate, but now that was over. Dave Stewart, the perennial Oakland number-one starter (he was signed again by his old club in April, for perhaps the last year of his career), came walking in from the outer diamond beyond right field with a towel over his shoulder, and he gestured cheerfully to Harper. "Don't change a thing!" he called out. "You could always do that stayin' in *bed!*"

The sunshine and green tints of spring training show a darker tone as well, for this is also the season when fans must bid their farewells to some familiar, trusted figures on the field — veteran players who have come to the end of the line. This year, a trio of remarkable pitchers — Rich Gossage, Jack Morris, and Jeff Reardon — announced their retirements within two days of one another, opening within me freshets of memory in which their distinc-

tive individual styles and their collective stubborn will to triumph
took turns. Reardon, the burly and bearded right-handed reliever
(he rang up 367 saves while on hire to seven different clubs),
recalled himself to my mind as he always looked upon arriving once
again at the mound, where he radiated an aura of hostility and
unwelcome that seemed to cast a shadow over the batter's box and
its luckless waiting occupant and to spoil the general mood right
down the length of the other team's dugout. I remembered the
same Goose Gossage that everyone else does, I imagine — the mut-
ton-chop whiskers, the rearing stride and burning, "Try *this!*" fastball, and then, in the clubhouse, his odd, pale eyes and the appealing boyishness with which he talked about it all afterward, win or
lose. I see Jack Morris in front of his locker as well, with the writers
and photographers on every side, the drops of sweat on his bristly
mustache glistening in the TV lights, and his body sagging and
drained by his just completed effort — the ten-inning 1–0 shutout
of the Braves in Game Seven of the 1991 World Series, say, or one of
those flamboyant September shootouts that matched him up, inning after inning, against other doughty old warriors like Mike
Flanagan or Doyle Alexander. Morris's 254 wins made him the top
winning pitcher through the 1980s and '90s, but the easy ones
don't come readily to mind. All these pictures will still seem fresh
on the first weekend of August in the year 2000, I imagine, when
these three gentlemen, almost surely, will be sitting for the photographers again, up in Cooperstown.

Bob Welch departed the scene, too, after the Athletics sadly
found they no longer had room for him on their roster when they
broke camp in Arizona. He had seventeen years in the majors as a
starting pitcher but knew that he would always be first remembered
for the moment in the World Series of 1978, his rookie season with
the Dodgers, when he duelled the Yankees' Reggie Jackson, head
to head, over an extended, Cecil B. De Mille sort of at-bat, and
struck him out, swinging.

The A's opened their season on the road, playing brief and
unsuccessful consecutive series (they lost two of three) with the
Blue Jays, the Brewers, and the Angels, and when they came home
at last to Oakland Brian Harper sat down and talked at length with
his wife and their three young sons about the trip. (I had spotted
him knocking out ground balls to the boys back in Arizona, a
couple of days after that terrific ten-minute turn in the batting

cage.) The next morning, he stopped by the Athletics' front office
to thank them for their interest and the contract, and to say that he
had decided to retire from baseball. After fifteen years on the field
and on the road, he'd suddenly found that he'd had enough. The
fire was out.

Bob Mikel and I made each other's acquaintance one cloudy,
breezy morning in Mesa, at Ho Ho Kam Stadium, where we were
sitting in the third row of grandstand seats, a bit up the first-base
side, watching the Cubs take batting practice. Mikel is a Sacramento
lawyer and a lifelong Cubs fan. He is lean and cheerful and in-
formal-looking, with a gray mustache, and our exchanged first
glances, I think, registered identical readings: old fan, true fan,
serious about the game, not taken in by the owners, happy to be
here, can't *believe* that baseball is back, etc., and now what about the
Cubs' pitching? Mikel, who has regular spring-training seats at Ho
Ho Kam each year, is a better fan than I am, it turned out. This was
his second trip south from Sacramento this spring, for he had also
come down in March, to watch the replacement players strut their
feeble stuff ("They were willing," he reported, "and so were the
fans, but —" and he shook his head sadly), while I had obdurately
stayed home. He told me that he had grown up in Bloomington,
Illinois, which is serious Cubs country, and that he and his father
had sustained their almost daily Cubs talk even after the younger
Mikel moved out to California. When the Cubs at last made it into
the National League playoffs, in 1984, the two had cried together
over the telephone. And when Bob Mikel learned, not too long
ago, that Hoss Radbourne, a Pleistocene-era Hall of Famer, was
buried in Bloomington, he made a pilgrimage to the site.

Bob and I exchanged notes about the winter just past, and found
that each of us had encountered deep reservoirs of irritation and
anger over the strike among our friends and colleagues, almost all
of it directed against the players. "Everybody's mad," he said. "It's
like going with the same girl for a long time and then she turns you
down. You don't want to see her again *ever*, but then — well, you
know, these things can change. But right now the bulk of people
want to take it out on the players. I know one man who's sixty years
old and says he's never going back to the game. He's going to
boycott baseball."

It came as no surprise to me to find that Mikel himself did not agree with this response to the players' strike. "I don't think most people who talk this way have any idea how tough it is to play baseball in the big leagues," he said. "They don't understand how hard these young guys have worked to reach this level, and they don't notice that this isn't the way it is in other sports. The lesson of Michael Jordan is lost on them. Give him credit, but he couldn't play baseball *at all*. I tried to argue with them, but I didn't get very far. 'They're overpaid' is all I heard. I can understand how people might think that anything over three million a year is too much money for anybody to earn. On the other hand, I believe that most of the players care about the game, and I think Donald Fehr does, too." (Fehr, of course, is the executive director and chief negotiator of the Players Association.)

I told my new friend that I'd also encountered people over the winter — they were always men — who didn't want to hear about the difficulties of playing baseball at the major league level. They insisted that it was more of a game, more fun, than other professional sports. "They should get paid less *because* it's baseball," one man said.

Bob and I talked a little more about the game (the real thing, I mean, not its problems or its image) that day, and we got to see some lively, sloppy spring innings played by the Cubs and the Giants, with a bench-clearing near-brawl — a practice brawl — thrown in. I was happy for him when his Cubs batted around in the third inning and brought in six runs. He and I had enjoyed the comfort of our shared expertise and our insidey names and references — this is what baseball talk is all about — but I believe we also shared an unspoken suspicion that we had almost become superfluous. We are old fans (*my* mustache is white), and it looks more and more as if our passion for the sport doesn't count for much anymore, whether or not our view of things is on target. The mean season we have all been through has changed the sunshine game, and nobody yet knows how much.

Baseball — the clubs and the players together, for once — has undertaken a concerted effort to make it up to the fans this spring, with early-season bargain prices at ticket windows and team members unexpectedly lingering down by the front-row boxes after batting practice to meet the fans and sign the kids' programs and caps and team gear. Wherever I went, in Arizona and then back home once the season had started, players and writers and executives were talking about the common perception of major-leaguers as spoiled, greedy children and about what could be done to change it now. Bob Tewksbury, the right-handed veteran control artist (he is the leader among all current major-leaguers in fewest bases on balls per nine innings), who came over to the Texas Rangers this year, told me that he had found very few people back home in Concord, New Hampshire, who seemed to have any idea of what the players were striking about. "I talked about pitching to a group of Little League coaches one day," he said, "and when I was done I said 'Does anybody want to talk about *baseball?*' and they were like a bunch of caged lions. We talked about the issues and the players' position for about forty-five minutes, and they kept saying, 'I didn't know *that.*' I felt like I'd cleansed my soul. I think that a lot of this misperception comes from jealousy — from folks who can't play ball and don't have a lot of money. That's why they go in for lottery games."

Ron Darling, of the Athletics, who is now in his thirteenth year as a major league pitcher, said, "The owners have got to get past running down their product, and the players have to get past not trusting the owners. We have to find some kind of compatibility. This is a great game or it would never have survived what we've been doing to it. We can't keep doing this stuff. I think the Players Association has a terrible image. Most people out there have no idea that this was never about the players asking for more money. It was only about keeping our freedom in the marketplace. All the guys I've talked to think P.R. is their number-one problem. This past winter they found they had to keep answering questions, about the players and the issues and the money, from all their neighbors, all the people they know. They never should have to do that. All this should be black-and-white to anyone who knows about sports."

Another New Englander, the Mets' muscular new first baseman, Rico Brogna, told me that he had not encountered any such opprobrium or misunderstanding back home in Watertown, Connecticut, in the off-season. "If anybody was upset, they didn't mention it to me," he said. "They're knowledgeable fans there, and I think they were educated about the issues." I thought about this discrepancy after our conversation and guessed that it might have to do with the fact that, while Watertown is a fair-sized town (population 20,000), Rico Brogna, who rapped seven home runs for the Mets in his brief stint with them last summer, at the age of 24, was a football and baseball All-American at Watertown High in what must feel like the very recent past up there. In his case, the players' P.R. problem has never come up.

I had a chance to talk about the fans' view of players with a somewhat older star — Bob Gibson, the near-mythical Cardinal fireballer, who, as I'd expected, was direct in his opinions. "If baseball was easy, everybody would be doing it," said Gibby, who will turn sixty this fall, and who has just rejoined the Cardinals as a pitching coach after several seasons away from the show. "I was at one of those fantasy camps and there was a man there about thirty years old who thought he could play ball. He was a pretty good athlete, and he told me, 'If I knew which pitch was coming, I could hit major league pitching.' I said, 'Hell, I'm fifty-five years old and I could tell you every pitch and you still wouldn't touch one of them.' He said yes, he would, so we went out there and of course it was one, two, three. He never came close. I said, 'I haven't pitched in the major leagues in fifteen years. Come back fifteen years from now and I'll strike you out again.'"

Some management voices that I heard also expressed anxiety about the way the sport is now viewed by its prime consumers. The Cubs president, Andy MacPhail (he is the son of the former American League president Lee MacPhail and the grandson of the flamboyant old Dodger and Yankee executive Larry MacPhail, who is in the Hall of Fame), said, "If ever we needed it, we're getting a tangible lesson that we owners and players have a common concern with the fans. We have to be careful in this business, because the players aren't just one side in a dispute — they're the product. I resent it when people say that the players are greedy. They're not. They were being good soldiers, and they stood fast because they were thinking about the next generation of players. Both sides in the struggle got an A for resolve this time around. You just have to be sure that you're not putting your soldiers in a bad fight."

MacPhail, with his rimless glasses and his hair parted down the middle, looks like a young front-office friend of Christy Mathewson's. After emerging from one of the deadlocked bargaining sessions with the Players Association delegates last winter, he delivered a telling comment on the tenor of things in there: "I'm tired of being told that I'm evil and stupid, just because I disagree."

I asked him whether baseball should now perhaps consider placing more emphasis on the difficulty of the game in its promotional offerings, instead of relying on sweet evocations of its past — the "Field of Dreams" operetta.

"I don't know the answer," he said. "Michael Jordan did a lot for us, but part of the appeal of baseball is that all shapes and sizes can play the game well. Mo Vaughn and Chuck Knoblauch were roommates, back in the Cape Cod League — did you know that?" Vaughn, the massive Red Sox first baseman, moves in a magisterial atmosphere of clout and silence, while Knoblauch, the Twins' compact and combative second baseman, takes more of an infielder's view of the world: shorten up and swing. "The best players always make it look easy, no matter what size they are. But if we present the game as something that's extraordinarily difficult we're running the risk of losing that closeness that so many fans have for baseball — the 'I played this same game when I was growing up' feeling. You might be alienating your best customers."

MacPhail told me that Cubs fans, who have long been viewed in the business as paragons of loyalty and exasperated patience, were perhaps beginning to divide their attention between the two Chicago teams, depending on the teams' current levels of success. "Critical involvement is one of the reasons this game is so appealing," he went on. "As a baseball executive, you're always in the process of trying to improve your future at the expense of your present team, or vice versa, and fans can really get into that. They're always managing and general-managing the club for you. They want to know why we didn't pick up Kevin Brown or Terry Mulholland this year. I don't always appreciate the calls and questions, but that's a real part of the popularity of the sport."

Sandy Alderson, the president and general manager of the Oakland Athletics, has had a difficult time of it lately, for the club is being sold by the Haas family, and its operations are somewhat on hold until the negotiations are completed. (This spring, the club filled its roster by recalling or resigning so may stalwarts from its pennant-winning days of the late '80s and early '90s — Dave Stewart, Dennis Eckersley, Rick Honeycutt, Mike Gallego — that the crowd in the dugout, in those canoe-green warmup jackets, looked like a Dartmouth reunion class.) Alderson has known success and hard times in almost equal measure, and his opinions, in a business obsessed with yesterday's take and today's standings, are notable for their calm and distance. "There are always reasons for the fans to be unhappy with the players," he said one afternoon in Phoenix. "They look as if they're doing something easy that you could be doing, too, but for some odd circumstance. And society is so obsessed now with celebrity and destroying celebrity — that carnivorous response — that ballplayers are victimized. We want to tear down people who do things that we can't do, who have more money than we have, and we'll do it for any reason at hand — drugs, money, selfishness, laziness. There are always plenty of negatives to attribute to the players, if you want to look for them. We have to work to change this perception, because perception is reality in the entertainment business. I think it's going to be relatively easy to get this done, as long as the players go along. Every time a $5 million star offers to put up a couple of hundred dollars for some charity for every home run he hits, it gets amazing mileage. It also wouldn't hurt if we could eliminate the disdain that a few of the players show for anybody else, whether it's the fans, management, umpires, or less talented teammates."

Better public relations, Alderson thinks, is one area where the players and also the different clubs can easily benefit from a unified, un-Balkanized approach, as they have lately been doing with merchandising. He is enthusiastic about the new crop of television commercials — a $15 million "Welcome to the Show" campaign put together by Goodby, Silverstein & Partners, which is the agency responsible for a classy campaign for the National Basketball Association. The spots are clearly aimed at the recalcitrant, stay-at-home fan. In one of them, a "connoisseur of hot dogs" is seen wolfing down a Ball Park frank, and another spot presents Bill Lee, the old Fenway Spaceman, weirdly discoursing on the aerodynamics of the ball. My own favorite spot, produced by ESPN, presents a beautiful but sulky young woman pouting in a grandstand seat (she represents the game, of all things) who morphs into the looming, bearded phiz of John Kruk, the disheveled recent Phillies first baseman, leaning in to kiss the camera. "Don't you love it!" Alderson said. "It's not that 'Field of Dreams' approach — it doesn't patronize. Kruk's face is so disarming that you can't resist."

I came home from Arizona and unpacked, and in a twinkling, it seemed, found myself hurrying down the gum-blackened, malodorous steps of the I.R.T. 161st Street El station on my way to another season. Nothing had changed: the cops and Sabrett wagons, the TV tricks and pigeons and handball players, and, of course, Yankee Stadium itself, patiently waiting there for us — the same junky old high-wall sanitarium, and, inside, swarms of pale-faced fellow-inmates, released to the yard after our long stretch in solitary, gravely shaking hands and squinting in the thin spring sunshine. Except for the game, Opening Day went by without incident, and we were reassured by some ancient keepers and the ritual mild rounds of welcome and return. Eddie Layton, the senior-citizen happy-hour organist, did his between-innings (and between high-amp blasts of rock) showpieces, twiddling the dopey vox-humana cadenzas and beaming at us from his keyboards, via the big centerfield screen; and announcer Bob Sheppard, enunciating the pregame lineups, reminded us that we were not just catching the Knicks again over the tube, or visiting Barcelona or the Villa Borghese, but were safely home in the Bronx: "Daahnn-nee Taahrtt-a-bulll — rightt fieldd."

I chatted with scribe pals and sat for a while with Mel Allen, resplendent in a sky-blue tie, in the home dugout, where he told us, "On a day like this, your mind has got to go back to the good days." Mine was there already. Robert Merrill did the anthem once again, this time somehow bringing back memories of Bert Lahr; and Joe DiMaggio, waving and smiling at the stands as he never did when in uniform, threw out the first ball from the front of the mound and then made a little trot back toward home to retrieve the memento-pill from the catcher. Joe D., who is 80 now, could impart class to a K-mart ribbon-cutting. The Clipper was succeeded on the mound by Governor Pataki and Mayor Giuliani, there for a *second* first-ball ceremony. They got a nice fat round of boos for their pains. Ah, America.

All of us, I think, were waiting for the crowd to say something about the strike and the pains of our long exile, but it never happened. The official gate count, of 50,245, included about two hundred women, to judge by my quick binocular census, and the guys, in company with their sons and cousins and brothers-in-law (and the poor schlump from the hardware store — *you* know, he never gets to go anyplace, let's bring him along), in their gigantic sports windbreakers over their bulging gym-built or Bud-built upper bods, filled the tiered long rows to bursting, where they guzzled and stuffed their faces and laughed and yelled and bumped chests (the high-five is at last fading), and even watched the game a little, too. A visiting Dallas columnist, beside me in the press box (it was Yanks-Rangers, on this strange mid-schedule Opening Day), said, "God *damn*, this is an awful tame crowd for Yankee Stadium. Maybe it's a replacement crowd." But he needn't have worried. The right-field bleachers were in full late-August voice by the second or third inning, belting out their rapid-fire, evenly spaced, pissed-off-sounding "OHH-OHH! OHH-OHH! OHH-OHH!" battle cry, and then, after they'd spotted a little fracas in the lower-reserved section and some hapless responding security guards, switching over to the happy "AHHSS-OLE! AHHSS-OLE! AHHSS-OLE!" theme, which rolled across the long lawns and around the upper deck and came echoing back from the shadowed deep rows behind third. I was in Heaven — well, a back corner of it.

The baseball was all right — about what you'd expect, given the circumstances. Jimmy Key, the resident Opening Day southpaw (his record now stands at 6–0 in this peculiar specialty), set down the visitors in neat bunches while looking a bit below his best, until he abruptly ran out of gas in the sixth and was gone. He was apologetic in the clubhouse afterward and said he expected to be a bit more fine in the near future — which is to say that he will show the batters those Mozartean changes of tempo and location that send them back to their dugout in enlightened dismay. Tartabull and Bernie Williams contributed a home run each to the eventual 8–6 Yankee win, and second baseman Pat Kelly rolled out a gemlike bunt base hit in the sixth which helped build a quieter but no less material run. John Wetteland, the dominating new Yankee closer acquired in a trade this April from the impoverished Montreal Expos (he registered 105 saves for them over the past three seasons), came on in the ninth and shut down the proceedings in proper fashion, writing a "K" at the bottom of the page. He performed quickly, which is apparently not a work habit understood by an earlier toiler out there — the Texas starter, Kenny Rogers. During part of the Yankee third inning, I was able to crack, disrobe, and devour five peanuts, consult the Rangers' media guide to learn the whereabouts of their departed general manager, Tom Grieve (he has joined their cable television team), and conduct, via my stat sheets, a protracted study of the list of previous Yankee Opening Day pitchers, going clear back to 1946 (Spud Chandler, against the Philadelphia Athletics), all while Rogers was delivering himself of two balls and a foul to Paul O'Neill. "C'mon," I said at last, "throw the *ball!*" Baseball, if I needed further reminding, was back.

The fans, let's face it, are not in a mood to be quickly charmed back into ballparks by those suddenly affable big-league stars who have been handing out autographs before game time or tossing their caps into the crowds for souvenirs. Nor will they be instantly won over by a realization that the infielders and pitchers and batters out there are doing something perhaps more demanding than a Charles Barkley slam dunk. In spite of some deep discounts at the box office — the Mets offered all seats at a dollar for their first weekend at Shea, and the Royals gave away twenty thousand tickets outright, for instance — attendance was sharply down in most parks in both leagues, with actual attendance in some places comically or pathetically lower than the announced totals. The fans who did go were in an obstreperous mood, interrupting play with individual forays onto the field. In Tiger Stadium, where bleacher crowds can quickly turn ugly, play was nearly suspended when some fans out there began heaving bottles and batteries and the like at the visiting Indians outfielders. Whether this general sourness will last, or whether it will break down into localized glooms waiting to depress the gate the moment a home team begins to slip in the standings, is something we won't know until midseason. One thing that is already noticeable is that early attendance totals were heavily off in some of the cities whose franchise holders were known to be among the hardest of the hard-line owners in the recent debacle — in Houston, Kansas City, and Miami, for instance, and at Comiskey Park, the home base of the unbenevolent Jerry Reisdorf. His opposite among the owners is Peter G. Angelos, a Baltimore labor lawyer, who refused to prepare a squad of replacement Orioles players during the first round of spring training, and said he would not field such a team once the season started. (His stand infuriated his fellow-capitalists, and they may now attempt to punish him in the next round of league expansions by awarding a cut-rate franchise to Washington, where large sectors of the Orioles' fan base make their home.) The O's, whose assets include the delectable downtown Camden Yards — the very model of a modern major stadium — and the game's prime active hero, Cal Ripken, Jr., drew 97 percent of capacity for their home opener and have already sold 85 percent of the available tickets for the remainder of the season. The best P.R., one might almost say, comes naturally.

If my own state of mind about the immediate condition of the pastime is any indicator, bad feelings about baseball now center on the apparent indestructibility of the long feud between the two embittered parties, and the fact that the strike seems to have settled nothing. Negotiations between the owners and the Players Association, which had seemed to be edging closer to a compromise settlement just before Judge Sotomayor's intervention, have screeched to a stop, and there is persistent talk that both sides are now girding for another showdown at World Series time next year. For the present, both sides are left with a shattered economy that will continue to offer very high salaries to a relatively small number of star players — about 15 percent of the total, that is — and much less to the remainder. Major-market clubs like the Yankees and Braves and Colorado Rockies will continue to snatch up the available top pitchers and fielders and sluggers, as they have lately done with the likes of Jack McDowell and Marquis Grissom and Larry Walker, and have-not teams, such as the Expos and Mariners and Pirates — the small-market franchises whose plight the owners proclaimed was reason for a salary cap and a promise of subsequent revenue-sharing among the clubs — will cut their budgets and trim their talent even further, and still face deficits and renewed pressure to pull up stakes and move elsewhere. The Yanks signed McDowell, a top-of-the-class free-agent starter, lately of the White Sox, for a salary of $5,400,000, and acquired Wetteland, after outbidding several other teams equally in need of a tough closer, for players and cash. By contrast, many players of proved ability and experience — part of the bourgeoisie of baseball, so to speak — signed on last month for one-year salaries that were worth, in some cases, a fifth or a tenth of what they had been earning last year. As their agents pointed out, the strike had so depleted team revenues that there was no other option but to sign and play. This downturn in the salary scale has come as an unexpected prize for the owners at the end of a very rough journey, and they will undoubtedly wait and think about its meaning for some weeks or months before the notion of again sitting down across the table from the union begins to look like a useful or crucially imperative idea.

A week after the season started, I had a fax from a friend in Georgia, who wrote, "Yes, I've watched the Braves. Yes, I've read the box scores. I got tickets for August, damn them. Wuss City."

I absolutely understood this, because my wife and I had already accepted an invitation from friends of ours, another couple, for a Braves game this month, right here in New York, and I expect to catch the Dodgers at Shea later on this month, and the Mariners up at the Stadium early in June. I can always claim to myself that I'm *covering* these games, but it won't really be true. I'm in Wuss City, too — in fact, I may run for mayor. My own disaffection from baseball didn't make it past the top of the fourth inning of the Mets' home opener against the Cardinals — the moment when three young men jumped out of the stands and began scattering handfuls of paper money around the infield. Then they lined up in a row out by second base, with their fists in the air, and from the press box we could see that each of them had "Greed" inked across the front of his T-shirt. I was impressed — and even more so when it became clear that the greenbacks they'd thrown around weren't Monopoly money, as we'd assumed, but dollar bills. "Demonstration," I wrote in my notebook, but even before the field cops had taken the firebrands away and the grounds crew had swept up the loot, my effete, Eastern-liberal-humanist instincts of fanly solidarity had given way to the familiar upflow of irritation that comes over me whenever anything gets in the way of a ballgame — paper airplanes or a stray dog on the field, a descending parachutist or an earthquake, or even a passing August thunderstorm. Let's get with the program, God — this is *baseball*. In the act of proclaiming themselves fans, I mean, these bozos had disqualified themselves from membership in that company.

I had plenty of time in which to reflect on this discovery during the next few innings, when five or six other sans-culottes ran out into the middle of things (there to encounter that death-ray indifference of a big-league fielder or pitcher when confronted on the field by anybody in street clothes), although it seemed clear that the impelling sociopolitical force at work by now was beer. The crowd got a kick out of it, especially when still another fan scooted out from the stands while the bloodhounds were closing in on some idiots in center field, and wrenched the third-base bag loose from its moorings — a first, in my experience — and started to scoot back again, with the souvenir tucked under his arm. ("'FAN STEALS THIRD,'" three journalists near me in the press box murmured in unison.) With my binocs, I caught a glimpse of the miscreant's face just before he was escorted — heavily escorted — down the dugout steps, and it was clear that he was searching the stands for William Kunstler.

None of this, it turned out, was as entertaining as the game itself: a noisy, high-scoring, poorly played affair (the scorer was in a forgiving, spring-planting sort of mood) in which the pitchers handed out runs and home runs like — well, like dollar bills, and the fans' boos and cheers often seemed to overlap. The moment of the evening — the moment of this baseball year for me so far — came in the top of the seventh, when the Mets' rookie right fielder, Carl Everett, called off his center fielder on a fly ball and threw out the tagged-up Cardinals base runner, the fleet Brian Jordan, with an airmail, into-the-mitt double-play peg that nailed him a yard or so up the third-base line, ending the inning. "Wow!" we said in the press box, in chorus with 26,604 surrounding pairs of tonsils — a poor home-opener crowd, if truth be told, but now an extremely happy one. Inspired, the Mets came in to bat and responded with an instant home run (it was by Rico Brogna) and then two more runs that recaptured the lead and, it turned out, won the game as well.

If there is a retreat or a statement here, it has to do only with the limited opportunities that we fans have available to us during these plague years of baseball. We are never consulted by the opposing moneyed powers in the course of their ill-tempered maneuverings, and whenever a brief armistice does come along, their overtures to us, whether in the form of cut-rate tickets or extra autographs, are demeaning. I understand the impulse to stay home and shut the doors and windows against baseball (does this ever include the games that come in on the tube, I wonder), but no one suffers more from such an embargo than we do. Our remaining choices, it occurs to me, aren't all that bad. We can go to a game. Then we can go to another one, maybe with friends. We won't just stay home and catch the game on television again — where Don Mattingly shares time with Larry King, and the difficult two-on-and-one-out threat in the sixth is suspended by our click-click to old bits of *NYPD Blue*. We won't balk at the price: twenty-odd dollars for a pair of mezzanine reserved is a quarter of the hit for a Knicks game. We'll *go*. Then, along about the All-Star Game break, we might even take a chance and hurry back to the same park in the hope of picking up a pair of seats at the window, just before game time. Anybody who follows this plan — I semi-guarantee this — will stop thinking that he can play ball as well as or better than the guys on the field, and won't care by as much as an old peanut shell whether he is helping the plutocrat owners. He will be a fan again, and — for this season, at least — the proprietor of our amazing game.

ROGER ANGELL

The Game's the Thing

FROM THE NEW YORKER

BASEBALL, A SHABBY carnival for most of this season past, has folded its patchy tents, leaving us at the close with some unaccustomed feelings of pleasure and even clarity. The Atlanta Braves, in dominating the hyperextended postseason play (they won eleven out of fourteen games on the way to their championship) and suppressing the scary Cleveland Indians in the World Series, confirmed what had previously been only a statistical truth: they are the team of the nineties. Now their doggedly chanting and tomahawking fans can put away memories of the team's exquisitely painful defeats in the World Series of 1991 (in which they lost each of the last two games to the Twins in extra innings) and 1992 (four one-run losses to the Blue Jays), and even their unexpected fall to the grungy, overachieving Phillies in the 1993 league championships, and relish happier late returns. The Braves, late of Milwaukee and, earlier, Boston, are the first major league club to bring home the crown in three different towns; even better, they are the first major sports franchise in Atlanta to win it all in the end. For the rest of us, gratitude comes in plainer terms, for the Braves have now become the World Champions we were deprived of by last year's players' strike and, in a miracle of simplification, have made the preposterous 1995 season almost understandable. They are the Big Unit, as even Randy Johnson might agree.

The six-game World Series, which brought us some remarkable pitching performances, was absorbing and close and sometimes tense but, let's face it, a bit short on drama. It had few of the deep, bell-gonging overtones of that Braves-Twins matchup four years ago, and never came close to the amazements of the Mets and Red Sox' Ring cycle of 1986. *That* year, the Series was preceded by marvelous playoff championships in both leagues, featuring games and innings and at-bats (Don Baylor's and Dave Henderson's against the Angels in Anaheim; the day-into-night Mets-Astros du ellings down in Houston) that are still talked about whenever and wherever fans gather: taken together, those twenty postseason games felt like a sudden school holiday. I doubt that we'll ever get that sort of baseball back again, if only because there are so many games now that they are diminished in the sorting out. By arranging for an extra round of postseason meetings, with preliminary divisional playoffs that include "wild card" clubs which failed to win their regional sectors but outdid the other certified losers, the baseball planners have increased the chances that there will be some wonderful or god-awful games somewhere in October but in the process have destroyed the essential critical ingredient, which is rarity. They have also confused and driven away uncountable sports followers who once thought of themselves as baseball fans but, it quickly became apparent, could not understand how this new postseason worked (even the players had problems with this, to judge by dugout conversations I heard during the last week of the regular season) or quite remember who was playing. Many friends with whom I happily used to talk baseball at the end of the summer have fallen into this category. As things came down, there were thirty-one postseason games this time around (out of a mind-bending possible forty-one), which made for plenty of baseball entertainment, just as the owners and planners had hoped, but, inevitably, less that can be remembered. Baseball feels like the rest of America now: it feels like television.

Early on in the opening Mariners-Yankees divisional game, up at Yankee Stadium, I began to appreciate how many evidences of baseball good fortune were represented there that night. There was the stirring September work by both clubs that had landed them, each very late in the day, in this new tournament: the Yankees had gone 21–6 for the month, and claimed the wild card with eleven wins in their final twelve games; while the visitors had captured the American League West only after coming from behind in twelve of their winning games over the final month (this is unheard of), and then knocking out the Angels in a tacked-on, winner-take-all elimination. That game, completed only the night before, out at Seattle's Kingdome, had used up the Mariners' six-foot-ten left-handed ace, Randy Johnson, at least for the time being, which meant that the Yanks wouldn't have to face the league's best pitcher (18–2 for the season, and the eventual American League Cy Young Award winner) for these two home games in the short series. There was also the special pleasure of watching Don Mattingly, the Yanks' perennial storekeeper at first base ("Donn-ee *Base*-ball! Donn-ee *Base*-ball!" the bleacherites chanted), catching and throwing and batting in this, the first postseason game of his fourteen-year career. Even late in the evening, it felt fluky that the Yankees somehow remained tied, at 4–4, after the second of the two silencing home runs blasted by the visitors' Ken Griffey, Jr., each whacked off a dawdling split-finger delivery by David Cone. Mostly, though, it was the crowd itself that made me feel lucky — a 57,178 turnout, unmatched at the Stadium since 1976, which seemed determined to make up in one night for its mass silences and absences down the long Steinbrennerian twilight. The Yankees won, 9–6, but it was the fans that both clubhouses talked about afterward. "The loudest for a long, long while," said Seattle manager Lou Piniella, a trusted critic of this particular orchestra. The Yankee skipper, Buck Showalter, was almost voluble for once. "Such a passion and energy here tonight," he said. "I've asked Willie and Lou and Reggie and Stick" — imperial old Yankees all — "what it used to be like here in a pennant race, but I can't imagine it could be more electric." He sounded like a kid brother just home from a major date: the big first.

The outsize events on the field, the wild noises of the crowd, and the exclamatory excitement of the players and watchers seemed to flow over, unchecked, into the next night's event — a drizzly, unbridled, fifteen-inning, 7–5 all-timer that was concluded, eight minutes before one-thirty in the morning, by Jim Leyritz's two-run homer — the sixth round-tripper of the game. There were 27 hits, but the constant retyings of the score and changes in the lead — the Yankees fell behind and then bounced back four different times — did away with the sense of slackness that sometimes afflicts these marathon affairs. The abrupt turns of fortune and some outlandishly bad calls by the umps made for interesting changes in timbre from the bleachers. With a Mariner runner at third in the top of the sixth, Yankee shortstop Tony Fernandez threw himself behind the bag to stop a grounder and freeze the runner; face down in the dirt, he had no chance to finish the play but flipped up the ball to his second-baseman partner, Randy Velarde, who fired to first for the out. Nobody in the press box had ever seen it done before. A bit earlier, Griffey had slightly bobbled Fernandez's drive to deep left but had then whirled and thrown a fiery low strike to second base, to erase him there, silencing the bleacherites for only a moment. "Fuck you, *Ju*-nior! Fuck you, *Ju*-nior!" came their merry, choirlike response. Impossible, outrageous, hilarious, rocking and roaring its deafening anthems (the Village People's "YMCA" is the latest great yell-along), the crowd never quit. Like it or not, they were us: New York defiant, having the time of its life.

Long, loud games can go by very quickly, but even in this one there were plenty of those baseball pauses in which the looks and quirks of the dramatis personae impinge themselves upon our fanly attention: the glowering scowl of the slump-emerging Paul O'Neill; Griffey standing tall in the batter's box, with his black bat up by his ear as he begins his little toe-to-toe jiggle before the pitch; the placid, almost sleepy gaze with which the semi-anonymous Edgar Martinez — a semi-anonymous two-time batting champion — regards the arriving fastball; Lou Piniella, a little more popeyed and bullfroggy than we remembered him, wiggling his toes beneath the bench as he watches; the imperious Roman stare of young Andy Pettitte from atop the mound; Bernie Williams drawing that surveyor's line in the dirt with his bat before he steps into the box; and so on, right down to Don Mattingly's oddly twisted back leg after he swings and fouls off the pitch. All this and the wonderfully ornate and childish masquerade of Ruben Sierra after he has launched another homer — the bat dropped flat (I'm done with *you!*), the two-step backward shimmy that he finishes with a little pluck at his shirtfront (Be still, my heart!), and only then the unsmiling, nothing-to-it, slow-and-then-slower tour of the bases. We forgave him all this after he hit another dinger, his second in two days, to tie things up again in the bottom of the sixth, and it was forgotten in any case after Mattingly's instantly ensuing shot into the centerfield seats. Cheers and laughter and torn-up paper came out of the upper decks, and then some harder kinds of debris as well. Manager Lou,

who had been observed kicking and throwing things in his dugout,
took the occasion to pull his troops from the field — a brilliant
managerial ploy if there is such a thing as momentum in a ball
game. We resumed in time, and no harm done, but the pause
allowed a good many of us to wonder what sort of fans come to a
ball game carrying extra batteries to fling at the visiting outfielders.

Not much more need be said here to convey the breadth and
tenor of this long, quick evening, except about the weird moment
in the bottom of the twelfth when Sierra's smash to the top of the
left-centerfield fence scored a pinch runner, Posada, with the tying
run and brought Bernie Williams flying around second and then
third with the sure winner. The Yankee dugout emptied as everybody rushed plateward, waving towels and dancing up and down to
welcome him home, as — oop, as the relay (left fielder Diaz to
shortstop Sojo to catcher Widger) came flying past Bernie's slide
and nailed him cleanly at the plate, where the ump punched him
out, ending the inning. It was all done so quickly that for a moment
nobody quite knew what had happened. Stopped in their tracks,
the celebrating Yankees slowly turned away and walked in the other
direction; and the rest of us (What! Wha?) stared at the replay
screen, and only then took our seats again. All right, we're tied.
Bring us more baseball.

After the last of the baseball, which was, as noted, Leyritz's two-
run homer in the fifteenth, the catcher talked lengthily with the
media (the morning writers were looking for something quick for
their editions) in front of his locker. He is a veteran Yankee, tattooed and crew-cut — a biker catcher — but he couldn't get over
the game. Don Mattingly got to the heart of it more quickly: "We'd
stay up all night for this. People rise up."

The games resumed on the opposite coast, where the Mariners,
within the vast, gloomy closet of the Kingdome, dismissed the
Yankees in three clangorous meetings — a huge present to their
success-starved fans, who were facing the loss not just of this pre-
pennant series but of the franchise itself. In a plebiscite conducted
before the M's attained the American League West title, local voters
had defeated by a narrow margin a plan to finance a new baseball-
only stadium in Seattle — an outcome, the team's owners had
warned, that would lead to the sale of the club and, almost surely, its

removal to another city. But the thrill and noise of winning — no wonder those splendid Seattle rooters yelled so loud — are unanswerable politics, and while the M's were putting up their valorous losing struggle against the Indians in the American League Championship Series the Washington State legislature reversed the voters' decision and worked out a ballpark deal — Build It and They Won't Go — that will keep baseball and Boeing and *caffè latte* on the same waterfront. The Yankees, in any case, first ran into Randy Johnson out there (he struck out ten of them, on an otherwise off night); then suffered an appalling meltdown of their bullpen while losing a game in which they had led by five runs; and then expired in the eleventh inning of the finale, with the Big Unit, on one day's rest, taking the win in relief. I was watching at home, and the presiding image of these games — the most vivid series of the entire postseason — was the combative, icy-faced David Cone, utterly spent after 147 pitches, bent double on the mound in agony after walking in the game-tying run.

Malcontent fans who persist in viewing big-league ballplayers as a pack of spoiled millionaires never seem to recall moments like this, but the truth remains that we demand a lot of these samurai late in the year — especially the guys out on that little hill. This year, we saw the Conean tableau in several variations: the Angels' Mark Langston clutching his temples in the dugout after being outpitched but not outfought by the Unit in that earlier, one-game elimination, only to see his chances go glimmering with a broken-bat, bases-clearing double that ended up under the Angels' bullpen bench; and later on, inexorably, Randy Johnson himself waving forlornly to the Kingdome fans as he took his leave in the sixth game of the ALCS, down by four runs to the Indians after giving up a home run to Carlos Baerga. It was his first defeat since August first, but even tyro fans there must have been able to see that after his fifth appearance in fifteen days that marvelous left arm had turned to Kleenex. He had said this might be coming. "I need a rest," he told the media-swarm after his prior outing and third postseason appearance. "You guys think I'm invincible, but I'm not. I'm in uncharted waters."

Orel Hershiser, who went 16–6 this year for the Indians and then won four of his five starts in the postseason, gave the expected answer when asked how he felt about pitching on three days' rest:

"Whatever they want me to do, I'll do it." As it came out, this was the only time this fall when Orel was asked to work on short rest — and almost the only time when he was heard to utter a baseball cliché. When I pressed him a bit about the strain on pitchers' arms imposed by the special demands of late-season ball and now by the extra burden of an added round of playoffs, he said, "It gets you into a risk/reward area. . . . The deeper the playoffs are, the more risk you're willing to take. There are going to be times when a manager will have to stay away from a hot hand in order to protect a pitcher's career." Conversations between pitchers and managers about the state of the pitcher's arm on the eve of a big game tend to be short ones, he admitted. "Tommy" — Lasorda, his old manager with the Dodgers — "wasn't one to mince words," Hershiser said. "If he got a yes out of you, he wouldn't try to talk you out of it."

Hershiser delivered all this with his customary optimistic cool, but his message had a certain weight. He is an adult, and not just in years (he is 37 now, though he scarcely looks it), and is thus in a minority in his profession, and it was a treat to be around him this year while he was enjoying a return to something close to the peak he had enjoyed during his glory years in Los Angeles. Back in 1988, he delivered one of the game's historic sustained pitching performances: a 23–8 season for the Dodgers which included a stretch of 59 consecutive scoreless innings; a Cy Young Award as the top pitcher in his league; and then successive Most Valuable Player citations in the league championships and the World Series — he was 3–0 in six games, with a shutout in each series. Not once in his 42-plus postseason innings that year was he granted more than three days off between starts, and at one point came on to close out a game in relief on the day after completing seven innings as a starter. These things can befall particularly tough and successful pitchers, and so can some other things. In April of 1990, Hershiser underwent extensive shoulder surgery on his pitching arm, from which, as he said late this summer, he is only now nearing a complete recovery. This is a happy story, as such matters are counted.

Hershiser's surprising decision to remove himself from the proceedings in the midst of the first game of this year's World Series is to the point here, in that it tells us how rarely pitchers, however smart and experienced, become participants in the hard decision about when they should pitch and when they should sit down. With the score at 1–1 in the bottom of the seventh, Hershiser, after walking the first two Atlanta batters, received a routine visit at the mound by Indians pitching coach Mark Wiley, who was startled to hear Orel say that he had lost the release point for his pitches and was thus probably not the right man to face the dangerous Ryan Klesko, now coming up to bat. Hershiser did not claim to be out of gas or hurting; he was out of kilter. Cleveland manager Mike Hargrove, though unhappy about the turn of events, had no choice but to take him out, and controversy grew deeper when the men Orel had walked subsequently came around to score the tying and, it turned out, winning runs of the game. The loss broke his string of seven wins without defeat in postseason play. Hargrove stood behind his starter in the subsequent interviews, and while no one wanted to question Orel's heart, the matter hung oddly in the air for the rest of the week.

Given another start in Game Five, Hershiser threw eight strong innings and won (thereby returning the Series to Atlanta for the final weekend), and then cheerfully reopened the case in the postgame colloquy. He'd had the good of the team in mind, he said, and he'd "checked out on ego" in asking to be relieved. Next time, though, given the same circumstances, he would probably say nothing. "Maybe I should have been less of a manager and more of a player," he conceded. Asked, perhaps with a trace of cynicism, how he had recovered his release point for this day's start, he delivered another strikeout. "The number-one thing was that I stood taller on the mound," he said. "That allowed my hips to get out from under my shoulders. I've been told many times by Sandy Koufax that you have to stand high to throw low."

The wavery time line of this account can be defended only as a reflection of one fan's state of mind while under bombardment by so many critical games and at-bats, plays and pitches. Nor can I excuse the omission of other accomplished teams, whose arrival into and sad departure from the various postseason tourneys will not be expanded upon here: the Colorado Rockies, who came bounding into the playoffs after coming back from a six-run deficit in their very last regular-season game but fell quickly to the Braves; or the Cincinnati Reds, picked by many as the club most likely to go all the way, who knocked off the Dodgers without strain but were shut down (and shut out, four games to none) by the Braves in the National League championship. I should point out that even a reporter with heroic staying powers could not have taken in all these games this time around, because of the ridiculous scheme imposed by the baseball planners which gave us "regionalized" television coverage of the postseason, thus confining watchers to a single, arbitrarily selected game from the two or three or four being played on a given October evening. It will not happen again next fall, someone having convinced these same bumblers that hiding the product may not be a viable strategy for a declining national industry.

All this and the Red Sox, too — my old gang, who enjoyed such a brilliant August this year and went belly up once again in October. Their trancelike state during the last of their three-and-out defeats by the Indians, and particularly the hopeless at-bats of the inestimable Mo Vaughn, sent me home from Fenway Park with a nearly empty notebook: nothing to remember. Some of my Sox-benighted friends have mentioned the ancient Curse of the Bambino in whispering about this new debacle, but I suspect that a more hideous spell is at work: the Curse of the Boot. The Sox have lost thirteen straight postseason games, going back to the instant in the tenth inning of the sixth game of the 1986 World Series against the Mets when Bill Buckner allowed Mookie Wilson's little bouncer to go frisking through his legs out behind first base. It's time for Max von Sydow.

Another hovering occult mystery was the simultaneous disabling of *two* team mascots in the postseason — the Mariner Moose, who broke an ankle when his all-terrain vehicle dragged him into the Kingdome outfield fence, and the Indians' Slider (a ripoff of the Phillie Phanatic, if there ever was one), who fell off the right-field wall in mid-somersault and blew out his right knee. I suspect the hand of God.

I feel less compunction in passing over just about the entire 1995 schedule of games — a shortened season that began after an injunction by a federal judge barely saved the game from the presence of strikebreaking "replacement players" on the field, and was played out in many cities in half-empty stadiums as the fans continued to show their displeasure with the ongoing labor standoff between the owners and players. The boring and ill-tempered wrangle remains no closer to solution than it was on Opening Day. Attendance during the regular season was down about nineteen per cent, over all. Winning teams and some fresh stars — the Dodgers' writhing Japanese pitcher Hideo Nomo among them — brought some of the customers back, and so did the August celebrations in Baltimore surrounding Cal Ripken, Jr.,'s 2131st consecutive game, which eclipsed Lou Gehrig's old road marker. It was a blue-collar sort of achievement in a limo and luxury-box era of the sport — satisfying and irrelevant in equal parts, since Ripken is a modest hero who earns $6 million a year. I share in the general amazement that he was able to endure without serious injury while fulfilling the difficult and risky requirements of a shortstop. On the other hand, I don't believe he would have lasted anywhere near such a distance if he'd been playing, say, right field. What keeps a man eager to punch that time clock day after day is an interesting job.

The passing of Mickey Mantle — he died of cancer in August, after surviving a liver-replacement operation necessitated in part by his years of alcoholism — also brought back thoughts of a sunnier era in the game. He was a sad and perhaps a tragic figure, but right to the last he retained a sweetness and directness that made his struggles for a little sobriety near the end of his life as much of a feat as anything he achieved on the field. There was no fakery or P.R. about him, and that made it easy for us to remember the shy, blond Oklahoma kid who turned up at the Stadium in 1951 and began slugging the ball and running the bases in a fashion that took your breath away. I've heard people say what a shame it was that Mantle happened to play just across the Harlem River from the only better player in the city (and in that part of the century), Willie Mays, but it wasn't like that at all for us fans. It was a kick.

Indians fans had a carefree summer in their dandy new downtown ballpark, Jacobs Field, where they watched their bullying hitters power the club to its 100-win season, a marvel in an abbreviated year like this one. Each game won and every run-up, lopsided score must have been candy for the hometown faithful after their have-not, tenement upbringing: it had been forty-one seasons since Cleveland's last pennant. The Tribe led the league in hitting, homers, runs, total bases, stolen bases, sellout crowds, and ear muggings — the last committed by the stadium's postmod-

ern sound system and its idiotic, prizefight-style announcement
("CARRRR-LOHSSSSS BAEERRR-GGAAAH!") of each and every
home-team batter. The team's avatar and driving force was the
antisocial, ferociously intense cleanup batter Albert Belle, whose
52 doubles, 1 triple, and 50 homers this season made him the first
major-leaguer to rap 100 extra-base hits since Stan Musial turned
the trick in 1948. I think the Mariners must have felt a little shiver
at the prospect of watching Belle let loose in the championship
series while surrounded by the likes of Baerga, the senior-statesman
slugger Eddie Murray, the exuberantly muscular, short-swinging
third baseman Jim Thome, and the baby-faced outfielder Manny
Ramirez (the Cleveland batting order regularly included seven
players who batted .300 this year, and five with better than twenty
home runs), but what caught one's attention as the games wore on
was the Indians' pitching. Squeezed and parched, the Seattle batters could put up only a couple of frail one-run innings in their last
three games. Edgar Martinez, repeatedly pitched to in the up-and-
in, low-and-away pattern, resembled the victim of a curare-tipped
dart while he was in the box, feebly and politely expiring (he batted
.087 for these games) while his friends and family kept insisting
that he would feel better any moment now.

    With no prior loyalty to either of these teams, my incorrigibly
boyish attachment went automatically to the underdog M's, in
those stylish navy and green caps, who rewarded me with their dash
and grit, and entranced us all with their melodramatic, eleventh-in-
ning comeback win in Game Three at Jacobs Field — more of a
movie than a ball game. With Randy Johnson again out there in the
middle, his lank locks fluttering in the lakeside breezes, and the
Seattles up by 2–1, matters appeared to be in hand until Jay Buhner, their goateed, egg-bald right fielder, muffed a deep fly ball in
the eighth, putting aboard what eventually became the tying run.
From my perch in the auxiliary press box, directly behind this
street accident, I saw Buhner start to backpedal casually, then more
anxiously as the approaching ball grew in size. He disappeared
below the rim of the wall an instant before an incredulous 43,643-
breath, collective shout, which gave me all the news or replay that I
needed. Buhner had knocked an earlier solo home run, but it was
his second one, with two runners aboard in the eleventh, that
chilled the locals (the Indians had been previously undefeated in

extra innings this year) and also, as he told us later, took care of the awkward little social silence that had surrounded him in the dugout after his mistake. "Relief?" he said. "Disbelief? All of the above."

Televised baseball, to which I again had recourse at home, has its discontents (one of them is named Brent Musburger), but its details can add a texture and filigree that you sometimes miss at the park. Watching Hershiser's habitual cricking of his head off to his left in mid-pitch, for instance, you suddenly notice how it opens up the entire right side of his body for the full-sweeping, forward and downward delivery. From Seattle we were given closeups of Baerga's earplugs (defense against the Dome din), and also of a pleasing earlier moment, when 22-year-old Bob Wolcott, the Mariners' surprise starter and winner in Game One, was found sitting next to Johnson in the dugout after giving way in the eighth to the bullpen relievers, who would sew it up for him. Both men were smiling over Wolcott's outing, and then the Unit gave him a little slap on the thigh with the back of his glove: Great game, kid. The hovering camera eye has trained us to keep close watch on the dugout after ugly moments as well. Sometimes we can actually pick up the magic word in the act of formation, as when the manager's lower lip is placed just behind his upper teeth and the famous fricative takes wing. Mike Hargrove gave us a demonstration when his left-handed reliever Paul Assenmacher, inserted in a game expressly to get rid of the left-hitting Tino Martinez, threw ball four instead. And who can blame him?

The Braves, on arriving at their third recent World Series, reminded me of the old Yankees, not just because they won but because they have learned the trick of changing while seeming to look like the same team. Only nine players among the new champions were on the Atlanta roster that fell before the Twins in 1991. The additions include some established players picked up by trade (first baseman Fred McGriff, center fielder Marquis Grissom) or free-agent signing (Greg Maddux), and an equal number of home-grown, carefully brought-along young stars like Javier Lopez, Ryan Klesko, and Chipper Jones, who have begun distinguished major league careers. More kids are on the way, including the center fielder Andruw Jones, who was named minor league player of the year while playing for the Class A Macon Braves. The pitching rotation — Maddux, Tom Glavine, Steve Avery, and John Smoltz — has been intact for three years, an eternity in modern baseball, and accounts for the stable, well-ordered feeling that surrounds the club, and for its habit of success. What matters about the Braves' championship isn't just the loot and the glory but the confirmation of general manager John Schuerholz and manager Bobby Cox (who preceded Schuerholz as general manager) in their painstaking, one-game-at-a-time way of conducting their operation. It is a model for a business that continues to find room for embarrassing relics like George Steinbrenner and Marge Schott.

The Indians' two victories in the World Series and their grudging resistance throughout could never quite free them from the numbing efficiency of the Atlanta pitching. Greg Maddux, the current holder of the Braves' tenured Cy Young chair (he has just won the award for an unprecedented fourth consecutive year), opened the proceedings with a suffocating two-hit win, and Glavine (with an assist from Mark Wohlers) wrapped things up a week later with a one-hitter. Only the closeness of the competition (five of the six games were settled by a single run) made us believe from time to time that a different outcome might be possible. The Clevelands, in batting .179 as a team, arrived at a Zen-like understanding of the recent plight of the Mariners.

It's hard to know how the Atlanta pitching played to a national audience that has lately proclaimed itself disenchanted with the old game. Neither Maddux nor Glavine is a pitcher in the gasping, edge-of-your-seat Sandy Koufax or Bob Gibson mode. Rather, they conduct their business in the style of actuaries — studious collectors of numbers and patterns and opportunities, who arrive at a plan and then ride it through to the end. Maddux, who has a glazed, pallid stare, studies hitters and hitting styles so obsessively that he confessed, after his masterpiece, that he hadn't found it necessary to look at most of the dossier compiled by the Atlanta scouts. He did consult his brother Mike (who pitches for the Red Sox) about some details. And after that? "Well, you just try to make pitches, you know?" He shrugged. "Yes, I was very pleased, but . . ." He sounded less bored than removed (he claims he doesn't watch the games he is pitching during the interludes spent on the bench) but then seemed to sense a need to apologize. "What was I *thinking?*" he said. "Well, uh, just make my pitch. That's what you do."

Those pitches, you could see in the replays, were in the standard repertoire: fastballs that moved in or out; cutting and sinking
breaking stuff inside to left-handed hitters; pitches away to set up
their opposite; and so on. Every one of them arrived just on or just
off the outer inch or two of the plate — a strike zone that became
wider late in the game as home-plate umpire Harry Wendelstedt
grew bemused by Maddux's work. Maddux said he had made perhaps twenty bad pitches, but they were hard for us to remember.
"When he misses, he misses out of the strike zone," said his catcher,
Charlie O'Brien. Atlanta errors led to unearned runs for the visitors in the first inning and then in the ninth of that opening game,
but what my boringly clear scorecard says is that Jim Thome's single
in the fifth inning was the only break in a string of twenty-five consecutive Cleveland batters retired by Maddux, eighteen of them
on ground-ball outs. Not much there for the home-towners to
moan or tomahawk over, but for pitchers, of course, no news is the
main idea.

The Indians were more considerate, capturing both of their er-
ror-filled, adventurous wins before their home crowds with noisy
late-night outbreaks — a clean, game-winning single by Eddie Murray in the first one and a homer by Thome for a lead that barely
held up in Game Five, keeping Hershiser's win intact. Maddux, in
his second start, continued to entertain us, though less austerely,
giving up a first-inning home run into the right field seats to Albert
Belle, and then throwing a purpose pitch past the throat of the very
next batter, Murray, who glared and pointed, and even took a few
steps toward the mound, emptying the dugouts and bullpens. The
ruckus had all the ferocity of a "Sesame Street" party, but it did
permit the rival pitchers a unique (in my memory, at least) opportunity to exchange views out on the field, where the peerless Maddux explained that the pitch had been intended to move Eddie
away from the plate but never — perish the thought — to hit him.
"But you have better control than that," replied the gentlemanly
Orel. "I'm going to have the ball, too," he added, gnomically.

To second-guess the managers here — an ancient privilege — the
experienced Bobby Cox gave us a running seminar on the need for
alternate nerve and patience in a short set of games, to my way of
thinking, while his opposite number, Hargrove, managed by the

book, which works well when your team is a dozen games ahead in its division in August but perhaps not so well when you're down a run to Greg Maddux late in a World Series game and decide to pull back your infield with the aim of giving up another run in return for a double play. He won't do it next time.

But it is the baseball itself that seizes us when innings and chances run down near the end. There is always more: Rafael Belliard's mouse-quick squeeze bunt; Kenny Lofton's six times on base in the third game; the vivid Indians shortstop Omar Vizquel bare-handing another ground ball at short; the whipping night wind lashing at the Cleveland rooters' fan-banners ("O MY OMAR" and "B-LEVELAND" and the rest) around the upper-deck facade at the Jake; Dennis Martínez, with a white towel wrapped around his neck, expressionless and elegant on the bench after his failed final effort, back in Atlanta; Dave Justice's ringing, Series-winning solo homer; and the suave Glavine pitching away and away all through *his* amazing game, feasting on that sliver. But such flashing moments recede quickly once the season ends, and we must let them go. Both of these teams, we should reassure ourselves, have been built for the long haul and will return, more or less intact, for our pleasure next spring, if we care to come back. This autumn, they reminded us once again that it isn't the games that let us down, but perhaps only ourselves. Attention, as somebody once said, must be paid.

DAVID REMNICK

Back in Play

FROM THE NEW YORKER

NEARLY ALL THE old American basketball arenas have been abandoned or razed, victims of the corporate demand for more "luxury suites," more room to hawk the beer and the cheese dogs and the "regulation" Nerf balls. Boston Garden is scheduled for demolition (the Celtics have played their last season on the exquisitely warped floor), and Chicago Stadium, once a graceful barn on the West Side, is already gutted — four walls in search of the wrecking ball. The Bulls play their games now across the street at the United Center ("United" as in the airline, of course), and the place features all the new amenities: lots of bathrooms, nice parking, no rats. The United Center is huge, cool, and white: a mobster's mausoleum, the world's largest freezer unit. It is a distant place to watch an intimate sport; the "luxury suites" are so far from the court that the plutocrats keep their televisions on during the game. All around the National Basketball Association, the geniuses who own teams seem to have no faith in the audiences or in basketball itself. At an ordinary weekend game at the Brendan Byrne Arena, in the Jersey swamps, not long ago, I sat through more low-end entertainment than Liberace knew in a lifetime. It was like Vegas Night at the chamber of commerce: fireworks and strobe lights during the introduction of the starting lineups; a karaoke contest; a recorded voice urging us to "stand up and cheer"; a recorded laugh mocking the efforts of a player at the foul line; two guys dressed in mattresses who declared themselves "sumo wrestlers" and jumped on top of each other during time-outs; dancing "Jersey Girls"; prepubescent "Junior Jersey Kids"; a mascot called Super Dunk who shot foam-

and-plastic sticks into the crowd. It's this way just about everywhere — Chicago included.

Michael Jordan once promised that he would never play at the United Center — Chicago Stadium was his Old Vic, his artistic home — but, with his decision to rejoin the Bulls after his midlife sabbatical as a minor league baseball player, he has deigned to enter the vulgar hall, and thus transform it. Just when the sports pages had become little more than labor reports and police blotters, Jordan stepped in. He has saved the spring.

Jordan, who is the most self-conscious of performers, began his unretirement from basketball March 19th with a gig in Indiana. Except for some brief thrilling moments — a breakaway dunk in the first half, a ferocious struggle for the ball with Reggie Miller in the second — he proved rusty against the Pacers: errant on the jump shot, winded at times, out of synch with his new teammates, barely reacquainted with the old. The Bulls' Croatian forward, Toni Kukoc, who had been heartbroken two years ago to discover that Jordan was leaving the team just as he was joining it, seemed daunted now by the return of his hero. Kukoc spent much of the Indiana game with his feet glued to the floor, his jaw slack. Like so many millions of others, Kukoc was delighted just to be watching Jordan — even a temporarily mortal Jordan — play the game again.

Jordan's first game in Chicago came five days later, against the Orlando Magic, a first-place team featuring two of the best young talents in the sport: Shaquille O'Neal, a Goliath with grace, and Anfernee (Penny) Hardaway, a silky guard who, with his preternatural sense for the flow of the game, reminds everyone of Earvin (Magic) Johnson. An hour before tipoff, I was talking with Hardaway in the Orlando locker room. The United Center's locker rooms are, admittedly, very new, very clean, like a suburban den. Ordinarily, teams play tapes of the night's opponents, but the Orlando players seemed determined to convince themselves that it was Michael Jordan who ought to be concerned about them. An episode of *Star Trek: The Next Generation* played on the television. Hardaway, for his part, wore a T-shirt bearing the hermetic logo

> Step Up, I Lay You,
> Step Off, I 'J' You,

Foul Me, I Trey You,
I Gotta Get P.A.I.D.

In-your-face braggadocio is the lingua franca of the NBA, but
where Jordan was concerned Hardaway did not mimic the rhetoric
of his T-shirt. He was worshipful, even wary. To play against Jordan
"was something I always wanted," he said. "When he retired before
I had a chance to play against him, I felt cheated. It's strange.
One guy comes back and everything changes. Everybody's *thoughts*
change." It was amazing how readily the players and coaches
around the league deferred to Jordan. Indiana's coach, Larry
Brown, suggested that Chicago, barely a winning team through
mid-March, could now win the NBA championship. Chuck Person,
of the San Antonio Spurs, used a mystical vocabulary. "He's like a
poltergeist," he said of Jordan. "He's an incident by himself."

Out on the court, a few players were getting limber, taking desul-
tory jump shots, walking through moves they would later attempt at
frenetic speed. Unguarded, unhindered by an opponent whacking him in the ribs or waving a hand in his eyes, even a backup
player like the Chicago forward Corie Blount hit 70 or 80 percent
of his shots. It means nothing. In baseball, players are competing mainly against the difficulty of the sport itself, the almost laugh-
able improbability of hitting a speeding baseball with a flame-
tempered twig. Baseball is such a hard game that small children
modify it (they hit off a tee) and the middle-aged *enlarge* it (calling
it softball). In basketball, the fundamentals — shooting, passing,
rebounding — are relatively easy to manage, at least in the solitude
of an empty schoolyard; the difficulty comes in competing against
the athleticism, the obstructions and wiles, of an aggressive opponent. Anyone can hit a 15-foot shot, sneakers to the floor; only a
professional can manage it with a leaping lump of muscle in his
face. That's why Jordan is so much better than anyone else who has
ever played the game. He plays as if in solitude. High in the air,
his legs splayed, his tongue flopping out of his mouth, he seems
weirdly relaxed, calm, as if there were no one special around and
plenty of time to think through his next move, floating all the
while. Faced with double coverage, as he almost always is, Jordan
finds a way to wedge between defenders, elevate as if on an invisible
forklift, his legs dangling, and then drop the ball through the hoop.

The ease of his game makes the rest of the players, all of them stars in college, look rough, somehow — clumsy, a step slow. "Scoring is scoring," Jordan says serenely in *Rare Air,* his autobiography. "If I want to average thirty-two points a game, I can do that easily. It's just eight, eight, eight, eight. No problem. I can do that anytime. That's not being cocky. That's confidence."

In the late '80s, the Detroit Pistons, coached by Chuck Daly, seemed to find a way to stop a Chicago team that was, at the time, so lopsided in talent that it was often known in the papers as "Michael Jordan and the Jordanaires." With a jaunty bounce of pride in his voice, Daly told me, "Michael is a player with no weaknesses — he has all these skills, great intelligence, a bionic physical presence — and so when we played him we devised a strategy called the Jordan Rules. We committed ourselves to double-teaming him and, if we could, steering him to his left, his presumably weaker hand. But you know what? Jordan outgrew the Jordan Rules. He just learned to play through them." Others are more dubious, and remember that it was the Pistons' brutality — their stray elbows and surreptitious shoves — that worked so well. Frank Layden, the former Utah Jazz coach, once said to Jordan's biographer Jim Naughton, "The Jordan Rules? You know what the Jordan Rule is, don't you? Knock him on his ass. They can talk all they want, but the one thing they did — when he got in midair — they knocked him down."

The crowd is desperate to set eyes on Jordan. Four huge video screens above the court are playing a tape loop of his greatest hits — scenes from his career in high school, at the University of North Carolina, and on the Bulls. The screens are also playing his collected commercials — McDonald's, Gatorade, Nike, Coca-Cola — as if these, too, were part of his game. The film will have to do for a while. Jordan, who has been trying to get used to this alien arena's bright lights and tight rims with solitary workouts in the afternoon, is out of sight, hanging back in a room reserved for players having their ankles taped. No Press Beyond This Point, the sign says. In the open, main part of the locker room, many of the Bulls come and go, dressing, watching film of old Orlando games, wearily answering questions about their returning leader.

The Bulls have handed out hundreds of press passes for this game, and everyone's mandate is the same: Get Jordan — Jordan pictures, Jordan quotes. Both the *Tribune* and the *Sun-Times* published special pullout sections in the morning; the local television stations have been broadcasting live from courtside since late afternoon. The press cannot afford to miss a Jordan sighting. A pack of reporters and half a dozen cameras all cluster near his locker. As a group, we gaze at his open closet and the vestments dangling therein: a mustard-colored sports coat on a hanger, slacks and shirt on hooks. There is, as well, a heap of basketball shoes, a box of Bubble Yum. We all stare, as if doing so would draw Jordan into the room.

It is a strange tableau, and on the other side of the room one of the Bulls' centers starts laughing. At first, it is hard to tell which center: Luc Longley, the Aussie; Bill Wennington, the bearded one; or Will Perdue, who wears a Hannibal Lecter mask to protect his face. All three are big, bulky white guys; they look like bouncers at a very tough club.

"Hey, boys, you never look at my locker that way!" It's Wennington, the one with the beard.

Then, under deadline pressure, one of the cameramen says, "I gotta have something!" He angles his camera lens toward the closet floor. He is filming a jockstrap. Written on the waistband is "Jordan, #45."

Michael Jordan leads one of the grandest and most peculiar American lives since Elvis left the building. His return this spring has been big news in Chicago, and in Chengdu, too. The *China Sports Daily* said in its story, "This flying man, Qiao Dan" — M.J. in Mandarin — "is still the most popular sports star on earth." He may also be the most valuable human commodity in sports. He earns about $30 million a year endorsing products — nearly eight times his basketball salary. Every detail of his return has implications. The mere rumor that he might return to basketball caused Nike stock to soar. Simply by changing his jersey number from 23 to 45, he spawned an industry. Every kid in the country wants the new shirt. Champion, the company that makes the official shirts, has ordered its plant in Winston-Salem to add a midnight-to-eight shift to fill the demand.

At the age of 32, Jordan is the subject of picture books, a shelfload of biographies, and countless videocassettes, and his face appears on lunch boxes, drinking cups, sneakers. In Chicago, his image is everywhere, like Kim Il Sung's in Pyongyang. Every one of Jordan's endorsements is designed to make him (and, therefore, the product) heroic, available, pleasant, elegant, "beyond race." Even academe has turned its eyes to the Air. ("Finally, there is the subversion of perceived limits through the use of *edifying deception,* which in Jordan's case centers around the space/time continuum," Michael Eric Dyson, of the Chicago Theological Seminary, explains in his essay "Be Like Mike? Michael Jordan and the Pedagogy of Desire.") So that Jordan can get his teeth fixed without causing a commotion, his dentist comes in on a day off. His barber used to do the same, but Jordan shaves his own head these days, giving it the pleasing burnished look of an antique desk. Once, Jordan was out on the golf course and paused to finish eating an apple. He threw the core into the woods, and suddenly a group of kids, who had been following his foursome, ran off in search of the remains. "Please, please don't do that," Jordan said. Jordan receives between forty and fifty letters every week from dying children who tell him that it is their last wish on earth to meet him. He obliges as many as he can; to the rest, he sends a pair of Air Jordans that he has worn in a game. One child, who died of leukemia, was buried wearing the size-13 shoes that Jordan had given him.

On October 6, 1993, Jordan announced that he was quitting professional basketball to spend more time with his family. (Jordan and his wife, Juanita, have three children.) "I'm going to watch the grass grow and I'm going to have to cut it," he said. Basketball fans accustomed to watching aging superstars lurch on until the last possible paycheck were shocked — Jordan's skills had not fallen off at all — but, with time, his decision began to make some sense. The Bulls had won three championships in a row, putting to rest the shibboleth of Jordan as a ball hog incapable of giving up some shots for the good of the team. In the end, Jordan had raised the level of every player on the Bulls, including the mysterious and pouty All-Star Scottie Pippen. There was nothing left to prove on that score.

Jordan's decision to retire also had an artistic dimension. His career was his œuvre, and he refused to tarnish it with an autumnal slide into repetition or self-parody. In the short run, he was depriving us of his presence and weakening the entire enterprise of professional basketball, but in the longer view we would never have to remember him logy and diminished as he closed in on middle age.

Jordan had long been a student of the career of Julius Erving —
the purposeful flamboyance on the court, the studied grace when
dealing with reporters and advertisers — and he did not want to
end up as Erving had in his final years, reduced to ordinary standards of play. Jordan's art would know no senescence; our memories
would remain pure.

What was more, his closest friend and adviser — his father, James
Jordan — was killed in a robbery that summer. It was hard to argue
with the decision. The man was just worn out in every way. After so
many years of playing the perfect gentleman for the press, after
enduring the sanctimonious criticism of his gambling, Jordan revealed in his retirement news conference a Nixonian prickliness, a
mock gratitude that he would no longer have to put up with "you
guys," the reporters.

Jordan was getting out before his desire or his legs or his grace
abandoned him. If fans did not like it — well, then, we would have
to learn to live with it. In an issue of *Sport* that appeared at a time
when he was already reconsidering his decision to retire, Jordan
was asked if it concerned him that he had left behind an "empti-
ness" in his fans and in the game itself. "I'm sorry, but it doesn't,"
he said. "Unfortunately, people are going to be thinking that way
for years because I'm through. I'm not coming back. At least, that's
my feeling right now. I know there are people who wish I was still
playing basketball, but at some point in time, either now or twenty
years from now, those people will get over it. I apologize if some
people think that's selfish of me, but that's the way it is."

Of course, Jordan's retirement had little to do with his desire to
play catch in the back yard with his children. Having satisfied his
familial longings in a matter of a few months, he signed on to play
baseball for the Chicago White Sox, who assigned him to their
Double-A club, the Birmingham Barons. It was something like a
lark — Jordan had not played baseball since he was in high school
— but not quite. Jordan is a competition maniac — his friends have
seen him get hysterical when he loses at golf, poker, or Ping-Pong;
he has lost hundreds of thousands of dollars betting with shady
characters on the golf course — and he cannot, it seems, live without the rush. James Jordan often said, "My son doesn't have a
gambling problem. What he does have is a *competition* problem."
Unfortunately, he had chosen for his lark the most impossible of

games, and one he had little hope of mastering. In countless feature stories on television and in print we were witness to the spectacle of Michael Jordan as George Plimpton, the amateur at play, and
it was not an entirely pretty sight: Jordan fanned at curve balls, he
lost fly balls in the sun. He was game and serious, but as a baseball
player he was never more than a novelty act — and, in his own way,
he had the decency to admit it. "This has been a very humbling
experience," he said.

Meanwhile, the vacuum in Chicago was becoming increasingly
apparent. The Bulls did well enough without Jordan in the 1993–
94 regular season — they won 55 of 82 games — but, faced with
the New York Knicks in the playoffs, they found their limits. They
lost, four games to three. This year, the slide was more precipitous:
suddenly the Bulls were not much more than a .500 team, a mediocrity. Pippen remained a star, but, unlike Jordan, he could not
make stars of his more earthbound teammates. The yearning for
Jordan was painful to witness. Every night before Bulls games, fans
would come early to the new arena and mill around a statue of
Jordan — a soaring construction of the master about to dunk, and,
underneath, the inscription "Michael Jordan 1984–93. The best
there ever was. The best there ever will be." Even in the worst
Chicago cold, fans would trade Jordan stories, remembering particular moments in his career: the change-of-hands-look-I'm-still-up
here-floating lay-up that blew everyone's mind and ruined an aging
Lakers team in the 1990–91 finals; the eyes-closed foul shots; the
kiss-the-rim slams.

Jordan's absence from the game left the league with middling
champions and no leading man. The NBA is full of young players
with fantastic potential: O'Neal and Hardaway may turn out to be
the cornerstones for a dynasty in Orlando; a rookie guard in Dallas,
Jason Kidd, has made a team out of the beleaguered Mavericks;
Glenn (Big Dog) Robinson is a hit in Milwaukee; and Detroit's
Grant Hill, a player of rubbery grace and fine manners, is already
the league's official answer to the spoiled stars who skip games and
practices with bogus injuries and then demand salaries in the tens
of millions of dollars. But none of these players were ready to
fill the Jordan gap, and everyone in the league office and in the
press knew it. The NBA, which had been so ascendant with Jordan,
Magic, and Bird in the game, was in a slump.

Late last spring, while the Knicks were attempting to slug, shove, and trash-talk their way past the Houston Rockets in the NBA championship series, I sat in the Madison Square Garden press section with a friend — Michael Wilbon, who is a columnist for the sports pages of the *Washington Post*. Wilbon's life, as far as I have been able to read it, is a nonstop busman's holiday. He is a basketball fan — a basketball *fanatic* — who is paid by his editors to follow the game as closely as he can. He complies. He has racked up a million frequent-flier miles, mainly in the pursuit of basketball games, but he is not likely to use his off-season to hit the beaches in, say, Tahiti. As Wilbon would say, "You can't get no goddam ESPN in no goddam Papeete." And yet, as we watched the Knicks and the Rockets pound up and down the boards in quest of the NBA title that night at the Garden, it was clear that Wilbon was taking no pleasure in this series. He despised its artlessness. He frowned at every collision, sneered at every turnover. For me, as for nearly everyone else at the Garden that night, the possibility of a Knicks triumph was a chance to relive the singular thrill of an age ago: the championship of 1969–70, when Willis Reed, his injured leg shot up with painkillers, limped out onto the Garden floor (El Cid of Louisiana) and led the team to its legendary victory over Wilt Chamberlain and the Los Angeles Lakers. But Wilbon is not of this city — he is Chicago born — and he was having none of it.

"This game is a dog," he declared.

"Why's that?"

"Michael's hitting .200 in Birmingham and these fools think they're winning a championship."

My illusions were now shot. The Knicks were suddenly there before me in all their limitations — plodding, erratic, hysterical, a squad of lager louts trying to scare their betters by whacking their hands on the bar and talking too loud. The Rockets were more obviously a limited flock, a team with an extraordinary center — the Nigerian Hakeem Olajuwon — and four guys named Ed. In the end, the Rockets won the misbegotten series, and everyone except the participants and their dependents has long forgotten the whole thing.

Michael Jordan's return has rescued basketball from more mediocrity. He reminds us why we buy the tickets, why watching is not a waste of time; and the degree of gratitude is not just great but strange. In early March, while Jordan was merely reconsidering his status, I read a Mike Wilbon column in the *Post* in which he declared, without irony, that he would gladly give two years of his life if Jordan would only return to the Bulls.

Not long afterward, Wilbon, the league, the city of Chicago, even Knicks fans — all of us — got our wish. Jordan announced his intention by sending a fax through his agent's office. "I'm back," Jordan wrote, and that was all. Wilbon, pay up.

The Orlando game was a bust. Jordan shot too much and he shot too long. Seven of twenty-three from the field. His jumpers kept banging off the butt of the rim. Over and over. He was like a man who keeps pumping the gas pedal until the engine floods and the car dies. And then he turns the key again and pumps, just to make *sure:* 106–99, Magic. But, in a sense, Jordan was right to shoot as much as he did. Chicago had no prayer of going far in the playoffs unless Jordan got his timing back. A regular-season loss to Orlando was a small price to pay.

Jordan walked into the interview room trailed by a presidential-size security detail. (He does not do the naked-interview thing. He showers and dresses first, and all await him.) He managed to look spectacular in that mustard-colored jacket, but he could not hide his frustration. He was more bewildered than anything else. "I just can't turn it on," he said. "As much as I want to, I just can't turn it on. It will take time."

Jordan was in a five-week, seventeen-game race before the playoffs to retune himself to basketball. He had been away from the professional game for 636 days — nearly two full seasons — and in that time he had hardly touched a ball bigger than a baseball. "When I was down in the minors, every guy wanted to play me in basketball," he said. "I used to play on Sundays with some of the guys in Arizona. We'd go and rent a gym and play pickup games. And I think these guys thought I'm retired — or maybe they're like me, they think they can be a basketball player just as much as I think I can be a baseball player. But, really, each time I played, my appetite got a little bit greater."

Jordan himself never doubted that he could return and average 30-odd points a game — in other words, lead the league in scoring — but the *Chicago Tribune,* which chronicles the Life of

Michael with definitive attention, pressed some medical experts on the nervous question. "We tested Michael at our biochemical lab during his previous playing days," Dr. Charles Bush-Joseph, of the sports-medicine section of Rush-Presbyterian-St. Luke's Medical Center, told the *Tribune*. "He was off the charts in his ability to generate power in the legs. At 32, he is a bit past a man's physical prime in terms of quickness and explosiveness, but his high level of skills can more than cover any such loss. He just needs time to get back his neuromuscular edge — more commonly known as timing."

For my own peace of mind, I talked with two of Jordan's precursors at the guard position — Bob Cousy and Walt Frazier — and neither had any doubt that Jordan would scrape off the rust in time for the trials of May. Retired ballplayers — especially players of a certain level — are often touchy about the subject of the current crop. They can be grouchy, deliberately uncomprehending, like aging composers whining about the newfangled twelve-tone stuff. But not where Jordan is concerned. Cousy, who led the Celtics in the '50s and early '60s, and Frazier, who led the Knicks in the late '60s and the '70s, would not begrudge Jordan his eminence.

"Until six or seven years ago I thought Larry Bird was the best player I had ever seen," Cousy, who works as a broadcaster for his old team, said. "Now there is no question in anyone's mind that Jordan is the best. He has no perceptible weaknesses. He is perhaps the most gifted athlete who has ever played this foolish game, and that helps, but there are a lot of great athletes in this league. It's a matter of will, too. Jordan is always in what I call a ready position, like a jungle animal who is always alert, stalking, searching. It's like the shortstop getting down and crouching with every pitch. Jordan has that awareness, and that costs you physically. If you do it, you are so exhausted you have trouble getting out of bed in the morning. Not many athletes do it. To me, he hasn't lost a thing."

"Leapers are usually not great shooters, but Michael is the exception," Frazier said. "If you give him a few inches, he buries the jump shot. When he gets inside, his back is to the basket and he's shakin' and bakin' and you're dead. When he drives, good night. He's gone. Now that the league has made hand-checking illegal — you can't push your man around on defense any longer — it's conceivable that Michael could score even more. I don't think he's even sensed that he has more license now. When he does, he'll be scoring sixty if he feels like it."

For the next few weeks after the Orlando game, I followed Jordan, at various arenas and on the tube. Game by game, he was playing his way into condition. He hit a game-winning shot against the Hawks in Atlanta. He iced the Celtics in Boston. Most important of all, even when his shot was off he did enough of the other things — passing, rebounding, defending, and exhorting his teammates, his eyes narrowed with impatience — that suddenly the Bulls were once more a top-rank team. Pippen was getting the ball enough to satisfy his sensitivities; Kukoc was realizing he could play with, and not merely worship, Jordan; even the three amigos — Wennington, Longley, and Perdue — seemed smoother, professional, in the game.

Curiously, the only deficiency in Jordan's game was his tendency to shoot poorly at the United Center. "I guess I'm used to playing across the street at the Stadium," he said one night. "This is a new surrounding. But the court dimensions are the same." He had faith in his own powers of concentration. Suddenly his life was strange and cluttered again, a mass of requests and fans and commercials. "But once I step on the court I'm having fun," he said. "That's the good part."

On March 28th, the Bulls played the Knicks at Madison Square Garden. No crowd at the Garden had been this jumpy since the playoffs last year. Most of the new arenas diffuse the noise of the crowd — spread it out and turn it into a muffled undertone, a murmur. The Garden on a good night still rumbles, and once Jordan stepped on the floor the crowd kept up a steady roar — half in pleasure, half in fear for the home team. Against New York, Jordan is guarded by the most temperamental of the defenders he faces — John Starks, a young man who is capable of brilliance one night and errant rage another, and then a long, inert period of funk; he is maddeningly inconsistent, more talent than player. To be a Knicks fan is to be forced to live with the moody vacillations of John Starks. It is no way to live. And yet five minutes into his encounter with Jordan I felt for Starks, felt for him deeply. From the opening tap, Starks did the best he could, steering Jordan to his supposedly bad hand (the left), guiding him into other defenders, jumping high with the shot. It was all for nothing. Jordan opened the game with a jumper, shot as casually as tossing a stone into a lake. The next time Jordan had the ball, he palmed it, and waved it up and down, teasing Starks, as if this were a Globetrotters act and Starks were the paid dupe. Another score. Not long after that, Jordan caught a pass on the baseline and, before putting the ball on the floor, did a little trick in which he began arching his back, rocking back and forth, mesmerizing Starks. Suddenly, as Starks fell into the sleepy rhythm, Jordan spun and dashed around him. The lay-up, of course, was good. Starks trotted up the court on offense blinking, stone-faced, determined not to betray the frustration he was feeling.

From then on, my notes are a whacked-out mess — a stream of underlinings, exclamation points, hieroglyphs, each centered on another Jordanian amazement. By the end of the first quarter, he had twenty points. What was, secondarily, so thrilling about the game was that the rest of the players on the floor (Starks included) were at their best. I don't know that I have ever seen a better game in the regular season. The Knicks were freed of their psychoses. No one kicked the scorer's table. No one dissed the coach. There were no head butts, body slams, or petty screeds. Derek Harper drew a harmless technical foul. (As usual, he earned it, and then pulled off a theatrical palms-up protest of innocence, the way professional wrestlers do when they are accused of producing a "foreign object" from their shorts.) The Knicks were doing all they could to win. Were it not for Jordan's performance, Patrick Ewing might have been the morning headline.

But, of course, it was Jordan's night, and, as the game went on, Starks — alas, poor Starks! — began to wear the mask of infinite pain. Jordan hit shot after shot. There have been times in the past when his teammates, wearied of their role as supporting players, have rebelled against their leader's dominance. At one point against the Knicks, Scottie Pippen, a player of remarkable talents but delicate ego, seemed to ignore Jordan, who was open for a lay-up, and instead threw up an absurd bomb from long range, as if to say, "No, Michael, I will not *always* yield to you." Except for that moment, the Bulls meshed as well as they had in two years.

For the Knicks, and for the rest of the teams in the NBA that may face the Bulls this spring in the playoffs, the final play was the most

dangerous — the one that sent out a reminder of Jordan's dimensions as an athlete. Part of why we cleave to sports and fandom
(besides the sheer escapism) is that excellence is so measurable, so
knowable in numbers. The .500 shooter averaging 25 points and a
dozen rebounds a game is an all-star; the .410 shooter averaging
fewer points and boards is a mediocrity. Jordan's numbers — his
seven consecutive scoring championships, his stats as a rebounder,
passer, and defensive thief — easily identify him as among the best
to play the game. The last play against the Knicks shades in the
picture; it identifies him as — well, supernatural.

There were fourteen seconds left. The score was 111–111. By
then, Jordan had 55 points. I was somehow relieved that the game
would soon end. Jordan was performing at such a level that it
seemed inevitable that he would find a way to score and end it. And
to go on watching Starks continue his futile mission had about it a
quality of voyeurism, cruelty. Jordan was humiliating a weaker opponent. At times, it was beautiful to witness; at others, it was like
watching a man poke a wounded dog with a stick.

Jordan handled the ball. After letting a few seconds melt off the
clock, he closed in toward the side of the lane. He drove hard to the
right, dipping his shoulder, and then cut sharply to his left and
toward the basket. Starks stumbled. He was beginning to lose his
man. Suddenly, Ewing, all seven feet of him, stepped forward to
help smother Jordan. Now there were just five seconds on the
clock. Jordan coiled and jumped, leaving his feet as if to shoot. As
he would admit later, shooting had been his intention all along.
How can you not shoot with 55 points already? ("I'd be lying if I
said I came out to pass the ball.") But now the logic of the moment
had changed. Ewing had gambled — it was a smart gamble, for
there are times when Jordan is sure that he has a better chance of
scoring over two men than a teammate has of scoring unattended.
Not now. In the huddle, Jordan had advised Wennington, the slow-
footed center, that there was a chance — not a *big* chance, but a
chance — that he would get a pass if the play broke just so. Which is
how it broke. Even in midair, in the tensest moment of a game,
Jordan has a look of both concentration and calm, as if he knew he
was capable of suspending himself until the proper decision is
finally made. Meanwhile, everyone else is frantic, flailing. And now,
after passing up what would have been a low-percentage shot, even

for him, with Knicks leaping all around him, Jordan shoveled a pass
to Wennington. The center gathered the ball in, jumped, and hit
the point-blank shot: 113–111. Game.

Afterward, the Knicks coach, Pat Riley, said that yes, of course he
admired Jordan's performance, but he betrayed, as well, an over-
tired testiness. "You're gonna talk a lot about Michael tomorrow,"
he told the reporters surrounding him. "But it would have been a
hell of a thing if he had scored fifty-five and we'd won. It would have
been a different story line." Three weeks later, at the United Center
against the Knicks, Jordan did not need to play half as well as he
had in New York. This time, he shared the ball with Pippen, and the
two of them destroyed New York. Jordan is right. He's back.

Jimmy Thompson's
Fallen House of Cards

FROM THE COURIER-JOURNAL

HE'S NOBODY, REALLY. A small-time swindler who isn't even very good at breaking the law.

Outside of a steroid-inflated chest and an all-natural gift for gab, there is nothing particularly distinguished about him.

He is a 32-year-old white male with little education and less work history. He doesn't own a home, a car or even a phone.

It is, unfortunately, not uncommon for young men raised in South Louisville's Iroquois Homes housing project to quit school early, find good jobs rarely and learn their way around the Hall of Justice someday. In this respect he is an ordinary man.

So how did Jimmy Thompson create such an extraordinary mess?

How did a man whose police record portrays him as a wife-beating, petty-thieving, drug-selling, drug-using recidivist pierce the sanctum sanctorum of University of Louisville basketball?

How did a one-time bigamist and criminally negligent deadbeat dad become a trusted source of information for two local TV stations?

How did a chronically unemployed high school dropout pop up in more newsreels than Forrest Gump? He appears in the weight room with Keith LeGree. On the basketball court with Brian Hopgood. In the airport with Clifford Rozier. At a news conference with Mark Blount.

And most of all, how did Thompson's House of Cards come crashing down? How did his singular pursuit of becoming somebody ultimately lead to his being shunned by everybody — although the NCAA might become interested in him very soon?

The answer, unlike most things about Jimmy Thompson's tale, is rather simple:

He played both sides against the middle until he got crushed at the intersection.

From about 1988 to 1992, Thompson was a fixture in U of L's locker room, weight room and dormitory rooms. He was the Cardinals' Boy Friday. When Greg Minor needed a ride, Jimmy provided the car; when Rozier shot free throws, Jimmy shagged the rebounds.

Other services Thompson might have provided are a matter of conjecture.

"God knows all that he was doing," said Doug Semenick, a former U of L strength and conditioning coach who brought Thompson on board as a volunteer assistant coach in 1991. "What he would do is he would show up with things. He just was kind of the candy man."

Those favors put Thompson in position to cull information about the U of L program, and that information was his key to the other kingdom. He routinely provided tips to local media, especially to longtime sports anchors Bob Domine of WAVE and Fred Cowgill of WLKY.

Thompson traded info for access. Domine says his department frequently furnished Thompson with press passes to U of L games. Perhaps it was no coincidence that Domine landed the first and longest interview with Thompson when the story broke two weeks ago.

Cowgill says there were no free passes from WLKY, which has aggressively reported the Thompson story. But he says he did give Thompson complimentary tickets to Churchill Downs on three or four occasions.

"Everybody in [media] circles grew to know and understand and realize that he was a good source of information when it came to U of L basketball recruiting," said Rick Redman, WAVE sports director from 1987–93.

Thompson, the team and the media cozily coexisted until the middle of the 1991–92 season, when U of L officials say they banned him from the program for misrepresenting his relationship with the school.

But how effective was the ban? Two months ago a provocative piece of information came to light that indicated one of two things:

• Thompson had not gone away.

• Thompson had gone away but come back.

He said he had made about 150 calls to Blount, a U of L recruit. Those calls are a potentially serious violation of NCAA recruiting rules, and they put the Cardinals and the media on a collision course.

On June 21 the *Courier-Journal* made an open-records request that triggered an avalanche of action and reaction. While other media scrambled to catch up, U of L announced it had launched an internal investigation of the program.

The key question was whether Thompson still had ties to U of L and whether those ties led him to call Blount on the school's behalf. While the *Courier-Journal* searched for connections to Thompson, old ties scurried to disconnect:

• Domine, who estimates he has known Thompson for only three or four years, said: "What hurt me the most is when [associate athletic director] Mike Pollio saw me [the day the story broke] and said, 'Your friend Jimmy Thompson . . .' I said, 'Whoa, wait a minute. He never has been a friend. He's been an acquaintance.'"

• Cowgill, who has known Thompson for nine years, said: "We became . . . I don't know what we became. We became two guys who talked a lot. I would never call him. I would never ask him for anything, because I did not want to be put in the position of being seen as using him."

• Rozier, whom Thompson greeted at the airport when he arrived for his official recruiting visit to U of L, said: "I didn't even know the man's phone number. He'd come by and just watch [practice]. I treated him like any other fan."

Head coach Denny Crum has made no comment at all other than to acknowledge that U of L is looking into Thompson's activities.

Athletic director Bill Olsen, who had no previous association with Thompson, said: "I don't know the fellow that you're talking about. Denny Crum said he might recognize him when he saw him, but we cannot make any comment about Mr. Thompson."

Nor would Olsen comment on why U of L's lead recruiter, sixth-year assistant Larry Gay, apparently made five cellular phone calls to Thompson during April — the peak of Blount's recruitment.

At least one person couldn't completely swear off Jimmy Thompson no matter how much he might have wanted to.

"If I called Jimmy Thompson, they were just to return phone calls," Gay said.

If anyone ever knew Jimmy Thompson, they don't want to know him now. The mass exodus from his heaving ship has left him feeling alone, embattled and deeply wounded.

"I've been hit by Tyson, then Holyfield," Thompson said. "But I'm still standing."

But for how long? He has no job, yet he says he owes up to $3,000 in phone bills. And as of last September, the state of Indiana said he also owes at least $11,625 in back child support to his second wife.

"And as far as I know, the man ain't got no income," said Thompson's first wife, Rhonda, who married him at age 16 and still bears his name.

Thompson always has lived a transient existence, moving from home to home, family to family and courtroom to courtroom. Now the lone abiding constant — his tenuous but fulfilling association with the U of L basketball team — likely has been lost forever.

"I know I'm done," he said. "I know I'm gone."

Louisville basketball was in the early stages of its ascendancy when it captured Thompson's heart, and for most of his life he worshiped the Cardinals from afar.

As a child he perched atop his brother's shoulders and watched the Cards dazzle crowds at the Dirt Bowl in Shawnee Park. As a teenager he turned his bedroom into a shrine to his ultimate idol, Darrell Griffith.

"I'm a U of L idiot," Thompson often says.

He entered the program through the front door of Crawford Gym, which is open to all. In 1985 he began dropping by the Cards' old practice site to watch the legendary pickup games, taking advantage of an extraordinary level of public access that is highly unusual among programs of Louisville's stature.

Though virtually anyone could get into the gym, almost no one manages to get inside the program. But by 1988 Thompson had achieved his goal of catching a ray of the team's reflected glory.

He strolled among the stars in a way most fans can only dream of. Just ask . . .

• Former forward Tony Kimbro: "He's pretty cool with everyone who went to U of L."

• Former guard Kip Stone: "He'd just, like, pop up sometimes. It was supposed to be a twenty-four-hour quiet dorm, but there was a lot of visitors and noise. Lots of guys partying and stuff."

• Semenick: "I'd see him in the locker room all the time. . . . Sometimes the left hand doesn't know what the right hand's doing, and a guy like that can kind of slip between the cracks."

Thompson's entrée was a blue-collar combination of chutzpah and charisma that enabled him to riff with suit-and-tie broadcasters and baggy-jeans hoops heroes alike.

"Domine thinks I got ghetto talk or something," Thompson said. "He said, 'You've got a way of talking to these people that I can't.'"

Thompson talked his way in, put down roots, then blossomed into the Hanger-On from Hell.

"He really helped us out with our weight training," former guard James Brewer said, "then he started trying to get us to sell our tickets and stuff like that. It got to the [point] where everybody was like, 'Oh yeah, here comes Jimmy,' and everybody would shut their doors and turn their phones off."

Brewer and his teammates weren't the first to take evasive measures against Jimmy Thompson, who's a bruising six-feet-three, 245 pounds. Other aggrieved associates, mostly former wives and girlfriends, leave a cold trail of disconnected or unlisted phones. Few will discuss him openly for fear that he will inject himself into their lives once again.

Said Don Stiller, father of Thompson's second wife, Dana: "He was just hell from day number one."

Like nightshade, Thompson's benign appearance belies a dangerous nature. He's a generally friendly fellow, but his affability can be usurped by a quick, malignant temper.

Five of the twelve cases on his Jefferson County court record involve violent or menacing behavior such as spouse abuse, wanton endangerment and terroristic threatening.

An ex-girlfriend accused Thompson of poking her in the eyes when she was four months pregnant. He threatened to kill another ex-girlfriend whom, according to the arrest report, he embroiled in a prolonged car chase that forced her to flee to a police station.

He punched Rhonda Thompson and threatened to kill her, too. That's why she was granted an emergency protective order long ago.

"As long as I have it renewed, I know that I'm pretty safe," she said. "He's went off on me before."

Thompson's criminal record was clean until he was 28, rather late to join the ranks of repeat offenders. But it was around that time that he ventured into chemically enhanced bodybuilding.

"Once he started taking steroids, he went downhill," Rhonda Thompson said. "He built up, but his mind went down. When he used to live with me, he left a needle on my dresser. Excuse me! I've got two small children."

Thompson fathered a child by another woman, Dana Stiller, and married her in June 1987 in Floyd County, Indiana. He had checked the "never married" box on his marriage license application.

One problem. Thompson married Rhonda two years earlier in Louisville. Indiana records show Jimmy and Rhonda were divorced in Floyd County on October 30, 1987, but that's nearly five months after he married Stiller.

The illegal union was merely one of several flim-flams Thompson has engineered.

In June of '93 he was busted for selling $105 worth of suspected crack cocaine in the Park Hill projects — a fairly serious matter, if it weren't for the fact that the crack turned out to be fake.

But the coup de disgrace occurred six weeks later.

In a bind after having sold $250 worth of real cocaine to an undercover policewoman, the cash-starved Thompson dreamed up one of his most outrageous lies. He told Shirley Stiller — his ex-mother-in-law — that he had to "pay off some police officers." He told her that he had paid them $1,200 already but that they were demanding another $700 posthaste.

Outraged, Stiller confronted the police. She was promptly informed that there was no such shakedown, then was given $700 in marked money and wired for sound.

The sting was on.

Stiller gave the money to Thompson at about 5 P.M. August 2. About an hour later, police pulled Thompson out of Stiller's Ford LTD and fished the bankroll out of his sock. He quickly confessed to defrauding Stiller and was convicted of theft by deception, a felony that, along with the cocaine-trafficking conviction, landed him in the county jail in August 1994.

If Stiller was mad, she didn't stay that way for long. Last October, about two months into Thompson's jail term, she submitted a handwritten letter beseeching Judge Tom Knopf to "please shock him out." Knopf declined, and Thompson was released in January after serving out his six-month sentence.

He currently tools around town in Shirley Stiller's Nissan Maxima, complete with a U of L license-plate frame and window sticker.

Thompson's scams fared better at U of L. For at least four years the Hanger-On from Hell was in heaven.

"He was around the program a long, long time," Semenick said. "It's not like he was persona non grata out there."

Semenick says Thompson's media contacts helped point him toward a job he landed in the weight room in the fall of '91.

"The guy that kind of put him on to me was Bob Domine," Semenick said. "Bob didn't really come give me any type of reference, but I guess [Thompson] had told him he wanted to get into the field, and [Domine] said, 'Well, I know Doug. Go talk to him and see what you can work out.'"

"That's not true," Domine said. "I wouldn't recommend Jimmy for anything. Now I'm trying to remember: Did [Semenick] ever ask me that question? . . . If he sat there and said, 'Bob, what do you think?' I'd say, 'Well, you know, he seems to be real friends with the players. Might help you guys to have somebody who seems to get along with them.'"

However, Semenick and Thompson barely got along at all. Thompson was dismissed in short order.

"What really soured me with him . . . is he'd be up in the dorm," Semenick said. "And [with] these basketball players — and all of the major college athletes, for that matter — there's some pretty colorful things that go on, and he was right in the middle of it. I am a bit ashamed to say it took me six weeks to see all that, but it did."

Semenick said Thompson "still hung around the team for quite a while," providing rides and companionship until he wore out his welcome.

"He gave me rides, yeah," Minor said. "And at times we'd hang out, go places and maybe he'd show me off to his son. But I didn't get no stereos, no VCRs, no illegal stuff."

Minor and Brewer both say Thompson asked to broker their complimentary tickets, which is an NCAA violation. Brewer says he reported Thompson's offer to Crum.

Thompson says he made no such offer, but the coaches apparently thought otherwise. Semenick says assistant Scooter McCray scornfully introduced him to some men who claimed that "your boy in the weight room" had promised them tickets he could not produce.

If such an incident occurred (Thompson says it didn't), then it might further explain why he was banned (Thompson swears he wasn't).

"Banned? You got to be kidding!" Thompson exclaimed. "If somebody's banned, you've got to sign a piece of paper — something — that says this guy can't come on campus."

U of L has declined to cite specifics or offer documentation, indicating that it will be addressed in a forthcoming NCAA report — a report likely to feature Thompson prominently.

Though once enticed by the flame of fame, Thompson is now being consumed by it. He still loves the attention, but he loathes the scrutiny. Andy Warhol's guarantee was good for fifteen minutes, but Thompson's clock still ticks after two weeks.

"I'll be glad when it's done," he said. "When the truth really comes out, you see who your friends are."

While waiting for the truth to emerge, everyone is choosing sides. No one is choosing Thompson's.

The whole wild story was told to sports reporters all over town, but once they began digging into his record, many wondered if they were being duped.

It seemed at times as if the lifelong hustler simply was pulling the hustle of his life. But slowly evidence emerged that suggested Thompson might not be the complete liar that so many have accused him of being.

"People probably think I'm a crazy, wild ——," he said, "but you don't get to know all these people and not be something."

Players *did* know him. Broadcasters said his tips had been "incredibly accurate" before. And while looking into allegations attributed to Thompson, this newspaper turned up at least five unrelated potential NCAA violations in Louisville's previously untainted program.

But the most intriguing corroboration is this: the cell phone records that revealed communications between Thompson and Larry Gay — the chief recruiter of Mark Blount, who Thompson says is the chief reason for his $3,000 phone bill.

Unreachable for ten days, Gay finally was tracked down via that same cell phone. He said, "What's wrong with calling Jimmy Thompson?"

So the Hanger-On from Hell has likely seen his last press pass and had his last look inside a Cardinal's dorm room.

Yet even now, while he regrets that his checkered past has been trotted out for the city to sneer at, Thompson can't resist the thrill of finally being noticed. He is no longer nobody, but neither is he famous.

He is infamous.

As a reporter walked off from an interview the other day, Thompson called out. A red and black bandana covered his head. His bare, chemically altered chest was on sad display. He eagerly inquired:

"How big do you think the headline will be?"

LARRY DORMAN

Small Colleges, Big Game

FROM THE NEW YORK TIMES

Intense Football Rivalry

WILLIAMSTOWN, MASSACHUSETTS, November 8 — All around
the room, alumni living and dead are staring at the kid. On one
dark, oak-paneled wall, a picture of the 1901 football team —
smallish players with their hair slicked back and parted in the middle in the style of the day — looks down. From the folding chairs
crammed tight around tables, old men with hair either gray or
gone, look at him and nod.

In a clear, strong voice, the tailback addresses the room.

"I'm Jamall Pollock," he says. "Number 33. I'm an English major,
from Brooklyn, New York. After I graduate, I hope to teach and
coach for a year or two, then go to law school."

There is a burst of applause from the audience at the The Log,
an ancient tavern that sits right in the heart of this bucolic village in
the Berkshires. This is the weekly gathering of the Williams College
Sideline Quarterback Club, a collection of alumni and friends of
this college that was founded in 1793 here in the northwest corner
of Massachusetts. In an annual tradition, the seniors from the team
are introducing themselves and discussing their goals. Right now,
things are as they have always been, ever since this whole football
thing started more than a century ago.

There is more than the usual amount of electricity charging on
the chill winds this week. It is Williams-Amherst week, the season
finale for both football teams. This will be the 110th meeting of the

two schools, colleges that share a common ancestry and a common bond — and a temporary, though quite genuine, mutual dislike.

For this one week, there is nothing more important than The Game, when the undefeated Ephs of Williams (7–0) and the Lord Jeffs of Amherst (5–2) take to the turf at Weston Field and try to beat the holy hell out of one another in football.

To come here is to breathe clean air once again. This has less to do with the remote location of these colleges than with their priorities. It is here that the nomenclature "student-athlete" is no oxymoron. To be sure, this is the "biggest little game in America," as Dick Quinn, the Williams sports information director, has dubbed it. But it is even more than that.

It is really the essence of what college athletic competition can be. It is Division III, but it is first rate. Football is not a business here. It might be a very important piece of the fabric that is woven into the whole way of life at Williams, and down the road at Amherst. But it is only a piece. There are no scholarships, no red shirts, no pressures on the coach to win or leave, no pending investigations by the National Collegiate Athletic Association, no slush funds, no failed drug tests, no bowl games and no agents lurking in doorways.

About the only big-time you will sniff around Williams is that the time of Saturday's game was switched to 10 A.M., to accommodate the telecast of the game on ESPN2.

There are no other compromises. What there is, though, and in abundance, is excellence. It is everywhere, on the athletic fields and off. One feeds the other. Of the 1,982 undergraduates at Williams, about half play on one or more of the 31 varsity teams, 15 junior varsity teams or 7 club teams. Last year, every one of the varsity teams had a winning record (combined mark was 406–178–12). There were 66 All-Americans, 23 academic All-Americans and 69 academic All-Nescac (New England Small College Athletic Association) honorees.

At a school where the *average* Scholastic Assessment Test score is 1,300, that is no small accomplishment. And, of course, the football team is unbeaten, untied and trying to improve on its 60–45–4 overall record against the Lord Jeffs.

Obviously, most of these football players will not make a career of the sport. Some might. There is a good chance that Williams defensive lineman Ethan Brooks, six feet five inches and 275 pounds, will get drafted somewhere in the middle rounds. And Amherst has a lineman named Scott Curry, who is six-foot-seven and weighs 315 pounds, who is attracting quite a bit of notice from the National Football League. He also is getting recognition for his senior thesis, "The History of the Internet."

For the most part, these are young men like Pollock, an outstanding athlete who has gained 1,246 yards this year but who came here to get an education in both academics and athletics, to play their part and to become a part of the history that reaches back to Colonel Ephraim Williams (hence, the nickname Ephs, pronounced Eefs) in 1793.

Tradition is what brought Pollock here from Poly Prep in Brooklyn, where he carried a 3.4 grade point average, hopes, SAT scores of better than 1,300 and high hopes of going to Harvard, where he wanted to study, wrestle and play football, basically in that order.

He wasn't accepted at Harvard, but it so happened that Tom Parker, the head of admissions at Williams, had also attended Poly Prep. Parker's father had coached there. He convinced Pollock this was the place for him. It took him a while to adjust to the less-cosmopolitan surroundings, but Pollock is a true believer now.

"The great thing about this place is the people," he says. "We've all grown together, become closer, learned to support one another."

The roots that are set here grow deep. A three-year fundraising effort that ended two years ago set $160 million as a target. The total raised was $173 million. Alumni often come back and retire here. The togetherness draws them back, and then they wind up at the Wednesday lunches, reflecting on what they did and how it made them what they are.

They see people like Jamall Pollock, a player who was overlooked for his first three years here, and they nod. Because he persevered and now the 1,226 yards he gained this year are just 189 short of the career conference record set by Eric Grey of Hamilton in 1991. More important than that, though, is the GPA of well over 3.4 that will put him where he needs to be in the future.

Dr. Wayne Wilkins, class of '41, is among the attendees at the Sideline Quarterback Club. He was a blocking back and linebacker on that team, and can remember almost every play from the 16–8 victory over Amherst in the fall of '39. He went on to Harvard and got his medical degree and for sixteen years he was the team doctor for the Boston Bruins. It all goes together, the athletics, the academics, the excellence, the achievement.

"Some of the greatest friends I've had have been the people I played with and against on the football and baseball fields," he says. "That's what you take with you from a place like this."

And one of his best friends was a player from Amherst.

"Once you get beyond this game this week," he says, "then they're all your friends. Once you get beyond this."

Where Linemen Muse In Between Hard Hits

AMHERST, MASSACHUSETTS, November 9 — The wind is gusting and eddies of fall leaves twist in little tornados of color. On this very early and very cold autumn morning, the sun has barely climbed above the bleachers at Pratt Field, but Amherst College football practice is at full boil. Coaches are hollering, whistles are blowing, receivers are sprinting, with puffs of breath shooting like steam from beneath their face masks.

It seems an odd place and moment to be discussing a novel. These are supposed to be serious football times, what with the season-ending game against unbeaten rival Williams College coming on Saturday, with the Little Three Championship and eternal bragging rights at stake. But Greg Schneider is more than happy to oblige, since he's between drills right now. He slides his helmet back off his forehead and smiles.

"The plot is actually about a guy from a middle class family who marries into a sort of Yuppie lifestyle and realizes after a couple of years that it wasn't really what he bargained for," Schneider says. "He heads off on a bit of a soul-searching journey to go find himself.

"In some sense, it's my own nightmare for the future — to be funneled into some kind of secure, really easy lifestyle. You know, you think about the number of people who go to a good college, go right into a secure job. And off they go — and never look up for the rest of their lives."

Ah, youth and the search for truth and self. The author of this as-yet-untitled tale is Schneider, Amherst Class of '96, offensive tackle and part-time jazz saxophonist, guitar player in the band "Medicated Groove," a formidable-looking man of six feet five inches who has no aversion to throwing his 250 pounds around a football field. At most institutions of higher learning around America, this would be more than a novel encounter.

But at Amherst and Williams, such discourses are the norm. Still, it would be stretching it a bit to aver that the only polls that count to the players here are the *U.S. News & World Report* academic rankings — which have placed Amherst at number one for the third straight year followed by, also for the third straight year, Williams. Make no mistake. The scores of the games in this 110-year-old football series mean plenty to the minds under those helmets, and right now these Amherst seniors are 0–3 against Williams.

"That has to change," says Scott Curry, the massive offensive tackle who is working on a thesis about the history of the Internet. "I think we match up pretty well with them. Who knows? We might be able to surprise them."

Williams is trying for its fourth undefeated season since 1989, and Amherst lost its second game, 33–10, last week to Trinity. All that is meaningless in the face of what is to come. On this morning, Amherst coach Jack Siedlecki is presiding over a spirited workout. He assembled the troops on the field at 6:30 A.M., in part to acclimate them for the 10 A.M. start on Saturday, a time change made to accommodate the ESPN2 telecast.

The players are responding. Wide receiver Chris Miller tests his sore hamstring by laying out for a deep pass from quarterback Rich Willard. His teammates spontaneously cheer the effort. Curry, six feet seven inches and 315 pounds, shows why there is interest among scouts to make him Amherst's fifth National Football League player — he would be a project, but he has quick feet and a good base. Cornerback Sam Bartlett, also the captain of the squash team, knifes in front of a pass and bats it down.

If this didn't actually happen, it would seem too hackneyed to believe. But there stands the five-foot-nine Bartlett, who is preparing a senior thesis on the Civil War, in the spartan Amherst locker room, and the theme song from *Rocky* really is blaring, and he is pulling himself to his full height at the thought of beating Williams.

"It would be the biggest win of my life," he says. "It would cap off a great rebuilding process that we've been a part of, a great culmination to four great years."

In many respects, these liberal arts institutions mirror each other. Amherst was founded when Zephaniah Swift Moore, Williams' second president, decided to leave Williams and set up academic shop on the other side of the mountains. For this, the folks at Amherst are still referred to as the Defectors by some in Williamstown. The first building at Amherst is a direct copy of the first building at Williams.

What goes on in the classrooms and on the athletic field is so similar that, really, the only way to differentiate between the schools is to see who prevails on Saturday.

Tom Gerety, the Yale man who is the president at Amherst, recognizes this as well as anyone. He has a stock reply for the few alums who question the importance of athletics in general and football in particular.

"They are," he says, with a trace of resignation, "the sweatiest of the liberal arts."

And for this week, at least, they are the most vital. Even at Amherst.

For Seniors, It's the Football Game That Will Last Forever

WILLIAMSTOWN, MASSACHUSETTS, November 10 — Some things in life you never forget. They are indelibly etched into your consciousness, mental and emotional touchstones, like your first love, your first car, your first kiss and, in these parts, the last time you played football for Williams or Amherst.

Evidence of this abounded on those two campuses this week as the Division III teams prepared for their 110th meeting Saturday, the season finale and Williams' homecoming game at Weston field. There was a little extra ardor at the practices, there were motivational T-shirts — the best one, seen hanging in St. Pierre's barber shop on Spring Street, reads, "How Good Is Williams Football? Good Enough to Lower the Admission Standards at Amherst!" — and there were football alumni everywhere, strolling down the streets and giving pep talks from the bulletin boards.

At undefeated Williams (7–0), there was a letter from Ken Hollingsworth, director of athletics at Tilton School and Williams

Class of '79 co-captain. Every year for the last sixteen, he has written, exhorting the Williams seniors:

"Make no mistake, your season begins this week. You'll remember this week for the rest of your lives." He closed with an admonishment to kick Amherst "right back over the mountain!!" and signed the letter with his jersey number, 82, in parentheses.

Down at Amherst (5–2), Dick Carrie, Class of '45, held the players and coaches in thrall with his keen recollections from the 1942 game, in which Amherst upset the previously unbeaten Williams team. He shook down the thunder with a litany of participating Amherst alums that included Stansfield Turner, former head of the Central Intelligence Agency.

"We have had fifty-three years to relish that glorious victory," Carrie wrote in his letter. "Fifty-three years to savor it, to talk about it, to reminisce about it, to enjoy it for our lifetime. Will your team this year have the same lifelong thrill?" He added a postscript, "Do I smell an upset?"

Throughout the week, Amherst players drifted past the bulletin board in their musty old locker room — clearly it isn't the athletic facilities that draw these players here — and marveled at the vehemence of the letter and the vividness of the memories.

"I think I'd remember it for the rest of my life if we could do it," said offensive tackle Scott Curry. "Can you believe that letter? Fifty years later and he's writing that? A man in his seventies? That's a pretty special thing."

This is a special game, and there have been many singular speeches made about it all week. At the Williams Sideline Quarterback Club luncheon on Wednesday, the Williams assistant coach Renzie Lamb wasn't really joking when he said, "If you wish to be happy for an hour, get intoxicated. If you wish to be happy for three days, get married. If you wish to be happy for eight days, kill your pig and eat it. If you wish to be happy forever, beat Amherst."

If an Amherst upset were to occur on Saturday, it would be among the biggest, perhaps matching the 12–6 shocker Amherst pulled in '42 or Williams' 31–14 upset of the unbeaten Lord Jeffs in '73. The Ephs' current victory streak of 21 games is the longest in Division III. The Lord Jeffs, soundly defeated last week by Trinity, have lost three fullbacks to injury, including the co-captain Josh Mason.

Stranger things have happened in this series. In 1951, a stu-

dent and sports columnist for the *Williams Record* by the name of
George Steinbrenner — yes, *that* George Steinbrenner — was out-
raged that Amherst was ranked in the top 30 in the nation "ahead
of Yale, Navy, S.M.U. and so many other great football teams."
Steinbrenner, who was rough on coaches even then, took a shot at
Amherst coach Tuss McLaughery and then picked Williams to beat
Amherst by a score of 34–13. If only he could apply such prescience
to picking managers. Williams won by 40–7.

Like Steinbrenner and Turner and Fay Vincent and the countless other Williams and Amherst alums who have achieved in other
endeavors, the vast majority of current football players at the two
colleges will play their final football game as seniors. They will be
left with the indelible memory of the result. Fifty years from now,
there will be a letter on a bulletin board here, possibly from running back Jamall Pollock of Williams or center David Shapiro of
Amherst, and beneath the letterhead of some prestigious law firm
or medical practice it will recall in vivid detail the struggle that took
place at Weston Field.

No Points, No Victory, But Something to Celebrate

WILLIAMSTOWN, MASSACHUSETTS, November 11 — Down in
the mud and the blood and the sawdust, on a squishy surface at
Weston Field that looked like an aerial view of the Okefenokee
Swamp, Amherst College accomplished the impossible today.

It beat undefeated Williams, 0–0.

That's right. Amherst won the game, prevailed in the 110th
meeting of these Division III rivals. The score was tied, but the Lord
Jeffs were the winners. There was no mistaking it, no doubt about it.
Although Williams' historians were trying to convince everyone
that this was the first time the two teams had tied in eighty-seven
games dating back to 1906, no one was buying it.

When it was done, when the two teams had finished slamming
into one another and going just about nowhere on the sodden,
almost impassable field, there were tears on the Williams side and
cheers on the Amherst side.

"Yeah, I feel like we won," said Dan Milazzo, an Amherst running
back who sloshed for 48 yards on 16 carries. "Any other team, any

other game, a tie, and you don't feel too good about it. But this team has had quite a losing streak against Williams, and after the way we played our hearts out today, to keep them from scoring, to hang in the way we did, to me, that's winning."

Standing nearby, Amherst offensive tackle Greg Schneider was pumping his big fist.

"The reign is over," he said.

He was talking about Williams' dominance of the series. He was talking about the last eight straight, all of which ended in Williams victories. When you're down so long that bottom looks like up, you take your wins with your ties, even playing on a field that, had it been a road, would have been closed to all traffic.

Just how bad was the playing field? Well, record rainfalls over the past two weeks left puddles of standing water as late as Friday. Williams officials placed the obligatory call to the turf guru George Toma who told them there was nothing much they could do. This field made the legendary Mud Bowl — when the New York Jets were beaten by the Miami Dolphins in the American Football Conference championship game at the Orange Bowl in 1982 — look like a fast track. Punts fell from the sky and stopped dead, like sand-wedge shots into a soft green.

"It was like trying to run on wet sand at a beach," Williams quarterback Mike Bajakian said.

And so, the two teams tread water all day. Each blew its one and only opportunity to score. The Lord Jeffs, who finish the season at 5–2–1, had a chance to kick a field goal in the second quarter, but the 27-yard attempt by Dave Bobruff came up short. Amherst had penetrated to the Williams 10 because of a 13-yard punt by Williams' Matt DeCamp — a play that actually was one of Williams' finest in the game.

The ball had been snapped over DeCamp's head on fourth down from the Williams 23-yard line. He somehow scrambled back into the end zone, scooped up the ball, ran to his right and got off a line drive kick on the run that was downed at the Williams 36. It was the greatest 13-yard punt in the 110-year history of the game.

"For him to pick that ball up and kick it the way he did, it was a bit miraculous," said Williams coach Dick Farley, who finished the season with a 7–0–1 record and has a 17–0–1 record in Little Three play. "You know, this is a disappointing way to finish an outstanding year, but I'm not as disappointed as people might think. I mean, when you have a snap go over your punter's head, and you fumble another punt, and you don't lose?"

The Ephs best chance to score came in the fourth quarter. Held to 101 total yards in the first half (and 269 for the game), the Ephs finally got a big play with 11 minutes 14 seconds left in the game when Bajakian, the senior from Bergen Catholic High School in New Jersey, found tight end Mike Gardner running alone in the middle and hit him for 60 yards to the Amherst 18. Jamall Pollock, who had been held in check all day and who wound up with 67 rushing yards, had three straight runs to the 1-yard line.

But a pitch lost 4 yards, Pollock gained just 2 up the middle and the Ephs had a fourth down from the 6. Field goal or touchdown? The field was so bad where the placement would have been that Farley said, "There really was no debate. We had to go for it."

Bajakian took the snap and his center, Medley Gatewood, stepped back to pass block. Bajakian's foot stuck in the mud; Gatewood's foot stepped on top of his, and the quarterback tripped and fell. After the game, tears were streaming down his face. Did it seem like a loss?

"I think so," he said. "It sure doesn't feel like a win. I guess it's not quite a loss, but it's a lot closer to that than it is to a win."

Williams' star defensive lineman, Ethan Brooks, felt that way, too. He was bent over at the waist, inconsolable. Mark Colella, the Williams flanker, also had tears in his eyes. Just across the field, Amherst was celebrating.

As seriously as the players took the proceedings, there is more to a Williams-Amherst game than winning and losing, or, in this case, tying. The Amherst band, which bills itself as the "Mucho Macho Moo-Cow Marching Band and School of Cosmetology," is worth the price of admission. As much a quirky cheering section as a band, the members delight in hurling peculiar barbs — "The ref is a wonderful guy, the check is in the mail," they chanted after one call favoring Williams — and playing offbeat songs, such as the theme from *The Muppet Show.* In all, it's a delightful departure from the usual fare.

And, for that matter, so was the game. True, it was inartistic at times. There was stumbling and there was bumbling, attributable more to the condition of the field than the abilities of the players.

Surveying the scene afterward, Dick Quinn, the Williams sports information director, looked at the quagmire and frowned. "By Wednesday," he said, "we'll probably have enough money in the alumni office for a new field. We talk about how we do everything first-class here at Williams and this field was definitely not first-class."

True enough. But the effort put forth on it by both teams was.

"I know Williams is disappointed," said Amherst coach Jack Siedlecki. "I can understand that. For us, to a certain extent, we felt like we won. This was a big accomplishment."

It was that. Call it the first non-loss in nine years for Amherst, and, in a rivalry like this, that's a victory.

PETER DE JONGE

A '90's Kind of Rivalry

FROM THE NEW YORK TIMES MAGAZINE

EARLY ON THE morning of March 27, Pete Sampras, then the number one–ranked tennis player in the world, and Andre Agassi, number two with a bullet, boarded a Concorde jet in New York City to fly to London and then on to Sicily to represent the United States in a Davis Cup match against Italy. Not since 1984, when Jimmy Connors and John McEnroe seemed to own the sport, had two Americans been locked in such a furious competition. Sampras and Agassi had each meticulously planned their schedules, therefore, to give them the ideal proportion of action and rest needed to peak at the year's four Grand Slam tournaments. The Davis Cup was a huge disruption, and each had agreed to participate only if the other would. Even then, they had to be cajoled into playing and promised the use of a private plane from London to Sicily.

Unlike Connors and McEnroe, however, Sampras and Agassi didn't need a straw-hatted emissary from the United States Tennis Association, beseeching them to place love of country over contempt for each other. Despite the one-on-one nature of tennis, a conflict of such focused and intimate emotional violence that a single exchange can leave a permanent ridge of psychic scar tissue, Sampras and Agassi have always got along just fine.

It is true that Agassi once said of Sampras, whose long arms make him play several inches taller than his six-foot-one height, that he looks as if he had swung onto the court from a tree. And last year, at a Nike shareholder convention, Agassi suggested that company engineers come up with something to keep Sampras's tongue in his mouth. But in each case, Sampras accepted Agassi's hastily faxed apology. On the credit side of Agassi's ledger, after all, is the time that he graciously agreed to delay a match so that Sampras could recover from food poisoning. Even Agassi's girlfriend, the actress Brooke Shields, and Sampras's girlfriend, a law student named Delaina Mulcahy, are friendly: during Wimbledon this year, they shopped together at Harrods.

And so less than eighteen hours after Agassi had beaten Sampras in the finals of the Lipton Championships in Key Biscayne, Florida, a victory that would help propel Agassi to the number one ranking two weeks later, they sat side by side on the Concorde, Agassi by the window and Sampras on the aisle. Relishing the rare opportunity to talk to each other's only true peer rather than the coaches and surrogate friends on their payrolls, they dissected their respective games and psyches like a pair of friendly hackers.

Recalling the conversation several weeks later in separate interviews, both were still struck by the starkness of their differences. And while Agassi confessed an appreciation for Sampras that borders on awe, Sampras was less generous, bringing up only the parts of the conversation that reflected better on him. "Andre mentioned a point in the first set at the Lipton, where I dove for a volley," Sampras remembers. "He told me that if he ever dove for a ball, he'd look like a fool."

Sitting with Agassi in a hotel restaurant in Washington as he picks at a bowl of sliced fruit, I ask him about Sampras's recollection. "Pete's the kind of guy who can just decide you're not going to hit a lob over his head, even if he has to jump four feet into the air to get it," he says. "Me, I'll probably let it drop, and then wrack it." Besides, Agassi adds, "If a ball is about to go by me, I figure I've already done something seriously wrong."

What most impressed Agassi was how little Sampras leans on his coaches. (Agassi is now coached by Brad Gilbert, who helped him climb from number 32 to number 1 in a little more than a year; Sampras's coach is Paul Annacone, who replaced Tim Gullikson seven months ago when Gullikson withdrew to battle brain cancer, for which he is now undergoing chemotherapy.) "Pete said, 'Regardless of what Brad's done for you, you're the one who has to go out there and do it,'" Agassi told me in the restaurant. "I said, 'I totally agree with you, but he's given me a lot of important insights.' He said, 'Like what?' And I was like, 'Well, he's directed me here

and directed me there, and given me a game plan.' And Pete was
shocked to think that's what a coach does. All he knows is someone
who makes sure his toss is on line and helps with the fundamentals
on some very basic level. But nobody tells Pete how to play. Me, it's
the opposite. I have all the shots, but what the hell do I do with
them?"

Agassi, whose need to get naked is at the heart of his enduring charisma, continued: "The one thing that Pete has over me, or
I shouldn't say over me, but that I wish I had, is such a simple
approach and raw belief that he is just better than everybody. With
me, it's different. Even at the level of being number one now for
a while and winning tournaments and winning Slams, I still could
convince myself that, Geez, maybe I'm just not as good as I think
I am."

Between them, Sampras and Agassi have won the last four Wimbledons, three of the last five U.S. Opens and the last two Australian
Opens, not to mention about $20 million in official cash (and un-
knowable millions more in endorsements, much of it from Nike).
They represent opposite routes to the top of the tennis ladder.
Agassi, programmed since birth to be a champion, only started to
fulfill his talent after finally conquering his resentment over the
lack of say in his own fate. Sampras, a "natural," suddenly bloomed
at 19 with a straight-set thrashing of Agassi at the 1990 U.S. Open,
becoming its youngest-ever champion, and has suffered nary a mis-
step since. Their rivalry, which has come to a boil this year, hasn't
just rekindled interest in a dying game — it's the whole show. Every
major tournament begins with a fervent collective prayer that Sampras and Agassi will meet in the finals. If they do, it's Aeschylus; if
not, it's *Waterworld*.

So far, unfortunately, it's been a pretty sodden summer. After
three memorable encounters at the start of the year, including
Agassi's dramatic win over Sampras in the finals of the Australian,
the year's first Grand Slam event, Sampras and Agassi missed their
date in both Paris and London. In a fitting end to his disastrous
clay-court season, Sampras lost in the first round of the French
Open while Agassi was beaten in the quarterfinals by Yevgeny Kafel-
nikov, a big, blond Russian who is number six in the world. (Agassi
then blamed the loss, rather unconvincingly, on a strained hip
flexor.) At Wimbledon, the two seemed certain to meet in the finals

after Sampras struggled past Goran Ivanisevic in one semifinal, with Agassi set to play Boris Becker, whom he'd beaten eight
straight times, in the other. But after shooting out to an early
lead, Agassi crumbled, losing to Becker in four sets. In the
final, Sampras, showing his best form in a year, dominated Becker
and became the first American man ever to win three straight
Wimbledons.

With the late-summer return to the hard courts, the rivalry has
slipped back into gear. On July 30, Sampras and Agassi played for
the title in the du Maurier Ltd. Open in Montreal, their first meeting in more than four months. Agassi pulled out a three-set victory,
squaring the pair's pro records at eight wins each. Still, it is only
fitting that their battle for supremacy, at least for 1995, should be
settled on an American hard court, at the U.S. Open, the year's
final Grand Slam event. "On a medium hard court, you can win
from the back court and you can play serve and volley," Agassi
says, "so it's the perfect surface on which to test our two different
games." Starting tomorrow, they will each try to slog their way
through the 128-man draw while contending not only with the
August humidity but also with the singular stress of playing for all
the marbles in New York City, where the late-night crowds bay at the
moon and howl for blood. The Open is by far tennis's most gladi-
atorial spectacle, where two men enter and only one can leave. If it
were staged by Aeschylus, of course, the two men would be Pete
Sampras and Andre Agassi.

You might think that, the more time one spent observing and
talking to a pair of extremely wealthy young athletes, both of whom
left high school in their midteens and stand without rivals at the top
of their sport — as well as the marketing pyramid that props it up
— the more you would find they had in common. But under such
scrutiny, Sampras, 24, and Agassi, 25, emerge as mirror opposites.
Their games and heads match up strength for strength, weakness
for weakness, with perfect interlocking symmetry: Sampras has the
best serve in tennis, Agassi the best service return. Agassi has the
nastiest down-the-line backhand, Sampras the best running forehand. Agassi has the most effective and best-concealed topspin lob,
and Sampras, who is the sport's best leaper, the most explosive
overhead.

Agassi's skills are oddball, eccentric and not even inherently athletic, based on an ability to see and react to a tennis ball with
uncanny speed and accuracy. In a rally from the back court, Agassi
uses his hands and eyes to make the type of adjustments to the ball
that most players make with their feet. For a long time, Agassi, who
has a barrel chest and no-account legs, was criticized for his obses-
sion with weight lifting, and in fact for a couple of years, he did
appear more interested in bench-pressing twice his weight than in
winning tennis matches. But watching Agassi swing at the ball with
his short arms, you notice that he hits every ball just out in front of
him and no more than a couple inches on either side of his spinal
column — in effect, each stroke is like a small bench press.

Everything about Agassi's game is tight and compressed. Agassi
reaching for a ball as little as a foot away is a crime against nature.
He is the only player on the pro tour who never stretches; the only
time he got a rubdown at Wimbledon was before the semifinal
match that he lost to Becker. Even Agassi's smile is tight.

Sampras, meanwhile, is the sweetest, most fluid big cat in the
jungle, with tremendous power in the thighs and calves. When he is
playing well, everything is loose, flowing, silent and deadly, and
Sampras seems to simply kick back and delight in what his body can
do. For Sampras, tennis is a sensual experience. After a four-day
layoff following his Wimbledon victory, he sorely missed moving
around a court and hitting balls. "I like the feel of the ball coming
off the strings," he says. "I like the sounds. I just like to get out there
and groove a little bit." Whereas Agassi's every second of court time
is grunt labor — with his sweaty bandanna and pigeon-toed strut,
he'd look right at home on a construction site — Sampras is a pure
athlete. He plays.

The greatest difference between the two, though, may be that
Sampras operates from an unshakable belief that he has not yet
laid eyes on the man who can take him down when he is playing
well, while Agassi seems to be motivated just as effectively by in-
eradicable feelings of insecurity. That's why Agassi plays with such
instant ferocity, trying to strip his opponent bare within the first
few games of a match. Sampras, meanwhile, starts more slowly, is
less impressive in the early rounds of a tournament and plays with
leonine languor until he gets in a bit of trouble. It's why every
time Agassi steps on the court, it's personal, while Sampras believes
that whoever is across the net is irrelevant as long as he plays his

game. As Brad Gilbert notes, Agassi remembers practically every point of every match, but Sampras often forgets he has even played someone.

Perhaps the reason why Sampras plays with so much more equanimity is that, while tennis has deeply hurt Agassi, and at several times all but broken him, Sampras's career has been a stroll in the park. Agassi has had to clear one psychic obstacle after another, but for Sampras, Agassi is the first real challenge, the first opponent who he knows can beat him even if he plays well. "Pete needs someone who can give him a mental test," says Mats Wilander, a former number one player now finishing up his career. "Pete needs Andre more than Andre needs him."

In many ways, their well-marked public personas run exactly counter to the way they play. Agassi may seem daring when he screws in his earrings or laces up his black sneakers or shaves off all his body hair, but on the court, he is the far more conservative and repetitive player of the two. He is also the harder worker, the more compulsively prepared, and as some of Sampras's recent matches have shown, the better conditioned. And while Sampras may look like the boy that every father wants his daughter to bring home, he is all but uncoachable and plays with almost reckless abandon. "Sampras is the more artistic player," says Todd Martin, the number seventeen player in the world, "Agassi the more solid."

It is Agassi, the putative bad boy whom Nike pitches as the creator of rock-and-roll tennis, who is the born-again Christian and, if you can take his old pal Barbra Streisand's word for it, a "Zen master." A therapy graduate and a voracious reader of pop-psych authors like Marianne Williamson and Tony Robbins (whom Agassi has called "one of the most evolved people I've met"), Agassi is constantly seeking reassurances that he has changed, that he is getting better. Sampras, whose favorite line from literature is "Don't ever tell anybody anything," from *The Catcher in the Rye*, sees little need to change and seems perfectly content with who he is.

Five days after Wimbledon, Sampras is dripping onto the cement beside the East Hampton pool of his coach, Paul Annacone, talking about the subdued reaction to his third straight Wimbledon title. But he might just as well be referring to the uninformed reaction to himself in general.

On the court, Sampras turns himself into a conduit for his tennis, his personality all but erased. You could watch every pro match he has ever played and not know a thing about him. Off the court, however, Sampras has no lack of personality. Muscular, hirsute, his kinky jet black hair swept back, he's juiced up, bristling with opinion and cynical wit, the very picture of brutal youth. Sampras "couldn't believe" that his Wimbledon victory didn't rate the cover of *Sports Illustrated*, which instead ran a story about the return of Monica Seles, who two years ago was attacked by a crazed, knife-wielding tennis fan. "I mean, she's playing a freaking exo," says Sampras, referring to her comeback exhibition match against Martina Navratilova.

And Sampras offers an explanation for his scant postmatch praise of Greg Rusedski, whom he beat in the Wimbledon quarterfinals. (In a brazen act of self-promotion, Rusedski, a Canadian player whose mother is British, became a British subject just before the start of Wimbledon. After three early-round victories, he all but declared himself the savior of British tennis.) "Ninety-nine percent of the time," says Sampras, "even if I think a guy is worth [expletive], I would say he's got some talent, and has some time to improve. But I was so tired of hearing about Rusedski and listening to the British media that I decided, if I kick his [expletive], I'm going to be a little more opinionated."

One of the many revelations of the time I spent with Sampras is his foul mouth. Obscenities are such a weight-bearing element in his terse syntax that with the expletives deleted, often all that's left is the name of the guilty. "[expletive] Rusedski!" he blurts out, for the sheer joy of it; later, when I remind him how frequently Brad Gilbert, Agassi's notoriously gregarious coach, brings up the fact that Gilbert is four and four in the eight times he met Sampras as a player, he says, "[expletive] Brad!" He tries to point out the meaninglessness of the statistic. "I mean, this [expletive] guy here is 1–0 against me," Sampras says, pointing to Annacone, who is wading in the shallow end with a silly grin, not quite sure whether to look proud or insulted. "You want to humble Brad, just ask him about the Slams," says Sampras, who is well aware that, despite the $5 million in prize money that Gilbert has earned in a long career as a sort of overachieving bottom-feeder, he never advanced beyond the quarterfinals in any of the four major tournaments. "Just ask him about the Slams."

I pass along something that Pete Fischer, Sampras's first and most influential coach, recently told me: Gilbert, Fischer believes, has the greatest mind in tennis and he was always Fischer's first choice to coach Sampras if he couldn't do it himself. Sampras rolls his eyes. "Brad's got a good heart, but I couldn't take all that talking, discussing every angle, every shot," he says. "Whenever we used to practice together, I'd say, 'Brad, would you just shut the [expletive] up for thirty minutes.'"

"Brad's got a lot to offer," Annacone throws in graciously.

"Yeah, too much," says Sampras.

Sampras has gone out of his way to give credit to Tim Gullikson for helping him get from number five in the world to number one, and his feelings were painfully obvious when, after learning that Gullikson had cancer, Sampras broke down and cried on the court during his semifinal match in the Australian Open. But since splitting with Fischer when he was 18, Sampras has seemed to value his coaches more for their company than their wisdom. When Annacone, still wading nearby, starts expounding tennis theory, saying that a player is always plotting to take away the amount of time his opponent has to return a shot, either by hitting the ball hard or hitting it early, Sampras, without taking his eye off the little poolside basketball hoop he's shooting at, just says, "Nonsense."

"Nonsense," in fact, may be Sampras's favorite word, a blanket assessment that covers just about everything his eye takes in. Not without reason, he has come to see himself as tennis's one truly sane man, trying to navigate a sea of posturing lunatics; for all its prerequisites, the job is starting to try his patience. Sampras refers to his time in Sicily with Agassi as "the whole Davis Cup nonsense," pointing out that although players like to milk the international competition for all the patriotic P.R. they can, "no one in America really cares about the Davis Cup. Do you even know how the systems of ties and everything works?"

The more Sampras reveals of himself, the more it seems that his admiration for Agassi does not extend much beyond his ability to hit a tennis ball. When I ask what he specifically likes about Agassi, intending him to cite some attractive human quality, he draws a blank, then says, "I like the way he travels," referring to Agassi's private jet.

Just as all the tennis talk is getting laborious, Delaina Mulcahy,

Sampras's girlfriend, wanders out toward the pool. She's got a towel wrapped around her thin waist like a sarong, and she's waving her arms in the air. "The best thing about Pete and Andre," she announces, "are the girls."

She sits down next to Sampras. "Pete, it's beautiful here. We should get a place here."

"We hardly spend any time in our one house and you want to get a second place," says Sampras. "Nonsense."

Sampras and Mulcahy, 30, who is entering her final year of law school, live in Tampa in a huge house beside a golf course. She is Sampras's first girlfriend and they have been together five years.

"Darling," she says, "tell him how we met."

"After I won the Open, she saw me holding the check and said, 'I'm going to get me some of that.'"

"No, seriously," says Mulcahy.

"Seriously?" says Sampras. "I was doing this exhibition and we went out one night, and she fell totally in love with me."

"He always gets it backwards," says Mulcahy, examining her manicure.

The real version seems to be that Sampras, who was 19 and had never been on a date before he turned pro, called Mulcahy the day after they met and asked her to spend a week with him in Myrtle Beach, South Carolina. "Our first date lasted a week," says Mulcahy. (Agassi, by contrast, exchanged faxes with Brooke Shields every day for three months before risking the exchange of anything more intimate. Perhaps because they have so much in common — former childhood stars who both survived an overzealous stage parent — they have since locked into what they each describe as a solid and happy relationship.)

Sampras and Mulcahy start to goof around by the edge of the pool. He throws her in, twice, the second time eliciting a warning: "I'll remember this when it's time to get horizontal." At this moment, at least, Pete Sampras seems like an exceedingly normal 24-year-old.

In fact, his only eccentricity may be the sacredness with which he regards his sleep. Under the right circumstances, he can go for twelve hours at a stretch. He turns the air conditioning on full blast, snaps the sheets as tight as a drum, and insists that Mulcahy not so much as touch him until he wakes up. It's as if Sampras doesn't let anyone, even his girlfriend, near his subconscious.

Andre Agassi, on the other hand, tends to run his psyche like an open house, particularly if a visitor can help him play better tennis. On an early Friday afternoon in the middle of this year's Wimbledon tournament, Agassi and Gilbert were working out on the grass practice courts at Aorangi Park. In his first two overpowering wins, against Andrew Painter and Patrick McEnroe, Agassi had hit two or three stone-cold service return winners each game, often sending the ball back twenty miles per hour faster than it had arrived. But for Agassi's third-round opponent, David Wheaton, Gilbert was preaching the rewards of moderation, and Agassi was listening intently.

"If you rip it, he just keeps charging in, where all he has to do is react," Gilbert explains. "Slow him down, make him hesitate, and he's got to think about it. That's when he gets nervous." Instead of whaling on the ball, Gilbert says, Agassi should hit low, dipping topspin returns that will freeze Wheaton. Gilbert serves a half-dozen balls and Agassi responds as instructed.

Agassi's first tennis coach was his Armenian-born father, Mike Agassi, who had immigrated to the States after competing in the 1948 and 1952 Olympics for the Iranian boxing team. On the day that Andre first opened his eyes, Mike Agassi tied a tennis ball to a string and dangled it over his crib — "to get him to follow the ball." When Andre was old enough to sit in a high chair, Mike taped half a Ping-Pong paddle to his hand and tossed balloons at him, "to teach him timing." And a few years later, Mike put Andre on the cement court he had built in the back yard of the family's Las Vegas home and began bombarding him with hundreds of balls a day, spat out by eleven machines capable of manufacturing every kind of spin or angle.

Mike Agassi had long harbored the goal that one of his children would be a champion. After the first three Agassis burned out early, Andre was his last, best hope. He was a pure prodigy, a toddler who hit with topspin, moving into the junior-tournament circuit at 7 and, before he turned 13, rallying with at least half a dozen pros who came through Vegas.

Through the lens of psychotherapy, Agassi now sees the earliest stages of his tennis education as a mild form of child abuse. In an interview with *Tennis* magazine, Jim Courier recalled a junior tournament at which Mike Agassi took Andre's runner-up trophy and threw it in the trash. These days, communication between father and son is cordial but sparse. When I ask Mike Agassi what advice he might offer if his son were to meet Sampras in the finals of the U.S. Open, he says: "Why should I tell him anything? He hasn't listened to a thing I've said for three years."

At 13, Andre was shipped off to the Nick Bollettieri Tennis Academy, the notorious Florida tennis factory. Two days after his 16th birthday, Agassi turned professional, with Bollettieri, a law-school dropout who had never played competitive tennis, as his coach. In one early stretch as a pro, Agassi lost in the first round of nine straight tournaments, an experience that left him bawling on a Washington park bench, where he was comforted by a minister who traveled with the pro tour — the same minister who not long before had helped Agassi become a born-again Christian.

By the time Agassi was 18, he was number three in the world, having made the semifinals of two Grand Slams and won several smaller tournaments. Still, except for his victory at Wimbledon in 1992, he spent the next six years going either sideways or down, losing three Grand Slam finals in which he was heavily favored. And yet, his celebrity grew ever higher, even when he was losing and showing up overweight for tournaments. The media began to think of him more as marketing phenomenon than tennis champion.

Bollettieri, expressing disgust with Agassi's lack of commitment, very publicly severed their relationship, although Mike Agassi insists that his son's "firing" was a preemptive strike — that Andre had offered to keep Bollettieri on contract, but had told him he needed to work with someone who knew what it was like to deal with on-court pressures.

That someone was Brad Gilbert, whose own career was in its late stages. In jumping from Bollettieri to Gilbert (after experimenting briefly with a handful of other ex-pros), Agassi went from a coach with zero competitive experience to one of the most astute strategists ever. And because Gilbert was still playing, he had a current book on every player on tour.

Gilbert immediately went to work on Agassi's head, addressing the Grand Slam opportunities that Agassi had blown. "First of all," recalls Gilbert, "I told him those suckers are gone. There's nothing you can do to get them back." Then he convinced Agassi that all his failures were essentially due to lousy coaching. "When he came to me, he was a diamond that was uncut," says Gilbert. "He could play some great tennis, but there were flaws all over the place."

Perhaps the most central flaw was Agassi's apparent lack of grit, evidenced by his history of giving up once he got behind in a match. Gilbert, a ferocious competitor who as an apprentice pro won twenty-eight straight matches in qualifying events, has no tolerance for quitters. But instead of delivering his message as an ultimatum, as Mike Agassi might have, Gilbert reminded Agassi how interminably painful it would be to look back on his career with regret. When Gilbert took over, Agassi was floundering badly and seemed destined to go down as one of the game's most underachieving great talents. Within a year, he won the U.S. Open and the Australian Open; so far this year, he hasn't lost a single match short of the quarterfinals, nor to anyone outside the top twenty. "If Brad had been my coach earlier, I think I would have been number one in the world when I was eighteen," Agassi says, with more regret than hubris.

One of the most fascinating aspects of their collaboration is the way that Gilbert has built the new Andre without extirpating the old one. Gilbert isn't denying that Agassi got tight at the end of his Wimbledon match with Becker ("Hey, everybody chokes sometimes — *everybody*," he says) or even that Agassi got that old spooked look in his eyes; but he makes the valid point that Agassi never stopped fighting. "There was no point in that match where I thought Andre was going to lose until they said, 'Game, set, match: Becker.' If I ever thought Andre wasn't trying in a single match, I'd have a real problem with that."

Because of Agassi's fragile feelings about himself, Gilbert is just as concerned with keeping him from getting too pumped up too early in a tournament as he is with him going down — particularly because his toughest competitor, Sampras, often looks sluggish in the early rounds. "I tell Andre that it don't matter that you're crushing everybody and Pete's struggling," Gilbert told me at Wimbledon, "because second place don't mean nothing to either one of you. Pete's like a pitcher who wins 7–6 because that's all he needs to pitch that day, and then the next day, when he has to, goes

out and throws a 1–0 gem. I keep telling Andre to beware of the
wounded bear."

Now, as Gilbert and Agassi are nearing the end of their workout
at Aorangi Park, still plotting how to knock off David Wheaton,
Agassi asks, "What percentage should I serve to his forehand?" as if
he'll be toting a calculator in his shorts. They keep hitting as Gilbert spews out a steady stream of exhortation and non sequitur.
"When the bell goes off, you got to come strong!" he shouts across
the net. And: "Steffi's looking thin, she's looking razor-thin." And:
"I swear, I couldn't get that broccoli soup out of my mind last
night," to which Agassi responds, "Yeah, that can give you a foot
cramp." The talk always returns to strategy, though, and Agassi
can't get enough.

Despite the nearly miraculous results, there is something about
Gilbert's nonstop coaching and Agassi's rapt attention that is just a
little much, suggesting that the whole exercise serves more as an
emotional balm than a point-for-point battle plan. This seems especially true when, a few minutes later, Gilbert and Agassi are replaced on the same court by Paul Annacone and Pete Sampras,
who, in their own practice session, casually hit for forty-five minutes
without exchanging a single word.

According to Sampras family lore, Pete taught himself to play by
hitting against a wall with a racquet he had found in the basement.
One weekend morning when Pete was 9, his father, an engineer
for NASA, took him to the Jack Kramer Tennis Club in Manhattan
Beach, on the outskirts of Los Angeles. Pete Fischer, a pediatrician
who grew up in Yonkers, was just getting off the court, and Sam
Sampras asked him to hit with his son. When they were through,
Sam asked how much Fischer would charge to do it regularly.
"Nothing," said Fischer. Thus began one of the least likely coach-
athlete pairings in the history of sports.

"You have to see him," says Sampras of Fischer. "He's bald with
glasses, about six-foot-two, has a bad back, is kind of hunched over
and a little overweight. He's like a mad scientist. He tried to put his
brain in my body."

Fischer, 53, still lives near Los Angeles, and works about eighty
hours a week caring for critically premature infants at the Kaiser
Foundation Hospital. He recalls that before he met Sampras, he

had speculated with a friend what might happen "if a pure athlete, somebody like Willie Mays, had taken up tennis." And now here he was, rallying with a silent little kid whom Fischer sensed with frightening surety might indeed be tennis's Willie Mays. "He hit every ball square center, where he wanted to hit it," Fischer says. "You can't conceive of how good he was unless you were there." (In fact, until Sampras won the U.S. Open, Fischer often feared that he had disastrously tampered with history by encouraging him to play tennis instead of baseball.)

Fischer's own tennis education was limited to six lessons he got one summer, courtesy of his father, a toy salesman. Still, he was immediately aware of the responsibility with which he had been entrusted, and applied himself to Sampras's development with the dispassionate objectivity of a scientist and the unshakable confidence of a New Yorker. "Pete doesn't sugarcoat it," Sampras says. "He tells the truth."

With his parents' blessing, Sampras started spending all his free time with Fischer. They played on the hospital's courts three or four days a week after school, and at the club on weekends. Fischer's first step was to establish appropriate goals. "From the very beginning," he says, "the competition was always Laver, and it still is." (Rod Laver holds the record for the most major singles crowns, eleven, and he is the only player ever to win the Grand Slam — all four major tournaments in the same year — twice.) "Pete is still five majors and two Grand Slams behind Laver," Fischer says, "and he knows it as well as I do."

Fischer was blunt in his criticism, but his emphasis was always on the long term; to discourage Sampras from obsessing about junior trophies, he had him play a bracket or two above his age. "That might have been the difference between him and Mike Agassi," Sampras says. "Andre's father was more concerned with winning."

Sampras was 9 when he first ran into Andre Agassi, who was 10, at a tournament in Northridge, California. They were both tiny for their age, and Sampras recalls that Agassi beat him easily, hitting almost nothing but trick shots. "He toyed with me for about two hours," Sampras says.

By the time Sampras was 13, Fischer was showing him tapes of Laver, and talking very specifically about winning Wimbledon. Until he was 14, his best shot was a two-handed backhand, but after

Fischer concluded that a serve-and-volley game was necessary to dominate the majors, and that no player with a two-handed backhand had ever been a great volleyer, Sampras was obliged to drop it. "I was losing matches and losing confidence," Sampras says, "but Pete insisted that this was something that hopefully was going to help me win the U.S. Open and Wimbledon one day, and I trusted him."

Sampras's game changed so dramatically that his psyche had to adjust. "When I was 14, I was such an intense little kid," he says. "I played just like Chang, grinding from the base line. When I started serving and volleying, I became much more laid-back." Sampras discovered that there is an entirely different psychology between being a serve-and-volleyer and a base-liner, puncher and counter-puncher. And he found that being the puncher was a whole lot more pleasant. At the same time, Fischer began banging home the message that Sampras's only opponents were himself and history. "He's Pete Sampras," says Fischer. "He shouldn't care who is on the other side of the net."

The transformation of Sampras's game would ultimately account for his stunning success, but it was probably also responsible for the collapse of his relationship with Fischer. "Until I was 16," Sampras says, "I did everything Pete said. But then I started to rebel." The biggest struggle was over Sampras's serve. Fischer never intended for it to become as huge as it has, and believes that its dominance has fouled the harmony of Sampras's serve-and-volley game. Fischer still thinks that Sampras should take some speed off his first serve, get a higher percentage in and win more points with his first volley. As it is now, he thinks Sampras is too dependent on how well his serve happens to be working on any given day: "Pete should realize he doesn't need free points to win," Fischer says.

"Nothing is more demoralizing than getting aced a lot," counters Sampras. "We have this discussion every time I go to Los Angeles and we go out to dinner. He knows how I feel; I know how he feels. I just think he's wrong."

Fischer's reply: "I've always said that Pete is like my Doberman, Hitler. You've got to hit him with a two-by-four to get his attention."

Since Fischer, Sampras's coaching has consisted of little more than tweaking and polishing. Joe Brandi, who was coaching Sampras when he came out of nowhere in 1990 to beat Agassi and win the U.S. Open, was a quiet caretaker of Sampras's game. Even Gullikson, whom Sampras hired in 1992 and who helped him make the jump to number one, instituted very few significant changes. Like Fischer, Gullikson wanted Sampras to play more serve-and-volley, but it was hard to argue with Sampras's success. Last year, until a foot injury essentially wiped out his summer, he was having one of the most dominating years in tennis history, winning at Australia and Wimbledon and six other tournaments. Even Gullikson's illness, while it plainly affected Sampras, hardly distracted him from his tennis. In fact, in the five years since he won his first Open, he has been almost numbingly excellent. The result is a confidence that is as genuine as it is low-key. "The guy has just never said an arrogant thing, even in private," says Annacone, who is still considered Sampras's interim coach in anticipation of Gullikson's eventual return. "When he won Wimbledon this year, all he said was, 'I feel really good.'"

One way that the soul of professional tennis reveals itself these days is in the parceling out of seats in the players' boxes at Wimbledon and the three other majors. One seat goes to your coach, one to your trainer, one to your agent, one to the person you're most publicly having sex with, and one to the administrator of your sneaker contract. For both Sampras and Agassi, that is Ian Hamilton, Nike's director of sports marketing, tennis division.

Nike has so insinuated itself into the Sampras-Agassi rivalry that one occasionally wonders if it is really just some elaborate plan to hawk sneakers. (At Wimbledon, Nike plastered its oversize images on a double-decker bus that shuttled between the tournament site and the train station, and throughout the summer, Nike has broadcast a television commercial called Guerilla Tennis, in which Sampras and Agassi jump out of a cab, string up a net, and start going at it in the middle of a city street.) For all the prize money that each player earns, about $2 million a year, it's only a fraction of what Nike pays them. So beyond being competitors, Sampras and Agassi are fellow employees competing for the affection of Phil Knight, the chairman of Nike — who, after Sampras's Wimbledon victory this year, gave Sampras and Delaina Mulcahy a lift home in his private plane.

Each year, Nike rents an exquisite stone manse in Wimbledon, which, for the duration of the tournament, is known as Nike House. One morning during this year's tournament, Ian Hamilton ushered me past a security guard, a burly Brit with tattooed knuckles, and into the huge Nike House living room. In very broad strokes, he declared just how important Sampras and Agassi are to his company.

While Sampras didn't sign on until just before the 1994 Wimbledon tournament, Agassi has been with Nike since the beginning. In fact, Hamilton was one of the first people Agassi called from the Bollettieri Tennis Academy when he was about to turn pro, and Hamilton immediately dipped into a pile of discretionary money he calls "my gut-feeling fund." Two years later, a marketing juggernaut was born when Agassi made the semifinals of the French Open in a pair of denim Nike shorts that John McEnroe had refused to wear. Agassi, relentlessly colorful and highly quotable, recently signed a ten-year contract with Nike, reported to be worth between $100 million and $150 million. One reason why Hamilton won't name the exact figure is probably because Sampras is paid so much less — although Jeff Schwartz, Sampras's agent, says that each player's Nike compensation is tied to various performance clauses, making it impossible to predict exactly how much Sampras — or Agassi — will actually earn.

Hamilton invites me out back to the garden and opens a tool shed. Neatly stacked are hundreds of pairs of grass-court sneakers, which Nike supplies to its players at Wimbledon and Queen's Club, the Wimbledon tuneup. The surplus sneakers, says Hamilton, will be airlifted to Africa when the tournament is over. Arranged by size, they are available in just two models: the Andre Agassi and the Pete Sampras. The Agassi is a three-quarter-height model covered with odd little weltlike bumps; the Sampras is a more traditional low model. "Andre appeals to the young and the young at heart," Hamilton recites, "while Pete is the perfect ambassador for our new Swoosh collection."

There is an intriguing footnote, as it were, to Nike's role in the Sampras-Agassi rivalry, having to do with the sneakers that the company hastily prepared for Sampras last year when he jumped to Nike. According to sources close to Sampras, the new sneakers didn't fit him quite right and were the start of the foot problems that sidelined him last summer. Which may be why Sampras resorted to the sort of trick that has long been practiced by tennis pros who are cynical or reluctant endorsers: until Nike came up with a shoe that truly fit, Sampras briefly went back to his old sneakers — with a Nike swoosh painted on.

Even without Nike's boosterism, the Sampras-Agassi rivalry would have become a riveting one, all the more so for the inevitability with which it has unfolded. As far back as the junior circuit, astute tennis observers — Pete Fischer among them — saw Sampras and Agassi as the two best talents of their generation; even then, Fischer had no trouble picturing them fifteen years down the road, number one and number two in the world, settling the score on the hard courts of the U.S. Open.

For Agassi, the Open is where, as an 18-year-old semifinalist, he first displayed the scale of his talent and charisma, later showed the weird chinks in his competitive psyche — and then last year startled everyone by finding the will to overcome them. For Sampras, the Open is where, in one two-week period in 1990, all the careful plans of a street-smart pediatrician bore fruit, and the teenage Sampras revealed what most authorities consider the most devastatingly complete game ever. The Open is also where Sampras suffered his most painful defeat, to Stefan Edberg in the 1992 finals, which five months later was still keeping him up at night. "That loss really burned my stomach," he says. "It made me realize just how bad it feels to lose a Grand Slam final, how the only player that people care about is the one who gets his name engraved on the trophy."

Coming into the Open, Agassi couldn't be riding any higher: as of last week, he had won all of his hard-court tuneups. In the sticky heat of Washington, he beat Edberg despite vomiting four times during the final. In Cincinnati, after Sampras wilted in the heat during a quarterfinal match, Agassi pounded Michael Chang for the title. And in Montreal, Agassi outdueled Sampras in the final, 3–6, 6–4, 6–4.

Although Agassi and Sampras are now dead even in head-to-head competition, they're not quite equals. As Agassi put it after his win at Montreal: "The first thing you do when you get on the court with Pete is try not to be embarrassed. Once you've done that, you think about winning." It almost seems as though Agassi, even more than

Sampras himself, acknowledges that Sampras is the more talented player, and that if Sampras is playing and particularly serving at the top of his game, there is very little that Agassi or anyone else can do to affect the outcome. But rather than being paralyzed by this knowledge, Agassi is liberated by it. Every time he steps on the court against Sampras, he plays like someone who has very little to lose, while Sampras, who feels that he absolutely should win, tightens up. Agassi has lost the first set in each of their last four matches, but came back to win three.

"Pete is the best player of all time," declares Mike Agassi. "He's got the best serve, the best volley — the way he moves, nobody knows how fast he is. If he is serving well, the match could be over in fifty-three minutes. But if Andre stays with him, then mentally Pete starts to fall apart."

If all goes according to seed, at 4 P.M. two weeks from today in Flushing Meadows, Queens, Agassi and Sampras will make the 100-yard walk from the locker room to the Louis Armstrong Stadium Court, toting their huge bags filled with some dozen racquets each, surrounded by terse security guards with sunglasses and walkie-talkies. For all the middle-class trappings of the game, the atmosphere at ground level will be as raw and electric as when robed boxers make a midnight walk to a raised ring. As Agassi and Sampras make their way, it will certainly not occur to them that they may represent the one exception to the winner-take-all notion of sports, which is that over the course of their careers, two athletes can become so intertwined that what is remembered is not the outcome of their various matches, but the quality of their rivalry. If both players can each hold up his end of the bargain long enough, no one has to go down in history alone. They can make the walk side by side.

WILLIAM GILDEA

A Shot That Resounds in Hoosier Hearts

FROM THE WASHINGTON POST

Indianapolis

"I'LL MAKE IT," Hickory High's Jimmy Chitwood tells the coach, played by Gene Hackman, in the '50s-era movie *Hoosiers*. It's the final huddle, eighteen seconds remaining in the Indiana high school state championship game. Mythical little Hickory has battled the big-city favorite to a tie. Hickory has the ball; Hackman needs a shooter. He looks up quizzically at a kid called Jimmy Chitwood, then seems to bore straight to the dark-haired hotshot's soul as if divining the outcome. And Hackman says to Jimmy, almost too softly to be heard the way the crowd is screaming, "All right."

Jimmy dribbles out deep in the middle of the court as the seconds tick down and his four teammates set up a "picket fence" on the left side of the floor, clearing out so he can beat his man by driving to the basket or pulling up and taking the jump shot he learned as a boy on winter's frozen earth in southeastern Indiana. Jimmy fakes left and drives right and, precisely at the right end of the free-throw line, stops, jumps and shoots, and the ball rips through the net. Hickory is the champion of all Indiana.

Stop the tape. Eject. Put in "Milan vs. Muncie Central. 1954 State Finals." This is the game that inspired the movie. Milan, pronounced My-lun, is the tiny downstate school and Muncie Central the big-city favorite and still the record-holder for state titles. The black-and-white reel is sometimes jerky, sometimes blurry, filmed from the rafters. A play-by-play voice cries, "Can you hear me out there?" The background noise sounds like 15,000 people scream- ing all at once into a tin can. "Hoosier hysteria," it's called. Eight- een seconds remain and the score is tied at 30 and the real Jimmy Chitwood will take the shot. His name is Bobby Plump.

The slender, crewcut Bobby dribbles out deep in the middle of the court in his black uniform with the knee-high socks as the seconds tick down and his four teammates clear out to the left so he can beat his man either by driving all the way to the basket or pulling up to take the jump shot he learned behind the frame house in which he was born three miles outside of Milan. Bobby fakes left and drives right and, precisely at the right end of the free- throw line, stops and jumps and shoots, and the ball rips through the net. Milan is champion of all Indiana.

Fast forward about forty-one years.

"I'd shot that shot a hundred times — ten thousand times prob- ably," said Bobby Plump, leaning back in his suburban Indianapolis office — Bobby Plump Insurance. At 58, he still looks slender, in a gray-checked suit, though his sandy hair is graying. In November 1993 he felt chest pains and underwent angioplasty. Last February he had a double bypass. The morning after Christmas, atrial fibril- lation sent him to an emergency room. But even as Bobby Gene Plump grows older, his last shot is lodged in the forever-present of Indiana basketball.

"I was a very shy kid," he said. "I never would have said, 'I'll make it.'" Milan's 1954 coach Marvin Wood recalled that he designated Plump the shooter, and the team's center, Gene White, suggested that he and the other players clear out and give Plump most of the floor. "I love Gene, too," said Plump. "Woody said, 'Yeah, let's do that.' And he told Ray Craft, the other guard, 'Throw it on to Bob. Bob, hold the ball, then drive or take the jumper.' I said, 'Let's go over that again, Coach.'

"I still didn't get it right. *I* threw the ball on to Ray. But he gave it back to me and I still had my dribble when I looked up and saw their defense floating to the left. I faked to the left and took off to the right. Mr. Hinkle" — Paul D. "Tony" Hinkle, Plump's future coach at Butler University — "said I had the fastest first step he ever saw. When I went up and let it go I knew it was going in. You know the feel."

That shot — the most famous shot in basketball in Indiana — made Bobby Plump a legend in the Hoosier state, etched in memory with the nationally known likes of John Wooden and Oscar Robertson and Rick Mount and Larry Bird. Plump was ahead of his time with his jump shot, and in the grainy film of players shooting two-handed and one-handed set shots he soars just above the high-leaping defender. The first time Plump saw *Hoosiers* at a preview showing and Jimmy Chitwood went up to take that shot, he stayed settled in his chair in the dark theater and smiled. "I knew it was going in," he said.

Pleasingly Plump

It almost seems that Bobby Plump was destined to make that shot with three seconds left on the Saturday night long ago that caused anywhere from 20,000 to 40,000 celebrators, depending on the account, to descend on Milan, population 1,150, the next afternoon. Of the five starters, of the ten players for the 1954 Milan Indians, Plump was the best — although he was not the best that night at Butler Fieldhouse in Indianapolis. "It was the worst game I played in two years of tourney play," Plump said. He shot 3 for 11.

Still, the others wanted him to be the shooter. "All of his teammates were comfortable with him — they had faith in him, trust in him, so much so that sometimes they'd get into trouble because they'd force the ball to him," recalled Wood, who lives upstate now in Mishawaka and coaches the St. Mary's College women in nearby South Bend.

But more than the likelihood of his making the shot, Plump seemed fated for a fame that continues to grow even in the distant after-game because, as Hoosiers statewide tell it, no one could have handled it quite the way he has. His enthusiasm is enduring, he's eager to please. Invitations to speak come often, especially around this time of the year and tournament time. "I don't call 'em speeches," he said. "They're conversations."

Hope Never Dies

Wherever he goes, he drops in the message, as softly as his old basketball lay-up, that an underdog is not a nobody but somebody who can come out on top, or close enough, anyway. "I say that a person, no matter what he's doing, may be having a positive effect on someone, and that's the most important thing."

"He's a very caring young man," is how Wood put it. Plump is a boon to the countless numbers who phone him or write him, seeking advice or encouragement. He handed over a recent letter: "I teach in a high school . . . not a big school . . . The basketball coach is a friend of mine and a really good coach. However, the team is doing badly, 1–6 at this point. The other day he said . . . 'I guess I'd better bring out *Hoosiers* and show them how they really can win when they're down.' When I told him I know Bobby Plump, he said, '*The* Bobby Plump?' He uses you as inspiration for his team every year. He asked if I would write and ask you for any type of inspiration that you could provide for his boys . . . ."

Plump had to postpone eight "conversations" during his double-bypass recuperation. The flood of requests is a phenomenon that can be explained only by the importance of basketball in Indiana. It is part of life's fabric, woven with a lore dating roughly from tiny Thorntown High's state triumph of 1915 to a consuming presence of Bob Knight and his Indiana University Hoosiers, the pro Pacers, the other colleges and the high schools whose titanic clashes come crackling over the air waves almost nightly. Basketball always has been Indiana's winter game, played by youngsters in towns so small the numbers were better suited to basketball than football. They hung a hoop against a house or barn; often, a kid played alone, making open jumper after open jumper, tipping rebounds to himself.

The success story of a school with only 161 students, 73 boys, loses nothing in the retellings because nothing like it has happened since. Milan's triumph was possible only because Indiana crowned a single champion. Today, Indiana, Kentucky, and Delaware remain the only states whose tournaments are not stratified by enrollment. In 1954, 751 schools started the four-week event. In the foreword to a 1993 book by Greg Guffey titled *The Greatest Basketball Story Ever Told: The Milan Miracle, Then and Now,* Indiana sports writer Bob Hammel uses the word "afterglow" to describe the feeling that settled across the state following Milan's victory. The glow remains.

Bobby Plump: Milan's Miracle Man, a biography by Marty Pieratt, is due out soon. Plump and his son plan to open a restaurant to be called Plump's Last Shot or The Last Shot.

Humble Beginnings

Plump came from Pierceville, three miles outside of Milan. Maybe fifty people lived there. "I kiddingly say the 'in'-and-'out'-of town signs are on the same pole," Plump said. He was the youngest of six. His mother died when he was 5, and his sister Dorothea, then 20, took over raising the others. His father, Lester G. Plump, taught in one-room schoolhouses, but gave it up because he couldn't make enough money. He got a job in a factory in nearby Lawrenceburg crating deep-well pumps, and in his spare time worked a chicken-and-egg route from Pierceville to Cincinnati.

When Bobby was in fourth grade, Lester gave him a basketball and nailed a hoop and backboard to the front of the smokehouse. By chance Pierceville produced four of the ten players on the championship team — Plump, White, Roger Schroder and Glen Butte. Growing up, they played two on two in one yard or another. They played in snow.

"Milan was a big place to me," Plump said. "The kids weren't real receptive at first. You know, they came to like us a lot better when they found out we could play basketball."

Plump grew to be about five-foot-ten, 155 pounds when he played for Milan. After his sophomore season, the coach, Herman Grinstead, known as "Snort" for his temper, was fired. The official reason given was that Grinstead ordered new team uniforms without the approval of the school board. Wood got the job. Only 24, he had begun high school coaching at French Lick. In 1952–53 Wood took Milan to the state's final four. So in 1953–54 Milan did not come from out of nowhere as Hickory did in the movie.

But winning the title still was improbable because Milan had to beat several larger schools with top-ranked teams. One was Indianapolis' Crispus Attucks, with Oscar Robertson. "We were lucky," Plump said, "that Oscar was a sophomore." Plump scored 28 and Milan won, 65–52; Robertson led Crispus Attucks to state titles the next two years.

Milan's title-game victory over Muncie Central set off a celebration that produced its own heroes. A Milan auto dealer named Chris Volz provided three Cadillacs in which the players were driven to the finals. An Indianapolis police officer, Pat Stark, who had fallen in crazed love with the team, escorted the team in the Cadillacs and gave them a victory lap around downtown Indianapolis' Monument Circle the wrong way. Stark, who got into trouble but not enough to lose his job, also escorted the team home the next afternoon. Nobody remembers a Sunday afternoon in Indiana like it. The drive began with five cars and ended in a thirteen-mile-long caravan.

"We couldn't believe the number of people," Plump said. They had parked on all the roads leading into Milan, and had walked. The throng pushed forward to the school, where the principal spoke, and the superintendent, and the coach, and some players, and even the policeman Stark, who welled up with emotion and couldn't get many words out. Plump didn't say much — he didn't want to, because of his shyness. "It took me years to get over it — years," he said.

Plump went on to play for Hinkle at Butler University, site of "the shot," and set several school records. Hinkle then helped Plump hook up with the Phillips Petroleum Company in Bartlesville, Oklahoma, where he worked and played with its then-powerful industrial league team, the Phillips 66ers. Plump stayed for four years, then came home to Indiana and got into the insurance business. He has hung on his office wall a piece of his old high school's wooden gym floor shaped as the state of Indiana (at home he has a piece of the floor with the *scuff marks* still on it).

One player, Ron Truitt, who'd been a high school principal in Houston, died of cancer in 1988. Bill Jordan moved to Hollywood and became an actor. Like Plump, the other 1954 Milan players stayed fairly close to home. They and their coach get together almost every year, and every year Plump's shot is replayed. "It's sold him a lot of insurance," laughed former teammate Glen Butte, who'd been talking on the phone with Plump. Butte said to meet him in the morning downstate, in the Dairy Queen in Batesville. It's on the way to Milan.

In Milan, Heroes and Legends Live On

When you drive out of Indianapolis, you reach the country quickly. Only an occasional house or barn checkers the land southeast on the interstate. In 1954 it took much longer to cover the seventy-five miles to Milan, longer still on the March Sunday that year with thousands of cars blocking the country roads, people shouting and waving along the route. Milan's ten high school basketball players were coming home as Indiana state champions.

Visitors ever since have followed a psychic tug to Milan, drawn by images of the small school's epic triumph against much bigger schools, and by the town itself as a testament to life's improbabilities. No school that small — it had 161 students — has won the Indiana championship since, and many believe that none will again. Coaches, old athletes, writers, the curious in general trek here to see the place that inspired the movie *Hoosiers*, even if, to the townspeople's annoyance, not a single scene was filmed in Milan.

"You'd think they could at least have gotten a shot of the water tower or something," said Glen Butte, reminiscing at the Dairy Queen in nearby Batesville about his days on the '54 champions. The tower would have been perfect; "State Champs 1954" is painted on it. And on the wooden sign at the edge of town: "Welcome to Milan. 1954 State Champs." As Ron Corfman, sports editor of the neighboring *Versailles* (pronounced Ver-sales) *Republican and Osgood Journal*, said: "It's one year that will never end."

Corfman's job once was held by Tiny Hunt, a huge man who chronicled Milan's finest days and talked basketball with the crowds at Rosie Arkenberg's restaurant in downtown Milan. Rosie's used to close for the games and reopen afterward and stay open until everyone had his fill. Tiny is long dead and Rosie's is closed, though she still roots for Milan and keeps a photo of the '54 players in her living room above her sofa. Businesses in Milan have shut down over the years — the furniture store, the movie theater. But, among others, Chester Nichols's barbershop, American flag out front, still thrives. Nichols has been cutting hair here since 1948, and his father worked in the same place before him. Recently AT&T made a commercial in the shop, which caused a welcome hubbub in town with its main street blocked off.

A Place on the Map

"We go back five or six times a year," said Ray Craft, a guard who teamed with Bobby Plump in the '54 backcourt. Craft married Virginia Voss, a Milan cheerleader; they lived in Indianapolis. "Last

Fourth of July we rode in the Milan parade. It's good for Milan to be able to keep the memories." Craft, the assistant commissioner of the Indiana High School Athletic Association, appeared in a cameo role in *Hoosiers* as the tournament official who welcomes Gene Hackman and his team from "Hickory" to Butler Fieldhouse in Indianapolis, site of the finals.

Greg Guffey writes of Milan in *The Greatest Basketball Story Ever Told: The Milan Miracle, Then and Now.* "What will never change is that thousands of people, most since the release of *Hoosiers,* have made this tiny spot on the map a stop on their vacations. One couple from Kansas City saw the movie twenty-seven times before deciding it was time to see the real thing. Another couple called Craft . . . and said they were having trouble finding Hickory on an Indiana state map. He explained that Hickory was just a fictional school in the movie. So the couple visited Milan."

Many find Roselyn McKittrick's antiques and collectibles at the corner of Carr and Franklin. Inside the old double doors is a shop of treasures, and plenty of Milan basketball memorabilia. Books. Tapes of the '54 title game between Milan and Muncie Central. And stories. McKittrick is the town's unofficial hoops historian.

"We had a couple here recently from Pittsburgh," she said. "I had a letter from New Hampshire. A writer from Cincinnati was here. Another writer in Texas did an article. We have a lot of big older men who used to play — you can just see 'em when they're coming. And coaches. There was this young coach a while back who was starting off his career at Crawfordsville. He said he had heard his dad talking about Milan. You could see the dream in his eyes.

"It's one of those stories that's passed down from fathers to sons. People come and they talk about the David and Goliath aspect of what the '54 team did. It's the dream of a small town, to do what they did. It's a feeling that goes deep in all of us — the great upset. The team just kept picking up steam through the tournament, and life then was built around the high school and the team." About 900 of Milan's 1,150 residents then followed the team to the finals. Everyone else clung to their radios.

One can imagine it, standing on the vacant street outside the Railroad Inn restaurant as a freight rumbles just a few yards away through the heart of town. Inside the Railroad Inn, the black-and-yellow Milan letter jacket once worn by Gene White, who played

WILLIAM GILDEA243

center on the '54 team, is displayed in a lighted case. A painting of
the team hangs on the wall. The town is just a few hundred larger
than forty years ago. It almost seems like 1954.

It surely does out in nearby Pierceville. Turning off Route 350
onto a narrow road, one crosses the railroad tracks into the community that produced four of the ten players on the '54 Milan team
— Plump and Roger Schroder and White and Butte, the Pierceville
"Alley Cats," who played in the "alley" behind the Schroder store.
The Schroder house is there, but the store is boarded up. White's
feed store is gone. Beyond some dead cornstalks is the two-story
yellow frame house Bobby Plump grew up in; behind it he honed
the jump shot that he used to beat Muncie Central for the state
title. "You had to be careful not to fall into the manure pile near the
basket," Plump said.

"We were like brothers," recalled Butte, a big man with glasses
and gray hair, athletic director of nearby Batesville High for twenty-
five years before retiring last year. "The four of us grew up together.
We could see each other's houses. In the summers we'd go fishing
and camping on the creek near Versailles. There was hardly a day
when we didn't play basketball."

Others in the Dairy Queen talked of an Indiana University defeat
the night before, how it could have happened, what Bob Knight
might do to get his Hoosiers winning again. Butte was talking about
1954. "It could have been Craft's game," he said. Craft tried for a
clinching lay-up with a minute to play and missed and Muncie tied
the game at 30, leaving the heroics to Plump. "Plump became quite
a legend in Indiana," Butte said. "People ask, 'Where's Plump?
What's Plump doing?'"

Forty Years Later

Milan's old high school has been replaced by a large brick building
on the road into town. It has 325 in the high school grades, and
includes a fine gymnasium. There in the lobby is the championship
trophy. The '54 banner hangs above the court; photos of the '54
players are prominently displayed. It's a lot to live up to, and Craft,
for one, feels a bit awkward about it. "I think some of the kids at
Milan get tired of hearing about it. I think there's still some pres-

sure. But we certainly don't want to put any on them. We just want
them to play to the best of their ability, that's all."

Milan has been tough on coaches since Marvin Wood — Hackman in the movie — left after the championship season. No coach
has lasted longer than six seasons. Milan has not been very successful since White coached and his team won the 1985 sectionals. The
last winning season was 1988–89. At one stretch Milan went two
years without winning a home game.

"People told me this is a graveyard for coaches," said Randy
Combs, 31, the new man in town with the assignment of turning
Milan into a winner again. He's the new Marvin Wood. And one
can see the dream in Combs's eyes too, although realistically, the
dream can't be another state title.

Milan was his chance to become a head coach. So he moved his
wife, Lisa, and year-old son, Cameron, from Greenfield, near Indianapolis, where he had been an assistant, and bought a house in
Milan three blocks from school. He knows what it is to win in
Indiana, having played on a state champion at Vincennes Lincoln
in 1981. He wears the championship ring. He also knows the pressures faced by high school basketball coaches in Indiana.

"My coach, Gunner Wyman, was one of the best," Combs said.
"But when I was a sophomore, there was a petition to fire him. He
had to go before the school board. He said he wanted just two more
years. So his last game, he won the state. He got the last laugh. He
went home to Kentucky. And he remembers every name on that
petition."

The dark-haired Combs looked up and said, "I fully intend to get
the program turned around, and when it does get turned around I
think the kids will have the feeling of satisfaction, reward. There is
an undercurrent attitude [among the students]. They get tired of
hearing about the '54 team. But what the '54 team represents is
kids coming together for the common goal, blending their talents,
sacrificing individually for the good of the team. Let's build on
what lessons were taught by that group."

Juniors make up most of Combs's team, and it's a good thing:
Milan's record is 1–9. But he encourages them. Coming home from
a loss at the Ripley Country tourney, he turned on WIBC, Indianapolis, and he and his players listened to Indiana playing out in
Iowa. As they rode through the dark they could hear the Iowa

crowd roaring because the Hoosiers were being beaten. Milan had just lost. Combs tried to make a point in the bitter night. "I told them, 'Here's IU playing before 16,000, 17,000 people and this is happening to them. You think they're going to cry in their soup?'"

Combs said he wants his players to be leaders: "A role model for a kid in this area ought to be one of the high school basketball players."

And yet — the other morning he got a call from the bus company that drove the team to its last game, about an hour away in Hanover. "Somebody had spilled a Coke in the bus and made a mess," Combs said. "So I decided instead of holding afternoon practice, the team would clean the bus." He laughed. "I sat there thinking, 'Is this where life is taking me?'"

And then: "We're going to get there."

Heavenly Hysteria

On any night in Indiana a person can find "Hoosier hysteria." Zionsville was playing at Avon, west of Indianapolis. The gym was small, the ceiling full of beams, the noise piercing. The two schools' girls teams battled into overtime. A slender man with a crew cut, Phil Isenbarger, sat in the stands, rooting quietly for Zionsville. Isenbarger too knows what it is to win; he played on Indiana's 1981 national championship team headed by Isiah Thomas. Isenbarger's older brother, John, was a football All-American at Indiana. Phil, a lawyer in Indianapolis, is a volunteer assistant for the Zionsville boys — not quite ready to give up the game.

"She's a friend of Brandon Monk's," said Isenbarger, as Anne Johnston scored a winning lay-up with time running out. "Brandon probably has less natural ability than anyone on our team, but he plays about six hours a day. He's slow, he can't jump. It would be nice if he could win it for us." Isenbarger moved across the floor to a seat amid the Zionsville boys. But Avon prevailed as the school band — "The World's Meanest Pep Band" — played "Rocky" from a balcony behind a basket. A man leaned down from up there and yelled something almost directly into an opposing player's ear. It was just another night of basketball in Indiana.

DAVID ALDRIDGE

A Team's True Colors

FROM THE WASHINGTON POST

IN THE INNER SANCTUM of Redskin Park, next to the whirlpool and across from the showers, Washington Redskins tight end Scott Galbraith is getting a haircut. The subject isn't cut blocking, or which young quarterback is doing better. The subject isn't football at all. It's race relations.

"I admit that this is not the real world," Galbraith says. "Why is it not the real world? Because if a guy 300 pounds is rushing at you, I don't care whether you're pro-choice or pro-life. Block that [guy]. And when you block him, I'm going to love you for it. And once I love you for what you did in a working relationship, it can't help but open up the door to my inquisitive nature to find out more about you."

Galbraith continues, hypothetically:

"What is the origin of this person who just laid it on the line for me in a pressure, high-stress situation? Who is this person? Well, I found out he was a redneck from Idaho, who went to the University of Wyoming, and all people from Wyoming ain't prejudiced like I thought. You tell me — how else would I have found that out? How else would I have wanted to have found that out?"

If the American church at 11 A.M. on Sunday mornings is one of the nation's more segregated places, a National Football League locker room that fills up an hour later could be one of the more integrated. In that room, black men and white men put aside their racial differences for three hours for a common cause: in this case, winning football games. They are asked to do what many others struggle to do on a daily basis: make race in the workplace irrelevant.

Each week's game is the end product of a nearly year-long training regimen in which black and white players live in their own mini-society. They spend most of their time with one another. They lift weights together, take part in spring mini-camp together, endure summer training camp together in the blistering July and August heat, and live together during camp in college dormitories.

Then the regular season begins and the relationship intensifies, with players spending the next six months in one another's company, at least eight hours a day, five days a week. They practice all week, and then for sixteen Sundays (and the occasional Monday night), they sacrifice muscle, bones and blood together, some of them veterans, some of them just out of college, but all of them scrutinized daily — by coaches, by media and by fans.

At its best, a football team is a meritocracy, the quintessential level playing field, where excellence is measured objectively and then richly rewarded. At its worst, a sports team can be as troubled a workplace as any in America. Camaraderies forged on the field can be shattered by other kinds of competition: who gets paid the most, who plays and who doesn't, who's the boss, on or off the field, who's a star and who's not.

The Redskins locker room offers another way of looking at how well we all get along — and whether a functional, if not utopian, relationship between the races is possible.

"It is, relatively, two teams," said Terry Crews, 27, a reserve linebacker. "On every team I've been on, it's always at this table, it's all black, and at one table there's all white, and when the workday's done, black guys go one place, or party at one place, and white guys go to another. I think it's always going to be that way, as long as there are the differences."

Culture Clash

Of the fifty-three players on the Redskins' active roster as of November 1, 42 (79 percent) were black and 11 (21 percent) were white. That's a little higher than the average team racial makeup of 68 percent black, 32 percent white, according to figures from 1994 in the annual Racial Report Card of professional sports by the National Rainbow Coalition. So if there is an adjustment to be made in this world, it frequently is by the white player.

Redskins quarterback Heath Shuler, 23, grew up in Bryson City, North Carolina. One black student attended his high school. So when he went to the University of Tennessee, and to a football team with lots of black players, Shuler had to adjust.

"A lot of it, I was shocked about," he said. "Just little things. One time, a guy asked me, 'You going to your crib this weekend?' I'm like 'Uh, no.' I didn't understand what he was talking about. Cliff Dutton was a black guy on the team and I told him 'Cliff, you've got to help me out. These guys are saying stuff and I have no idea what they're talking about. They want me to *go to the crib* this weekend. What kind of place is that?' It was hilarious. Then he told me that means going home."

Many Redskins told less humorous stories about their college days. Kicker Eddie Murray, 39, who like Shuler is white, recalled driving from New Orleans to a beach an hour or so away near Biloxi, Mississippi, while a freshman at Tulane University in 1976, and seeing Klansmen on the side of the road handing out pamphlets. And running back Reggie Brooks, 24, said that at Notre Dame, some white players "just came right out and called you nigger in your face."

In the NFL, that sort of thing is rare. But there are occasional clashes of taste and style. In the weight room, more often than not, the deep bass beat of rap music, or other black popular music euphemistically called "urban contemporary" by radio stations, provides the background for arm curls and dead lifts by the black players. Only when most of the black players are out of the weight room — and there are as many white players as black — is the station changed to a country music station.

A Subtle Segregation

The pro player's daily life is filled with dozens of team-mandated interactions — meetings and practices, on the plane and on the trainer's table, at team parties during training camp and voluntary Bible study sessions on Monday nights. But when players are in less structured situations, blacks and whites often don't seem to integrate. Like in the cafeteria.

"I'm not going to say 'I'm not sitting there because there are three black guys over there, and there are three white guys sitting over here,'" Murray said. "Although that does happen. Is that a conscious thing? I don't know if it is or isn't."

In one corner of the Redskins locker room sits the "Dog Pound," an informal area where, every day, players get together to trade gossip, insults and jokes. All of the players in the Pound are black. Yet the players who populate the Pound insist that the division is along economic lines.

"It's a lot of guys that came off the waiver wire [players released by other teams and claimed by the Redskins], a lot of guys that are free agent rookies," defensive tackle Marc Boutte, 26, said. "It's a time to get away from football, have a little fun, joke and have a good time. We call it the 'hood, the ghetto. You go across the locker room and you see the Rod Stephens and the James Washingtons, all those guys [with big contracts]. It's totally economic."

But players of both races acknowledged that their workplace is like many others: When the day is done, many go their separate ways. They cited numerous reasons: differing backgrounds and interests, length of service, marital status.

"Most of the people here have families, or are married," said guard Tré Johnson, 24, who is black and single and a Redskin only two years. "They're all old."

Linebacker Crews, who played in Germany this past spring for the Rhein Fire of the World League, pointed out that many black players with the Redskins now live in neighborhoods in Loudoun and Fairfax counties near Redskin Park in Ashburn, where they may be the only black person on the street, and may bond with black players in the locker room to be around people like themselves again. Other players are self-described loners, who don't pursue any football friendships.

James Washington, 30, and linebacker Marvcus Patton, 28, are both black, and were fraternity brothers at UCLA. They both came to the Redskins this season. Yet when the day is over, they frequently go their separate ways.

"It all depends on what you have going," said Washington, who counts players of both races among his closest friends on the team.

"Personally, I don't hang out with the defensive backs [all of whom, like him, are black]. They like to golf, and I don't know how to golf that well."

One for All

The main concern of the team, however, is for its players to work together in the meeting room and on the field, not necessarily to be fast friends.

"I talk to our team about it," says Coach Norv Turner. "You can look at it from a racial deal, black and white, but . . . my feeling was the one thing we know we have in common is that we want to win. That's the one thing that's going to bring us together."

Yet outside influences can still split teammates. Money is one. Sixteen-year veteran Murray recalled his rookie year of 1980: "I got $10,000 in a signing bonus, so when I see guys getting $13 million, or $6 million just to put their name on a piece of paper, it can create some animosity because of the unproven factor. I never saw the reasoning behind that, and sometimes, that creates tension."

Shuler got a $5 million signing bonus last year. He said he was encouraged by teammates during his contract negotiations to get as much from the Redskins as he could. But there were, and are, occasional grumblings about the financial commitment the Redskins made to Shuler that aren't necessarily good-natured.

But friendships between black and white players are not unusual. Linebackers Matt Vanderbeek, 28, who is white, and Darrick Brownlow, 26, who is black, are close. Centers John Gesek, 32, and Vernice Smith, 30, became closer during training camp. Both were married but their wives were back home. And both of them started to get closer with Trevor Matich, 34, the team's special teams center. Gesek and Matich are white; Smith is black.

"Vern and I, we'd be friends off the field if we'd have met working for A&P," Matich says.

The three of them would eat together, and sit together in the whirlpool, working out their numerous aches and pains. And they'd talk. They still do.

"We talk about politics, we'll talk about the welfare system in politics, we'll talk about Republicans and Democrats," Smith said.

"A lot of times, we'll find that we want to end up in the same place, in the same area. We just have different ways of getting there, different opinions of how to get to that end."

Gesek, who grew up in San Francisco, is baffled by the notion that there could be something special in his relationship with Smith because they are of a different race. And Matich takes great pains to discuss the irrelevancy of race in football.

"You'd have to make a concerted effort to be a racist in this kind of a setting," Matich said. "When you look at what we go through together, starting with the off-season and working hard and going into training camp and sweating and bleeding and playing hurt next to one another, and then getting into the season and playing games when your teammates are all you've got, and you're all they've got . . . it's hard to look at anything except character and performance, and that's it."

But various forces work against the creation of longtime friendships of any color. The Redskins of the 1980s spent nearly a decade together, establishing ties in the community. Now, with the advent of greater free agency — the ability of a player to sign with another team once his contract expires — players come and go from year to year. There are sixty-five new Redskins on the roster from just two years ago, and that constant movement impedes friendships.

Harsh Reminders

And while black players constitute the racial majority on their teams, they are still a minority in the real world — and very much reminded of it.

Defensive tackle William Gaines, 24, a six-foot-five, 294-pound defensive tackle, has been stopped by police more than once driving home in suburban Virginia from Redskin Park.

"Being a black American, you see [race] everywhere," Gaines said. "You're more [likely] to see it than a white American would. Because I've been pulled over here a couple of times in my truck, doing the speed limit. Just riding on 66 or whatever. Once they pulled me over, though, they didn't give me any trouble. They checked to make sure it was my truck. . . . I guess because I had my truck fixed up, they thought it maybe was a drug thing or whatnot."

Linebacker Ken Harvey, 30, an African American who played in Phoenix for six years (the godfather of his children is Italian) before signing with Washington in 1994, felt a double standard for athletes there — and here — as well.

"If you're an athlete, you're O.K.," Harvey said. "Whereas if you weren't an athlete, you might experience [racism] a little more. Because I'm big, and I look like a player, people automatically assume you're a player, so you get treated a little bit differently. But I've had people follow me in the stores, and get nervous when you come on the elevator with them. It's there, no doubt about it." Athletes could be the wealthiest collection of black men on the planet. But when it comes to speaking out on issues in sports and outside the field, where their words could have as big an impact as their play on the field, most are usually silent.

The Struggle Continues

One rare exception was the recent Million Man March on the Mall in October. More than a dozen Redskins attended, despite criticism of the march and the participants in it because it was organized by Nation of Islam leader Louis Farrakhan, the controversial minister who many feel is anti-Semitic and homophobic.

Turner let them attend the march — and miss scheduled meetings and film study that Monday — as long as they came in early on Tuesday to make up for the missed time.

"I think in any situation, if people are going to be given something, then they have to give something back," Turner said.

Most white players said they didn't have any problem with the black players going, though some didn't understand the need for it.

Said quarterback Gus Frerotte, 24: "It's hard for a person like me to understand that, because I haven't been put through that, or my heritage hasn't been put through something like that. . . . But I didn't have a problem with it. It's something they believe in."

Another American racial controversy made its way into the locker room this season — the O. J. Simpson trial. During the months of testimony, little was said about the trial. But as the verdict neared, tensions increased.

On one memorable day during closing arguments, a debate

about Simpson's guilt or innocence started in one corner of the locker room between Matich and Galbraith, bounced to the Dog Pound, continued toward Brian Mitchell's locker, came out of the locker room and up the stairs and wound up back in the locker room.

The verdict did not polarize the locker room, though Turner said a few players had to "stand up for themselves" and explain their views to others who disagreed with them. Some white players, like Shuler, thought enough reasonable doubt had been established for acquittal. But there were differences that fell along racial lines.

"It got heated up in here at times. It did," fullback Marc Logan, 30, said. "There were some arguments going on. I thought it was good to hear people's viewpoints, and some of them, I thought they were crazy."

Mitchell, Leslie Shepherd, and Terry Allen had frequent talks with Matich about the trial. In most cases, they agreed to disagree.

On occasion, the strange world of pro football produces relationships that would be welcomed outside the locker room doors: a connection between black and white in which there is mutual respect for one another, some moments of closeness, and few of racial rancor.

"Vanderbeek is a country western rocker that drives a hyped-up Chevy and fits every qualification that you have, stereotypically, as a white boy," Galbraith said. "And I would go to war with Vanderbeek, and I would spend my time with Vanderbeek . . . because he's a person of integrity, he's a person of character, a person of honesty. I respect him because he's a tough guy, and I've seen him run around here and knock the hell out of people. We're in an occupation that — beautifully or tragically — allows us to see people as people."

Galbraith said "beautifully or tragically," as if there was something wrong with seeing a person as a person. But why make that qualification?

"Because of the experiences that I've had, and the kindred I've had with [Cowboys tight end] Jay Novacek, and other people I've been with, it leaves me vulnerable," Galbraith said. "Because I kind of go into the world with a false sense, thinking that everybody . . . is nice and kind. It's not true. . . . When I go over to the mall, those aren't my teammates, those are white people. And I'm black."

Belittled Big Men

FROM THE NEW YORK TIMES MAGAZINE

DARYL BUSH, A FLORIDA STATE UNIVERSITY LINEBACKER, reads the Bible every morning sitting on his bed beneath a poster of his girlfriend, a bikini-clad blonde who is a dancer with the school's Golden Girls at halftime. Dirty clothes are strewn on the bed across from him. "My roommate's clothes," says Bush, six feet two inches and 230 pounds. "The Jim Beam bottles on the shelf are his, too." Bush wants to make sure there is no misunderstanding about the dirty laundry (cleanliness is next to godliness), and especially not about the liquor bottles. He doesn't want to get in trouble with his coaches or the NCAA, since at 20 he is not old enough to drink in Florida.

Bush's teammates call him Psycho. He claims he doesn't know why, yet even in normal conversation his blue eyes glare with a barely restrained . . . what? Passion? Fury? He writes poetry in his spare time because he has "so much energy, I have to channel it by expressing myself." His poetry all has the same theme: bottled-up emotions that he tries desperately not to unleash until absolutely necessary. "I have an overwhelming desire to be my best," he says, which is why he plays football.

Over the last twenty years, his team, the Seminoles of Florida State University in Tallahassee, has won more regular-season games (171) and more postseason bowl games in a row (10) than any other team. The Seminoles won the national championship in 1993, have finished in the top four for the last eight seasons and are rated the eighth-best team in the country, with a 9 and 2 record. They'll get a chance to extend their record with their New Year's bowl game.

But this status has not come without a price, and as is the case with all major college football programs, the price is paid by the players. They have to perform flawlessly on the field, in the classroom and in the public eye. They have to adhere to strict, often nonsensical NCAA rules. They have to produce national championships, which bring their schools millions of dollars and their coaches generous salaries. (Bobby Bowden, the Seminole coach, makes about $1 million a year.) If they expect to move up to "the next league," the NFL, their performances must be nearly perfect. So they build up their bodies with weightlifting. They develop an aggression suited to the playing field but ill-suited to life off it. They try to avoid the temptations of sex, drugs, alcohol, and illicit cash payments.

For years, Florida State players were more successful than most in not cracking under these pressures — until the late 1980s, when a series of scandals hit: a player was shot and killed, an ex-player was accused of being a drug kingpin. In 1994 three players in the span of nine days were arrested on sex-related charges; at the same time a report was published saying that a group of players had accepted cash and gifts from agents' representatives trying to curry their favor, in violation of NCAA rules.

Florida State is not alone among major college football programs when it comes to scandals. The University of Nebraska, last year's national champion, has on its team a player awaiting trial for attempted second-degree murder. Another recently pleaded no contest to misdemeanor charges for dragging a former girlfriend down three flights of stairs and is awaiting sentencing — and playing ball. The University of Miami has also had its problems with off-field misconduct, including a financial-aid scandal and publicity about drug use.

In fact, the Seminoles' problems are typical, except in one respect. Their coach, Bobby Bowden, is a born-again Christian whose stated goal is his players' "eternal salvation." Bowden prides himself on having a "clean team" and players whose success on the field glorifies God and is a testament to the players' and the coach's righteousness. Bowden's aspirations for his players make the Florida State football program a more extreme version than those of other schools, with the pressure to be devoutly Christian amplifying the pressure to be great.

One former Seminole, Terrell Buckley, now with the Miami Dolphins, says the glory that college athletes receive isn't enough compensation for what they have to go through: "They try to tell us how to walk. Don't do this. Don't. Don't. When you hear 'don't' so much, it's human nature to rebel. [They] make it seem like a business. Well, then we ought to treat it like a business." Jesus Hernandez, an offensive tackle with the Seminoles this year, says: "Everyone makes money but us. I hate the most that we don't get paid."

In the closing minutes of the third quarter, Florida State is on its home field battling Georgia Tech. Eighty thousand fans are chanting the Seminoles' war cry. They swing their hands forward in the tomahawk chop, their trademark. (Both chant and chop were adopted by Braves fans when Deion Sanders, the former Seminole cornerback, went to Atlanta to play some baseball.) A booming drum beats.

Bush and his defensive unit take the field. At the snap the Tech quarterback hands the ball off to his running back. The ball carrier bounces off one, two Florida linemen until out of nowhere, Bush drives his shoulder into the runner's gut with such force he seems to deflate. The football is dislodged; players from both teams dive for it. Florida's ball.

Bush rips off his helmet, his eyes wide and glassy. "Now we're having fun!" he screams. Football helps Bush release all those pressures football has created. "The pressure is not in performing," he says, "but in all the demands on my time."

Bush leaves his dormitory room at 8 A.M. every weekday to sign in for breakfast at Moore Athletic Center, even if he doesn't eat breakfast there. He steps outside into the fall air. The players' dormitory is set far apart from the rest of the student housing. Bush walks across the parking lot and says: "We have a cop patrolling every night. He makes sure no girls or sports agents knock on our doors."

Athletes like Bush have little contact with anyone outside their team. They and their coaches like it that way. The players disdain their fellow students for not being athletes, for not being dedicated and disciplined, and at Florida State, often for not being born-again Christians.

The coaches try to regiment every moment of the players' day; virtually the only sanctioned free time is Sunday and after games, which are held on Saturdays. The players' days are filled with classes; interviews with reporters (morning and afternoon sessions); meaningless check-ins for breakfast, lunch, and dinner (the players have their own dining area and the talk is always about football); team meetings, and practices, all designed essentially to bottle up their rising aggression until game day, when they can unleash it on their opponents. ("Basically," says Greg Frey, a lineman, "what we do is hit people for four years.") The coaches' control is also intended to insure that players don't break any of the arcane NCAA rules.

When a reporter invites Bush out for a meal, he panics. "I don't know," he says. "I have to check. Make sure it's legal." He finds out it is "legal," as long as he pays for his own meal. He mentions this three times to the waitress. "Separate checks," he says. "Make sure." He insists on leaving his own tip, which he places conspicuously on top of *his* bill. When a teammate is late picking him up for class, Bush refuses a reporter's offer of a ride because it is against NCAA rules. Even coaches, if they see a player walking in the rain, cannot give him a ride to class.

At Florida State, a player becomes ineligible when his grade point average falls below 2.0 for two consecutive semesters. Roger Grooters, the director of academic support services, says in his two and a half years at the school, no football player has flunked out. The team's graduation rate is 71 percent for players who entered the school in 1988 compared with 53 percent for players who entered in 1987.

While Bush is practicing, Potbelly's, a campus bar, is filled with handsome fraternity boys flirting with pretty sorority girls. Intellectual kids with shaved heads, earrings, and tiny sunglasses are snickering at the frat boys. A group of drunken alumni, here for the weekend game and an opportunity to relive their college days, sit at another table.

The football players never go to Potbelly's. The fraternity brothers might badger them about the game coming up. The intellectuals might make loud comments about "dumb jocks." The drunken alumni might try to goad them into a quarrel. So they hang together, like cops.

Before every game, the players are kept isolated until a few hours before kickoff. "It doesn't get much better than game day," says

Bush. "There's no bigger thrill than hitting someone, beating them physically. When you hit someone and take control of them, you can see the fear in their eyes. The only fear I have is injury. I hurt my knee recently and missed a few games. It made me realize I wasn't invincible. So I began to play more relentlessly. I took hold of that fear because there's always the chance I might never play again."

Not all Florida State football recruits can "take hold" of that fear, says Randy Oravetz, the university's trainer. He says that when freshmen arrive, "they feel pressured to play with pain," adding that some "can't raise their pain threshold to the college level and push through it."

On an October afternoon, Warrick Dunn, the Seminole tailback who is one of the team's Heisman Trophy candidates, is wrestling with avoiding pain and playing with injury. Sitting on a cot in the trainer's room at halftime of the Florida State–Wake Forest game, he points to his arm and says in a barely audible voice, "It hurts up here." Oravetz applies an ice pack. "No, higher," Dunn says.

"I hate to get hit," says Dunn, who at five feet nine inches and 178 pounds looks too slight to play football. "I never lower my head to hit the other guy. I try to bounce off him, not run through him."

Dunn wants an NFL contract that will provide financial security for himself and his family. But NFL scouts have told him he might be too susceptible to injury to play in "the next league."

So when Dunn leaves the trainer's room to start the second half against Wake Forest and a teammate asks him how his arm is, Dunn shakes his head. But still, he will play this half. Bowden wants him to run for at least 100 yards this game to enhance his Heisman Trophy chances. And Dunn has to play to prove he is not injury-prone.

Scott Bentley looks like Jay Gatsby. Tall, slim, handsome, with straight blond hair that would fall over his eyes if not for the baseball cap he always wears around campus, pulled low over his forehead so no one will know him.

When Bentley enters a game to kick a field goal, Seminole fans boo him. When he misses, they boo louder. Bowden, on the sidelines, kicks dirt and mutters, "Kick the damned ball right!" Bentley trots back to the sidelines, head down, and stands apart from his teammates with his helmet on. He begins to pantomime kicking that missed field goal over and over, his leg high above his head like a Rockette.

In 1993, Bentley, who grew up in Aurora, Colorado, was Florida State's most celebrated recruit. His picture was on the cover of *Sports Illustrated* before he ever kicked a ball for the Seminoles. Bowden said he would be the key to the team's winning a national championship that year. In 1991 and 1992, Florida State had lost its chance for the championship by losing games to the University of Miami by one point each when its kicker missed a goal in the closing minutes.

"My dad wanted me to go to his alma mater, Notre Dame," Bentley says. But Bentley believed Bowden when he said he was "the final piece to the puzzle to win the national championship."

On January 1, 1994, in his freshman year, Bentley trotted onto the field at the Orange Bowl in Miami with 21 seconds left in a game the University of Nebraska was leading, 16–15. Bentley faced the ball on the 22-yard line. "I was like on an island," he says. "I couldn't hide. The whole world would see me mess up." When Bentley strode toward the ball and swung his leg in a right-left arc, Bowden put his hands over his eyes. After the kick, he said to Bentley, "I knew you'd get one sometime."

"Everyone said that's why I was at FSU," says Bentley. "And I did it. I won Coach Bowden's first national championship."

That spring, Bentley had a sexual encounter with a girl, which he audiotaped to protect himself, he says, because "my teammates had warned me she would get back at you if you got her mad." Then he played the tape for some teammates. She filed charges. Bentley was arrested for interception of aural communication. He pleaded no contest, performed community service, and was suspended from the team during the summer. He was reinstated again in the fall, but when he missed two field goals in a game against Clemson, he was benched for the rest of the season.

"I was devastated," he says. "I think they were punishing me for the sex thing. I felt like a complete failure."

Bentley's roommate, Danny Kanell, is also tall and handsome. But he looks more like Tom Sawyer than Gatsby. He walks around campus with the blissed-out smile of someone who has absolute certitude about his life.

Kanell was the second-string quarterback who held the ball for Bentley's winning field goal in the Orange Bowl. He is Florida

State's record-breaking quarterback, one of the four best in the country, the team's other Heisman Trophy candidate. He seems always to have a Bible in his hand and says he reads it for at least twenty minutes every day to ward off temptations. "Girls will do anything for football players," he says. "Guys always want to challenge us to fight. Agents are always calling, like putting candy in front of our faces." Kanell is perhaps less vulnerable than most of his teammates to some temptations. His father, Dan, is an orthopedic surgeon and the Miami Dolphins' team physician. Danny drives a $30,000 Toyota 4-Runner around campus.

Though Kanell, a senior, became the team's starting quarterback in the 1994 season, he says he still fears standing in the backfield to pass while "six guys are coming at your throat to knock your head off" and adds, "It's chaos around you. Someone's hand in your face. Things going so fast. I'd be shaking in my shoes."

When Bentley and Kanell first roomed together in Bentley's freshman year, they became close friends. Kanell held the football for Bentley for the *Sports Illustrated* cover. When Bentley was about to kick the field goal in the Orange Bowl, Kanell said, "When you make it, jump into my arms so I'll be on TV, too." Bentley did. Today, however, though they are still roommates, they no longer hang out together. A player who requested anonymity says maybe it is because Bentley was the Florida State hero as a freshman, but now Kanell has overshadowed him. He adds that Kanell thinks Bentley has a complex about him, that Bentley tried to steal his girlfriends. Which is an odd complaint from a youth who claims he prays every day to ward off the temptations of the flesh. The same player says he thinks Kanell's religious activities are for public consumption, not done out of a private conviction. (Kanell gives sermons at churches to youngsters about the evils of drugs and alcohol.)

Today, Kanell hears mostly cheers from Florida State fans, even when one of his passes is intercepted. Bentley hears mostly boos — he's in a kicking slump, and he embarrassed "the program." But he is expected to perform despite the pressure. "Scott said he feels like he's kicking against 80,000 FSU fans," says Kanell, smiling. "I told him, 'That's why Coach Bowden recruited you.'"

It is almost midnight after the Wake Forest game. The stadium is dark. The players have all left with their girlfriends and families.

Everyone's gone except a lone figure crossing the street, heading for the stairs that lead to the players' dormitory up a hill. The dark figure is Enzo Armella, short and bulky with a bull neck. He steps onto the first step and swings his left leg up after him. He steps onto the next step and swings his left leg up. He moves painfully up the flight of stairs.

Armella was never afraid of pain or injury when he played on the Seminoles' defensive line a year ago. "I was a mean player," he says. "No one ran up the middle on me. I was a bad guy. I thought I was tougher than anyone else."

Armella, who was raised in Miami, remembers experiencing "culture shock" when he got to the university: "Coach Bowden made us go to these white and black Baptist churches. People were yelling 'Amen!' and jumping up and down. I went with the flow. I never missed chapel but once, and you know what? The next game I blew out my leg."

It was parents' weekend, September 24, 1994, in Armella's junior year. He was pursuing a University of North Carolina receiver about to catch a screen pass, when one of his own teammates speared him in the leg with his helmet. "It was the worst pain I ever felt," Armella says. He was carried off the field on a stretcher while Florida State fans cheered him. He had surgery to repair ligament and nerve damage in his left leg, but it wasn't successful. He still walks with what he calls "a dropped foot." He needs another operation to transplant nerves and muscles if he ever expects to walk normally again.

"I was devastated," he says. "My career was over."

Jesus Hernandez was a boy of 9 in 1980 when he sat between his mother's knees on a small boat filled with two hundred refugees fleeing Cuba for Miami during the Mariel boatlift. Today he is a mammoth man, six feet two inches, 297 pounds of startling, dark handsomeness that always seems to take women's breath away.

When Hernandez arrived, he was shocked, he says, by the amount of pressure from coaches and peers to win. "You can't sleep after a bad practice," he says. "In class, you're thinking about how you messed up. You have to do better or you won't play. It could lead to the good life in the NFL. So you develop this tough-guy attitude. You think you're invincible. Then you remember what happened to Pablo and it's a reality check."

Pablo Lopez, also from Miami, arrived at Florida State to begin his freshman year in 1983 as a six-foot-four-inch, 240-pound offensive lineman. Two years later, he had added forty pounds of muscle to his frame and had acquired an aggressive attitude. He liked to hang out with his teammate Ed Clark, a linebacker who, according to one of his coaches, "was a fighter."

On September 13, 1986, while hundreds of students were milling about outside a gymnasium where a fraternity-sponsored dance was being held, Clark happened to drive by. One of a group of townies kicked Clark's car, and words were exchanged. Lopez saw what was happening and walked over to check on his friend. At one point, Clark waved a pistol around, and the townies left. They returned in the car an hour later with a shotgun stowed in the trunk and parked behind the gym.

Clark, still angry over the car-kicking incident, walked with Lopez over to the townies and punched one of them. The other man, Byron Christopher Johnson, a five-foot-ten-inch, 160-pound short-order cook, immediately pulled the shotgun from the trunk and pointed it at Lopez, who took a few steps toward Johnson and shouted, "You don't have the heart to shoot me!" Johnson fired; Lopez fell and then died on the way to a hospital. Shortly after his death, Florida State lost a crucial game to the University of Nebraska. Bowden said at the time: "We lost Pablo, and we lost our best lineman, to be honest. It might have made a big difference had we not lost Pablo."

Lopez wasn't the last Florida State football recruit whose macho attitude got him into trouble. Randy Moss, a six-foot-four-inch, 180-pound wide receiver from Rand, West Virginia, lost a scholarship to Notre Dame because, he says, "in high school, one of my home boys took it out on a white boy who'd written some racial things. When the dude was on the ground, I kicked him."

Moss was arrested and plea-bargained his felony charge down to two counts of misdemeanor battery. He served three days in jail.

He appeared to be damaged goods until the Notre Dame coach, Lou Holtz, a longtime friend of Bowden, recommended he accept Moss. When Bowden was asked by reporters why he accepted a player with Moss's background, he said, "Trust me. I found out what a good kid he was."

In the afternoon, before practice, Bowden likes to walk alone, halfway up the university's deserted home stadium. He says he needs that time by himself to "clear his head." He may well need that time because of all his activities beyond the stadium, which he spends more time on than most college coaches do.

He sells himself and Florida State nonstop, seven days a week. He gives speeches to civic groups, businesspeople, teachers, coaches, at conventions, at sports-card shows. Sunday mornings, after he tapes his television show, after a breakfast answering reporters' questions about Saturday's game, he often hurries off to give a sermon at a local church. On Thursday evenings, Bowden broadcasts his radio show from the Buffalo Connection restaurant near the campus. The restaurant is mostly filled with families, since virtually all Tallahasseans are Seminole fans. They wait patiently for Bowden to pose with them for pictures or to sign posters of himself.

Just about every day, after practice, Bowden sits in the lobby of the athletic center and answers questions from reporters. He has always been accessible to the press, he says, because "we are in the selling business and we need the press."

He is paid to endorse Nike athletic merchandise, Lykes hot dogs, Bobby Bowden's Seminole football camp, Ford automobiles. Before all home games, during halftime and after the games, the public-address announcer reminds fans to watch Bowden's TV show, listen to his radio show, buy the Ford cars he recommends. Bowden was even paid $50,000 by a sports writer, Ben Brown, for unlimited access to the Seminoles for Brown's book, *Saint Bobby and the Barbarians.*

Last April, Bowden's lawyer wrote a letter to Florida State's athletic director, Dave Hart, in an attempt to negotiate a "lifetime" agreement for the coach, saying that Bowden "brought the football program from the brink of disaster to the position it enjoys today as one of the top programs in the country." To retain Bowden's services, the lawyer suggested the school give Bowden a base salary and various supplements totaling well over $1 million. The coach wound up with a $150,000 base salary, a $225,000 salary supplement from Nike for endorsements, $275,000 for media programs, $200,000 for speeches, a $100,000 annuity, and a $25,000 life insurance payment. His five-year contract awards him $975,000 a year.

For years, Bowden was underpaid at Florida State compared with other major college coaches. But now, approaching retirement, he sees that money simply as the gold star on his coaching exam. "It's a matter of pride," he says.

Bowden is not unaware of how his salary demands appear to his players, without whom he couldn't make those demands. "My boys are reminded daily that they bring in huge sums of money for FSU," he says — $11.5 million a year, to be exact. "That's why I recommended that all college football players be paid for playing. I recommended to the NCAA they be paid $75 a month."

At practice, sitting high up in the bleachers, Bowden watches the players below like God as personified during the Industrial Revolution, a great clockmaker who simply taps the pendulum once to begin time.

His son, Jeff, an assistant coach of the team, says: "He leaves the coaching to his assistants. He doesn't care what we do as long as we get the ball in the end zone." Chuck Amato, assistant head coach, says that the assistant coaches formulate each game plan and that "Coach Bowden doesn't know what we're going to do." The only time Bowden intrudes in a game, says Amato, is when it's close in the final minutes. In one game against Penn State, Bowden wondered why Penn State opted to go for a two-point conversion after each of two touchdowns, until Amato explained the strategy. "Oh, that's why," said Bowden. And Bowden's legendary recruiting skills are brought into play only after his coaches have scouted a prospect. "Coach Bowden recruits who we tell him to," says Amato.

Before the game with Georgia Tech, the high school recruits are standing along the Florida State sidelines, watching the two teams do calisthenics at opposite ends of the field. The white recruits are tall, thin quarterbacks and linebackers. The black recruits are huge, big-bellied linemen and tiny, trim, wide receivers. All recruits are accompanied by student hostesses called Garnet and Gold Girls.

One pretty hostess looks up at a huge recruit and says, "So you're a tackle?"

The recruit smiles sheepishly and looks down at his feet.

"You're sooo big!" she says with wide-eyed wonder. Then she reaches up a languid hand with long, red fingernails and lays it seductively on his shoulder. The hint of a promise she will never have to keep.

Most black players at Florida State, which has a mostly white student population, don't date fellow students. They date girls from

Florida A&M University, the predominantly black college that lies alongside Florida State.

Kamari Charlton, an offensive tight end, who is from the Bahamas, dates an A&M girl. When they go out on her campus, he says, "FAMU girls come up to me and say I sold out by going to white FSU. I say my being here is not a black-white issue. I don't see black and white. I never experienced racism in *my* country."

At Florida State, Charlton has always considered himself "a loner." He used to chafe at his coaches' constant reminder never to embarrass "the program." He says, "It was like being under a constant microscope." When he tried to break up with his girlfriend one night, she pleaded with him not to. Then they had sex. The following morning he found himself in jail, charged with sexual battery.

Charlton was suspended from school in June 1994 and went on trial that fall. He was acquitted of all charges after less than two hours of jury deliberation. "Everyone said I had embarrassed the program. I said, 'Forget the program. This is my life. I embarrassed *myself.*' The program, the program."

Forrest Conoly, a six-foot-six-inch, 328-pound offensive tackle, also embarrassed "the program" last year. He was one of a group of Florida State players involved in the so-called Foot Locker Scandal, which earned the university the nickname Free Shoes U. and an NCAA inquiry yet to be completed. On a Sunday in 1993, a Las Vegas freelance agent not registered in Florida paid for $6,000 worth of sports merchandise (sneakers, caps, sweatsuits) for a group of football players at a Foot Locker store.

"Oh, when it rains, it pours!" wailed Bowden at the time. He was referring not only to the Foot Locker incident but also to the fact that two of his players (Bentley and Charlton) and one of his ex-players (Sean Jackson, a tailback) had just been arrested on sex-related charges. Jackson had exposed himself to a 22-year-old female student and asked her to perform a sex act on him. He pleaded no contest.

As if that were not enough, Corey Sawyer, a cornerback, was discovered to have bought a new $30,000 Nissan Pathfinder only days before the Orange Bowl game. Sawyer claimed he got the money from his mother, Lydia Clark, a part-time cashier at a school in Key West. She told reporters she earned $8.22 an hour. (Sawyer now plays for the Cincinnati Bengals.)

Before the Wake Forest game, the players assemble in the weight room for the chapel service. They're handed prayer cards for today's sermon. They move silently, big, hulking men in their shoulder pads and padded pants, while Clint Purvis, team chaplain, stands in their midst and searches for the spotlight. He moves a little to his left until he feels the overhead fluorescent light bathe him in a surreal orange glow. Finally, he begins:

"I want to talk to you today about Jesus Christ when he spoke to his team at the Last Supper. He told them he was proud of them but they'd have to play the game without him. Walking out of that locker room to the field, he said: 'I'm the true vine and every branch will bear fruit, but no branch will bear fruit by itself unless it remains on the vine. You'll bear much fruit if you remain on the vine with me.' This is like Coach Bowden telling you what you have to do on offense and defense. . . . Now remember, your coaches love you. The greatest thing you can do for them is to play the best you can and then say: 'God made that tackle, not me, because I am connected to the vine. I will produce fruit and give glory to God.'"

After their days at Florida State, a select number of players will "give glory to God" on the NFL playing fields. In the 1994–95 season, eleven players were drafted into the league. Eight of those draftees remain. Grooters, the director of academic support services, acknowledges that "some kids don't have it all together when they leave here. I know of a few who are doing nothing now with their lives." Yet many former Florida State players who learned to deal with the pressure of big-time college football used what they learned and took jobs in business, law enforcement, or the criminal justice system. Others did not fare as well. One graduate was just arrested on state and federal drug charges. He faces a thirty-two-count federal indictment.

As Bowden enters yet another locker room for his usual pregame pep talk, the players assemble around him. They sit while he stands, shuffling his feet, chewing gum, his eyes shaded by sunglasses. "Today I saw some of y'all struttin' in warm-ups like cool cats," he says. "There's no place in football for cool cats. Football needs intense people. I want you to tire them out. Fatigue makes cowards of men. You won't dominate them unless you're mean."

FRANK DEFORD

Trouble on the Court

FROM VANITY FAIR

IT HAS BEEN FIVE YEARS since Teddy died, so I assume he is back by now. He was a strong believer in reincarnation, Teddy was, and he feared greatly that this next time around he would return as either a four-legged animal or a Russian. Teddy found Russians so terribly boring.

While he was alive, Ted Tingling spent much of his time trying to make women's tennis less boring. Teddy had been a hugely success-ful society couturier in London, and after the war he decided that women's tennis clothes were too mannish. In 1949 he dressed Gorgeous Gussy Moran in lace panties; unfortunately, for that inde-cency he was banished from Wimbledon. But he never left the sport. Instead he became its historian, an official MC at many matches, and an unofficial ambassador for the sport. When Billie Jean King sallied forth against Bobby Riggs, she was dressed in Teddy's sequined armor. "How sick can a sport be when it depends on a dress-maker to solve its problems?" the *Daily Mail* of Lon-don inquired once, commenting on Teddy's many roles. But, God, Teddy did love women's tennis — may have loved it more than any woman ever did.

His involvement with the sport began when he was only 13, in 1924 on the Riviera, as personal umpire for Suzanne Lenglen. She was the first tennis champion to have been a prodigy driven by an obsessive father. "Papa" was all he was called, for he gave up his own life to, as he put it, "devote myself entirely" to his daughter's tennis. Tall, bent, usually dressed in a heavy greatcoat (even on the Riviera), he would stand by the practice court, forcing Suzanne to make two or three hundred shots to the same spot. It was, Tingling himself wrote, "to the total sacrifice of all natural life," but The Goddess, as Lenglen became known, kept up the appearance that she was having a fabulous time. She wore daring dresses to mid-calf, drank cognac at the crossovers, even entertained the press as she bathed. By 39, though, frail and distracted, she died of pernicious anemia, and it was speculated for the first time that perhaps an unfulfilled father had driven his tennis daughter too hard, too early.

The sport would see many grand seasons, but as Teddy approached his death he began to proclaim to us all that the sport was in the last opera of Wagner's *Ring*, "The Twilight of the God[desse]s," where all must perish because of the avarice of the principals. In rare optimistic moments, though, he would assure us that a child from Yugoslavia, who grunted and screeched, slugging two-handed from both sides, could yet save women's tennis from its Götterdämmerung. And, indeed, just days after Teddy died on May 23, 1990, the kid, Monica Seles, only 16 years old, won the French Open, her first grand-slam title.

Alas, Paris lied that spring. The game degenerated into monotony on the court as charges arose that the little girls were being rushed into anguish and abuse by men who profited from their talents. Mary Pierce, a French-American teenager, had for a father an ex-con who reportedly had schizophrenic and paranoid tendencies and took his daughter out of school when she was 14, sold the family house, and lit out for tennis fortune. Mary's father screamed at her opponents, screamed at her — "Mary, kill the bitch" — fought in the stands, even, Mary says, hit her and was finally barred for his menacing behavior.

Jennifer Capriati, the American crown princess, was rushed onto the tour by her father, Stefano, when she was only 13, but already, with endorsements, a millionaire. Soon she would leave school and Stefano would approve exhibition bookings — "exbos," the players call these lucrative divertissements — for his daughter literally half-way round the world. She started faxing in her homework, such as it was, grew quickly disillusioned, and by 18, fat and sullen, she had been nabbed for shoplifting and, later, drugs. The charges were dropped; the problems were only more evident.

The golden age was over. Chris Evert was gone by 1989 to have babies, and Martina Navratilova would follow her into retirement five years later. The leadership of the sport was in tatters; for several months last year, political infighting left no one in control. Virginia Slims had bankrolled women's tennis for years, but as antismoking activism spread, public opinion forced it out. The parent company, Philip Morris, brought in another subsidiary, Kraft, in 1989 as a sponsor, but women's tennis wanted more money out of Kraft, and less input. Finally, Kraft quit, leaving the circuit without a major commercial name, advertising, or financial support. As the sport's reputation nosedived, Tampax emerged as the only potential sponsor, but the Women's Tennis Association Tour felt that it was just *too* womanly. The situation was so bad that the omnipotent sports-and-talent agency representing many top players, IMG (International Management Group), threatened to start its own women's circuit.

Then, worst of all, in 1993 a deranged German fan stabbed Monica Seles in the back as she played a match in Hamburg, so that her German competitor Steffi Graf might ascend to the number one ranking again. She did. The players refused to let Seles keep her number one ranking while she recuperated. "They treated it like some injury — like only a sprained ankle or something," she cried out to me. For its part, the German justice system freed the assailant as a misunderstood fellow who had meant no harm. Fondly, *Der Spiegel* likened him to Samuel of the Old Testament: "The poor man owned nothing sweeter than a single lamb. . . . Günther Parche is even poorer than the man in the Bible."

International indignation, however, was so great that the German courts agreed to review the sentence, and Seles and her family took renewed hope that he might go to jail. Tentatively, she edged out into public, hitting on the new indoor courts at William and Mary College. The occasion was a special weekend to honor her agent, Mark McCormack, the chairman of IMG and an alumnus of the college, who had given the money to build the Nagelsen-McCormack Indoor Tennis Center. Attending a brunch with McCormack that weekend, she never seemed to mind that where she sat her back was exposed. Afterward, when we talked, her eyes sparkled with youth, hope, and health. "My dream in tennis — do you know what?"

I shook my head.

"My dream is to be like Suzanne Lenglen, to fly through the air and hit a volley flying — both my feet off the ground." She laughed at the sheer joy of that, and I could not help but think that if Teddy were back already, even as a bunny rabbit or a baby in Novgorod, he must have felt some twinge of delight at this moment.

But then, the next morning, the German courts declared that world opinion be damned: they had not changed their minds one iota about Günther Parche. Seles got the news over the phone in the Atlanta airport, and, swooning, fell back into her mother's arms.

The dirty little secret of women's sports is that women don't much care to watch other women compete. Except for figure skating, men watch women's sports on television in higher percentages than do women. Live audiences for women's tennis are weighted toward males about 55 to 45 percent. Ruefully, Martina Navratilova, who now serves as president of the WTA Players Association, recalls an experience at a club in Atlanta where she played last summer. "I'd see women who'd keep on playing while we were having a match, and I'd think, Would a man stay on the driving range if Jack Nicklaus were out on the course?"

Now, the good to all this is that women remain a great untapped sports-spectator market. Plans are in the works for two all-women's sports channels. You see, once gender equality is achieved and, just like men, women start parking themselves on their sofas all weekend, swilling beer, and clicking from one game to another, the popularity of women's tennis is bound to soar. IMG, which had so recently threatened to start a competing tour, was hired by the WTA Tour to find a sponsor. "It's not a very expensive price," Mark McCormack says. Only four or five million for the major women's sport in the world.

IMG has a huge investment in the sport already. It owns six women's tournaments and represents a dozen top players, including Pierce and Arantxa Sanchez Vicario, plus Capriati and Seles. (Of course, it also represents the men's tour and many of its top players.) A new Virginia Slims Legends tour — starring Evert, Navratilova, and King — started this spring, and IMG handles that too. IMG signed Anna Kournikova at the age of 9, and brought her over from Moscow to Florida, to Nick Bollettierie's Tennis Academy, which, of course, IMG also owns. IMG signed 11-year-old Martina

Hingis of Switzerland and put her in the Wimbledon 18-and-under juniors the next year. She's 14 and a pro now. And although it hasn't yet signed Venus Williams, the 14-year-old African American phenom, IMG arranged for her first pro appearance, at one of its tournaments. IMG pretty much owns women's tennis — yesterday, today, and tomorrow.

But then, is there another business in the world so dominated by one company as IMG controls the management of all sport? "I'M Greedy," the players have been known to call it. "International Money-Grubbers." "Darth McCormack and the Evil Empire." But, say what you will, nobody keeps better company. IMG has even represented the pope. And the Nobel Foundation, Raggedy Ann and Andy, Itzhak Perlman, Rolex, Wimbledon, Pat Conroy, Jose Carreras, and scores of the best athletes the world over. McCormack was international when international wasn't cool.

By now, the tale of how McCormack conceived a major international business that hadn't previously existed has been repeated so reverently and so often that it has the ring of an epic poem. It all started when Arnold Palmer, who had played golf in college with McCormack, went to him for a little business advice; soon Jack Nicklaus asked Palmer if he might not share McCormack's wisdom, and from there a cottage industry of athletic representation exploded — tennis players, racecar drivers, figure skaters — and IMG was born. Eventually, it began to spread its grasp beyond mere sport.

In 1990, for example, IMG ventured into "cultureland." "We intend to be number one in classical music," McCormack declared at that time. "We figure the competition is nonexistent." And, sure enough, soon IMG was one of the two leading international agencies in the field. More recently, IMG has made a considerable foray into the world of modeling.

Betsy Nagelsen, McCormack's second wife, was a journeyman tennis player when he met her (she is still an IMG client, as a sports commentator). She is credited not only with heightening his interest in her sport but also with softening the intensity of her 64-year-old husband's life, which still begins almost every day well before dawn and lasts late into the night — usually ending in a city other than the one in which it began.

A manic organizer, McCormack is sort of an ambulatory day-book. He maintains an endless list of personal statistics on a fiscal-year basis — July to July — and he can report such authoritative personal minutiae as: until he took a ninety-one-day Pacific cruise a couple of years ago (booking four cabins, for secretaries, friends, and family) he had not slept for more than seventeen consecutive nights in the same bed for twenty years. Most people have heard of his enormous bestseller, *What They Don't Teach You at Harvard Business School*. His new book is *Hit the Ground Running*, a numbing compendium of travel tips, which will be just up your alley if you require an exhaustive analysis of the perfect location for tele-phones in a hotel room.

Nevertheless, McCormack is indisputably more at peace now, even serene. He actually — this bowled me over — hands out snap-shots of the magnificent love nest that he and Betsy built near Orlando. Bob Briner, a contemporary and former competitor (he is a retired executive of another large tennis agency, ProServe), says, "The last times I've been with him I've seen even more of a spark of warmth. We've even talked about spirituality. Clearly, Mark's dealing with what's the endgame now. 'What's the capstone to my life?'"

McCormack smiles, then grins, then actually laughs at the sub-ject. "You know, I think I've spent more time in the last five years talking about my death and who's going to pull the plug than anything else." He may have designated the next-in-line equals at IMG, but he remains adamant about not retiring.

"Mark has changed a great deal recently," Betsy says. "He's paid more attention to things I value — and, yes, some of that is involved with faith, Christian belief. Sometimes in the past he's overlooked people's feelings to reach his own goals." Sometimes he still does. In *Hit the Ground Running*, McCormack blandly advises you to dou-ble- or even triple-book airlines for your convenience; make hotel reservations for days more than you need, just in case; reserve a restaurant table for three when it's really only two of you, to give yourself more space — and (unsaid) damn the airline, the hotel, the restaurant, the other patrons.

Yet if many people disapprove of McCormack and his global domain, which includes 60 offices in 26 countries, the most in-trepid sleuths have found no evidence of any IMG impropriety. A

British-government commission once did conclude that IMG was "pregnant with conflict of interest," a stupefying revelation equivalent to discovering that a saloon was rife with spirits. With tennis (or golf), IMG can own the tournament, control the rights (down to hiring Betsy Nagelsen as one of the announcers), produce the best players, and even give out, to its undeserving young recruits, the "wild cards" — those medieval indulgences of tennis that allow the tournament sponsors to use a few spots in the draw to insert anyone they please. Meanwhile, IMG can also schedule exbos for its stars when someone else is sponsoring a tournament. And now, of course, IMG controls both the men's and women's tours. Not to mention the advertising encircling the stadium — signage, so called in the business.

But McCormack will not back down an inch in any discussion of conflict of interest. "The fact that we own a tournament [as well as many of the best players] makes the sponsor more comfortable," he declares. "The fact that we own it makes our clients more comfortable. The fact that we own it makes our *young* clients more comfortable. They know we might get them a wild card."

But, I inquire, is that fair to everyone else? Shouldn't sports be the one sphere in which merit alone rules?

"Wait a minute," McCormack replies, shaking his head in exasperation at this tiresome old line of interrogation. "That's not conflict of interest. That's favoritism."

Fine — whatever you call it, should there be inequality in sports?

"If you take the risk, if you put up the money. That's what free enterprise is all about."

And that, in one form or another, is the defense McCormack always applies on behalf of IMG. "I keep telling the players," says Billie Jean King, another IMG client, "don't be scared of IMG. They're the ones who've taken the risk."

Anne Person Worcester, the young woman who was finally promoted to fill the void as the head of the Women's Tennis Association Tour, says, "Ultimately we felt comfortable that because IMG has so much invested in women's tennis that it's in their best interest to respect the rules. Because they're the big giant, everyone has them under the microscope." Moreover, because Worcester used to work at IMG, she knows she must endure the same scrutiny.

Clearly, the potential for dictatorship — even a benign one —

for manipulation and cover-up, is indisputable, and while nobody puts it quite this way, IMG is so dominant in this one sport that it is really beholden only to its own sense of a commercial noblesse oblige.

McCormack himself professes simply not to understand what all the fuss is about, and eventually he just shakes his head in polite exasperation at me. "You're so far away from me," he sighs, "that I just don't know where you're coming from."

I try another tack. Recently figure skating has become so successful that it has cut into women's tennis audiences. Sponsors that previously supported the court now work the rink. McCormack nods. Nobody disputes this. In fact, IMG's Discover Card Skating Tour is a prime rival for the women's sports dollar. How does it serve the WTA Tour to hire a direct competitor to save it?

"Oh, that's more of an advantage," McCormack replies sotto voce.

It's an *advantage* for women's tennis to be run by a company that has helped develop a major competitor? "Exactly." Well, why?

"Because, for example, our people know Discover Card, and that can wash over." And, more carefully now, he explains to me again the gospel of bigness, risk, and unfettered free enterprise. A few years ago, he would have been abrupt and arrogant. But, sitting in the beautiful new building at William and Mary with his name on it, while his wife is down on the court introducing his clients, who have come from all over the country to play before him, he is patient. He wants me to understand the IMG way of the world. Says Betsy Nagelsen, "Mark has always known there is a purpose in life beyond signing the greatest golfers and tennis players. But until now he has only looked to the future so far as he could control it."

Thirty years ago I was walking along the beach in San Juan, Puerto Rico, with two of the best women tennis players in the world — both of them complaining how lonely they were and how much they hated life on the tour. Soon, one of them, Margaret Court, the number one, would chuck it all and go back to Australia to be a shopgirl. The other player suffered something of a nervous breakdown. Burnout doesn't have to involve blatant abuse or exploitation. It has simply never been easy being a woman tennis player — all the more so when the player is young and naive. With the huge amount of money involved these days, it's even worse, because the children start younger. Bela Karolyi, the despotic girls' gymnastics coach, let the truth slip once: "The young ones are the greatest little suckers in the world; they will follow you no matter what." Monica Seles still remembers fathers at tournaments, pushing their unenthusiastic daughters upon her. "You can see," she says. "They're thinking about money first and love second." Often, the fathers become coaches. "When the father quits his job, you've got trouble," Evert says. She — as Tracy Austin did after her — went to school and lived a quotidian life off the court, even as she became a teenage champion. At 13, Austin was on the cover of *Sports Illustrated*, and at 16 she won the U.S. Open, but she remained an A student throughout high school, living a normal existence much of the year.

Andrea Jaeger, two years her junior, dropped out of school, though, and that became the norm. "I think we thought that if we put 150 percent into tennis we'd get it all back later on," Jaeger says. "But what I'm afraid is that we became too programmed ever to enjoy it."

McCormack defends the agents' role in encouraging young players to drop all else in order to play: "You can't stop a kid from wanting to play tennis if the parents want it. The child can provide financial security for the rest of the parents' lives. But if you let them go to high school, if you let them live a quote normal life unquote, fine, but who knows what will happen?" Agents, of course, have no authority to stop greedy parents from pushing their daughters; if they interfere, the parents may simply hire a new agent. Concomitantly there is a strong commercial incentive to go along with such parents. Indeed, there is implicit pressure to overbook the children because tennis has become such a high-turnover business — although everybody suspects that the lucrative heavy scheduling is what causes the high turnover.

Both Austin and Jaeger were physically washed up before they were 21. Austin believes she was merely "injury-prone," but Jaeger says, "Some pediatricians have told me that your bodies aren't supposed to be doing that at that age." Too often, though, the decisions about how to develop a young player's talents are passed, to parent, to coach, to agent, to destiny. Of the 13-year-old Kournikova, Bollettieri says helplessly, "She's perhaps as good as any student we've ever had. We've got to slow this one down, but I don't think we can."

The psychological strain of the tour may be the hardest challenge of all. Once, the players hung out together, sharing, gossiping, and having fun. Now there is little camaraderie. King, Evert, and Navratilova had all set a certain standard by being outgoing, gregarious leaders, but Steffi Graf, who succeeded them in the number one rank, was almost pathologically shy. Embarrassed by her father-coach's drinking and womanizing, sometimes she couldn't even bring herself to say hello in the locker room. Says Betsy Nagelsen, "I know a young player. The last time I saw her, she was in a little bit of a slump, had a few problems. But she had no one to talk to. She didn't even have anyone to go out to dinner with."

A few years ago lurid stories circulated that sex-starved lesbians hung about the showers ready to ravage lonely virgin tour rookies, but in truth the predators have invariably been the male camp followers. McCormack and Nagelsen are hardly the only example of a romance between a man in sports management and a female client — there are others even at IMG. Of a particularly notorious former top agent, one older player says, "I'm sure I was the only one of his clients he never could screw." McCormack protests, though, that IMG agents would never take advantage of teenage athletes. "IMG has no written policy about dating under-age clients, because it is not necessary," he says. "It is the basic understanding that this behavior would not be tolerated." Under pressure from the public, the WTA Tour has tried to develop ways to protect its young girls from the pressure — physical and psychological — that they must deal with. "We've taken a lot of the decision-making out of the legal guardians' hands," Anne Person Worcester says. Maximum playing times — for tournaments *and* exbos — have been set. An indoctrination session this year will even include a cautionary speech from Denise Capriati, Jennifer's mother, who is separated from her husband.

Maybe Jennifer will be back. After all, even now, she's still a teenager. The players do tend to be resilient. Tracy Austin gives motivational speeches. Mary Pierce, who surely had the most nightmarish time of all, is remarkably sweet and balanced. After her father was banished from the tour two years ago, she left tennis for a time, staying with a friendly family. "That was the first time I ever got to know myself," she says. "The first time I could just be someone normal — shop, watch TV. That was when I finally became Mary Pierce, and it made me feel good and confident, knowing who I was at last."

For others it takes longer. Andrea Jaeger still loves tennis, but she adds, "God, I hope no one has to go through what I did." She traveled on tour with her father, Roland, a former boxer. "But from 13 on, he really wasn't my father," she explains, "just my coach. People thought he was a psychopath, I know — or in it for the bucks. But no — my father did it all out of love for me. He wanted me to have a better life than he'd had."

She was so lonely. Often, she would play with the ball girls, and once, when she was honored at a March of Dimes dinner, she spent the evening with her only contemporary there — the poster child. Sometimes, she would leave practice and go visit the nearest children's hospital because already she felt she could identify more closely with the sick children than with the glamorous players.

Then, in 1984, when she dislocated her shoulder at the French Open, she had to give up tennis. She attended college, and, after an automobile accident, went to Aspen to recuperate, working as an airline agent. There an old idea of hers came to the fore. Andrea Jaeger, who had had her childhood taken from her by tennis, would devote her life to caring for children who can have nothing but a childhood.

Using $500,000 she had left from her tennis earnings she established the Kids' Stuff Foundation for boys and girls with life-threatening illnesses. Coincidentally, both Navratilova and Evert had also moved to Aspen, to grand houses there. Jaeger kept a smaller, two-bedroom house. When the bulk of her money ran out, she didn't even have a car.

By this time people had begun to hear about her mission. Gabriella Sabatini and John McEnroe made major gifts. IMG and McCormack came through handsomely, and Prince Bandar of Saudi Arabia, who has a magnificent chalet in Aspen, has matched funds — $225,000 so far.

But Jaeger's big break came when a mutual friend suggested she contact Fabi Benedict. Just before Jaeger called, Mrs. Benedict had been walking by a brook on her property praying to the Virgin Mary about a happy dilemma she had: Benedict and her husband, Fritz, owned choice Aspen real estate they'd bought years before, cheap, and she had been thinking about what to do with it. When she returned to her house the phone rang and it was Andrea Jaeger, and the older woman believed the Virgin had just heard her. So the Benedicts gave ten acres, and soon sick children began to arrive at what Jaeger named the Silver Lining Ranch, to boat on the river, to walk in the woods, to sing and dance, to ski in the winter, to go over to Navratilova's place to feed her horses, even to play tennis with Andrea.

The kids who come to the Silver Lining must stay in a hotel for now, but Jaeger's trying to raise money to build a ranch house with medical facilities. "God did bless me," Jaeger says. "I was very good at tennis. And fundraising is the most difficult thing I've ever done. But now I'm sure He thinks I'm going to be better at this from here on in my life."

Already, though, some of the kids who have spent vacations here have died. We get out of the rattly old station wagon somebody gave the foundation and trudge onto the Silver Lining Ranch. There has been a late-spring snow and the robins appear put out at this turn of events, but just over the brook, the skiers are happily riding up in the gondolas. Andrea says she can feel Rhea Olsen's spirit here, because this is where Rhea played with the other kids, where she took off her chemotherapy wig and slapped it onto Jaeger's head. Rhea suffered with rhabdomyosarcoma, a rare cancer. A few weeks before, Jaeger had flown to Chicago, where Rhea lived, because her health had declined so. She was almost blind, in excruciating pain, and so Jaeger moved into the trailer where Rhea was dying, putting up a cot next to where she lay. For six or seven hours a day Andrea and Rhea would talk about life and death. Rhea said it would probably be just like going into a long sleep, but Andrea shook her head. "No, every day you're going to be with me at Silver Lining," she told her, "and when I'm having a tough fundraising day, I'm going to hear you." And then Andrea said good-bye and left Rhea to die with her family.

We walk through the snow over to a good vantage point from which to view the land where the building will be erected when they have the money. When she was a young player, her face, beneath the pigtails, was drawn and hard. Now it is soft and warm, her pale blue-green eyes reflecting peace as much as determination and grit. "Ever since I was a little girl," she says, "hotels have been my life. Holiday Inns, Ramadas, Marriotts. All my life. But when I was in Rhea's house in Chicago — that little trailer . . ." She pauses, and what she says next may be the sweetest, most haunted thing I have ever heard an athlete say: "That was the place I finally felt at home."

"My dad let me decide," Monica Seles told me when we chatted in April. His name is Karolj. In Yugoslavia he was a cartoonist, but with Monica as his creation, he has compared himself to Michelangelo. "No, Dad never pushed me, and somehow I was always able to understand when he was my coach and when he was my father. I was the one who always said, This day, I want to go out and practice."

In fact, it seems that young Monica has often made major decisions for the whole family. "I think I had to be very strong just to get where I was," she continued. "Just coming here from Eastern Europe, not speaking English. Yes, there's always been a lot of strength in me. I was not afraid of a lot of risk. Yes, to come out of where I was required strength. And then he . . ." Suddenly Monica's mind twisted back again to Parche and him stabbing her, and she had to pause and gain control of herself.

Yet however much Seles misses playing tennis, there is the oddest, most conflicted way that she looks back on the very point of the game — winning. Coincidentally, too, this is the one thread that seems to connect so many of the players who learn the rote mechanics of the game so well so young but never seem comfortable with the spirit of competition. Seles won eight grand-slam titles, but she said that, unequivocally, the *only* time she ever truly enjoyed triumph was her first major-tournament victory, the Italian Open of 1990, when she thrashed Navratilova. "That was the closest I've ever come to a perfect match," she explained. The next week, in Hamburg, she whipped Graf, and, to herself, she thought, "Wow, I can beat these [players]." But that victory was not so satisfying as the one in Rome, and thereafter, no matter what she won, there was never any sense of fulfillment.

In fact, Seles concluded this sad part of the conversation by saying how much she preferred playing exhibitions. "Everybody is on their best behavior around you," she explained. "That's what's so great about them. I have more fond memories for exhibitions."

So many women tennis players who are indoctrinated early tend to be more robotic than athletic, to cling to the baseline, hitting textbook ground strokes, rather than venturing forward like Suzanne Lenglen, daring to gamble, volleying. They are perfectionists, the presentation more important to them than the outcome.

From talking to Monica, then, I do believe that at least part of the reason she has found it difficult until now to return, even though she is healed physically, is her fear of being unable to perform at her best in public immediately — and the companion fear that security can't be airtight. Seles's psychologist, Jerry Russel May, testified at Parche's retrial that she continued to suffer post-traumatic stress disorder, that even "when she would go to the grocery store and someone would look at her, she was frightened that this person would attack her."

I cannot believe that the judge would not have understood the terrible emotional damage done to Seles had she heard the victim herself speak. But, of course, Seles could not endure the agony of traveling back to Germany and facing Parche. She remembered that she had seen him a few days before the assault, evidently stalking her already. "He gives me this smile," she said. And, even clearer, she still sees his face, because as she turned reflexively, after the knife had been driven hard within her, she saw him raise the dagger again, just before he was thwarted by a security guard.

It remains, too, so difficult for her to fathom how Parche is free, a sympathetic figure to many Germans, while she herself is the one in confinement, and while her colleagues, the players, denied her. "I talked to a couple of them," she said, "and, of course, they say it wasn't them. But I know the truth. I know Gabriela [Sabatini] was the one who said, 'This is not to vote for' [letting Seles keep her number one ranking as she recovered]. I will never forget that. She's a human being." The other players? Monica bows her head, and I fear she may begin crying again.

Seles does not want to remain at home, behind the walls. "I do love this sport so much," she says. "I was growing as a person, too. But he hated so much." She can never bring herself to use Parche's name. "How can one person have so much hatred? I just love the game, and for somebody to take it away from me. . . . For hate! And he got everything he planned!" Softer now: "His dream came true."

Finally, early in June, after a visit from Navratilova and a trip to Europe with the McCormacks, Seles made the decision to attempt a comeback — in that controlled situation of an exhibition, which she prefers. It is set for July 29, against Navratilova. At least it is a start. There is still time for her dream, to soar toward the net like Teddy's Goddess.

JAN REID

Big

FROM TEXAS MONTHLY

IN A ROOM OFF a narrow hallway on the forty-second floor of mid-
town Manhattan's Four Seasons hotel, heavyweight boxing champion George Foreman is talking to Ben Kinchlow, the dapper and
urbane host of *The 700 Club,* the religious news and talk show. They
touch lightly on matters of faith and George's penchant for naming
many of his children George, but mostly they talk about fighting.
Like nearly everyone else, Kinchlow doesn't call him Champ or
even Mr. Foreman. One handshake and he's "George" — at 46, he
brings that out in people. From his homes in Houston and Marshall, George has come to New York this third week of December to
host *Saturday Night Live* and to move along an autobiography now
in rush production at Random House, but he's plenty in demand
elsewhere. The National Father's Day Committee wants to declare
him father of the year. *Gumbo* magazine wants him as its gumbo
marshal. A magazine in France wants to interview him on the subject of poise. *Life* magazine wants him to pose with a ballerina from
the New York City Ballet (the hook is fitness and weight control).
George's agent boasts that these days George commands a larger
speaking fee than Norman Schwarzkopf. Since his knockout of
young Michael Moorer in early November, the world has beaten a
path to his door.

Both George and Kinchlow have deep, rich voices. They laugh a
lot. But it's hard to hear too much of their conversation because
bedlam has broken loose in the hallway. Certain hotel guests are
allowed to register their dogs, and at this moment three Labrador
retrievers are baying, snarling, throwing their chests against a door.

The dogs are vexed because their owners are out, and for half an hour a camera crew from a South Korean TV network has been muttering and moving gear around in the hall. A hotel security chief steps off an elevator with a look of polite, intense displeasure. He wants those cameras to disappear — now. The Koreans acknowledge that they understand him but stand their ground: their boss, a correspondent whom George's handlers know only as Mr. Soo, is in there with George and Kinchlow, and he has just stuck his head outside and told them to be ready.

The door opens and George ambles out, grinning. He is nattily attired in a size 50 extra-long sport coat. The man is vast — six-foot-four, about 250 pounds — but it is not the bigness of obesity. He has an odd, slow gait, as if his feet hurt. Over his shoulder he remarks to his courtly publicist, Mort Sharnik, that Kinchlow looks like a movie star. The grin vanishes when George hears the howls of the dogs and their hard thumps against the door. Then, to the horror of the hotel security chief, the hall is ablaze in TV lights. The Koreans crowd into an elevator with George, shooting all the way. Pressed into a corner, towering over six men, George goes stiff. Beads of sweat pop out on his shaved head. "Please," says Sharnik. "Sorry," replies Mr. Soo, and the lights go out.

Down on the seventh floor, in a room reserved by Mr. Soo, George takes a chair and offers a few pleasantries as the harsh lights reignite and the camera rolls. Mr. Soo suggests a prayer. Everyone bows his head. "Heavenly Father," Mr. Soo begins, "we thank you for the time to interview Mr. Foreman," and the conversation warps off from there. Mr. Soo commends George for his missionary work and for his practice of fighting on Saturday night and flying back to Houston to preach the next morning. "Preaching is my profession," George responds, smiling. "I just moonlight as a boxer." Mr. Soo says that it has been reported in the North Korean press that George will fight next in that country against a prominent Japanese wrestler. "Oh, I don't know about that," says George, after a slight pause. "But I've always wanted to go to Korea."

"*Norss* Korea?" cries Mr. Soo.

One can tell that George would like to slip his publicist a pleading look. "I just know it's one big beautiful country," he says gamely. "Always wanted to go there. And the food! I just love the food."

Mr. Soo leans forward, greatly pleased, and in a torrent of Korean wants to know what delicacies have teased his palate. George is running now, praying for the bell. "What's that soup?" he says. "Something about sparrows?"

"Sparrow?" says Mr. Soo. He reels off the names of several soups.

"Yeah," says George, trying to remember. "Like . . . saliva of the sparrow."

At the end of the interview, George shakes hands all around and strides through the door and down the hall with lights and a camera three feet from his shoulder. In the elevator he turns and faces the orb of yellow glare, and Mr. Soo takes a long lateral step, centering himself. Just before the doors shut, Mr. Soo's head plummets forward, and he bows at the waist.

On, then, to the thirty-fifth floor, where George is doing a public-service spot for Martin Luther King Day. George has been asked to join actor Edward James Olmos, singer Tony Bennett, and model Lauren Hutton in a campaign that will, at Coretta Scott King's urging, attempt to redefine the holiday as an occasion for public service. All George knows is that he's supposed to say something about the importance of doing good. But now a starched young federal bureaucrat is asking him a long list of complex questions about the value, message, and meaning of King's life.

Though the smile popularly associated with George's big round face comes to him easily, it's not his continuous pose. The casual look is not a glower either, but it suffers no fools, or anybody who might take him for one. George studies the bureaucrat a moment, then interrupts him. "Have you got a script?"

The man hands him a fact sheet. George reads it and hands it back. On camera he begins: "To me, Martin Luther King represented pure patriotism. And nonviolence. You actually can turn the other cheek. There would be forced change, but not through violence. It wouldn't happen with a fist, or a stick." Onlookers gasp with admiration. He never stammers or has to start over. He nails it. Knocks them dead.

The irony of George's celebrity, which is hardly lost on him, is that it's lavished on a prizefighter — one who deeply loves his game. Though the populace honors the king, it harbors deep misgivings and class disdain for his bloody realm. But the element that enthralls people who care nothing about boxing transcends a seemingly quixotic seven-year quest that ended with an unmatched athletic achievement. The greater comeback of George Foreman spans four decades, and it is a stirring tale of a human being's reclamation.

He grew up effectively fatherless, first in Marshall and then in Houston's Fifth Ward, where his mother moved in search of work. When he was 14, she was hospitalized for an emotional collapse brought on in part by his bad behavior. She sent a letter home that contained forty-five dollars to pay for his sister's graduation ring. George, who soon after that dropped out of school, stole the cash and bought a hat, a sweater, and a bottle of Thunderbird wine. For the next two years he mostly lived on the street, sleeping in abandoned shells of houses, playing dice, and rolling winos. His chums called him Monkey. One night, after mugging somebody, he slid under a house, hiding from the police. He could smell himself and kept thinking that they were going to send dogs after him, and that the dogs would smell him too.

A public-service TV spot by pro football star Jim Brown prompted him at seventeen to sign up for the federal Job Corps program. First in Oregon and then in northern California he learned how to lay bricks, and though he brawled and caused trouble in the camps, there were glints of maturity and conscience — every month he sent home fifty dollars to his mother. At the second camp a coach named Doc Broadus got him interested in boxing. Two years later, following a relapse among the Fifth Ward muggers and winos, George won the 1968 Olympics by clubbing several youths senseless in Mexico City. It was a year of political rage and black power; on the medalists' stand United States sprinters ducked their heads and raised black-gloved fists of protest during the national anthem. By contrast, George captivated the nation (which had no idea he had recently been a base Houston thug) by waving a little two-dollar American flag when he received his gold medal.

As a young pro, George spent $10,000 of his first substantial payday to buy his mother a house in nicer northeast Houston. He disposed of two great heavyweights, Joe Frazier and Ken Norton, in such quick and savage fashion that he was deemed invincible. But he was an unpopular champion. The public found George surly, which he was — but in retrospect, who could blame him? He was the one who had waved Old Glory in Mexico City. During the Vietnam War, he was prepared to enlist in the navy or air force, but he drew a high number in the draft lottery and, like countless others, chose to pursue a civilian career. Yet it was Muhammad Ali, stripped of his title because he refused to be drafted, who emerged from Vietnam as a folk hero. In 1974 George played the dope, as he cheerfully puts it now, in Ali's rope-a-dope brainstorm in Zaire, which ended with George exhausted and being counted out in the eighth round.

He dealt with it by trying to sleep with a different woman every night and by walking around his Marshall ranch with a lion on a leash. In 1977, maneuvering for a return fight that Ali was none too eager to grant him, he lost a decision to a clever Philadelphian named Jimmy Young, and after the match, in the throes of heat prostration, thought he was dying and found God. At 28 he walked away from boxing. He got fat and happy (except for a bitter divorce and child-custody battle) and became a street-corner preacher. He stopped hating Ali and realized the man was a friend. If George hadn't been the greatest, he could look back and know he had stepped high in history's most gifted peerage of heavyweight fighters. For ten years he seldom even shadowboxed. Then, at 38, after begging for money to keep a Houston youth recreation center open, he started fighting again in places so far from a major airport that TV crews couldn't find him. Unlike many old fighters who try to make another go of it, he hadn't abused himself since his teens — aside from overeating — and except for Ali, Young, and a Denver slugger named Ron Lyle, nobody was ever in the ring with him long enough to damage his brain cells much. During his comeback, George fought every six weeks, shed forty pounds, and got some skills back: first the left jab, which, in his prime, opponents likened to being thumped in the face with a telephone pole; then the straight right that comes behind the jab; then the left hook that sweeps in after the right. He could shoot the jab out, dip a knee, and follow hard with a left uppercut — a difficult combination, yet critics said he was ponderously slow.

In twenty-four bouts, George fought and stopped four quasi-contenders; the rest were targets. Boxing insiders were laughing at him, but he was a big name, and all at once the public loved him. What a nice and funny guy he had become! Such a pleasant contrast to bad Mike Tyson. Of course, nobody believed the fantasy. But then, to the consternation of Tyson's only credible rival, Evander Holyfield, Tyson first let himself get knocked out by journeyman Buster Douglas and then was doing time in Indiana on a rape conviction. Prizefighters stay in the business for the prizes, not the joy of getting hammered; for poor Holyfield, George was the only big payday out there. At 42 George put up a splendid fight, but the younger and faster hands prevailed. Public sentiment shifted: Give it up, old man. It's not funny anymore. You're going to get hurt. Yet George kept fighting, risking the fate of his historic soul mate, Muhammad Ali. He lost a decision to mediocre Tommy Morrison and took a turn in a short-lived TV sitcom, in which, for religious and marital reasons, he declined to kiss his co-star on the mouth. He claims that one day the actress stormed off in a huff, shouting, "Well, I never!"

Then, last April, chance and market conditions rose up again. The gallant Holyfield — weakened by his fight with George, two epic bouts with Riddick Bowe, and a heart condition — lost a close decision to an undefeated but little-known Detroit fighter, Michael Moorer. Holyfield retired the next day. There were other able heavies, such as Bowe and Tyson, who is nearing the end of his prison term, that Moorer might choose to hazard down the road. But in the meantime, the new champ desired a big, easy payday. Once more, George was the biggest draw out there, and he was getting older every day. In fact, to force the World Boxing Association to heed Moorer's wishes and sanction the Las Vegas fight, George and his Beverly Hills lawyer, Henry Holmes, had to go to court in Nevada and win an injunction on the basis of inconsistent rules enforcement and age discrimination. Only in America. George, who had received $5 million for fighting relative nobodies, accepted about $2 million to get one more title shot.

George's trainer and strategist for the Moorer fight was a portly man named Charlie Shipes, who owns a small long-haul trucking firm in northeast Houston. In the late '60s, George, Shipes, and Sonny Liston, who was still in the game following his two losses to Ali, were stablemates in Oakland, California. Shipes was a flashy undefeated welterweight, billed by his handlers as the uncrowned champion, until Dallas's Curtis Cokes, the crowned champ, dismantled him in his one title fight. George's other guru was Bob Cook, a brown-haired man who in the late '70s was a standout La Porte High School running back. College football didn't work out for him; he first bulked up as a competitive bodybuilder, then started working out at George's youth center. They struck up a friendship, and Cook fought eight pro bouts as a middleweight. George now relies on Cook for weight training and nutritional advice. (All that business about hamburgers in both hands is for show; George eats more sensibly than most people.)

Before the fight, the sports media couldn't get a fix on Moorer's personality and thus decided the star in his corner was his voluble trainer, Teddy Atlas. But the 26-year-old champ was no soup can. Moorer carried 222 pounds impressively, and after beating Holyfield, his record was 35–0 with 30 knockouts. Moorer is a left-hander and the first one to hold a heavyweight title; that's because right-handers hate them, almost never see them, and as champions, seldom give them a shot. It's like boxing a mirror image: if both men jab at once, their fists collide. It's awkward, as the punches zoom in from angles right-handers are not used to seeing. After watching tapes of Moorer, Shipes and George came away even more devoted to an old axiom of how to fight southpaws: straight right hand every time he wiggles.

Of course, he had to be close enough to land it. Though analysts scoff at George, inside the ropes he incites real fear. According to *Sports Illustrated,* Don King once proposed a Foreman bout to Tyson, who replied, "You like him so much, you fight him. No!" Several observers thought they saw that fright in Holyfield. George knew he couldn't win a decision against Moorer if the young man punched in flurries and danced far away from him. So he feigned a personal animosity toward him, suggested he was a coward, wouldn't look him in the eye. The message was: Come on in here. Atlas knew what George was doing. At center ring for the referee's instructions, the trainer ordered his fighter to look at nothing but George's chest. At the end of the first round, when Moorer took the stool, Atlas told him, "The hardest part of this fight is over. He's just a guy. Our sparring partners were better. Am I right or wrong?"

Moorer basically fought a one-handed fight. With his right he threw multiple jabs, hooks, uppercuts. His left was little more than a guard against the threat of George's right. Gaining confidence, he bobbed and weaved and talked to George. "Pop! Pop! Pop!" he said, landing punches. Though George was staggered several times, he knew he couldn't let himself get knocked down. "They'd just say, 'Oh, no, George is old. Stop it,'" he later said, explaining his thinking. But his height and bulk were a problem for Moorer. He held his arms high and vertically, and he deflected punches with his gloves and forearms. Moorer wasn't eager to burrow inside, so he often found himself looping punches over George's arms. Though more than half of his blows landed, many glanced harmlessly off the top of George's head.

George relied on jabs and straight rights — some soft, some hard, but he just kept coming. At the end of the sixth round — a rousing toe-to-toe brawl — Shipes suggested, "Try moving over to the right a little. Get away from that right hand." He was concerned about the damage to George's left eye. A round later, Atlas nagged Moorer to keep up the pace. "Remember what I told you about an old car? This is an old car. Let him go slow, he can make it down the road. Make him go faster, he'll start to break down."

In George's view the eighth round was pivotal. He surprised and wobbled Moorer with three quick rights. Moorer gave him a curt nod of acknowledgment. "The only way anybody ever gets a title shot," George said afterward, "is to convince the other guy, 'Aw, he's just in it for the money.' Then he gets in there and realizes he's in a *fight*. But you don't want to communicate that too soon, 'cause he'll change his plans. Way he took that hook, I thought, 'Ah, now I got him. I questioned his courage. He's not gonna run.'"

Angelo Dundee, the 70-something trainer who worked Ali's corner in Zaire, had joined George's team a week before the fight. He's a good luck charm, he has seen it all, and he's one of the best cut men in the business. After the eighth he asked George, "You all right?" George: "Yeah." Dundee: "You sure?" But in the ninth George was pooped. Later he said that his cornermen were voicing fears about the scorecards, and after the ninth he snapped at them, told them to shut up. Whatever was discussed, he walked out in the tenth and turned it up. After two left-right combinations, he again crossed Moorer up with a right lead and left hook. Another hook missed so wildly that George almost spun himself in a circle. "Give him all the credit in the world," sympathized HBO commentator Gil Clancy, "but he's a 45-year-old man in a young man's game."

Then George landed another jab and right. Stung, Moorer stayed put and dropped his hands slightly. George had been stepping to his right, which is difficult for a right-handed fighter. He did it, as Shipes said, to escape Moorer's punishment, but he was also looking for an angular lane. The last right hand George should throw in his life — the one he could never land against Ali — sloped downward about two feet. Moorer dropped like a sack of flour, flat on his back, struggling to raise his head, as blood pooled in his mouth.

Pandemonium. George was on his knees praying. His brother Roy fainted. HBO's Jim Lampley, who had ridiculed the contest before it began, shrieked, "It happens!" Moorer, who fought artfully and won seven of nine rounds on points, found a likable public persona as a loser. Seated on his stool with the gloves off, he looked up at the camera, nodded gamely, and raised a thumb. He gave it all he had. George, with sunshades hiding a badly swollen eye, spoke into a microphone. "When you wish upon a star . . . doesn't matter who you are . . ." Ali, who later sent George a congratulatory note with a hand-drawn happy face, no doubt admired the poetry.

Moorer leaned through the shoulders and gibberish and planted a kiss on George's bald head. Pops.

High in NBC's office tower in New York, I am parked on a sofa with Mort Sharnik and Terry Sparks, a pleasant young man who travels with George and is sometimes referred to as his bodyguard, though the boss outweighs him by forty pounds. This, in its entirety, is Foreman's entourage. Sue Leibman, a *Saturday Night Live* associate producer who ushers guest hosts through the drill each week, hurries out of a meeting with the writers and approaches us. "George's title," she says briskly. "He is the . . . ?"

After a second we reply in a chorus, "World heavyweight champion."

Oliver McCall, a former sparring partner of Mike Tyson's, actually holds one of the three major sanctioning bodies' titles, but Leibman doesn't need to get into that. She nods and hurries back to the writers.

From another office, where George is holed up, comedian Carl Reiner emerges and is instantly crowded by the young staff. Reiner, who seems to have been making a courtesy call, walks off happily, twirling a forefinger. "If George Foreman says you're a genius,

you're a genius!" It's seven at night, eleven hours since George
started his day with an hour on the hotel's exercise treadmill. Suddenly Leibman rushes out to Sharnik, this time with a greatly troubled look. The bear in George has finally gotten riled and spoken
sharply: he's still here because they want to take him out to eat?

Ushered down the elevators, we walk to a limo provided by the
network. A Christmas shopper gapes and exclaims, "That's George
Foreman!" George wears a topcoat and muffler over his dress wool-
ens and a short-billed cap pulled down toward his nose. In the car,
he stretches out his legs as the lights and street steam of Manhattan
glide by. "TV," George says moodily when Sharnik asks him how it's
going. "They don't know it's about eyesight. About visual. They've
got all these writers who know they got to be funny, so they think
and think and all they can come up with is dirt. It's just a constant
battle. And you know you're in trouble because not one of 'em has
a gray hair."

The limo stops in front of a deli, and Sharnik goes inside to get
George's favorite New York supper: a pastrami sandwich on whole
wheat with mayonnaise, lettuce, and tomatoes. The order frequently draws a laugh or double take; Sharnik sheepishly explains
that the guy's a southerner. As we move again, the conversation
turns to boxing. "How good was Charlie Shipes?" I ask George.

"Best I've ever seen," he replies, animated for the first time since
we left NBC. "He could do everything. Moving left jabbing, moving
right jabbing: he was precision. And he wore these red trunks and
red headgear; he just looked like a boxer. I used to say, 'I don't want
to turn pro yet. I want to learn to box like Charlie Shipes.' Sugar
Ray Robinson was like that. Except he had bad habits. Archie
Moore was the best at defense." George raises his arms horizontally
and ducks his head behind them. "Like this, but Archie was throwing punches all the time. He never hit hard" — George snaps his
fingers loudly — "but they *rained* on you. Joe Louis: they used to
talk about his devastating combinations, but the only punch he
threw hard was the last one. That was the hardest thing for me to
learn. You don't have to hit hard just because you're able to." He
floats a big soft hand toward my face. "That's how I did it with
Michael. Just let him see the jab. If you hit him too hard with the
left, he'll start to worry about the right. And it'll put him too far
back. When the time comes, I won't be able to reach him."

He lowers his head and looks at a brightly lit toy store. The building is flanked by three ledge steps of white rock. "See that?" he says. "One time in Houston, I watched Sonny Liston balance on a ledge like that on the ball of one foot. He did a deep knee bend, picked up the other foot, and stretched his leg straight out. Then he held his arms straight out and just stayed there, like a statue." George smiles at the memory. "Never seen anything like it."

Before the New York trip, I had gone to Houston to meet Charlie Shipes, whose home and trucking yard is tucked away in the pines off U.S. 59. Charlie's affable wife, Barbara, told me he was out trying to find a truck part and then let me through the security fence; she advised me to keep an eye on the pit bull that walked along at my calf. The Shipeses live in a mobile home surrounded by several tractor-trailer rigs. The only evidence of Charlie's lofty position in boxing was a couple of heavy bags under a shed and some photographs on the mantel. Barbara said she had been a friend of one of George's late cousins, who introduced her to Charlie at George's church. She said she'd never seen a pro fight. "I hope George'll quit now," she told me. "He's got his health and all those kids still at home."

Just then, Charlie walked through the door in coveralls and a soiled cap. Smoking a cigarette, he reminisced about his own 53–5 record and the time Doc Broadus delivered them a huge youngster from the Job Corps camp in Pleasanton, California. "Sonny was good to George," he said. "George would bloody his nose, and Sonny wouldn't unload on him like a lot of fighters will. He was just bringing him along. George got his puncher's reputation because of the way he took apart Joe Frazier. But, hell, he did it with jabs, hooks, rights, and uppercuts. The man can box."

We talked about George's second ring career. The public adulation is no less intense in Houston; George has been saying he'd like to go out with a gift to his hometown: a title fight that fills up the Astrodome. He talks about Tyson, who'll get out of prison this spring — a fight that promoter Bob Arum says could gross $200 million. "Whatever George decides to do," said Shipes, "he's got my blessing."

But . . . Tyson? To me, the thought was terrifying: an angry creature who believes himself wronged and has spent three years in a cage. "Well, yeah. Tyson's good," Shipes said, now on his feet and shadowboxing. "Great hand speed, and he's kind of a switch-hitter. He'll step to the left and double hook, high and low, then do the same thing to the right. Ain't ever seen anything like it. But if a man's still got his legs under him, and there ain't no *nerve damage*, I'll take the experience. See, George came up with Ali, Frazier, Kenny Norton, Jerry Quarry, George Chuvalo. That's like going to Harvard. This young crowd now, they just been to junior college."

The next morning, the Sunday before the New York trip, my wife and I went to George's Church of the Lord Jesus Christ. It's west of U.S. 59, south of Intercontinental Airport, in a poor and neatly kept neighborhood that looks forgotten. Just down the street is George's youth center. Inside, the church is well furnished but spare. George doesn't evangelize much, even in the neighborhood, for fear of turning his church into a circus. Many of the people who go there are related to each other. George's nephew Jody Steptoe, who is an assistant pastor, sat on a chair tuning an electric guitar. There were about sixty people, all but four of us black. Steptoe stood up and started playing the guitar. "Glory, glory, hallelujah," he sang slowly, "I'm gonna lay my burden down . . ." A few women were on their feet swaying, two or three with tambourines. "Softly and tenderly Jesus is calling," they sang.

When the music stopped, George walked in, resplendent in a camel blazer. Approaching the pulpit, he kissed a child on the top of her head. George doesn't write his sermons. He selects a passage of Scripture, reads it in segments, and reflects on whatever comes to mind. This day his text was Luke, Chapter Twelve. He told stories about how badly he hurt his mother when he was growing up and how he periodically resolved to stop stealing — at least from her. The congregation burst out laughing when he pulled down his lip and mimicked a man with no front teeth. "Wake up from being dead drunk and my best friend says, 'George, look what you did to me.' 'I did not do that!' 'Yeah, you did . . . but it's O.K.!'"

He read some more Scripture, then recalled a low point in one of his five marriages. "Sometimes they just don't want you. I mean: you. I went up to my ranch, and all I could think to do was cut grass. Mow and mow and mow. I ran my tractor over a stump. I was trying to fix my mower with a sledgehammer and come way up over the top. Whomp! Hit myself right on the knee." He danced across the church on one foot. "Thank you, baby Jesus, thank you for all this pain! Take my mind off the mess I have made of my life." He limped on as the laughter subsided. "Amazing grace," he said, shaking his head. "That saved a wretch like me."

George looked again at the Bible in his hand and read loudly. "Take heed, and beware of covetousness, for a man's life consisteth not in the abundance of the things which he possesseth." In the sermon he fashioned the parable of the rich fool into a biting comment on the temper of these times. George knocked out Moorer the Saturday before Election Day. Many comeback candidates invoked his name in their acceptance speeches, but politically George is a fish out of water. He endorsed one candidate: Ann Richards, who was trounced. George is the poster boy of the much-maligned Great Society; he has often said that LBJ saved his life by creating the Job Corps. He once reflected on his flag-waving impulse at the Olympics: "What I did in Mexico City wasn't no demonstration. I was just happy and proud to be an American. When I looked at America, I saw a compassionate society that didn't give up on its underclass."

On this day, he didn't sound so confident of that fundamental generosity. "I'll tell you about middle class," he said. "Their mommas and daddies used to be poor. Now they've had a job ten years and have a credit card. Hear 'em talking at the barbershop. 'Look at all those people getting rich on welfare. All that stuff they buy.' Why, there's people in this country that don't have fifteen cents."

"Amen. That's right," several people said. George chewed on his lower lip, and he did not look happy. "You don't have to reform 'em," he said sarcastically. "Just don't give 'em nothing. *Shut up!*"

George has nine kids, ages 22 to 3. One son runs the ranch in Marshall, his eldest daughter is in college, and the rest live in a home in the Houston suburb of Kingwood. On Thursday afternoon during his week in New York, in his *Saturday Night Live* dressing room, he picks up a phone and calls home. He talks to his wife, Joan, who was born on the Caribbean island of Saint Lucia — yet he makes no mention of glitzy things and famous people. The conversation dwells on antibiotics and the child who's running a fever.

When an intercom booms George's name, he goes out in the

studio to tape some promotional spots that the producers and network officials will review and air before the show. "Watch *Saturday Night Live,*" he commands in one, "or I'll beat you up and eat all your food!" In the studio there is genuine laughter as he tries out various routines. Later, he is joined by the show's musical guest, the rock group Hole. Hole's lead singer is Courtney Love, a bleached-blond miniskirted young woman with a tattoo on her shoulder and runs in her hose. She is the aspiring empress of grunge rock and the widow of Kurt Cobain, a Seattle rock star who was depressed and had a heroin problem and dealt with it by putting a shotgun to his head. Courtney's shtick is Madonna to the max: all week she has been trying to prove that she's the baddest girl around. She and George shake hands, and the crew positions the band around him. As the cameramen line up the shot, Courtney stands below George. She primps by shoving her breasts upward with the palms of her hands. "Tits," she keeps saying. "Tits." George keeps his eyes on the cue cards.

In one promo, Courtney and George are supposed to begin by hyping the show and then get into a mild spat. On the first take, Courtney ad-libs. She turns and bangs her fists against his chest and then tries to jump and wrap her legs around his waist. George fends her off, and he leaves the studio laughing, but in his dressing room he plops on the sofa dejectedly. Sharnik asks him about the scripts. "So bad they can't be fixed," George says with a sigh. "Start trying to change this, cut that, it just gets worse. I'm not gonna say anything. I just never shoulda done this. No way. Not in this lifetime."

Leibman, the associate producer, knocks on the door, comes in, and rests a moment, waiting for the wardrobe man. Once more, talk of boxing revives George's spirits. He elaborates on his belief that tragedy is interwoven in all feats of athletic greatness. "In boxing we got this saying: 'I'm gonna put my head on your chest.' Means I'm gonna take the best you got and come right through all your defenses. The first fight against Muhammad, Joe Frazier *did that.* To a man as great as Muhammad Ali. After that, Joe never was quite the same. What else did he have to prove?"

I glance at Leibman. Her eyes have grown very wide.

As George tries on sport coats he talks about Tyson, whose imminent return to the sport will be watched as closely as Ali's was twenty years ago. "Boxing is a matter of who can fill the tent," says George, unbothered by the circus analogy. "Mike Tyson doesn't need the title. The title needs Tyson. But what he had, he can't get back. Because it was all speed. Tyson is not a powerful puncher." George shadowboxes, demonstrating his point. "Hit you in the ribs, and you say, 'My, that hurts,' so you bring down your elbow, and he comes right up to the head. But it takes at least two years in the gym to get that going, and then you got to fight constantly. Title fights don't get arranged that fast. Tyson is Humpty Dumpty. All the king's horses, all the king's men. Everybody gonna be whipping him."

George fiddles with his cuffs and looks in the mirror. "But there's a young one out there. Nobody's even heard of him yet. One day he's just gonna loom among us. Be like Tyson, when he first came up. People be standing around saying, 'You want him?' 'No, I don't want him. You want him?' I hope it's somebody like Joe Louis."

The halls leading into the *Saturday Night Live* studio are lined with photos of great comedians and great comic moments, and the production is amazing to behold: seven complex activities unfolding at once. But the dress rehearsal is painfully unfunny. The closest thing to humor involving George has him propelled by time capsule to Germany in 1939, where he changes history by knocking out Hitler and becoming World Führer. The producers have flown in ring announcer Michael Buffer to put on a Nazi uniform and do his basso "Let's get ready to rumble" routine. At George's request, bit parts in the sketch are played by fight promoter Bob Arum and Henry Holmes, the lawyer and agent who won the age-discrimination injunction and negotiated his book contract. ("Yeah, but Henry's stock is down," George grumbled at one point during the rehearsals. "He's the one who got me into this.")

The sight gags feature actors and crew members whose eyes are swollen shut. In a demeaning skit, George, cast as TV's Incredible Hulk, grunts and smashes things until finally he calls the show's writers out and observes correctly that nobody in the studio audience is laughing. They wrote that! But the joke's on him. Seated next to me in the audience is a young man named Mark Taffet, who works for TVKO, a network that airs boxing matches. During a break, Taffet excitedly tells me the concept of George's next match, tentatively set for April 22. "We find a real-life Rocky, see. White guy, deserves a shot. We're looking at two or three prospects now. Michael gave George a chance, so George gives somebody else a chance. The second fight is huge, but this fight . . . well, this fight is more of a celebration."

Below us the cast has assembled to close out the show All keep a wary eye on Courtney Love, who reportedly came of age with a trust fund and now is looking for somebody else to throw her legs around. The victim will be her guitar player; they'll fall in a heap, her panties bared to all. George isn't smiling as he waits for the camera light to come on. He towers above the others and has a pensive expression on his face. The champ. Earlier in the week he told one interviewer who pressed him about his plans in the ring and beyond: "Just don't tell me I'm too old. I'm blue-collar, and I've got nine kids. I've gotta work till I can't work anymore." He told another interviewer that he wanted to shake every hand, sign every autograph. But this is the longest time he has spent in New York since he was a young contender fighting in Madison Square Garden. He's a grown man now. In his mind he's already at the airport. It's time to go home.

Man of the Century

FROM GOLF WORLD

GOLF'S OLDEST LEGEND lives quietly in Marco Island, Florida, in a comfortable fourth-floor apartment flush on the Gulf of Mexico, with a view almost as expansive as the life he has led. He was born before the airplane, raised before radio, a star decades before television. He drops more names by accident than most people do with a full sweat.

Harry Vardon? Played with him. Bernard Darwin and Grantland Rice? Interviewed by them. Ed Sullivan? Caddied with him. Howard Hughes? Taught to fly by him. The sand wedge? Invented it. And for modern-day gladiators who gauge success by White House visitations: Warren Harding asked Gene Sarazen to stop by in 1922. "I'm the oldest living *everything*," Sarazen says.

Sarazen is 93, and if the weather is too hot or too cool or, as on this October day, too damp, he has to take the view from inside. His mind is still sharp, and he doesn't even wear glasses. His face, despite all those decades in the sun, is remarkably unlined. He still has a car and occasionally drives. But when recalling the past these days, he edits his stories for brevity, to save his strength as much as anything. Sarazen has lost some twenty pounds in the past years — he had to have his trademark knickers taken in two inches in the waist — and he is concerned about his ebbing appetite. "I don't eat much," he said, "but I like this new spaghetti, this angel hair."

He is also bothered by arthritis, particularly in his shoulders, an affliction that limited his golf to two swings during 1995 — sendoff shots to start the Masters in April and the Sarazen World Open a couple of weeks ago. "It's so painful that I don't like to do it,"

Sarazen said. "I don't know how I managed to get that ball off the first tee at Augusta."

The week prior to the Sarazen, Donald Panoz, who began the event in 1994 to honor the old pro, was concerned that Sarazen might forgo his duties as honorary starter. "But I was talking with him and asked how many people would be traveling up on the plane with him," Panoz said. "And he said, 'I'm traveling light. It's just going to be me, my grandson and my driver.'" For the record, Sarazen ended the season as he began it, with a drive down the middle of the fairway, never mind the cortisone shots he had to take just to be able to take his cuts.

Sarazen has lived so long that his annual appearance at the Masters — he became an honorary starter in the early 1980s, at first playing a full nine holes, and more recently, merely striking one tee shot in the presence of those whippersnappers, Byron Nelson and Sam Snead — is Sarazen's calling card to a generation of fans. There he is, almost visibly trying to will his joints to warm up in the early morning chill. There he is, getting Snead to tee up his ball. There he is, bunting one down the sprinkler line one more time, with just enough hand action left to illustrate why Harry Vardon — yes, *the* Harry Vardon — once said of him: "His swing is perfect, and he has that clasp-knife sort of snap in hitting iron shots that distinguishes the very great golfer from the merely good."

"I feel like an exhibit in a museum," Sarazen observed at Augusta a few years ago. That was about the same time he told Hord Hardin, then chairman of the Masters, that he was getting too old to hit a shot. "Gene," Hardin told him, "they don't want to see you play; they just want to see if you're still alive."

There wasn't a Masters when Gene Sarazen was born the youngest of two children of Federico and Adela Saraceni on February 27, 1902, in Harrison, New York. Golf was about as new to the United States as the Saracenis were. Gene Sarazen's birth name was Eugenio Saraceni, which he would change when he was 16 and starting his unlikely way in golf. "I made a hole-in-one, and the newspaper had a headline with Eugenio Saraceni," Sarazen recalled, pronouncing the name with a proper Italian accent, "and I thought that sounded like a violin player. So I changed it. G-e-n-e S-a-r-a-z-e-n. That wasn't in any phone book. I liked the way it sounded, and I liked the way it looked. It sounded like a golfer."

Sarazen became a golfer against all odds, not the least of which was Federico's opposition to the sport. Federico Saraceni had studied to become a priest in Rome, but had to change his plans when both his parents died in the same year. In America, he earned a living as a carpenter by day, then retired to his basement each night to read the Italian classics. He believed that his son's station in life would also be as a tradesman. "He wanted me to be a good carpenter," Gene recalled. "He wasn't for the country club crowd. I don't think he ever was in a clubhouse."

Sarazen's father saw his son play one stroke in his entire career. It was at the 1923 PGA Championship at Pelham Country Club outside New York City, a tournament Sarazen won. Federico stood on a road adjacent to the tenth hole and peered through a fence. "He was looking over from a highway," Sarazen said, "and I had about a forty-foot putt, which I missed. When I got home that night, he said, 'To think you get paid for what you're doing. You missed that putt.' I told him I was lucky to get down in two shots in that position, but he didn't know. He took a swipe at a ball once and he fell down. He almost broke his leg."

Despite the discouragement from his father, Sarazen loved golf almost from the time he was 8 and caddying for the first time at Larchmont [New York] Country Club. Because of better opportunities at nearby Apawamis Club, Sarazen moved there, where one of his fellow caddies was one Ed Sullivan. One day, Sarazen and Sullivan got called down for the next twosome, and Sullivan jumped at the bigger and flashier of the two bags. But by the end of the day, the sports writer Grantland Rice had given Sarazen $3 — three times what Sullivan got — and begun a lifelong friendship with him.

Sarazen's caddying money went toward the Saracenis' bills. His heart, however, got deeper into the game, inspired by Francis Ouimet's stunning victory in the 1913 U.S. Open and stoked by matches on a makeshift neighborhood course with tin-can cups and schoolyard games so persistent that his teachers would set fire to the kids' wooden-shafted clubs. Whereupon Sarazen, who used the interlocking grip favored by Ouimet, and his friends would retrieve the clubheads, scour up some replacement shafts, and have golf again.

Sarazen wasn't in school very long, forced to drop out in the sixth grade to earn more money for the Saraceni household. In

1917, when he was 15, the family moved thirty-five miles to Bridge-port, Connecticut, home of bustling wartime manufacturing. Gene caught on at Remington Arms, drilling holes in wooden crates in which shells were sent to Europe. In January of 1918, Sarazen caught a cold, which became pneumonia and later developed into pleural empyema. Sarazen was so sick he received the last rites. He stabilized, but to drain the fluid from his chest and to prevent the onset of tuberculosis, Sarazen underwent an operation in which two holes were drilled through his back between the ribs. When he was finally discharged from the hospital in May, his doctor, John Shea, told Sarazen to get an outdoor job.

To Sarazen, that meant golf, but the game, despite Ouimet's triumph, was still tough for homebreds to enter. The Scottish and English immigrant pros ran the roost. But Sarazen persisted, hon-ing his game at a nine-hole public course in Bridgeport called Beardsley Park. Before long, thanks to the help of its pro, Al Ciuci, Sarazen was able to get a job as a shopboy at Brooklawn Coun-try Club.

Two of Brooklawn's most prominent members, Archie and Willie Wheeler, convinced their pro, George Sparling, that Sarazen was something special, and he was on his way to a life as a competi-tive golfer, with one more detour. In the winter of 1919, Sarazen returned to Bridgeport Hospital during the middle of an influenza epidemic. He had the grim task of delivering the dead to the morgue. "The patients that were going to die during the night, the doctor would put a red light over their bed," Sarazen remembered. "And when they were gone I would take them down. I would take shots of whiskey so I wouldn't catch the flu. There was nothing else you could do. There was no vaccine, no pill to take."

Sarazen's game advanced quickly. By 1922, when he was just 20, Sarazen had tasted victory and life on what passed as the pro-fessional circuit. Working as the pro in Titusville, Pennsylvania, he caught the eye of Emil Loeffler, the greenkeeper, and William Fownes, the founder of Oakmont Country Club in Pittsburgh. Fownes bankrolled a trip for Sarazen to play Skokie Country Club in Chicago, in advance of the 1922 U.S. Open there.

"I got back to Pittsburgh," Sarazen said, "and I told Mr. Fownes that the course was built around my game. I was fortunate. But in order to win those things, you've got to be fortunate."

When Sarazen won the 1922 U.S. Open, he also started what

would be a lifetime of good relations with the press. He was a good quote when quotes weren't the lifeblood of newspaper stories. "All men are created equal," Sarazen said after winning the Open in 1922. "I'm just one stroke better than the rest." When Sarazen was in his prime, favorable attention affected the endorsements and exhibitions that a golfer might get to supplement his paltry purse winnings — to this day, Sarazen speaks fondly of his 1930 Agua Caliente Open triumph in Mexico that paid him an unheard of $10,000 — and he knew how to play the game.

When Sarazen insured his hands for $150,000, or suggested that the hole be eight inches in diameter instead of four and a half inches, it brought him headlines. His peers were jealous and at times suspicious of Sarazen. His publicity-seeking coexisted with a peppery on-course demeanor obscured at times by a Cheshire-cat grin. "That grin of his," wrote legendary British golf writer Bernard Darwin, "is the mark of a sunny and delightful nature, but not of an altogether placid one." If Hagen was the showman and Jones the gentleman, Sarazen rounded out American golf's troika of the 1920s as a competitor who gave no quarter.

Sarazen was, in fact, as solid as the calves that supported his five feet five inches, a man who always took care of his body. He strengthened his golf muscles by swinging a weighted practice club — an idea he got from a chat with Ty Cobb. But Sarazen's real heavy lifting was simply in blazing a trail as an Italian-American during a time when not everyone liked pasta. And if he had changed his name for reasons other than not to sound like a violinist, no one could have blamed him. But Sarazen was forever giving people a reason to pay attention.

When he traveled the world during the 1930s, taking golf to South America and Asia, Sarazen was not only making money but, as Donald Panoz points out, "being a globetrotter before globetrotting was cool." It was risky business and meant flying in dicey planes, driving on dangerous roads, and hitching a ride on the occasional freighter. He made friends easily in the foreign lands, and the Japanese (perhaps, Sarazen reasoned, because he was more or less their size) took a special liking to him. He can remember playing in Japan in the late 1930s, several years after he invented the sand wedge. Sarazen would play a bunker shot, and when he walked out of the trap, the Japanese would filter into the sand and take their place in the stance he had carved.

Every golfer who blasts out of a bunker and saves par ought to thank Sarazen for creating, in 1931 and 1932, the first modern sand wedge. His inspiration: the way the tail of the plane was adjusted upon take-off one day when he was learning to fly with Howard Hughes in Florida. Sarazen also credited watching ducks land on a pond, skimming the surface with rounded bellies.

A model with a concave face, eventually ruled illegal by the U.S. Golf Association, existed earlier, but Sarazen soldered a thick base, or flange, onto a niblick, creating a clubhead that would bounce, rather than stick, in the sand. The new design revolutionized the way pros viewed sand bunkers — they were no longer a crapshoot. Although the advent of steel shafts coincided with Sarazen's invention and has to be taken into account, the average winning score in the ten U.S. Opens from 1932 through 1941 was 6.6 strokes lower than the winning average in the U.S. Opens played from 1922 through 1931. For Sarazen, the only drawback was that he never made a dime off his invention. Since he was under contract to Wilson Sporting Goods — he was signed in 1923 and remains under contract to this day — the company reaped the benefits. The same thing happened when Sarazen popularized the use of "reminder" grips.

Sarazen once said that inventing the sand wedge was his biggest contribution to golf. It was a singular achievement, ranking right up there with a stroke he played during the final round of the 1935 Masters — at the time a fledgling little invitational tournament whose only real attribute was that golf's recently retired hero, Bobby Jones, had begun it.

Augusta National's par-5 fifteenth hole was then 485 yards, and as Sarazen reached his second shot, he knew he needed to birdie three of his final four holes in order to tie leader Craig Wood. Today, golfers routinely reach the green with a middle iron for their second shots, but Sarazen had about 235 yards to the hole, over the small pond that fronts the green. The distance called for his 3-wood, but the snug lie demanded a 4-wood club, a club not yet as popular with the golfing populace as the 2-wood, or brassie, but one that Sarazen had embraced for some time.

Although only twenty-three people were standing by the green — Sarazen's count, including Jones and Walter Hagen — Sarazen's stroke was one of the first "shots heard round the world." The double eagle got Sarazen into a playoff with Wood, which he won the following day for his last major title. His Masters triumph, combined with his earlier victories in the U.S. and British Opens and PGA Championship, also gave Sarazen the distinction of being the first golfer to win all four modern "Grand Slam" events. Ben Hogan, Jack Nicklaus, and Gary Player are still the only others to have done so.

At the time, Sarazen was hoping for a plaque to mark the spot from which he struck his historic blow, but the divot was merely filled in with grass seed. But twenty years later, in 1955, the small bridge on which golfers cross the pond on the left side was named in his honor. By then, Sarazen was 53, long removed as a regular player on tour, and fifteen years from his last serious run at a major, the 1940 U.S. Open, when Lawson Little beat him in a playoff. Sarazen was still fit, and would have made a killing if there had been a senior tour. He was doing occasional television commentary for NBC — Sarazen prematurely congratulated Hogan for winning the 1955 U.S. Open with the eventual winner, Jack Fleck, still on the course — but mostly spent his time on his farm in upstate New York.

Sarazen had lived with his wife, Mary, and their children, Gene Jr. and Mary Ann, on a farm since 1933 — first in Brookfield, Connecticut, and later in upstate New York. He got his nickname, "The Squire," in the process. He always liked the nickname, and the irony that it stuck on someone who grew up a poor city boy was never lost on him.

Sarazen was all but out of public view by 1961, when Shell Oil decided that a golf travelogue show would be good for business. *Shell's Wonderful World of Golf*, which ran on NBC-TV from 1962 through 1970, featured pros playing matches in exotic locales. It brought host Sarazen into the dens and grillrooms of a new generation of fans. It was a lot like his worldly travels decades earlier, only this time the ride was smoother and the seats in first-class.

"The show really gave him a new lease on life," said Fred Raphael, producer/director of the Shell series who later started the Legends of Golf, the precursor to the senior tour, in 1978. "He didn't just represent Shell, he represented golf. Because he had already been around the world, it was like that show was created for him."

Sarazen also had a hand in the formation of the Legends tournament. He and Raphael were dining after the second round of the 1963 Masters when Sarazen left the table to call for his starting time. "He came back," Raphael remembered, "and said, 'Tomorrow, the old legend, Gene Sarazen, will be paired with the future legend, Arnold Palmer.' The word 'legend' got me thinking."

Raphael has many memories of the Shell days, none more vivid than one particular trip to Rome. Sarazen's father, by then in his nineties, had returned to Italy many years before, disenchanted with American politics. He received a regular check from Gene, but the father and son who never got along hadn't seen each other in a long time. So Gene Sarazen went to have dinner with Federico Saraceni. Sarazen gave his father a television set. It was the last time he ever saw him. "That was a great moment for him," Raphael said. "He was as happy that night as I ever saw him."

Sarazen is about the age now that his father was then. But other than the bittersweet reality of outliving most of his friends, Sarazen has few regrets. "I wouldn't wish to start over again for anything," he said. "I won the four majors and I'm satisfied." Not factoring in the aging process, Sarazen's life hasn't been the same since 1986 when Mary Sarazen, whom he married in 1924, died shortly after suffering a heart attack. She had the formal education he never received and a love and trust in him that wouldn't quit. "Here I was, the Open champion, and I only had a sixth-grade education," Sarazen said. "Then I met this girl, and she was so well educated. I married her quick. I was very fortunate. But the last eight years have been lonely."

A housekeeper shares Sarazen's apartment. His daughter, Mary Ann Ilnicki, and her son, Gene Martin, live on Marco Island and see him often. Sarazen's grandson is particularly close to him, an aide-de-camp really, who travels with him on his infrequent out-of-town trips. Sarazen is looking forward to the reopening this year of the Island Club, at which he maintained an office that he visited daily to handle correspondence and eat lunch until a fire destroyed it almost two years ago. He lost some memorabilia in the fire — as he had in 1976 in a blaze at home in New Hampshire, where he summered — and if not for the quick thinking of some golf-savvy firemen, who covered some important articles with a tarp, the loss would have been greater.

Sarazen tends to his various charitable concerns — primarily a scholarship program at Siena College and the Urgent Care Center on Marco Island — and watches plenty of news and golf on television. He kept up with the O. J. Simpson trial and judiciously says, "When people ask me what I thought of the verdict, I say I believe in the American system. I don't want to take sides." He handles letters and autograph requests, the latter increasing after The Squire has made a television appearance because, he admits, it is evidence that he is still alive. "They say, 'I thought that guy was dead,'" Sarazen said.

Of the current crop of golfers, Sarazen enjoys watching Greg Norman the most. He also admires Corey Pavin, a man of similar stature who proved this year that he also knows what to do with a 4-wood. But Sarazen most enjoys watching televised senior golf. He is a little bit more familiar with that cast of characters, and they seem to play faster. Sarazen always champed at the bit when he played, and he believes everyone else should, too. He is uncertain whether he will attend the Masters next spring, when he will be 94. "That's a long ways off," he said.

Sarazen's life has been so long and so rich, it longs for something to tie it together. That would be the Marco Island phone book. Gene Sarazen is listed, the only Sarazen in its pages, just as he had diagrammed those many years ago when he picked a name that sounded like a golfer. Even a double eagle disappears into the dark, but how wondrous the ride.

GREG COUCH

What Might Have Been

FROM THE WICHITA EAGLE

"I REMEMBER BACK IN THE SUMMER of '93 . . . or maybe it was '94
. . . when I played Mats Wilander, who used to be the number one
tennis player in the world. That's right, number one in the world.

"It was a tournament in Connecticut, and we split the first two
sets. We get to the final set, and I'm up 5–3. I get a couple of match
points, but he hits some incredible shots to hold serve. You should
have seen these shots!

"By the way, he was one of the nicest guys on the tour. I got to
know him pretty well. He invited me to his house for his birthday
party once, and the next day we went golfing.

"Anyway, it's 5–4, my serve. And I get some more match points.

"Understand, there are ten thousand people in the stands. Half
are yelling, 'MATS! MATS!' the other half yelling, 'BUFF! BUFF!'

"I go to the back of the court to towel off my grip, but really it's
because I have chills. And the excitement . . . and my adrenaline is
pumping. So I'm standing there taking all this in and thinking,
'This is just about everything I've ever dreamed of.'

"A world champ, a big stadium, everyone screaming. And here I
am, one point from winning. Me, little Buff Farrow of Wichita,
Kansas.

"Then I hit my serve, chip a backhand down the line and come
to the net. He tries a passing shot with his forehand, and . . .

"It goes into the net. Game, set, match. I win.

"The greatest feeling I've ever had."

*

Someday, Buff Farrow may willingly tell stories like that, about his glory days in tennis. For now, you have to dig them out of him.

They are buried under the ones he tells most, of a career ruined by bad luck, bad timing and bad decisions. And by maybe his greatest betrayer of all.

His body.

Ten years ago, as a senior at Wichita Southeast, Farrow was the number two–ranked junior player in the nation. He went on to play number one for UCLA.

UCLA! And he advanced to the semifinals of the NCAA tournament. He was one of the fastest players in the world, had a big serve and strong, reliable groundstrokes. As a pro prospect, he couldn't miss.

But he did.

He never made the singles draw at the U.S. Open. Never made it at Wimbledon. And never was ranked higher than number 205 in the world.

"You can't look back and think about it," he said. "It would be too painful. I just wouldn't be able to function."

He does look back, though.

Today, at 28, he works for Omni Centers in Wichita, selling pagers and cellular phones, and managing three office buildings. He retired from tennis just eight months ago, but is so far removed from the game that when you ask what he thought of Chang's victory over Agassi the other day, he says, "Chang beat Agassi?"

Ask for the high point of his career, and he won't tell about his match with Wilander. Instead, he'll stall, squirm, fidget and struggle to dust off the memories.

Ask for the low point, and you'll hear one story after another. He tells of trying to have his rackets strung the night before a match in Brazil. The stringer boycotted the tournament, leaving Farrow with just two usable rackets.

He won the first set and was leading in the second when he broke strings in both rackets.

"So I played with broken strings," he said. And lost.

There was a tournament in the Caribbean where he got sick. They took him to a clinic in Jamaica and made him wait four hours before a doctor saw him.

"Then, finally, they put me on a wooden table and told me I had kidney stones and they needed to operate right away," he said. "I was like, 'No, no, no, no, no.'"

Good thing. It turned out he didn't have kidney stones at all but had contracted a parasite. He played the next few tournaments with severe stomach pain. And on a trip to the Australian Open, he had a headache that got worse and worse and WORSE.

"I thought my head was going to explode," he said. "I was pacing up and down the aisle on the plane. We had a stop in Los Angeles, and I got off the plane and said I needed to see a paramedic."

The blood vessels in Farrow's ear had burst; he was unable to fly for several days. Not only did he miss the Australian Open, but he also was unable to fly home.

These are the stories Farrow tells. For now, they're the ones he feels define his career.

"I've had players on the tour come up to me and say, 'I thought if anyone was going to make it, you were. What happened?'" he said. "I don't have an answer for them."

"One time, I'm sitting at home doing nothing when the phone rings.

"'Buff?' the voice says. 'This is John McEnroe.'

"He wants to know if I'd like to come out to his apartment in New York for a few days and practice with him. I had gotten to know him some when I was picked as a practice player for the Davis Cup team. I practiced with him, and with Andre Agassi.

"In fact, McEnroe and I played practice sets against Ken Flach and Robert Seguso, the number one doubles team in the world.

"We won.

"You know what they used to say about McEnroe: Who's the best doubles team in the world? McEnroe and whoever his partner is.

"Anyway, I figure the chance to go to his place and practice is probably something I shouldn't pass up. So I go to New York, and the first day we're playing at Central Park, and he kicks my, uh, butt. He wins the first set something like 6–2, then goes up 2–1 and stops playing.

"Just stops.

"We walk back to his place together and he chews my butt out the whole way. For twenty blocks. Nobody in my life has chewed me out like that. He makes me feel like I'm the worst player in the world.

"He says, 'I'm not even putting any pressure on you. What are you doing? You're not even making me hit one volley.'

"Berates me the whole way. And there's nothing I can do. We get back to his apartment and I don't even want to come out of my room.

"The next day, we go out again. I beat him 7–5 in the third."

Farrow tells the story about McEnroe only to show how things went wrong in his career. He tells how he had been on the Wichita Advantage TeamTennis championship team just before McEnroe called. Then, after practicing with him, he was at the top of his game.

He went back to Brazil, planning to play a series of events. He breezed through the qualifying rounds and the first two rounds of the main draw of the first tournament. He was in the quarterfinals, needing only one more win to qualify for the whole series.

In the big match, he won the first set, took a lead in the second, then fell and hurt his shoulder.

"I had to serve underhanded the rest of the time," he said. "I actually held serve once, and got up 3–0. But the guy came back. He won 7–6, and went up 1–0 in the third. By then, I was just wasting his time."

So Farrow defaulted the match.

You see, he'll tell you, here he was, playing well. And then something happened.

Again.

A broken foot, a bad back, a blown-out shoulder, a ruptured inner ear, a parasite.

"I'm burned out on talking about the injuries," he said. "I hate it when people blame injuries all the time, but it's just like, 'Damn.'

"The first person it has to fall onto is me. Me, and just bad luck."

Bad timing, too. Today, the nation's number two junior is likely to have big-dollar sponsors. And the National Team helps top juniors with coaching, expenses, and entries into tournaments' main draws.

In Farrow's day, just ten years ago, none of that was available. But he knows he wasn't just the victim of circumstances.

He blames himself for not realizing the importance of the business side of the sport. He didn't promote himself, didn't push sponsors for financial help, didn't hire an agent.

He also didn't travel to tournaments in countries such as Russia and Nigeria, which have few good players. That would have made it easy to advance in tournaments and gain a higher ranking.

"If I was to go out again," he said, "I'd treat it as a business instead of just a fun game."

"Bjorn Borg, John McEnroe, Mats Wilander, Jimmy Connors — all the guys I idolized when I was little. I can call them friends.

"Well, Connors and I aren't super friends, but we get along. We do now, anyway. I met him when I was at UCLA. He came up a few times and asked if I wanted to practice with him. It would be a hundred degrees, and he would run around like a machine, the whole time wearing a sweater.

"Meantime, I'd be dying.

"But when I was with Wichita in TeamTennis, we played his team in Los Angeles, and I had a bunch of friends in the stands. They were heckling him, and right during the match he runs up into the stands and starts threatening them. 'After the match. You and me.' That kind of stuff. So he comes back to the court, steamed, and we finish our set.

"I win, 5–1 in the tiebreaker.

"He didn't talk to me for a year after that."

The end of Farrow's tennis career took a year to unfold. It's the story that haunts him most.

It started in Los Angeles in late 1993. He had to move when the owners of the home he was housesitting returned.

Meantime, he had a sprained ankle that wasn't healing. He decided to move back to Wichita temporarily and stay with his parents.

"Then my girlfriend broke up with me," he said. "Oh yeah, and there was The Snowball Fight."

Some of his friends tried to lure him into The Fight, but with his history of injuries, he didn't want to get involved.

"Then, one guy nailed me in the eye with a snowball," he said. "I tried to get out of the way, and as I ducked, I sprained my knee."

Four months later, in March of last year, the knee had healed. So he decided to go to Oklahoma City to practice with a friend.

But there was a snowstorm that day, and someone ran into his car on the expressway, all but totaling it.

"All the windows were busted out," he said. "And my side mirror was on my lap."

At some point, you realize the gods are against you. Farrow was beginning to wonder. But he didn't want that to beat him. Talent overcomes.

Doesn't it?

So in the fall of last year, he decided to give it another try. He would play a tournament in Schenectady, New York, and then try again for the U.S. Open.

In the first round of qualifying in Schenectady, he won the first set 6–2. He was up 2–0 in the second, when he ran wide for a forehand.

"I felt a little twinge in my back," he said.

By the next point, that twinge had turned into full-fledged pain, sucking the breath out of him. He could barely move. But he kept playing. This was his last stand.

Then he lost the second set. The pain was stabbing him. He had no hope. Pain won; Farrow defaulted.

That's how his career ended.

He spent the next few days in bed, drove to the U.S. Open but still wasn't physically able to play qualifying. He asked for a wild card, didn't get one and went home.

That was a Wednesday. On Monday morning, he showed up for work at Omni in a coat and tie.

How much do you have to accomplish to be a success? Farrow said he doesn't have a lot of money. He doesn't have a deal with Nike or a series of TV commercials.

But he played number one for UCLA and had his education paid for. He traveled the world and took his shot at the tour for more than five years.

He went three sets with Jim Courier, played Stefan Edberg on TV, beat MaliVai Washington, lost a close one to Todd Martin.

He beat Mats Wilander in front of thousands of fans. John McEnroe invited him to his apartment to practice. Jimmy Connors charged his friends in the stands and didn't speak to him for a year.

At 28, he is armed with a lifetime of stories.

"It's tough for me to appreciate a lot of the things I did," he said. "I'm comparing my results with, say, John McEnroe's.

"It might take ten years before I realize, 'Hey, I beat Connors. How many people could do that?' I'm hoping in ten, fifteen years I'll say, 'I did pretty damn well.'"

For now, he has to concentrate on business. His father, who also works for Omni, helped him get the job. But he's quick to say he started at the bottom, doing everything from white collar work to grunge work.

"I started out wearing suits and ties," he said. "But after a while, when the tie gets caught in the toilet while you're plunging it, well . . ."

He doesn't know if this will lead to a career, but he has passed up tennis pro jobs at posh clubs. He wants to show he can make it without tennis.

Still, there are two rackets on the floor next to his bed. He picks them up occasionally, swings them, and dreams about what could have been.

What should have been.

"I like to think in the back of my mind that I could come back," he said. "Maybe I could."

He has been on the courts only three times since September. He helped out his coach, Mervyn Webster, by hitting balls with wheel-chair athletes. He practiced once before that.

And he was invited to play in a pro-am in Tulsa this month. A day of tennis, golf and country club life sounded pretty good to a working stiff, so he agreed to play.

He called a friend and asked to practice. They hit for half an hour and everything felt great. Then Farrow tossed the ball and hit his first practice serve in months.

And his back went out. He left the court, went home and withdrew from the pro-am.

MAT EDELSON

Cal on the Verge

FROM BALTIMORE MAGAZINE

AT 4:17 P.M. ON A BEAUTIFUL JUNE DAY, Baseball's Reluctant Messiah arrives in the cramped visitors' clubhouse at Toronto's Skydome. Rookie Gregg Zaun, who has been playing air guitar, suddenly takes notice. As Cal Ripken strides powerfully past Zaun, the tenderfoot major leaguer looks up. Ripken traverses the room, and Zaun's eyes lock on the superstar shortstop's back, as though he's taking a mental Polaroid.

Cal. Cal Ripken. And me. On the same team. Cool.

With the air of an efficient CEO, Ripken approaches the small sign-in table. He thrusts out his left elbow, balls his fist to check his watch, and signs a check-in sheet to begin his 2,067th straight day at the office.

Changing from a natty brown sports coat and blue turtleneck into a uniform that hugs his Atlas-like physique, Ripken dreads his day's first appointment — the ritualistic press conference. He'd rather stitch a baseball with his teeth than talk about himself, but fourteen reporters are anxiously awaiting a chance to gnaw at the corners of his personal world.

At 4:49 — four minutes after the press conference's scheduled start — Ripken emerges into the visitors' dugout to a blast of TV lights. His eyes catch the light and reflect a surreal electric blue. As with dad Cal Sr., Junior's dress uniform makes him look alarmingly perfect from head to toe: His face is shaven as clean as a baby's butt; his cleats look spit-shined.

During the first volley of warm-up questions, Ripken meets each inquisitor with a steady gaze, his answers delivered *sotto voce*. Once his hands hint at self-consciousness, especially when he finishes a drink and drops the paper container.

He's asked if he has special plans for the day he breaks Lou Gehrig's consecutive games streak — exactly the sort of question Cal's dad taught him to duck. "I'm someone who doesn't look too far ahead," says Junior, his left thumb and forefinger slowly digging into his smooth right palm. "I'm thinking about tonight's game. That's my only way to protect myself, to go out and do all the things I've done these years. Plain and simple. I don't know any other way of dealing with it."

As the questions pile up, Cal's hands discover the small cord that runs from the tiny mike pinned onto his chest, across his right thigh, and into a briefcase which feeds sound to the electronic media. He's jostling the cord lightly when a Toronto broadcaster breaks protocol. "Regarding your own privacy, you've talked about going to the Coke machine in the hotel at midnight and somebody came out from behind the machine and asked for your autograph . . . How 'bout the assault on your privacy? Has that changed you at all?"

The question touches on the down side of life inside "The Streak" — mounting security issues and Cal's vanishing private self. Ripken stares for a moment, his lips slightly parted. His right hand, plugged directly into his nervous system, is now mauling the mike cord, threatening to dislodge it from the black box that's going to deliver his thoughts across Canada.

Any other player might vent at a moment like this, but that's not Cal. When pressed, he typically reaches for his father's bits of working class wisdom: You do your job quietly and without complaint about the inherent responsibilities. "I'm a private person," Junior says finally, "but I recognize that when you're in the public [eye] and out here playing baseball, you have to be more of a public person."

The awkward moment is about to break. Somewhere, deep in the bowels of Skydome, someone has pushed the switch to open the three-piece roof for the game. Sun pours in, making a beeline for Ripken. He glances up, his attention drawn to the field of play. On his right, his teammates are emerging to begin their work day. After fielding one more question, Baseball's Reluctant Messiah excuses himself. "Thank you," he says politely, untethering himself from the mike and the media.

It's time for Cal Ripken Jr. to do his life's calling. It's time to play ball.

Understand this about The Streak, Cal Ripken's nearly completed pursuit of baseball's supposedly unbreakable record, the 2,130 consecutive games played by New York Yankee Lou Gehrig: the players and owners see it as a beacon shining through the dust still swirling around the game they blew up with last year's strike. The chorus coming from the Commissioner's office goes something like this: *Cal, Cal, he's our man, if he can't save baseball, nobody can!*

To the powers that be, The Streak touches on everything that's good about baseball. It is the American work ethic captured in freeze-frame, a shining example of loyalty and purity of purpose. It's little boys with runny noses spitting into their gloves at twilight while Coach Dad tirelessly belts out grounders. Or so the mawkish mythology goes.

Only in this case, all that romantic father-and-son working-class-values stuff is completely, unavoidably true.

So maybe it makes complete sense that baseball is turning to Cal Ripken Jr. for deliverance.

Hey, Cal. No pressure.

When 21-year-old Oriole Cal Ripken took to the field on May 30, 1982, he only had to look ninety feet for paternal support; Coach Dad occupied a secure piece of real estate hard along the third base line.

Neither of them could then fathom that a cosmic countdown to baseball immortality had begun, ETA September 6, 1995. "If someone told me years ago that I was going to play in two thousand straight games," Cal Jr. says now, "I would have told them they were crazy. It seemed impossible. Still does."

Ripken was just following in his father's footsteps, and the rules were simple. Practice endlessly. Play hard. Do your job right. "It's just as easy to do something right as it is to half-ass it," says Cal Senior, who spent a lifetime playing, coaching and managing in the Orioles organization.

The elder Ripken was one of the game's toughest warriors in his time. He treated his on-field coaching box like his private office, reserved strictly for baseball business. That became abundantly

clear during the 1979 World Series, when Rip Senior stomped
the Pittsburgh Pirate mascot for stepping on his turf. He threatened the Philly Phanatic with similar treatment if the mascot didn't
confine his antics to the stands.

Cal Senior's gospel was called The Oriole Way, and Junior became his finest disciple. Both of them espoused the cardinal princi-
ple that's made the Baltimore Orioles baseball's winningest team
over the last thirty-four years: *Every move you make, every ground ball
you take, every bunt you fake, you do for the team.*

Junior hasn't forgotten, even amidst the distracting occupational
hazards of contract negotiations. When he signed his $30 million
contract just before a game in 1992, the golden boy glanced at his
watch and bolted from the Orioles' third-floor boardroom in the
Camden Yards warehouse; he didn't want to be late for pregame
stretching.

But the Orioles Way also dictates that the job isn't finished when
the game is over. Senior carefully weaned his son on the idea that
baseball feeds on support from fans and the media. Even while
Junior was still a kid, his father's clubhouse was always open to the
press.

And Junior will never forget how O's great Brooks Robinson
placed the fans on a pedestal. "He was genuine in all his dealings,"
says Junior today. "He always had time for me. I picked up on that
and it impressed me. Outside of my dad's influence, he molded a
lot of who I am."

Now you can watch Junior coming out after games in uniform,
patiently signing Oriole paraphernalia late into the night, a solitary
white-clad figure indulging hundreds of fans. "A simple answer to a
simple problem," he says of these marathon autographings. And he
feels the same way about the pregame press briefings on the road.
"I'd still prefer not talking about [The Streak]," he says. "But I
found that, by talking about it the first day in a city, it minimizes
how much you have to talk about it. You talk about it for fifteen to
twenty minutes, you get good at it, and then for the next three days
it goes away. That's a freedom I like."

"I'm just a ballplayer," Ripken typically says of himself, eternally
expressing wonder at the attention surrounding The Streak, as if
he fails to truly comprehend that he's about to break the mother of
all sports records. For in The Streak, beneath the considerable lay-

ers of hype, is everything that both Cal Ripkens believe in. It is
a record caked with sweat and sacrifice, rooted in a single ideal
shared by father and son. "If you do things right, good things happen," says Cal Senior.

Can such a prosaic wisdom really be the stuff of greatness?

The old man's still at it at 59, coaching wannabe major leaguers. It's
a hazy, damp June summer morning, and the muddy baseball diamond on the Mount Saint Mary's campus looks more like a field of
cream than a field of dreams. It's so hot that even the birds have
taken the day off. But not Cal Ripken Sr.

Even in the oppressive heat, Senior cuts a military figure, a white
polo shirt starched onto his wiry five-foot-eleven-inch, 170-pound
frame. In a voice roughened from years of smoking Luckies, Senior
instructs a group of teenagers attending his annual week-long baseball camp. Standing near the entrance to the third base dugout,
Senior hikes up a pair of fine blue slacks, hunches slightly and goes
up on the balls of his feet. Three slightly goggle-eyed kids watch as
he demonstrates the right way to lead off first base. "You take two or
three steps off first," he growls, the weathered lines in his face
coming together like a country road map. "Now, as the pitch is
going to home, you start shuffling further off. When you shuffle off
you come down on your right foot" — Senior whacks his right thigh
for emphasis — "at the time the ball is reaching home plate. If the
ball goes in the dirt, then you keep on going."

Fifteen feet away, the Ripken family matriarch sits in the dugout
watching the demonstration. Vi Ripken's attention is focused on
the knee Senior dips within inches of the moist dirt. She shakes her
head. "I don't know why he wears those pants!" she laughs.

For 40 years, this has been the Ripken Way — Senior teaching
baseball, Vi providing comic relief and minding the store. It is the
world in which Cal Ripken Jr. was raised.

In the book *Cal Ripken, Jr., Quiet Hero*, author Lois Nicholson uncov-
ered a sixth-grade autobiography that Junior had penned. "My
father's occupation, baseball, requires a lot of travel," he wrote.
"Before I was a year old, we journeyed to Daytona Beach, Florida; Thomasville, Georgia; Little Rock, Arkansas; Leesburg, Florida; and Rochester, New York."

At the beginning of each season, mom Vi would pack the trailer with her four kids in tow and drive to Senior's latest managerial assignment. It was a baseball life, fun yet grueling, and, on $400 a month, hardly glamorous. "We managed to pay the bills, but we didn't save a lot," says Vi.

Vi and Rip (her nickname for Senior) raised their kids strictly, just as they were raised. Both came from humble, Harford County stock. Vi recalls accompanying her dad on late night oil burner calls. Rip's parents owned a gas station and grocery store. "Just because you felt bad, it didn't mean you didn't go to work," he says. "Mom was like that. Dad was like that."

Years later, Junior saw this credo at work. He was helping his dad, who was hand-cranking an old snowplow. The crank flew off, leaving a gash in Senior's head. Out came a bandana; on went a butterfly bandage. Senior finished his neighbor's walkway.

Rip's father died when he was just a youngster. With two older ballplaying brothers off in military service, he grew up in a hurry. "It was mother and I, and I became the man of the house at nine," he says.

His lifeline became baseball. "Rip was just as married to baseball as he was to me," says Vi of her high school sweetheart. "I'd like to be conceited and think that our marriage meant more. But I never tested it."

Rip recalls hitting pop-ups to himself when he was four. He went on to star at Aberdeen High (just as his namesake son would do a generation later). Senior signed with the Orioles in 1956, and when his catching arm crapped out in the minors, he turned to managing.

Like his father before him, Rip treated his occupation with respect, and demanded the same of his children as they went from baseball town to baseball town. Rip's team had a dress code, and so did his kids. No jeans. No tennis shoes.

"You didn't look like a ragamuffin, or wear sandals at certain times," recalls Cal Jr. He's relaxing on a black leather "players only" couch in the Orioles' spacious clubhouse, waiting to get his ankles taped before a game. His reminiscences are barely above a whisper. "You had to wear a shirt at dinner time. Sometimes on hot summer days, when you were out playing in the pool and you'd come in for a cookout, the last thing you wanted to do was change clothes. But there were certain rules."

The dinner topic was usually baseball. Senior would pontificate

on the seventy-three ways to turn the double play, and the kids
would act up. "He used to get so mad," says Vi. "[He'd say] 'Listen
to *me!*' and *bam!*" — Vi slams her hand down on an imaginary table
— "a fork would go flying. They'd do it just to make him mad."

All, that is, except Junior. "The conversation would start, and it
would be all baseball, baseball, baseball," recalls brother Billy, now
playing for Cleveland's top minor league team. "Some of us, we'd
basically say 'Uncle!' We'd had enough. But Cal could always take
more of it. He was completely interested the whole way through."

Junior even mimicked his dad's body language. "Rip would be
talking to somebody," recalls Vi, "with both his hands in his back
pockets. And there was Cal, a few feet away, just listening, with both
his hands in *his* back pockets."

Junior admits he first went to his dad's baseball clinics just to
have precious time alone in the car with him. It soon turned into
much more. In baseball, father and son found the outlet for their
overcharged competitive juices. "I guess you could say I was a fierce
competitor," says Rip, the remark causing a sudden commotion in
the living room of their Aberdeen house.

"You *guess?*" Vi shoots back.

"I went out and played hard," he returns. "That's the only way to
play the game."

Junior sometimes took his games a little *too* seriously. He once
bloodied his head celebrating a checkers win. Cheated his grandma
at canasta. Stole Monopoly money. "We played in a soccer league
that basically disbanded because we were fighting every team,"
laughs his brother Fred. "More often than not, [Cal] threw the first
punch."

Somehow, over time, baseball began to absorb Junior's temper.
Vi tells of a school field trip she chaperoned to Fort McHenry. On
the way back, the bus traversed Baltimore Street, and the kids went
nuts as they checked out The Block. Vi had a tongue lashing all
ready for Cal, but when she turned around there he was . . . study-
ing his baseball cards.

And baseball would continue to help Junior stay on the straight
and narrow. "When I was 11 or 12, everyone goes through a summer where they smoke cigarettes," he says. "We were returning
bottles for change, then going to the machines to buy cigarettes. All
of a sudden, out of nowhere, I made up my mind that I wasn't going

to do it anymore, and the reason was that I wanted to be a baseball player, and smoking was not good for baseball players. A lot of choices thereafter I was always able to ask myself 'Is this good, is this bad, and how will it affect my baseball?' If you have a good background on what is considered good and bad, you'll make pretty decent choices, and if you really focus on something you want bad, you'll know the consequences of your choices."

Slowly, Cal picked up the work habits — much of the time through osmosis — that would propel him through The Streak. Senior would lecture a group of kids or one of his minor league teams and Junior was there, soaking it all up.

In 1977, Rip — then a coach with the Orioles — had a rare opportunity to watch his son play for Aberdeen High. One play jumped out at Senior: Cal ranged far to his right at shortstop, setting his feet properly in anticipation of receiving the ball, then grabbing it, shifting his weight flawlessly and slinging the ball to first to get the out. It was textbook perfect. When Rip had to leave in the fourth inning to get down to Memorial Stadium, he passed his son on the bench.

"Where'd you learn to make that play?" asked Senior.

"You taught me," said Cal.

"No, I didn't."

"Yes, you did. At a clinic in Rochester. That's the way you instructed the infielders."

By Cal's junior year, his burgeoning talent caught the eyes of pro scouts, one of whom shared his last name. "I was very much aware of his interest," says Senior. "But with my background," — he's scouted thousands of players — "I didn't pay attention to his skills as far as going into professional baseball until he became a junior in high school. As a junior, I took Cal down to [Memorial] Stadium. I'd throw to him, and he'd stick that ball up there in the seats. He showed me the tools that you needed to go into professional baseball."

Like his son, Senior is shy of glorying in the accolades those tools have wrought. The only time Vi remembers Senior acknowledging his son's growing importance was way back in The Streak's first year, 1982, when Cal won Rookie of the Year. The night after the award was announced, Junior was on *The Today Show,* and the phone in the Ripken home didn't stop ringing.

Vi turned to her husband. "Rip, I don't understand this attention. It's his job. Am I wrong, or is he that good?"

The words passed quietly from Rip's lips. "He's that good."

It is a comment only an old, irreverent friend would make. "Fifty-nine more games to go!" shouts Minnesota Twins outfielder Kirby Puckett, spotting Cal Ripken in the catacombs between clubhouses under Camden Yards. Ripken's just finished filming a Nike commercial in the stands, to be aired the night of the All-Star game. Puckett, like Ripken a perennial All-Star, is filming next. The two close within arms' distance, the game's tallest shortstop in history towering over the five-foot-nine-inch fireplug. "Fifty-nine more games, man. Then you get a day off!"

Puckett is all laughs; Ripken is slightly aghast.

But such verbal jousting is increasing as Ripken closes on Gehrig. Opponents stopping at second base this year usually toss a quick "good luck" or "hang in there" in Cal's direction. "They've gotten more serious about The Streak than I'd like," says Ripken.

Though there *is* comic relief. In a recent game against Kansas City, rookie David Howard slid hard into second, colliding with Ripken as Cal completed a double play. "The next day I'm walking past their bullpen," says Cal, "and a few of them said they told Howard 'Do you know what you were *doing?* You can't run into *him!*'"

"If you asked a hundred major league players which player they most admired, a hundred out of a hundred would say Cal Ripken," says *Sports Illustrated*'s Tim Kurkjian, who has covered baseball for fifteen years.

Ripken's peers find his consistency mind-boggling. "A lot of players talk about [The Streak]," says Boston's oft-injured slugger Jose Canseco. "I don't know how he does it. I've been on the [Disabled List] so many times. I pray to stay off the DL. Some people, injuries just follow them. . . . Cal's blessed. He's got an angel."

Heavenly assistance aside, baseball insiders are generally even more impressed with Ripken's professionalism: he never misses a practice, never puts down a teammate, never humiliates an opponent. He signs endless autographs, plays nearly flawless defense and leads like a dignified general on the field and in the clubhouse.

Playing shortstop only adds to his luster. Next to catcher, it's the game's most physical position. Full of twists, lunges, dives and the occasional enemy moose who barrels into second base to break up a double play. Fortunately, as author George Will notes, "Cal's built like a piece of Stonehenge." At six feet four inches, 220 pounds, Ripken resembles a linebacker more than a traditional welterweight shortstop.

The extra heft may help him take a beating well. "If he gets hit by a pitch," says O's trainer Richie Bancells, "he'll have a bruise there at the time, but then it's totally gone the next day."

Then again, such resiliency may be in the genes. Veteran coach Elrod Hendricks recalls a line drive during batting practice smashing into Senior's eye, instantly ballooning his face. "It got huge," says Hendricks. "But he refused to sit. He coached that game. The next day the bruise was down, the day after it was gone. I was like 'Hey, New Guy!'"

Their peers also see both Ripkens as superior baseball thinkers. For about 150 pitches per game, Junior performs a high-speed analysis worthy of a NASA computer. He reads his catcher's signals, relaying to the infielders what pitch is coming for positioning purposes. With a runner on first, he'll shield his face with his Rawlings glove, look at the second baseman and either widely open his mouth or purse his lips just before the pitch — a signal that tells who covers second base if the runner tries to steal. All of it plays into the alchemy of a game that Ripken is tenaciously determined to brew in his favor.

Such intensive game-thinking might turn a mere mortal's brain to putty. Yet Cal's mind even stays in overdrive when he's off duty. He and teammate Brady Anderson sometimes play a game they call Mind Trap. "It has lots of mathematical quizzes," says Anderson, "like, 'In two years, a person will be twice as old as he was three years ago.' I'll figure it out in my head, but he'll figure out the *equation*, so he can figure out any age [given that problem.] That's him."

Beyond simply thinking fast, Cal's sheer knowledge has helped him keep The Streak alive. Knowing where players hit means he's rarely out of position, certainly a factor in injuries. Knowing their speed saves his arm; a Ripken throw usually beats the runner by only a step.

"Does he do that on purpose?" an umpire once asked.

Absolutely. Ripken's seen shortstops like Boston's Rick Burleson burn out their arms by throwing every ball hard to first.

Only once has Iron Cal looked into the eyes of a possible melt-

down. Ripken sprained his knee in the O's infamous 1993 brawl
against Seattle. The fracas came *this* close to ending The Streak.
"That was the only time he and I ever sat down and said 'It may be
today,'" recalls then-manager Johnny Oates.

To craft the perfect attendance record at work, you need to keep
family matters at home. For the most part, Cal Ripken Jr. has been
able to do that. Some of his distractions have been routine, others
more serious. Son Ryan was considerately born on an off-day, but
wife Kelly went through three years of mysterious medical scares
before doctors diagnosed her Graves disease in 1987. Caring for his
wife and juggling the demands of his job was quite a challenge, "but
every time I went to a new doctor, Cal was there. He hung in there,"
says Kelly.

Eventually, even Cal's work ethic became a distraction. When Cal
Senior came to the O's helm in 1987, his son hadn't missed an
inning in five years — over 8,000 innings. The press was going
bonkers; Senior wasn't so thrilled. He thought the media circus
posed a threat to his son's performance and silently began wondering if he should pull the plug. He stopped wondering in Toronto
that September 14, when a throng of reporters made it nearly
impossible for Junior to get to the locker room to change his uniform. That night, Senior summarily benched Junior in the eighth
inning of a blowout loss.

Four hundred and seventy miles away in their Cockeysville townhouse, Kelly Ripken was watching. "I was thinking, 'Who took him
out of the game? His *dad* took him out?! What's going on? *Has his
father lost his mind?!*"

But in retrospect, Kelly says now, "It was the right thing to do. I
asked Cal if he knew ahead of time. He said, 'No, Dad didn't want
to give me all this time to think about it. He just said 'You're out.'
Cal was stunned. He didn't like sitting there. He wasn't angry, just
stunned."

The anger would come five years later, for completely different
reasons. After the 1992 season, Senior was fired as an O's coach,
and brother Billy was released. All this came within four months of
Junior's August birthday signing of a $30 million contract, a deal
that then-owner Eli Jacobs insisted on wrapping up while the season was going on. The timing of the events shook the Ripken clan.

"He was upset. He didn't know what to make of it," says Kelly of Cal's reaction. "He didn't want to think the bad thought: 'Gosh, was this all intentional?' It was like, 'Nah, it couldn't be.'"

Vi Ripken confronted the same question. "Of course I am bitter. You go through some doubts. They went through this big hoopla of insisting on signing [Cal] before the season was over. You always wonder. Was this 'Let's get [Cal] out of the way so we can do [with Senior and Billy] what we want to?'"

For thirty-seven years, Senior had given his heart to the game and his soul to the Orioles. When he was fired as manager only six winless games into the '88 season, he accepted the decision without public complaint, returning as a coach the following year. But this proposed demotion — the Orioles offered Senior a minor league assignment — was too much. Cal Ripken Sr. retired. The Orioles? They gave him a one-page farewell.

"It was like the end of a marriage," says Vi. If so, the divorced partners have kept a wary distance. Cal Senior hasn't been back to Camden Yards since the day he cleaned out his locker. When Billy signed with the Texas Rangers, it was one of baseball's beautiful coincidences that Texas was to play the 1993 Camden Yards home opener. "I really wanted to go to the game, but Rip wouldn't go," says Vi Ripken. "I wanted to put on a Texas cap and walk through and wave at everybody. But we were sitting at the kitchen table, watching the opening ceremonies, and when they announced Bill, and that standing ovation, I cried. [The tears] kept coming."

Cal still feels the hurt. "Baseball in the early stages of my life took my dad away. Then baseball gave that access back, and I took that for granted. When it was taken away again, you realize how much you miss it, and that it's not normal. You could turn to your dad if you needed some help in a parental way. Or if it was too sensitive, you have your brother. I miss them being here. I miss the access to my dad," says Ripken.

Through it all, Ripken has played on. "Your performance is under scrutiny every day," he told the *Sun* in 1992. "You're considered a professional and that's what you do. Everyone has their life to live with their own individual problems, but you're supposed to come out and be able to separate it."

In this era of whining millionaire players, Ripken is a throwback to his father's time, evoking praise even from hardened baseball veterans of yore, men with sun-worn faces and cleats discolored from decades of tobacco spit. "Playing against him," says 58-year-old Toronto pitching coach Galen Cisco, "you come to love him, you might say, seeing his playing every day and wondering how in the devil anybody could ever do something like that."

And as G-day approaches, even Ripken's workplace is getting more familial. Manager Phil Regan says he can't even *think* about sitting down his shortstop. "We're not stupid," laughs the rookie manager, hinting at his job security.

Many of Cal's teammates are already angling for their place in this historical snapshot. Pitcher Mike Mussina's done the math; it'll be his turn to pitch that night. Phil Regan's got dibs on the lineup card; it's headed for his vault. Some players will bring their own camcorders — all eager to salute their unassuming comrade. "He didn't set out to break the record," says pitcher Ben McDonald. "His approach was to play every day. He didn't even think about The Streak. He learned that from Senior, who we all learned a lot from. Senior said 'Play,' and he played. Played it the way it ought to be played."

To Cal Ripken, there can be no higher compliment.

About 35 miles northeast of Camden Yards, a crowd has gathered to watch baseball's 66th midsummer classic, the All-Star game. Well, truth be told, the crew at The Bullpen on Route 40 is actually gathered to watch the American League's starting shortstop. Cal Ripken is Aberdeen's hometown hero, and many of the blue-collar types around The Bullpen's rectangular wooden bar know Ripken or his family personally. Welder Mike "Noodles" Nordell lives around the corner from Vi and Rip and was Cal's high school catcher. Bar manager Tommy Pluff laughs that he and Fred Ripken played hooky from school and drank Senior's Schlitz. Sign-painter Trish Hessler once had Billy as a substitute teacher: he spent the class chewing sunflower seeds and talking about big brother Cal.

As pints of Red Dog flow out of the taps, the postwork reverie is broken as smoothly as a play-by-play man's call each time Ripken's image floats across one of the bar's four 25-inch TVs. Cal lines a ball hard to right, a sure hit. *"AYYYYY!!!"* shout fourteen voices in unison. But wait! Right fielder Tony Gwynn sprints in . . . the ball sinking but not quick enough . . . as . . . he . . . picks it

MAT EDELSON

327

off his shoetops. . . . *"OOOOOOOoooooh"* goes the momentarily deflated crowd.

"Everybody here is proud of Cal, even more so now because he's getting the attention he deserves," says Byron Martin. "People who say he doesn't know where he's from, they don't know Cal. He knows where he's from, he knows everybody here. If he walked in here, he'd know everybody by name."

Despite his annual $6 million salary, Cal Ripken and his Streak have still managed to strike a deep chord in every lunchpail town in America. Steady Cal Ripken? He's the guy an AP photographer caught cleaning out the gutters the day after he won the Rookie of the Year award.

It is a clean, wholesome image. In hero-starved America, these days, you can take an image like that to the bank.

Cal Ripken may say he's just a baseball player, but he's not a rookie when it comes to business. After his 1991 MVP campaign, Ripken and agent Ron Shapiro formed the Tufton Group as a clearinghouse for marketing and media requests. "My goal was to put the process in place to take care of all the opportunities baseball's brought me off the field," he says.

Despite his juggernaut status at the moment, Ripken's never won a national endorsement. When compared with other megastars — Michael Jordan, for instance — Ripken's roughly $1 million a year in endorsement and licensing deals is light. That's partly because basketball simply brings higher endorsement clout, and also because Ripken is so self-effacing; in Madison Avenue's jaundiced eyes, substance never equals style. Ironman Cal's not flashy, and he's certainly not controversial, two of the more fissionable materials the ad folks like to see.

Sometimes, corporations don't quite get Cal's baseball-first mentality. Get this: Disney was hoping Cal would be willing to take off the day after he breaks the record — to star in a Disneyland parade.

Not.

Still, bigger bucks are coming. Last year, his general counsel, 28-year-old Ira Rainess, took two road trips to talk business with Cal. This year it's up to seven. The two pow-wow late at night at Ripken's hotel, which for security reasons isn't usually where the rest of his teammates stay. The meetings start at midnight and run until two-thirty. "We order room service," says Rainess. "Cal has an omelette, I have a chicken sandwich. I get a Diet Coke, he gets a Coke, and we go at it."

There's plenty to chew on. Last year, Cal had four commercial endorsements — all local and regional — and fifteen licensing arrangements. This year, Rainess figures Ripken will end up with four or five national endorsements and fifty licensing arrangements.

Then there's his signature deal. "Cal probably signs more autographs in one year than Lou Gehrig and Babe Ruth did combined in their entire careers," says Cal Senior, who rarely speaks specifically about Junior's streak or the man his son is chasing. "It used to be the kids that got the autographs, now it's a big business."

And how. Harry Bryant of The Score Board says he's visited Ripken on just about every Orioles road trip this year, horsehide and sharpies in tow. "We'll sit together from midnight until three," says Bryant, "watching HBO while he signs balls." Bryant says Ripken's autographed memorabilia is now on a six-week backlog.

In all, Rainess figures The Streak will double Ripken's annual take.

While this Cal-ification craze might initially smack of greed, Rainess points out that Ripken hasn't pocketed a penny of his off-field earnings in three years. After expenses for Tufton, much of the extra dough — over half a million dollars — has gone to the Kelly and Cal Ripken Jr. Foundation, which since 1993 has given over $150,000 to community programs, most notably The Ripken Learning Center. (Since 1988, the Ripkens have given $350,000 to the center, which last year taught 170 adults how to read.)

"Cal," says his father, "has his priorities in the right order."

Sometimes when he gets home from a hard day's work, Cal Ripken's wife can hear it in his voice. "Cal isn't one to speak freely about his emotions, and sometimes it's hard to read him," says Kelly, "but it's just the way he says 'I'm glad to be home.'"

It's been a year of pulling in the reins and circling the wagons for husband and wife. In Baltimore, nights out are out. "Because of what's going on, you're going out with everybody else. It's not 'Cal and I,' it's 'Cal, I and everybody in the restaurant,'" says Kelly.

Cocooning has included reprioritizing precious family time. As with most families, the kids come first; while the rest of the team flies between cities on a road trip, Cal will often take a detour through Baltimore to spend more time with Rachel and Ryan.

When Ripken's at home, daddy often plays school chauffeur for his six-year-old daughter. "That's their special time alone," says Kelly, "just the two of them, just like the car ride Cal used to have with his dad going to the ballpark."

Since summer break, the family spends most mornings together. Sometimes they're watching the movie *Grease* for the umpteenth time. (Cal used to sing Olivia Newton-John's part, until Rachel began to object.) Often they go for a romp in the pool. Cal hoists Ryan on his broad back and gets to play daddy, and Kelly welcomes the break. "He plays in the pool; he doesn't sit on the side and lounge. I'm taking advantage of 'Oh great, he's here, but he's leaving in an hour, so I'm gonna watch.'"

Afternoons used to be couple time, but interviews and other commitments have turned the Ripkens into ships that pass in the night. Kelly laughs that the only way she can make family decisions involving Cal is to lock him in the car, drive down a road and disconnect the cellular.

Life in the sports fishbowl occasionally tears at the couple — Kelly admits that sometimes they'll snap at each other, given that there's no real release from the unyielding media and public pressure — but the Ripkens know their moment in the sun will soon pass.

That may be why, for the first time, Cal seems to have come to peace with The Streak. Kelly gave him a word of advice in spring training. "I said 'It's a long year, but you know what? Enjoy it. Let them tell you how great you are. Normally you'd downplay it. Enjoy it, because after the fact, it's over. Let 'em think you're the greatest thing since sliced bread.'"

The words must have struck a chord.

"I used to fight the [media] notion that I was going out there playing for The Streak. I've come to a conclusion that people are going to have a strong opinion for or against," says Ripken. He's even come to a détente with those pesky press conferences, joking that they've proven to be "therapy" of sorts. "It could be a combination of my own maturity, or that The Streak's taken a turn for the positive," admits Ripken. "I think it's a positive. I've learned to come to grips with it."

Good. He's just in time to enjoy it with the rest of us.

At approximately 7:37 on the night of September 6, Cal Ripken Jr. will — rainouts and baseball deities willing — take to the field for the 2,131st straight time. The Ironman record will be Ripken's for all time, just as they said it would be with Gehrig. Over 47,000 screaming fans will surrender themselves to the moment; millions more around the world will bear witness through TV.

And there will be one face in the crowd Cal Ripken Jr. will be looking for. His father's.

Since his bitter 1992 dismissal, Senior has stayed professionally retired. The Orioles' only contact with him came last month; Peter Angelos wrote, expressing his wish that Ripken attend the record-breaking game.

Rip's anger at the O's is still evident. He attended Rex Barney's recent booksigning at the Babe Ruth Museum in the off-season only after he was assured that no member of Orioles management would be present.

Still, he shares a bond with his son that no management decision can tear asunder. "Even though he's not here, we have the ability to share baseball on a level that not too many people understand," says Cal Ripken Jr. "I can share my thoughts with him, without his witnessing something, and we've done that our whole lives."

On this night, for one moment as he stands atop the sporting world, Junior will turn to the stands, looking for one special witness. Cal Ripken Sr. says he plans to be there. "Everything I've ever done," says Senior, "I've done to help a player."

Among the thousands of cheers celebrating a job done right, their eyes will meet.

Two men. One incredible record. A monument to them both.

RICHARD BEN CRAMER

A Native Son's Thoughts

FROM SPORTS ILLUSTRATED

IT'S A STINKIN'-HOT NIGHT at the ballpark — near 100 degrees, the air is code red — and the Orioles are playing the cellar-dwelling Blue Jays. Still, it's got to be a big night: it's Coca-Cola/Burger King Cal Ripken Fotoball Night. That is, it's the sort of ersatz event that is a staple of baseball now that payrolls are fat, attendance is slim, and the game — well, no one trusts the game to be enough. These new Orioles yield to no club in the promotional pennant race. There's Floppy Hat Night, Squeeze Bottle Night, Cooler Bag Night. There's an item called the NationsBank Orioles Batting Helmet Bank, and there's the highly prized Mid-Atlantic Milk Marketing Cal Ripken Growth Poster. They are all a stylistic match for the graphics on the scoreboard that tell you when to clap or the shlub whose bodily fluids are draining into his fake-fur Bird Suit while he dances on the dugouts for reasons known only to him.

Still, as a celebration of the Hardest-Workin' Man in Baseball, the hero of this Old-Fashioned Hardworkin' Town, the Cal Ripken Fotoball is my personal favorite, perfect in every detail. There is the *F* in the name — gives it klass, and it's korrect, because there's no photo on the ball. There's a line drawing of Cal's face, with a signature across the neck. The signature is of the artist who made this genuine-original line drawing from a genuine-official photo of Cal. And then there's the plastic wrapper — says it's all Made in China. I like that in a baseball. And one key word: NONPLAYABLE. In other words, don't throw or hit it, or this fotobooger will come apart.

Hours before game time, I wanted to ask Cal about his Fotoball. I wanted to ask how it feels to be the icon for baseball and Baltimore. But he's hard to catch in the locker room. He has his locker way off in the corner, where his dad used to dress as a coach. The official-and-genuine Oriole explanation is that the corner affords him room for two lockers — one extra to pile up all the stuff fans send him. But it's also unofficially helpful that there's an exit door in that corner, and anyway it makes Cal plain hard to get to. (One day early in the season I was blocked entirely by the richly misshapen and tattooed flesh of Sid Fernandez.) And if you're lucky enough to catch Cal, you're still not home free: Even local writers — guys Cal knows — find that out. "Angle your story," he might say, without looking at the writer, his eyes still on the socks in his hand. "Yeah . . . but what's the angle?"

So the writer must explain what he *means* to write. "Cal, it's just about all the second basemen you've had to play with — you know, 30 different guys to get used to."

"No," Cal says to his socks. "Doesn't do me any good to answer that."

See, these days, just a handful of games from Lou Gehrig's record of 2,130 consecutive starts, he's playing writers like he always plays defense, on the balls of his feet, cutting down the angles: *How is this gonna come at me? Where should I play it?* Positioning (forethought, control) has always been his game. And streak or no streak, Cal still has to play the game *his way* — that is, correctly: He's got to click with his second baseman.

This new locker room defense is the only effect Cal permits himself to show as he surfs the hype wave into the record books. That and maybe some testiness toward umpires. Just a couple of nights before Fotoball, the second base ump missed Cal's tag on a runner, and for the next ten minutes obscenities and spittle flew out of Ripken's mouth. (Of course, Cal did it the right way, facing home plate while he manned his position, never turning his head, so the ump wouldn't be shown up and have to toss Cal out. Ripken, being Ripken, has to throw even imprecations correctly.)

The point is, the umps, the writers, even the Streak itself, they all get in the way of the goal — always the same goal — which is to play the game *just right*. The umps make mistakes. The writers don't care; they want controversy. Cal doesn't like controversy. And the writers take time. Cal doesn't have time, not now. He's got his wife and kids in the big country house; he doesn't get enough time with them already. He's got fans, he gives autographs — thousands of signatures. He's got press conferences at ballparks across the country and big, scheduled media hits — the *New York Times, Prime Time Live, TV Guide,* the cover of *Sports Illustrated.* He's got endorsement deals, his old ones (local hot dogs and milk) and new ones: Chevy Trucks, Coca-Cola, Nike, Franklin Glove, the Adventureland theme park, and assorted memorabilia, including a bobblehead doll. (You can't establish a deathless baseball record without a bobble-head doll.) It's not easy being an icon — when it *has to be done just right.*

And time before a game . . . well, forget it. That's sacred. That's Cal's time to prepare. He's in his routine — the silence, the planning, the discussion. And he wants to hit, take batting practice, correctly: first a bunt, then a ground ball to the right side (move that runner to third), then a fly to the outfield (bring that runner home) and then swing away, swing away, swing away. He wants to take grounders — has to take grounders — but correctly: You don't grab the ball any which way and close your mitt around it; you catch the grounder with an open glove, to get your throwing hand in. You catch it in position to throw. That's all part of catching the grounder correctly. See, Cal's dad, who taught him, has these sayings — said them all a million times — like: *If you want to play the game properly, you have to get ready to play.*

Or there's this one:

You have to know what you want to do before you can do it.

And even more often, there's this one:

Practice doesn't make perfect. PERFECT practice makes perfect.

So there's Cal on the Camden Yards ball field, trying to practice perfectly to get ready to be perfect, and I'm lurking in the dugout — *I wanna ask about the Fotoball.* That's the funny thing that happened to Cal: He landed in all this hype and distraction, the reporters and the shoe deals and about a thousand plaintive kids screaming, "Cal!" "Cal, pleeeze!" "Mr. Ripken!" "*Caaal!*" He's got hungry little Baltimore to feed with esteem. He's got Powerade and Fotoball. He's got me to deal with, and every other sideshow in the whole Hoopla Nation . . . because he was raised to pay attention to the game.

Here's the funniest thing that happened to Ripken: Now that the calendar, luck and stubbornness have made him Baltimore's hero, the team, the media and the city's nabobs have decided he's got to be a blue-collar hero.

Oh, young Cal . . . he was raised a Baltimore, you know. . . .

That's how the local song begins.

. . . So he grabbed his lunchbucket and went to work every day — the way guys do in this hardworkin' town. He did his job 13 years straight — like the fellas on the swing shift at Crown Cork 'n' Seal. . . .

Well, a workin'-class hero is something to be. But it just doesn't happen to be . . . him.

At $6 million a year, Cal Ripken Jr. lives in a house the size of a Wal-Mart, near the ninth jump of the Maryland Hunt Cup, in steeplechase country, the Greenspring Valley, along with the other rulers of Baltimore. Ripken goes to work in a chartered plane or in the Orioles' fashionably retro theme park.

And the town? Well, that's a complicated story — one that goes well beyond the Camden Yards theme park and the surrounding Inner Harbor theme park, with its rows of shoppees selling $20 T-shirts or crabs at $35 a dozen. None of that is meant for the man on the swing shift. In fact, there is no more swing shift. Crown Cork and Seal closed up its plants, like all the other big manufacturers.

The ball yard, Harborplace, the gleaming insurance and banking towers looming over the gleaming water — they were all designed (with forethought, control) to replace the blue-collar Baltimore that was crumbling like an empty row house. Or at least to distract attention: Here the rulers of the town would build the Baltimore you're *supposed* to see; they would stock it with family attractions — the shoppees, tall ships, an aquarium (Hey! How 'bout *baseball?*) . . . and plenty of parking, so the white people could jump into their cars and go back to the suburbs to sleep. They wanted the kind of place that *Good Morning America* would visit. *If you build it, Joan and Charlie will come!* And so they did! That worked like a charm. In fact, that's what they called Baltimore: Charm City.

But somehow that name never really stuck. See, the schools still didn't work, crime's a problem, taxes are murder. And even those new towers shining out there, beyond the centerfield fence, they're going empty. This town is literally shrinking up. Somehow, all the Disneyfication of the downtown didn't win for Baltimore the label that the rulers really wanted: big league. Now they've given up on the catchy nicknames. They've just mounted Cal up front, like a hood ornament, to symbolize what Baltimore's all about.

The truth is, Cal wasn't raised a Baltimore — nor even a true son of Aberdeen, Maryland, the town thirty-three miles up the highway where his parents still keep their house. When Cal was growing up, the Ripkens' home was baseball. Young Cal was raised an Oriole.

You have to understand what it meant. When Cal was growing up, the Orioles were the best club in the game. There were pennants: '66 (world champs) and '69, then '70 (world champs again) and '71. There were playoff teams in '73 and '74 and a pennant again in '79. These Orioles were stars on the mound: Jim Palmer, Dave McNally, Mike Cuellar. They were sluggers at the plate: Frank Robinson, Boog Powell. They were stars with the glove: Mark Belanger, Paul Blair . . . and for twenty-three years at third base, Brooks Robinson.

The great thing was not what they won but how they did it. This wasn't the richest club. As a business, it wasn't even good. The Orioles had to win pennants to draw a million fans. Any evening you could leave work at 7:15 and drive like a bandit through the neighborhood in northeast Baltimore that had as its centerpiece Memorial Stadium. Everybody had his own route through those tight streets. Everybody knew a kid who parked cars in his alley or his driveway. And for five bucks at the window, you could stroll through this comfy concrete pile and settle yourself to watch the greatest righthander to hit the league in thirty years, Palmer, mow down some visiting lesser lights. By midgame, if you had the wit and nerve, you could spot an empty seat in the second or third row . . . you could sit, for god's sake, a foot and a half behind the bald owner, Jerry Hoffberger, hard by the third base dugout, where it looked like Brooks was gonna dive straight into your lap for that ball. "Way to dig it out, Brooksie!" some fan would yell. Brooks would look up to see if he knew him. These were ball fans. They would hoot an outfielder out of the park if he threw some rainbow over the cutoff man's head. The Orioles were all about defense. Sometimes they made brilliant plays. But they always made the routine plays right. That was the Oriole Way.

There was actually a book. It had all the plays: where the cutoff men stood, who backed up where, all the bunt plays, the pickoff plays. . . . This was the codification of the Oriole Way. And this text was taught at every spring training and through the summer, in every ballpark throughout the organization. In Stockton, Knoxville and Elmira, they did everything the Oriole Way, down to the dress code (on the street), full uniform (on the field), batting practice *(first the bunt . . . one to move the runner over . . . one to bring the runner in . . . then swing away, swing away, swing away)*. The Orioles couldn't afford to *buy* pennants. When they had a hole, they had to fill it from the farm. But when those kids came up, they were Orioles already. The only thing manager Earl Weaver had to tell them was the curfew. On the field, they knew how to make the plays right.

And that's where the old man came in. Cal Ripken Sr. was a catcher whose playing career (1957–62) arced short of the majors. Then he was, for almost fifteen years, a coach and manager in the bushes, teaching the gospel to fledgling Orioles. For all the years of his famous son's life, Senior was preaching the Oriole Way. Living it, in fact, in Asheville, Rochester, or some other town where his wife, Vi, would rent a house and make a home for the four children during the summer. Wherever home was, the ballpark was the Ripkens' second home. Dad would set the kids to work in the clubhouse or hit grounders to them (Dad could run a perfect infield) — 100 grounders, 150, as many as they wanted — unless they started screwing around, grabbing at the ball, hotdogging throws, in which case he would pick up the ball bag and walk off. *(PERFECT practice makes perfect.)*

Cal Jr. didn't live in Aberdeen full-time till high school, in '75. (Senior didn't come up to the big club, as a coach, till '76.) But young Cal was already an Oriole. From the time he was able to read, the box score from Baltimore held names he knew — they'd been kids on his father's teams. *(Hey! Al Bumbry went 3 for 4! Junior had shined his shoes in the Asheville clubhouse!)* When Junior was drafted in '78 — and made it through the system, the Oriole Way, by '81 — he was just rejoining family.

And it *was* like family, the way the guys would go out after road games — or in Baltimore, they would babysit one another's kids, watch 'em all together in somebody's pool. Or everyone would go out to Hoffberger's house after Sunday doubleheaders: cookouts and laughter, players and ex-players, kids and wives, stadium ushers and secretaries, Weaver and the old coaches — Bamberger, Hunter, Ripken — grinning half-lit on National Bohemian beer (that was

Hoffberger's brewery), saying (like they always did), "It's great to be young and an Oriole!" And it would go from just after the game to . . . well, when the last guest left. Even on a weekday night Cal Jr. would come off the field, and there would be Dad at the table in the locker room, holding court — Senior never liked to leave too quickly after a game. And he would take apart that game, too, for a couple of hours sometimes, and you could learn some baseball. Cal Jr. liked to hang around like Dad. And even if he stayed for two hours, he'd still see guys — Palmer, Elrod Hendricks — in the parking lot, fans around their cars. Autographs were mostly for kids. When that was over, they could talk baseball.

And the baseball was splendid. In '82, Cal Jr.'s first full year, the Orioles took the pennant race to the final weekend against Milwaukee. That was the most exciting thing Junior had ever felt in his life. The next year they took it up a notch and won the pennant in the playoffs in Chicago. Attendance was sky-high. All of Baltimore was on a roll. There was a working mayor in those days — guy named Schaefer, he was kind of the Oriole Way of mayors — and he'd walk into some business in town and tell 'em, flat out, they had to buy season tickets. That's when he wasn't busy building somewhere. (Hell, he was rebuilding the whole Inner Harbor, said it was going to save the city!) It was exciting just to be there. And when the O's beat the Phillies in five games in October, and Schaefer had a parade through the streets, and the fans came out by the tens of thousands, yelling, "*Cal M-V-P, Cal M-V-P!*" . . . then everything seemed perfect. Nobody knew it was over.

No one had marked as a disaster the moment three years earlier that Hoffberger sold the team. (The new owner, attorney Edward Bennett Williams, was already whining about the tight streets around the ballpark. Fer crissakes, it took him *an hour* to get home to Washington.) No one knew the mayor was running for his last reelection; he was building his last towers, selling his last tickets. No one — certainly not Cal Jr. — knew that would be his last pennant, last Series, last parade. No one saw it was the end of the Oriole Way — not even Senior, keeper of the code — until four years later, when Williams gave him a thoroughly diminished team to manage and then fired him because he didn't win.

Sure enough, it's a big crowd for Fotoball. No surprise: Camden Yards is always near-sold-out. The field level is almost all season tickets. The club level, above that, is all bought up by businessmen who send young waitresses to fetch their crab cakes and designer beer. And it's big business in the skyboxes, where buffets and TVs are arrayed in cool darkness, behind plate glass. The rulers of Baltimore built this pleasure playground for themselves.

In the rest of the yard it's family entertainment — parents cajoling little Kim, Lee, and Ashley to keep their Fotoballs in the Oriole (promo) sports bag so they won't get cotton candy or frozen yogurt on them. It's a prosperous crowd, overwhelmingly white. The P.A. man, Rex Barney, yells his single, aged joke — *"Give that fan a contract!"* — whenever a customer catches a foul ball. There's the Bird dweeb, dancing with the ball girl down the left-field line. There's the Jumbotron in centerfield, flashing trivia quizzes (JeopBirdie) or guess-the-attendance or a picture of the player at bat, along with some cheery bio factoid: *Chris had 3 HR in one game with Columbus.* (Big deal.) The whole show is paced like a Saturday-morning cartoon: something has to happen every thirty seconds, or else.

Oh, there is a game, too.

It isn't a very good game — though Cal puts the O's on the board with a home run in the second inning. That revs the crowd for a while. They're up in their seats, rooting . . . till the third out, and then the P.A. speakers whine to life with a female voice like treacle: *Noo-body does it better.* . . . It's the theme song for the Jumbotron video on Cal: Cal hitting, Cal sliding, Cal high-fiving, Cal in the pivot, Cal as a kid, Cal with his kids, Cal getting a plaque, Cal in gauzy sunshine waving his cap. *Noo-body doezzz it bettttter. Bayyyy-bee yerrrrr the besssst!* The boys in marketing must have put that splendid tribute together. No one is rooting at all — they're just watching TV. Cal is already the favorite with all the suburban children. They wear jerseys with the big number 8 on the back and ORIOLES across the chest. (No official-and-genuine Oriole jersey, not even the road uniform, says BALTIMORE anymore. Regionalism is a Key Marketing Concept.)

Meanwhile, the O's are giving the game away — handing it over to a last-place club. On the mound Jamie Moyer has already walked in two Toronto runs. Now, two ground balls that the second baseman can't play and an error in left field turn into three more runs. The nearly 42,000 in attendance watch in murmurous passivity. They make noise when they're told to — though they did stand to

cheer for Bobby Bonilla on the occasion of his first Oriole hit; he
was o-fer his first two games. Still, everyone seems sure Bonilla will
put the O's over the top. Has to. He's worth millions! They're
pleased with the team's owner, Peter Angelos (another lawyer). *At
least he's not afraid to spend!* (And isn't it great? All they had to give up
for Bonilla was a couple of farmhands — just two of their best outfield prospects. Minor leaguers!)

Middle innings: Toronto now has six runs. It's always disturbing
to this crowd when their team of hired millionaires doesn't win.
And it's always somewhat mysterious.

The front-row box next to the dugout, right on third base, is now
held by Ripken's agent, Ron Shapiro. Those seats have a splendid
view of Toronto runners rounding third, but Shapiro couldn't be in
a better mood. He's gorgeous in his warmth — the kind of fellow
who'll reach over and hold your arm with his hand while he tells
you something nice about yourself. He's a lawyer by training, sports
agent by trade; he's the man who set up Cal's charity foundation
and created the Tufton Group, which handles demands on Cal in
this year of the Streak. As Cal's father is father to Cal's game, so is
Shapiro father to Cal's iconhood.

"To me," says Shapiro, "the bonding between a player and his
community is what it's all about." Ripken, he says, has made a
conscious choice to stay in Baltimore for his entire career. Yes, Cal is
committed to working with Baltimore. "He wants to be appreciated
for his totality as a human being . . . as a thoughtful, caring, committed and community human being." Shapiro is thoroughly hip
to the great divide in the ballpark — the family crowd, the corporate crowd — and alive to the possibilities this presents for
Cal. "Because, remember," says Shapiro, "they'll all come out for
Cal. Both constituencies." He sounds like an operative sizing up a
prime piece of political horseflesh. Politics is another of Shapiro's
games. He is the finance chairman for the current mayor's reelection campaign. Ron Shapiro is going to remain a ruler of Baltimore.

The Blue Jays have the bases loaded (again!) when their batter,
Alex Gonzalez, raps a clean hit to left . . . except it never gets
through. Ripken was moving before the bat hit the ball. He is so far
in the hole, it looks as if his weight will carry him into foul ground.
But he picks the ball on the bounce, backhand, with his body

somehow already turning, with his right hand already sweeping up to meet his glove at his hip. He is backpedaling, almost falling toward third, when he plants his big right leg, which lifts him into the air, whence he fires the ball in a white streak to second base. And the runner is out — inning over. It is the kind of play that stays in your head as a picture. At Camden Yards, no one yells. Polite applause. The fans are waiting for the next thing to happen. "Dad. . . . *Dad!* . . . DAD!" This is a kid on my left. He wears a T-shirt that says CHICAGO BULLS. His father turns. "Cal's gotta hit another home run! Dad! Can we get ice cream?"

This current mayor, guy named Schmoke, made a new slogan for the city: *Baltimore. The City That Reads.* No one knows what that's supposed to mean. But about the same time, Cal set up his own foundation and its literacy program: Reading, Runs and Ripken. Shapiro keeps everybody on the same page of the hymnal. Cal's always been willing to sing along.

Now that Blue Collar Cal's so famous across the nation, everybody's trying to pick up the tune. *Would you say there's something special about this town? Hardworkin' people?* It was one of those man-on-the-street ads, supposed to thump the tub for local Channel 11. They wanted to bill themselves as the Hard-Working News Team. Of course, it seemed like a small-minded play on Cal's streak — collusive, self-satisfied, and small-town. That's Baltimore too.

Though he'll never talk about it, Cal remembers clearly those times when the town chorus turned against him. There was '88, that awful year when his father was fired (the O's started 0–6 under Cal Sr., then Frank Robinson came in, and they lost 15 more in a row). And there was '92, when the team and the town gave up on his little brother, Billy (Cal's favorite second baseman, but of course he can't say that, either). In fact, every time Cal's hitting went south, those hardworkin' airwaves were filled with captious comment. People said Cal ought to sit down. Take a rest. Stop acting like Superman. *Stop putting his own streak ahead of the team!*

It hurt him. Confused him. In '88, when Brady Anderson joined the O's, he found Cal one day leaning alone against the left-field fence. "What's goin' on?" Brady said.

Cal just waved him away: "Not now."

Brady insisted. "No, c'mon. Tell me. What's wrong?"

Then Cal asked this near-rookie, this *kid*, "What does the Streak mean to you?"

What Cal couldn't figure was: How could they criticize *the best thing about him?* He always came to play. What was wrong with that? That's the way he was. Was there something wrong with him?

Still, he signed two contracts after that. Even in the middle of negotiations, he never made a threat to leave. That didn't have to do with Baltimore's values. It had to do with his values. He thought if you say you're willing to leave — if you declare for free agency — then you have to be willing to go. He wasn't.

And that's his real link with this town, with the people in the row houses. City councilman Martin O'Malley (who is to local politics what Cal was to baseball as Rookie of the Year) represents those old, tight streets around the silent Memorial Stadium. "People here don't care where he lives," O'Malley says. "Or how. They don't want him to be blue collar. And they're not waiting with bated breath for him to pass Lou Gehrig. You know, the city can ebb and flow. We've got racial divisions. We're best known for *Homicide* on TV. The population's at its lowest point since World War I. But number 8's still trottin' out to shortstop. People see that. He never gave up on them."

Cal does hit another home run. Two dingers on Fotoball Night — how 'bout that? But it isn't enough, not when the rest of the lineup hits nothin', and the O's give away three or four runs. Toronto 6, O's 3 — final. The Orioles have departed second place, heading south.

It promises to be a somber clubhouse scene when the writers are admitted ten minutes after the O's last strikeout. The pack makes for the manager's interview room. I am hunting Cal, still with my Fotoball, still without avail. Often after games he'll sit for a while in the lounge — players only — to talk about the game. But tonight it looks like the rest of the guys are getting dressed, heading out. Coaches, too. It is almost eleven o'clock. I watch Cal's corner. A camera crew, for mysterious reasons, is filming his locker, shining a minicam spotlight onto his shoes, his chair, his uniform shirts. (Maybe it's another Jumbotron tribute. Maybe they'll make this one scratch-'n'-sniff.)

"Check the field." This is whispered in my ear in the locker room. "He's out there. You better check it out."

I go out through the tunnel, under the empty stands. Except they aren't empty. There are thousands of people, all standing, looking down at the rail where Cal Ripken is signing Fotoballs.

Cal has one foot on the rubberized warning track, one foot on the padding of the rail. He has his own felt-tip. And he is signing — correctly, of course, down to the *Jr* and the period after his name. (Then he blows on his signature to make sure it won't smudge.) There are city cops around him and two dozen ushers to keep the crowd in line. But mostly they just stand there grinning. This is just Cal and the fans.

"Cal, would you put 'From B.J. to Kristin'?"

"Kristin with a *K?*"

"K-R-I-S-T-I-N. . . . Thanks, Cal."

"You're welcome," Cal says.

He signs their Fotoballs and then their programs — or their shirts, ticket stubs, popcorn boxes, whatever they want, as many as they want. If they want him to use their pens, he caps his and signs with theirs. (One guy's pen doesn't work, so Cal rubs the point on his palm till it satisfactorily marks up his hand.) If they don't ask him something, Cal asks them. "Favorite hat?" Cal says as he bends to sign one kid's sweaty headgear.

"It is now," says one of the cops.

Cal never lets a kid leave without a word from him. "You ready for bed?" Cal says to a yawning little girl. "I feel that way, too."

But he doesn't look ready for bed at all — stoked up is more like it, in high enjoyment. He doesn't just hold out his hand for the next ball and the next ball . . . he looks up and fixes each fan with the shock of his light blue eyes and a greeting. The cops warn him a couple of times that fans are still piling into line in the concourse — the line stretches now from the right side of home plate halfway to the left-field corner. "That's O.K.," Cal says. He keeps signing and talking.

"How'd you break your arm?" he says to a boy as he signs his cast, then his Fotoball, then his hat. "Your bike? Jumpin' a couple of cars? Or you just fell off. . . . How long you got to have it on? . . . Well, that's O.K. You can still play other games, can't you?" (The kid just shakes his head, mute with awe.)

The grown-ups, who didn't get Fotoballs, bring Ripken whatever they have. One woman hands over her shoe. "I'd like to sign it inconspicuously," says Cal, turning it over, "so you can still wear it." Says the woman: "I'll wear it." Maybe a hundred parents push kids forward and then back away, making motions of entreaty with their cameras. Each time, Cal leans in next to the kid — "Cheese," he says. ("Oh, didn't wind? Try again. Cheese and crackers.") Teenage girls are in that breathless, open-mouthed, near-tears state known to doctors as Deep Elvis. They want to kiss him. Cal demurs. They want to hug him. Cal leans in. "Not too close," he'll say. "I'm all sweaty." (They don't mind.)

At midnight it is still near 90 degrees on the field. The rest of the vast yard is silent and empty, in a strange surfeit of light. The grounds crew has finished with the mound, home plate and infield. The rest of the stands are clean and bare. Supper has long since been cleared in the clubhouse. The locker room is also empty save for a couple of attendants cleaning, putting laundry away. Still there are fans, stretched in a line down the concourse. And Cal keeps signing: "Is that Katie with an *i-e?*"

The polite lieutenant, Russell Shea, leans in behind Cal. "I'll be the bad guy, O.K.?" he says. Cal nods but keeps signing and talking. Shea calls Cal "the finest gentleman I've met, bar none — and I've been stadium commander for two years." So he lets Cal make the schedule. He leans in again: "You want anything? Cold drink?" Cal shakes his head. He is still in full uniform, his forearms shining with sweat, his ankles still taped. For most of the last hour and a half, he has stood on one leg while he propped each ball, photograph, or program on his left knee — so he could sign just right. Shea, unbidden, brings a bottle of Powerade. Cal keeps signing.

"Let me stretch out your shirt, so I can sign it right."

"Yeah, this picture's rookie year. You want me to sign on this leg?"

The way Cal describes it, he's too pumped up after a game to leave. His family's asleep . . . and the fans want so little — a picture, a handshake, a signature to remember the night. He likes it when they ask him to write their names too — or when they bring pure trash for him to sign (some lemon-ice wrapper that has been on the floor). That way, he knows: they never mean to sell it. (The one piece he won't sign is a pair of uniform pants brought down by a collector. The guy would have sold the pants for a fortune.) He likes it when fans ask if he remembers them or they bring up some name he's supposed to know. ("Do you know Pat Francis?" asks a big-haired blonde. "She useta babysitcha." Cal fixes the woman with an elfin smile. "We used to tie up our babysitters sometimes. We outnumbered 'em." And the woman is giggling.) The way Cal describes it, if he can talk with a thousand Baltimore fans, he'll find out he knows most of them. That isn't true. But it pleases him to think it's true.

It pleases him to see the excitement on their faces — and their shock. *(He talked to us! He was so nice!)* It pleases him to do this correctly. It pleases him, this power to give some bit of himself (as the kids yell to one another, as they run with their autographs: *We got Cal! We GOT CAL!*). This is a heady power: On this night or any night, at any hour, midnight or after . . . by his act alone, by his attention for one minute, by a stroke of his pen, he can give value to trash. He can make a night, or a town, feel big league. He can make even Fotoball something real.

Quarter after twelve. What he can't do is stop. Not easily. Not tonight. There are hundreds left in the concourse when Cal murmurs, "Pen's going." That means he is going — soon. But he signs a few more, till the collector with the pants shows up again. ("I didn't come to argue. Cal! Just these pictures!")

"I'm done," Cal says. He caps his pen.

"CAL! Ooooowww!" It is a moan of near-physical pain from a mother-with-son behind the collector — a kinda-cute mom, with curly brown hair. "Pleeeese, oh, god!" She's been waiting with her hyperweary kid for hours.

"I'm done," Cal says. "Sorry. I can't do any more." He is heading down the dugout steps. She is going to cry — you can see it. "But how 'bout if I give you my cap? Is that all right?"

The mother doesn't get it. She looks at her stunned son to see if that is all right. Cal ducks in the dugout and surreptitiously signs the bill. Then he pops up the steps, puts it in the kid's hands. The mother is still staring at her kid: *is it all right?*

But the kid can't look up. He is staring at this . . . *thing.* As if a meteorite had landed in his hands. Cal is already in the tunnel when the boy looks up — not at the mom but at the dark heavens — and says, "Whoa! YESSS!"

TONY KORNHEISER

He Told It Like It Was, Like Only He Could

FROM THE WASHINGTON POST

THE OLD TESTAMENT SPEAKS of the prophet Jeremiah, a right-
eous man lamenting the evil, decay and disaster around him, pre-
dicting calamity for those who won't heed his words. An arrogant
man. A scold. A crusader.

Our own Jeremiah passed away yesterday.

Sadly, we will never again hear these words: "This is How-wuhd
Co-sell, speaking of sports."

Cosell was The Key Figure in bringing sports upstairs out of the
furnished basement and into the family room. It was Cosell,
through *Monday Night Football,* who took sports from lazy weekend
afternoons into the white light of prime time, and in so doing
fastened sports on the cultural map forever. Roone Arledge may
have designed the plane, but Cosell flew it.

Television never saw anything quite like Cosell, with his toupee
and his Brooklyn Gothic puss and his unsinkable ego and his impossible vocabulary. How did he ever land in sports? With that
urban background the only thing he knew about splitting a seam
was: Afterward, you'd have to sew it. What was Cosell doing in the
same business with the jockocracy, as he called it?

Cosell took such pride in standing out like a sore thumb that he
called one of his books *I Never Played the Game* — though he sure
could talk it; he made you wonder if ABC paid by the syllable.

But his appeal wasn't just about being different. If Cosell was merely different, people would have tired of him quickly, and dismissed him. No, Cosell was one of a kind. A *TV Guide* poll named him concurrently the most liked *and* most disliked sportscaster, as if none of the others even mattered. People tuned in to see Cosell. Cosell turned a game into an event; his presence certified its importance. The next day people didn't talk about the game as much as what Cosell had said. If Cosell called someone "utterly functional," letting the phrase drip out of his tongue like battery acid, half the audience thought it was a compliment, and the other half thought it was a death sentence.

Cosell's prose was overripe, like Jimmy Cannon's, and he uttered it with the bombast of a tent preacher. He was quick to understand that on television the pictures would carry the action — what he had to do was dramatize the moment. Nobody was better at that than Cosell, who could make an ordinary fifteen-yard run seem like Jesse Owens spitting at Hitler.

Cosell became so big that he could no longer cover the story, because he *was* the story. At the ballpark, more people gathered around Cosell than around the players. Next to Johnny Carson, Cosell probably had the most recognizable face in America; he surely had the most recognizable voice — that unmistakable bucket of gravel spilling out like bursts from a machine gun. Friends tell of the time Cosell was in a limousine, being driven to Yankee Stadium for a *Monday Night Baseball* game. The car was cruising through Harlem, and Cosell noticed a crowd had gathered around two men who were fighting. Cosell allegedly ordered the driver to stop the car, whereupon Cosell got out, waded into the crowd, and began to announce the fight. The people were so stunned they stopped fighting and flocked excitedly to Cosell like he was the King of England. It's sad to think there's a generation of sports fans growing up now that doesn't take Cosell's fabulous, basset-hound mug for granted.

Cosell's celebrity was so vast that genuine stars clamored to get in the booth with him. You'd be watching a game, and all of a sudden there was Cosell jawing with Burt Reynolds or Glen Campbell. He became a world-class name-dropper. There was "breakfast with Liza," and "cocktails with Kissinger." Cosell shilled like crazy. He was a carnival barker, luring us into the tent to see the naked dancers (then sometimes shaming us for watching, like with a football rout or a one-sided bout, until he chucked boxing altogether after the 1982 Larry Holmes–Tex Cobb fiasco); he fell helplessly in love with the tacky "Battle of the Network Stars," an absurd athletic competition among jiggly TV starlets and prime-time pretty boys.

But when the public interest was at stake Cosell was our surrogate. He was the first to understand that Muhammad Ali was being railroaded, and he crusaded for Ali. Some sports writers would write that Cosell cynically attached himself to Ali like a barnacle to an ocean liner, but he and Ali became the Fred and Ginger of *Wide World of Sports*. Cosell was something unique to TV sports — a serious, intelligent man with moral principles. He was lacerated for his self-promotion in "telling it like it is," but for years the only real journalist TV sports had was Cosell. God help you if you didn't bring the sprinters to the Olympic track on time, Cosell was all over you like a December wind. Cosell was as feared on his side of the street as Mike Wallace is on his.

There was no in-between: you either loved Cosell or hated him. It started out that most people hated him, but by the 1980s that had turned. In his later years on TV Cosell became something of an American totem. Although he was not fond of many sports writers, Cosell was always friendly to me, and I was always a staunch defender of his. I fondly remember calls from him, at odd hours; I'd pick up the telephone, and Cosell would be on the other end, and I'd hear that familiar cadence saying something like, "To-ny, To-ny, To-ny, what are we to make of the National Football League now? They're scampering for their boats like mice in a Farmer Gray cartoon." You didn't have conversations with him, really; it was more like he was working out a speech. When it was over, he would say kindly, "Always good to talk with you, T," though all I'd done was listen. I'd put down the phone thinking I'd heard the voice of God.

Cosell had an amazing ability to extemporize. He did his brilliant five-minute daily radio show, "Speaking of Sports," without notes or a stopwatch — almost four minutes to the commercial, then fifteen seconds to wrap up; it was all in his head. I watched him do it a few times. He was awesome. I recall Cosell being engrossed in something completely unrelated to his radio show right up to air time. For example, he'd be on the phone with Sonny Werblin, and his radio commentary was going to be about Mickey Mantle. He'd put Werblin on hold, get his radio cue, and Cosell's words about Mantle would tumble out flawlessly. He'd end right on cue, with a Shakespearean flourish about the courage it took for Mantle to play on those gimpy knees. Then he'd go back to talking with Werblin, resuming their conversation, as if he'd merely put down the phone for a moment to light a cigar.

When Cosell left TV ten years ago it created a vacuum in network sports journalism that hasn't been filled. ESPN's *Outside the Lines* has a consistent edge, HBO's new magazine show is promising, and Bob Costas always asks good questions. But the fact is that network television is in financial partnership with big-time sports, and for all the hours devoted to sports on TV, mainly what you get is a tyranny of highlights.

Howard Cosell was usually the lone wolf of TV journalism, the only one who dared unlock the door to a real story. He'd unlock the door and walk down the long hallway, illuminating it only by the fire of his own conviction. He carried a glow that always suited television. In his passing, the picture is already a little dimmer.

Biographical Notes

DAVID ALDRIDGE graduated from American University in 1987. Most recently, he covered the Washington Redskins for the *Washington Post* from 1993 to 1995. In January 1996 he joined ESPN.

ROGER ANGELL is a writer and editor for *The New Yorker.* This is his fourth appearance in *The Best American Sports Writing.*

MICHAEL BAMBERGER is a senior writer for *Sports Illustrated.* Before joining *SI,* he was a reporter for the *Philadelphia Inquirer.* His profile of golfer John Daly appeared in *The Best American Sports Writing 1993.*

MARK COOMES, a University of Louisville graduate, has covered University of Kentucky sports for the *Courier-Journal* since 1992. He previously worked for newspapers in Florida and Louisiana, where he covered the U.S. Senate campaign for former Ku Klux Klan Grand Wizard David Duke. In 1995 Coomes and coauthor Pat Forde together wrote an award-winning expose on the improprieties of the University of Louisville basketball program.

GREG COUCH reports that his connection with sports began when his soon-to-be parents delayed inducing labor until the Bears-Giants championship game ended. In 1994 he was one of six writers in the nation to win three Associated Press Sports Editor Awards. A 1986 graduate of the University of Colorado, he writes for the *Wichita Eagle.*

RICHARD BEN CRAMER won a Pulitzer Prize for reporting. He is the author of *What It Takes,* a chronicle of the 1988 presidential race.

The sports editor of *LA Weekly* since 1990, DAVID DAVIS began writing the *Weekly*'s sports column in 1994. His work has appeared in *Sports Illustrated, Boxing Illustrated, Live!,* and the *Village Voice.*

FRANK DEFORD is the author of eleven books, most recently the novel *Love and Infamy*. He is a columnist for *Newsweek*, a sports commentator for National Public Radio, and a correspondent on the HBO program *REALSPORT*. In 1993 Deford served as guest editor of *The Best American Sports Writing*.

For the past six years, PETER DE JONGE has written frequently about sports and other topics for the *New York Times Magazine*. He lives in Manhattan with his sons, Matthew and Joseph.

LARRY DORMAN writes about golf and other sports for the *New York Times*. A graduate of Loyola University in New Orleans, Dorman formerly covered football for the *Miami Herald* and the *Fort Lauderdale Sun Sentinel* and golf for the *National Sports Daily*.

MAT EDELSON is a senior writer with *Baltimore Magazine* and a contributing sports reporter for National Public Radio and the Canadian Broadcasting Corporation. His sports writing has appeared in many publications, including *Sport, American Health,* and *USA Today*.

TOM FARREY formerly worked as projects and enterprise reporter at the *Seattle Times,* where he won six APSE awards and the Women's Sports Foundation Award for newspaper reporting. He is now an editor with ESPNET SportsZone, where he develops interactive content and explores the new media frontier. He still reads books and newspapers.

BILL FIELDS, a senior editor at *Golf World,* is a native of Southern Pines, North Carolina, and a 1981 graduate of the University of North Carolina. In 1986 and 1992 he received the Best Magazine Feature Award from the Golf Writers Association of America. He lives in Stamford, Connecticut.

PAT FORDE has worked for the *Courier-Journal* since graduating from the University of Missouri in 1987, and he's been a sports columnist since 1992. He was nominated for a Pulitzer Prize in 1990 for his investigation of academic failures in the University of Louisville basketball and football programs.

WILLIAM GILDEA of the *Washington Post* is the author of *When the Colts Belonged to Baltimore: A Father and a Son, a Team and a Time*. A former Nieman Fellow, his profile of Muhammad Ali appeared in *The Best American Sports Writing 1992*.

MICHAEL J. GOODMAN is a contributing editor to the *Los Angeles Times*. He was an investigative reporter for *Time* magazine from 1974 to 1985. He was taught news writing and investigative reporting at UCLA. He is the coauthor of *Your Best Bet,* a guide to international gambling.

This is PAT JORDAN's third appearance in *The Best American Sports Writing*. He is a frequent contributor to a number of national publications.

TOM JUNOD is a writer-at-large for *GQ*. He won the National Magazine Award for Feature Writing in 1995 and in 1996, becoming the first writer to win the award two years in a row. He lives in Georgia.

KAREN KARBO is a frequent contributor to *Outside*. She is the author of two novels, *Trespassers Welcome Here* and *The Diamond Line*. She is currently at work on a book about the female volleyball player and model Gabrielle Reese, entitled *Big Girl in the Middle*.

TONY KORNHEISER is a columnist for the *Washington Post*, where he has worked since 1979 after stints with the *New York Times* and *Newsday*. He is the author of two books, *The Baby Chase* and *Pumping Irony*. He hosts a morning radio show in Washington on the station WTEM.

A former Olympic marathoner, KENNY MOORE has worked on the staff of *Sports Illustrated* since 1980. A native of Portland, Oregon, Moore lives in Hawaii. He is the author of *Best Efforts: World-Class Runners and Races*.

Chicago native JOEL REESE wrote *Down and Out* as his master's thesis at the University of Montana in Missoula in 1994. He received his bachelor's degree at Lawrence University in Appleton, Wisconsin. After stints as a reporter with the *Missoula Independent* and the *Point Reyes Light*, Reese is now a free-lance journalist in Chicago.

JAN REID's profile of pitcher Roger Clemens appeared in *The Best American Sports Writing 1992*. Reid joined *Texas Monthly* at the magazine's inception in 1973, and his work has appeared in *Men's Journal*, *Inside Sports*, *Esquire*, and many other publications.

A native of Boulder, Colorado, RICK REILLY joined *Sports Illustrated* in 1985. He is the coauthor with Brian Bosworth of *The Boz: Confessions of an Anti-Hero*, with Wayne Gretzky of *Gretzky*, and of *The Wit and Wisdom of Charles Barkley*.

DAVID REMNICK is a 1981 graduate of Princeton. He joined the *Washington Post* in 1982, where he covered sports from 1984 to 1985. His books include *Lenin's Tomb: The Last Days of the Soviet Empire*, which won the Pulitzer Prize in 1993, and *The Devil Problem (and Other True Stories)*. He has been a staff writer for *The New Yorker* since 1992.

Before joining *Sports Illustrated* in 1993, TOM VERDUCCI served as a sports reporter and columnist at *Newsday*. A native of East Orange, New Jersey, Verducci led his high school football team to the state championship. He is a graduate of Penn State University.

Notable Sports Writing of 1995

SELECTED BY GLENN STOUT

Fritillary? *The New York Times Magazine*, September 3, 1995

NEAL POLLACK
Fish Heads. *The Chicago Reader*, December 1, 1995

RON POLLACK
Reach Out and Touch Someone. *Pro Football Weekly*, July 1995

S. L. PRICE
Your Words Against Mine. *Sports Illustrated*, December 18, 1995

SCOTT RAAB
Heaven Is a (Minor League) Hockey Town. *GQ*, April 1995

SCOTT RAAB
Wild Thing. *GQ*, March 1995

JONATHAN RABAN
Last Call of the Wild. *Esquire*, April 1995

MIKE RANDOLPH
What the Hell Am I Doing Up Here? *Outdoor Canada*, March 1995

PETER RICHMOND
The Arm with the Golden Man. *GQ*, September 1995

PETER RICHMOND
Exiles on Main Street. *GQ*, April 1995

JACK ROSENBERGER
Spain's Fiesta of Blood. *The Village Voice*, January 17, 1995

PAUL RUBIN
Golf's Missing Link. *New Times*, April 6–12, 1995

LUKE SALISBURY
Baseball Has Lost Its Past. *The Boston Globe*, April 26, 1995

ALAN SCHWARZ
The Holdout from Hell. *Baseball America*, January 9–22, 1995

TOBY SMITH
The Dukes's Tragic Shutout. *The Albuquerque Journal*, August 13, 1995

ANDREW TODHUNTER
Gale Force Kayaking. *The Atlantic Monthly*, August 1995

GEORGE VECSEY
And the Winner Is: Art Modell, Grubbiest Man of the Year. *The New York Times*, December 24, 1995

PATRICIA WEISS
The Green Season. *Northeast*, August 20, 1995

ALEX WELLS
Dragons in the Snow. *Men's Journal*, April 1995

L. JOHN WERTHEIM
The Dunks and Downs of Billy Ray Bates. *Rip City Magazine*, August 1995

STEVE WILSTEIN
There's Still No Quit in Jerry Quarry. The Associated Press, October 1995

JEFF WISE
Commies on the Ropes. *The Village Voice*, May 30, 1995

TOM WITOSKY
Back on the Streets with a Degree, Dream. *The Des Moines Sunday Register*, July 30, 1995

BOB WOJNOWSKI
Grant Hill: A View from the Top. *The Detroit News*, February 12, 1995

RODGE WOOD
Nancy and Tonya: The Opera. *Detroit Free Press Magazine*, January 8, 1995

MARK ZEIGLER
Boxer Gets First-Hand Look at Sport That Killed Father. *The San Diego Union-Tribune*, March 21, 1995